TENNIS

SPORT AND SOCIETY

Series Editors
Aram Goudsouzian
Jaime Schultz

Founding Editors
Benjamin G. Rader
Randy Roberts

*A list of books in the series appears
at the end of this book.*

TENNIS

A History from American Amateurs to Global Professionals

GREG RUTH

UNIVERSITY OF ILLINOIS PRESS
Urbana, Chicago, and Springfield

Library of Congress Cataloging-in-Publication Data
Names: Ruth, Greg, 1986– author.
Title: Tennis : a history from American amateurs to
    global professionals / Greg Ruth.
Description: Urbana : University of Illinois Press,
    [2021] | Series: Sport and society | Includes
    bibliographical references and index.
Identifiers: LCCN 2020056076 (print) | LCCN
    2020056077 (ebook) | ISBN 9780252043895
    (Cloth : acid-free paper) | ISBN 9780252085888
    (Paperback : acid-free paper) | ISBN 9780252052798
    (eBook)
Subjects: LCSH: Tennis—History. | Tennis players. |
    Women tennis players. | Tennis—Tournaments.
Classification: LCC GV992 .R88 2021 (print) | LCC
    GV992 (ebook) | DDC 796.342—dc23
LC record available at https://lccn.loc.gov/
    2020056076
LC ebook record available at https://lccn.loc.gov/
    2020056077

For Courtney

Contents

Photographs follow pages 80 and 180

Acknowledgments

Playing a tennis match may seem like only an individual effort. It is not. A whole team often works behind the scenes. The same goes for writing a book on tennis.

Archivists and librarians across the United States aided me in my research. A few deserve special recognition. Meredith Richards and her colleagues at the International Tennis Hall of Fame hosted me on more than one research visit. Kirstin Kay and her colleagues in Special Collections and University Archives, University of Massachusetts Amherst Libraries, went above and beyond during my many days there. This project would not have been possible without the efforts of interlibrary loan librarians Jennifer Stegen of Loyola University Chicago and Carolann Adams of the Collier County Public Library in Naples, Florida. For the many librarians who helped with image rights and reproductions, thank you.

Several historians also improved this work. Tim Gilfoyle's reading refined the project as a whole. He continued to offer excellent advice throughout the publication process. Michelle Nickerson encouraged me to sharpen my thinking on gender history in particular. Elliott Gorn saved me from several gaffes all the while encouraging me to tell a readable story. Ben Rader prompted me to think about where this project fits into topics of interest to sports historians. I extend special thanks to the three anonymous peer reviewers whose reader reports made the details and the arguments of this book much stronger.

Acknowledgments

An author could not have asked for a better publisher than the University of Illinois Press. From initial correspondence, acquisition, and into production, Danny Nasset skillfully guided this book to publication. Ellie Hinton speedily reviewed accompanying materials to move the book into production. Series editors Aram Goudsouzian and Jaime Schultz are true experts who shaped the pages that follow for the better. Tad Ringo and his colleagues managed production with great care. Dustin Hubbart created the exciting cover. Kevin Cunningham, Michael Roux, and Roberta J. Sparenberg helped promote the book. Jill R. Hughes skillfully copyedited the manuscript. Kate Blackmer of Blackmer Maps drew the wonderful maps. Sheila Hill prepared the helpful index.

A number of tennis players and enthusiasts also aided this project in less direct but still impactful ways. The online members of the Talk Tennis at Tennis Warehouse hosted community threads that inspired me to look further into historical newspapers to track down which professionals played when and where. Mike Terry was my first tennis coach, and throughout this project he remained an enthusiastic supporter of the history of the game. The many tennis players I have instructed over the years, my fellow United States Professional Tennis Association and Professional Tennis Registry teaching professionals, and my United States Tennis Association league teammates, all aided in this project by helping me to better understand how the game is played. The same goes for my college teammates.

Personal thanks go to my family. My parents, Jenny and Harry Ruth, unwittingly started this project by encouraging me to start playing more tennis than football. They have been beyond supportive to me from long before this project began. I love you both. My sister, Libby Campbell, and brother-in-law, Seth Campbell, also encouraged me along the way. Thank you both.

My wife, Courtney Burris Ruth, has blessed my life beyond measure. She, more than anyone, knows what this project took because she was with me every step of the way. I love you.

Abbreviations

AELTC	All England Lawn Tennis and Croquet Club
ATA	American Tennis Association
ATP	Association of Tennis Professionals
ELTA	Eastern Lawn Tennis Association
FFT	Fédédération Française de Lawn Tennis
FIT	Federazione Italiana Tennis
ILTF	International Lawn Tennis Federation
IMG	International Management Group
IPTPA	International Professional Tennis Players' Association
ITF	International Tennis Federation
ITHF	International Tennis Hall of Fame
LATC	Los Angeles Tennis Club
LTA	Lawn Tennis Association (of Great Britain)
LTAA	Lawn Tennis Association of Australia
NTL	National Tennis League
MIPTC	Men's International Professional Tennis Council (aka Men's Tennis Council)
PLTA	Professional Lawn Tennis Association (of the United States)
PSLTA	Pacific States Lawn Tennis Association
SCTA	Southern California Tennis Association
TPASC	Tennis Patrons Association of Southern California

USNLTA   United States National Lawn Tennis Association
USLTA   United States Lawn Tennis Association
USPLTA   United States Professional Lawn Tennis Association
USTA   United States Tennis Association
WCT   World Championship Tennis
WITF   Women's International Tennis Federation
WLTM   Wimbledon Lawn Tennis Museum
WPT   Women's Professional Tour
WPTI   World Professional Tennis Incorporated (aka World Tennis Incorporated)
WTA   Women's Tennis Association / Women's International Tennis Association

Tennis Amateurs and Tennis Professionals

In January 2016, reports emerged from the Australian Open—one of tennis's so-called Grand Slams or four major tournaments—that the winningest men's tennis professional of all time, Swiss champion Roger Federer, would inaugurate a new tennis team competition named after the great Australian champion Rod Laver. Team8 and Tony Godsick, Federer's sports marketing agency and agent, respectively, would work out the details for a handful of top European players to compete against a handful of the best players from the rest of the world. Reports characterized the event as akin to golf's Ryder Cup, but Federer thought of the event as a way to honor the great champions of his sport's past.[1]

Widely thought of as a tournament-centric individual sport, tennis has seen events similar to the Laver Cup before. Before the days of so-called open tennis—which took place in 1968 and in which tennis professionals were first welcomed to play against amateur players in game's most hallowed venues and in the most historic tournaments—tennis was a sport divided against itself. Professional barnstorming players competed night after night across the United States and around the world to get paid for popularizing tennis while amateur tennis associations staged tournaments on expansive sporting club grounds. Jack Kramer, the most consequential of the professionals in shaping the sport in the twentieth century, put on the first Kramer Tennis Cup in the fall of 1961. Since the end of the Second World War, Kramer had led the professionals, first as a touring player and later as a touring promoter, only to find both the amateur and professional game ailing for want of spectators by the 1960s. His solution was to relinquish some of the contractual control he held over a half dozen touring professionals to a newly formed players union called the International Professional Tennis Players' Association (IPTPA). Made up of around twenty professionals, this organization decided to install Kramer as their first leader and to hold international tennis team competitions for the world's best professionals akin to the Davis Cup competition for the best amateur tennis players from the sport's leading nations.[2]

"The pro tours are a major factor in the development and growth of the game throughout the world," wrote William "Bill" Lufler in 1963. "The professionals continue to bring the best tennis in the world to the four corners of the globe." As head professional of the West Side Tennis Club of Forest Hills, New York, Lufler saw the best amateur tennis players in the world as his club hosted the U.S. National Championships. From 1963 to 1966 he also served as the president of the United States Professional Lawn Tennis Association (USPLTA). That organization represented around 550 tennis coaches and instructors in the United States, many of whom were affiliated with private clubs, few of whom ever traveled to play tennis matches for paying spectators, and none of whom had any say over the governing body of the game in America, the United States Lawn Tennis Association (USLTA), as that organization generally disallowed anyone who earned income from the sport of tennis from membership. Lufler made the relationship between the IPTPA players and the USPLTA coaches seem harmonious, but in reality the teaching professionals and touring professionals competed just as much as they cooperated with one another to secure the limited dollars in the professional game before 1968. Far stronger competition, however, existed between the touring professionals, the USLTA, and the various national tennis associations that made up the world governing body of the game, the International Lawn Tennis Federation (ILTF).[3]

Laver himself was the perfect player to honor both the amateur and professional tradition in the sport. He won the Grand Slam of the sport—that is, a calendar year sweep of the Australian Championships, the French Championships, the Wimbledon Championships, and the U.S. Championships—as an amateur in 1968. He repeated that feat as a professional in 1969, the first year that all four of those championships became open to professionals and amateurs alike. In between he led the Australian professionals in winning their third and final Kramer Cup before the competition ceased in 1963.[4]

As a participant observer, Laver has even made a compelling case that Australia dominated postwar world tennis from the mid-1950s up to and just past the beginning of the Open Era in 1968. Match results support much of that claim, just as evidence compiled by historian Kevin Jefferys also shows Great Britain to have exercised the major pull on the sport of tennis from the game's beginnings in the late 1870s through the mid-1920s. In a book focused on British tennis, Jefferys nonetheless concludes that when the entire history of the game is taken into account, the United States stands above all tennis nations.[5]

Sports historian Robert J. Lake has charted the recent upswing in tennis scholarship in a state-of-the-field essay in which he followed the number of articles that address tennis in two dozen leading English-language academic journals. He finds that no articles appeared in the 1960s, only a few in the 1970s, and just over a dozen each in the 1980s and in the 1990s. In the last twenty years, however, 126 social scientific articles have appeared that either address or focus on tennis in some capacity. Add to that the 45 essays that make up the recent *Routledge Handbook of Tennis*, in which his essay appears as the lead, and the time seems right to answer Lake's "call to arms" to continue to push the study of tennis in new directions.[6]

Book-length studies of tennis by academic historians are fewer but on the whole excellent in having deepened understanding of the sport. Heiner Gillmeister has traced European origins of the game in rich detail. Lake has used lawn tennis as a lens to view British social values during the late nineteenth century and throughout the twentieth century, in the process offering a nuanced view of major issues involving the governance of the sport. E. Digby Baltzell set a similar example for the United States following the celebration of amateurism in elite clubs and associations on the American Eastern Seaboard within a broader look at the sport in American society. Warren F. Kimball has plumbed internal records to produce a definitive institutional history of the USLTA that also explores the influence of that organization on many aspects of the game. Susan Ware has analyzed the impact that the match known as the "Battle of the Sexes," pitting Billie Jean King against Bobby Riggs in 1973, had on women's sports in late twentieth-century America. Eric Allen Hall has shown how Arthur Ashe used his status as a tennis champion to become a civil rights leader. Sundiata Djata has written about the remarkable successes of people of color in tennis in the United States and abroad. Elizabeth Wilson has looked at the game from a literary point of view and offered a strong overview of important cultural moments in the sport.[7] This book, by contrast, both partners with the above scholars and plays its own game in putting events like the Laver Cup and Kramer Cup into historical context, in the process advancing a periodization of the sport of tennis into three constitutive eras.

Period one began in 1873 with the first lawn tennis match hosted by British military officer Walter Wingfield in Wales. The game moved from there to America, Australia, and around the world but remained an exclusively amateur sport defined more by cooperation than competition among fledgling amateur tennis associations who codified the rules, established governance, and sponsored interclub competitions, matches, and tournaments. As the game diffused around the world, particularly from the East Coast to the West Coast of the United States, competition between amateur associations intensified while cooperation continued. The first era came to an end when Frenchwoman Suzanne Lenglen and her American promoter Charles C. "C. C." Pyle organized the first international professional tour throughout the United States in 1926, thus presenting professional tennis as a both popular and professional sport that rivaled the game as a pastime for the social elite.

The cardinal characteristic of the second era, which began in 1926 and concluded in 1968, was intense competition over the commercialization of the game. That competition existed between tradition-oriented associations who wanted the game to remain exclusively an amateur pursuit and professional players and promoters whose embrace of tennis touring was both an attempt to earn a living from the sport and a challenge to the authority over the game exercised by the tradition-minded amateur associations. Finally, after 1968 steady pressure from the professionals and occasional mismanagement by the amateur associations' leaders spurred the opening of competition between professionals and amateurs that has continued into the present. Money became the defining feature of this third period, but, as this book suggests, money matters always marked tennis as a sport both apart from and, in that way, crucial for understanding the history of sports and commercial entertainment in the twentieth century.

The string tying together these three periods was competition for control over the direction the game would take and the money to be made from the game. Nowhere else in the world did that competition come into such sharp relief than in the United States, which, as the twentieth century advanced, accrued more and more influence in shaping global popular culture, in which spectator sports were an important part.

The aristocratic prehistory of tennis as the sport for the royal court confounds more than explains why tennis remained primarily a pastime for amateurs long after so many other spectator sports embraced professionalism. The first court tennis championship in the world with matches between professionals and amateurs took place back in 1740. By contrast, boxing, the sport most associated with professionalizing first, did not do so until more than a century later, in 1882. As with boxing, horse racing and cricket were sports popular with gamblers. Money attracted and refined talent to a degree that both sports had strong professional elements by the 1850s and '60s. In the United States, cricket had morphed into America's pastime by the Civil War. The Cincinnati Red Stockings became baseball's first professional team in 1869. Two years later the Cleveland Forest Cities took the field against the Fort Wayne Kekiongas in the first all-professional game in the newly formed National Association of Professional Baseball Players. A YMCA physical education teacher named James Naismith created the game of basketball in Springfield, Massachusetts, in 1891. Five years later in Trenton, New Jersey, the players of the Trenton Basketball Team became the first paid professionals in a spectator sport on the rise. Professional soccer began in Great Britain in 1886. In the United States, British rugby had evolved into American football by the 1880s and soon became the centerpiece of college sports. That the game remained so popular and profitable on university campuses explained how football could so quickly make room for professionals with the formation of the American Professional Football Association in 1920.[8] At the same time that these sports embraced professionalism to varying degrees, the new sport of lawn tennis that began in 1873 maintained a near-absolute commitment to amateurism in all aspects of the game.

Country clubs boomed in Great Britain between 1873 and 1900 as England reaped the rewards of being the center of a global empire. Wealthy Americans looked across the Atlantic, saw the places of leisure that came with prosperity, and set about building the same sort of spaces in the United States. The proliferation of private clubs along American seaboards helped to organize sports like tennis into ostentatious pastimes rather than profit-making entertainments. The National Association of Amateur Athletics in America, founded in 1879; the Amateur Athletic Union, founded in 1888; the National Collegiate Athletic Association, founded in 1905; the American Association of Amateur Oarsmen, founded in 1872; the League of American Wheelmen, founded in 1880; the United States Golf Association, founded in 1894—all attested to the strength the amateur ideal had among moneyed men in North America. In the minds of these men, sports needed separation between amateur and professional players, and in the main they achieved that separation by 1900.[9] Despite occasional challenges from outsiders who wanted to earn a living playing tennis, the clubs and associations run by amateurs held firm control over the game for its first fifty years.

Government and individual responses to the major upheavals of the Great Depression and World War II greatly undermined the authority of the amateur associations by creating conditions under which a whole new generation of tennis players with social backgrounds different from those of the men who ran the amateur associations could take up the game. The best of those players held far more liberal views when it came to money in their sport, and they shared those views across the country and throughout the world year after year on professional barnstorming tours in the late 1940s through the mid-1960s. The visibility and viability of those tours eventually coaxed reluctant amateur association members to vote to allow the opening of tennis's major tournament venues to professional players in 1968. Almost simultaneously, sports marketers, professional promoters, sports publishers, and ultimately the players themselves popularized the game into much the same form that it retains today.

CHAPTER 1

Amateur Associations along the American Atlantic Coast

The first game of lawn tennis took place on the expansive green lawns of a Welsh country estate in the late summer months of 1873. Major Walter Clopton Wingfield patented his game in February 1874 with a rhomboidal rather than rectangular court demarcated by taped lines and a triangular net strung between two posts hammered into the ground at a distance of twenty-one feet apart. His patent proposed the spread of the game throughout the British Isles, and he purported that his new design took tennis outdoors for the first time and thus "placed within the reach of all" a game that only Europe's wealthiest had previously enjoyed. His patent approved, Wingfield wrote the earliest tennis rule book, where in that pamphlet's second and third editions, he changed the name of the game to *sphairistikè* before he finally settled on calling it "lawn tennis" in the fourth edition. In addition to patenting, writing the first rules, and titling the game, Wingfield produced the first pieces of tennis equipment for commercial use. His kits came in a wooden box large enough to fit four racquets, a net, two net posts, two tennis balls, and a rule book. Favorable press coverage helped Wingfield sell over a thousand of his tennis sets in the first year. Britain's proximity to France helped the game spread quickly to the European continent, via either British holidaymakers or expats.[1]

The ways the game's early players interacted with their racquets revealed the earlier roots of lawn tennis and its subsequent spread after 1874. Over the next quarter century, that diffusion resulted from the strong cooperation and gentle competition between members of the leisured classes on both sides of the Atlantic. During the first few years of the sport, most lawn tennis players held their racquets with a continental grip, which allowed for both forehand and backhand strokes without moving the hand position of the index finger knuckle pad on the second bevel of the racquet's handle.[2] The grip's name reflects the antecedents to the British lawn tennis found in the games of racquets and court tennis originating on the European continent. Played mainly in France, these games required participants to execute strokes off a wall or close to the ground, therefore necessitating a grip that positioned the racquet at such an angle so as to not scrape the ground.[3]

As with the racquet, the early manufacture of tennis balls made plain the origins of the global spread of tennis in British colonialism. The felt and stitching of the ball were all white. The cost of the balls prohibited all but the ruling class from purchasing them. The balls even carried names like the "Hard Court" ball, which signified where a player should play, and the "Demon Ball," which signified what kind of player should hit with them. The manufacturers made those linkages between British colonialism and British sports explicit in an advertisement for Slazenger's "Colonial Ball," made specifically for humid conditions in places such as "India, Australasia, Africa, and South America, and indeed all Countries situated at a great distance from where the Ball is made, and where extremes of temperature have to be contended with. . . . Its reputation, however, is world-wide, and it is an admitted fact that our Colonial Ball will retain its resiliency and wear longer than any other Ball produced."[4] The players themselves hoped the same could be said for their colonies.

The British Empire did not include the United States in the second half of the nineteenth century, but during those decades cultural exchange remained strong. As the ranks of the middle class swelled in Victorian America, a tension between a belief in personal industriousness and the desire of members of the middle class to define their identities as separate from the growing urban working class became more pronounced. Urban and rural recreation, restorative practices, and leisure were major avenues through which people could promote their class distinctiveness. Before the Civil War, most Americans never ventured much beyond their local county seat. The improved transportation network and homestead legislation that was passed during the war stimulated settlement west of the Mississippi River. More importantly, travelers to the West brought back fantastic stories of the wonders of the frontier to share with people living in the Midwest and the East. These stories in turn encouraged the growing middle class to travel on the developed rail lines to sites of natural beauty and a burgeoning network of camps and resorts in scenic locales. The American vacation was born.[5]

In the cities, the Gilded Age and the Progressive Era were moments for the first massive reorientation of the nation's recreation space by newly trained planning experts. Frederick Law Olmsted, the era's foremost landscape architect, designed America's most famous urban leisure ground in New York City. Occupying 843 acres of Manhattan real estate, Central Park embodied the growing importance that urban planners, municipal reformers, and city residents alike assigned to restorative and open space in ever more crowded cities. Moreover, urban parks could mirror class relationships found in neighborhoods, the workplace, and all walks of life. Central Park itself featured no fewer than four separate entrances, each for a different rank of person entering the park. In Chicago special promenading thoroughfares and private beaches were designated for the city's elites, but the city did not have a public swimming area along the lake until Lincoln Park opened one in 1895. The city center of Denver, the boomtown of the mountains, featured wide walking paths for the conspicuous walking of the city's new money merchants. In the last two decades of the nineteenth century and the first two decades of the twentieth century, cities from Boston to Cleveland and from Kansas City to Los Angeles increased their parkland by up to 600 percent, a massive reorientation of space catalyzed by a burgeoning middle class interested in assuming some of the authority to plan and the pleasures to play that previously had been enjoyed only by elites.[6] Within the cities themselves, parks simultaneously met the leisure needs of everyone and reminded everyone of their particular position in society.

In a far more discreet way, urban elites had long hidden themselves away in private men's clubs. In the first third of the nineteenth century, those clubs usually took the form of militia companies. Some exceptions, such as New York City's Union Club, were more social in nature. Beginning in the 1840s and '50s, cricket clubs sprouted along major thoroughfares and in wealthy pockets of cities such as Boston, Philadelphia, and New York. In these cities and secondary cities, like Chicago, baseball also grew in popularity, especially with the cadres of clerks and manual laborers who formed clubs and leagues comprised wholly of white-collar workers and mechanics.[7] Shooting and hunting clubs like the New York Sporting Association had origins in the antebellum years, but by the late nineteenth century, game was increasingly scarce in all but the farthest-afield areas of the country, leaving wealthy men with little alternative but to seek other recreational outlets.[8] These clubs shared a fondness for sport, they helped to reinforce male solidarity, and they expressed the awareness of class boundaries within urbanizing America. They also exposed the physical limits of recreation in the city.

Genteel resorts such as White Sulphur Springs, West Virginia, and Newport, Rhode Island, recreated and even enhanced class solidarity among the wealthy and socially connected when these people traveled away from home. Moreover, while most of the social clubs and workplaces in Eastern cities practiced rigid gender segregation, resorts brought women and men into daily contact on the croquet pitch, in the mineral spring, and on the dance floor. Starting around the turn of the century and continuing through to the Great Depression, many members of the urban working class increasingly looked to recreation outside the city in addition to the amusements they enjoyed within. Recent immigrants and African Americans also considered rural vacations viable, either by camping or by renting a room in an inexpensive boardinghouse. The oldest and most established resorts remained firmly in the hands of the upper- and middle-class elites, a grip that tightened when the Depression eliminated the little extra income most Americans relied on to visit an attraction.[9]

The same decades that witnessed the growth of scenic urban parks, secluded elite resorts, and middle-class vacations also saw a remarkable upswing in betting and games of chance. The Gilded Age gambler shot pool, rolled roulette, threw dice, and flipped cards, all the while pursuing a payoff through what historian Jackson Lears has identified as "providential arrangements of rewards and punishments" that were not unlike the creed espoused by the era's most notorious robber barons.[10] In growing cities, gambling dens catered to men of all classes. Blueblood resorts also indulged this ethos by building casinos and racetracks that catered to the wealthy people's appetites for cash and chance. In the millionaires' playground of Newport, Rhode Island, for example, craftsmen laid the last shingle on the magnificent Newport Casino in the summer of 1880, with the gaming tables opening to immediate acclaim. There the country's wealthiest men and women threw money hand over fist decade after decade until the music finally slowed with the onset of the Great Depression.[11]

At the same time that games of chance proliferated, a countervailing trend that championed games of skill took shape. Mastery of mind and body through vigorous exercise had origins in religious convictions such as the "muscular Christian" tradition, which began in England during the first decades of the nineteenth century before making it to America during the Civil War and in the postbellum years. No reformer espoused exercise for everyone more vigorously than Diocletian Lewis, who, during the 1860s and '70s, championed a "New Gymnastics" with men and women alike stretching limbs, grasping rings, lifting wooden dumbbells, and swinging Indian clubs. Exercise advocates suggested that team sports like football instilled young white-collar workers with industrious habits that led to a more productive workplace. Children too were encouraged to participate in structured play so that they could learn what it meant to be an American. Living in squalid tenements, recent immigrants and many in the working class felt the ability for self-betterment through athletics even more strongly. For these young men, individual accomplishment in team sports like baseball and individual sports like boxing served as a way to earn respect in a highly localized ethnic community and, in rare cases, a means of financial improvement for the most talented athletes. Throughout American cities, ethnic athletic clubs proliferated. The farthest-reaching consequences of the trend for masculine martialism came in the realm of foreign policy, where leaders of the United States believed outdoor exercise connected to the expansion of an American empire.[12] Tennis stood within all of these broader contexts of class, gentility, and leisure with one important exception. Women had played the game of lawn tennis from the beginning, and they would continue to play as the game grew in the late nineteenth and early twentieth centuries.

The conventional story of the spread of lawn tennis to America credits a woman. In under a year, Major Walter Wingfield's *sphairistikè* had gone out from his Welsh garden party to the British Caribbean with British military officers and colonial officials. In April 1874 Mary Ewing Outerbridge left Bermuda to return to the United States with a lawn tennis kit that included racquets, balls, net posts, and a net. Stateside, she introduced the game to her brother, A. Emilius Outerbridge, who, as director of the Staten Island Cricket and Base Ball Club, arranged for the marking of a section of the club's grounds for a lawn tennis court. Over the next two decades, the club grew from a dozen or so founders to six hundred members, many of whom competed in the yearly handicapped tennis tournament, which compensated for differences in player skills by giving weaker players a score advantage at the beginning of every game against stronger players. Much like getting strokes in match-play golf based on players' eighteen-hole handicap, handicapped tennis tournaments were the norm rather than the exception in the late nineteenth century, because grinding players' ability to the lowest common denominator rather than forcing them to play up to the skills of the best player in their group encouraged the growth of the game during its infancy. Over those same years, America's well-to-do continued to bring back lawn tennis kits from their transatlantic travels and mark off courts on the grounds of their sporting clubs, like the Germantown Cricket Club of Philadelphia, while in other instances they built private courts on their private estates.[13]

By 1880 the popularity of the game with the leisure class had risen to a degree that private courts and cricket clubs with a single lawn tennis court could no longer accommodate demand. Tennis-specific clubs began to proliferate in American cities, where a great density of wealthy citizens with the disposable capital necessary to purchase and hold large swaths of real estate in the quickly urbanizing United States could be found. This meant most lawn tennis clubs concentrated along the Eastern Seaboard of the Mid-Atlantic and New England. The West Side Tennis Club was one of the first and most prominent clubs in the country. Founded in 1882, the club had expanded to two locations by 1904. The clubhouse was located in the Bronx at 238th Street and Broadway, where members could also play on several courts. Female members had first claim on the courts at 117th Street and Amsterdam Avenue in Morningside Heights. Men were allowed to play there only through a formal petition to and with approval from the club's governing board. Victorian women generally had more opportunities to play tennis than other games offered by athletic clubs in America, and such cooperation and competition between the genders put tennis on a different path than other sports in the United States.[14]

The West Side Tennis Club capped total membership at 550, with the only stated requirements being that a potential member be older than sixteen and that two or more current members vouch for her. While not overtly stated, in practice this application process effectively barred African Americans from joining the club, as the all-white membership listed on the club's membership rolls perpetuated year after year until at least the eve of World War I. A similar class barrier was also in place, albeit with a little more malleability, as players who proved themselves talented in the many sanctioned tournaments held under the auspices of the Eastern Lawn Tennis Association and Metropolitan Association sometimes found their names listed on the membership rolls regardless of their personal equity. The wrong color skin or the wrong family kept someone out of the tennis club, but being a woman did not.[15]

Women members were in fact a draw to elite tennis clubs. In August 1890, along with benches full of male and female spectators, an elderly woman sat on a porch and watched four ladies play a doubles match on the lawn tennis court. The venue was the Brighton Beach Hotel, a popular spot with the Manhattan Park Avenue crowd. The woman grew frustrated with the women's poor play and divided attention. She believed the players were too interested in the glances of the young men watching the game; however, her scorn centered less on the "attention" they sought and more on the cumbersome outfits that hamstringed their tennis strokes. Their Victorian outfits fit so inappropriately that the servers used underhand strokes, as the tight-fitting sleeves restrained the extension and pronation of the arm that were necessary for an overhand service. "Hampered by graceful, but far too heavy skirts, big knotted sash, jaunty jacket, and a hat which will not sit just exactly straight if the head is moved violently," the old woman wrote, how could these ladies play any better? Her observations revealed the competing ideologies of style and success in the sport of tennis.[16]

Grace did not equal performance, but measures of both categories depended on whether the players were women or men. F. A. Kellogg, a leading writer on recreation and editor of *Outing* magazine, considered tennis an exceptional sport in three ways: First and foremost, tennis was the "youngest of athletic" sports popularized by the British that had spread to much of the world by the late nineteenth century. Second, more than most sports, tennis espoused refinement in the people who played the game and thus deserved to be played by the refined themselves—the lawyer, the doctor, the university student, the clergyman, and the college professor. Third, and most uniquely, the pioneers of tennis from the beginning had stressed the suitability of the game for "the gentler sex" and had worked tirelessly to make sure women participated.[17] Women participated as players in large numbers, but men reserved the governance of the game for themselves in the boardrooms of private clubs and in the tennis amateur associations they created.

Lawn tennis competition at and between urban athletic clubs and suburban country clubs was less well organized than cricket and baseball competitions because of the comparative novelty of the game compared to those older sports. That changed on May 21, 1881, when representatives from prominent athletic and country clubs sat in the Fifth Avenue Hotel in New York City and created the United States National Lawn Tennis Association (USNLTA).[18] The principal reason those thirty-four East Coast and Mid-Atlantic clubs agreed to meet in 1881 was due to a tennis match, or rather lack of a match, the year before. After visiting the Staten Island Cricket and Base Ball Club for an interclub meet, Bostonians James Dwight and R. D. Sears refused to compete in singles matches when they found that the balls the New Yorkers proposed to play with were far inferior to those they played with in New England. Other equipment differences concerned the nets, which varied in height, and the shape of the court, which varied in size. Different clubs even counted score in different ways. Club secretary E. H. Outerbridge realized that without a codification of rules and equipment, interclub matches would suffer, and without interclub matches, the game had little chance of growing as it had in England and throughout the British Empire.[19]

Outerbridge actually found garnering support from different clubs easy. Their boards of directors shared membership rolls that resembled one another's in terms of wealth and community standing. "I knew many of the members and some of the officers and directors of most of the clubs where lawn tennis was then being played, as most of them were cricket clubs, and I had been playing matches on their grounds as a member of the Staten Island Cricket Club, which practically every year visited Boston, Philadelphia, and Baltimore to play such matches," said Outerbridge. Urban elites along the Eastern Seaboard showed that shared leisure time reinforced their social and commercial networks when they quickly replied that they would attend Outerbridge's Fifth Avenue Hotel meeting. Chaired by the Staten Island Cricket and Base Ball Club's George Scofield, the attendees ratified the USNLTA's constitution in under half an hour. Most of the rest of the meeting then addressed the standardization of equipment and rules: the ball would now weigh between 1.87 and 2 ounces and have a diameter between 2.5 inches and 2.56 inches; all clubs would use the rules developed by the All England Lawn Tennis and Croquet Club at Wimbledon Village, which the USNLTA would distribute in pamphlet form; and the USNLTA Executive Committee would decide further tournament policy as the association grew. Fifteen additional clubs joined the association via proxy.[20]

Four years later the association had grown to include 51 member clubs, which competed in association-sanctioned tournaments and a year-end championship. By 1893, 107 clubs belonged to the association, with each and every one of them subscribing to the amateur ideal initially discussed at the Fifth Avenue Hotel first annual meeting. At the same time, the executive committee made *Music and Drama: A Journal Devoted to Sport, Music, the Drama, and Other Things* the official publication of the association. While that publication never really covered tennis, resulting in the association's quickly finding another publication to serve as the USNLTA's official organ, such short-lived action nonetheless revealed the degree to which the society types who ran the USNLTA thought of tennis not so much as a competitive sport but as just another leisure activity on their social calendars.[21]

Together with their British counterparts at the All England Lawn Tennis and Croquet Club (AELTC) and the Lawn Tennis Association (LTA), USN-LTA representatives in the late nineteenth century set out a basic standard of amateurism that held considerable sway in what historian Kevin Jefferys has called "the heyday of amateurism" in tennis.[22] In May 1882, at their first annual meeting, association members concerned themselves with the boundaries of amateurism and professionalism in the fledgling sport of lawn tennis. "None but amateurs shall be allowed to enter for any match played by this Association," members emphatically agreed by vote. Such a ruling positioned who and who was not an amateur in the early moments of the organization, both a symbolic and practical measure of the seriousness with which USN-LTA officials meant to patrol the social boundaries of the sport. The top of the organization, the executive committee, of which Dr. James Dwight was elected president, reserved for themselves the ability to rule on the issue of amateur status. Throughout the end of the nineteenth century and much of the twentieth, the most-senior members in the association would use their changing definition of amateurism as the gatekeeper that opened the sport of tennis to some and kept it closed to others.[23]

In its first decade of existence, the USNLTA laid out five basic provisions that if violated forfeited a player's amateur status and therefore removed the guilty member from the association: First, the guidelines prohibited a member from accepting any money in exchange for playing tennis for the enjoyment of others. Second, a member could not compete against a professional in any sort of public match that involved any recognition of a winner and a loser even without the involvement of money. Third, the teaching of tennis—or any other sport, fitness, or health routine, for that matter—was prohibited. Fourth, a player associated with a tennis club, as all players were in the 1890s, could not remain a member of a club if the player's association at the respective club benefited the club or the player financially in any way. Fifth, a player could not work for a sporting goods company because of his or her skills in tennis or any other sport. Members immediately challenged the amateur requirements with questions, such as whether or not a sportswriter, employed by a newspaper but participating as a player in an USNLTA tournament, violated provisions against material "gain" from tennis; in their replies, Dwight and other association leaders set the precedent of a hardline policy against money in tennis with the flexibility on the association's part to enforce that prohibition selectively.[24]

Criticism of the USNLTA's draconian stance against any money in the sport grew as the game grew. The most effective critique labeled the association as classist, a claim that prompted defensiveness from executive committee members. In 1899 Valentine Hall, the USNLTA secretary, addressed that criticism on behalf of the association when he published *Lawn Tennis in America*, the central section of which not only defended the amateurism of the game but also celebrated the aristocratic "parentage" that lawn tennis in the United States enjoyed from European court tennis. Hall went beyond royalty to draw connections between Greek and Roman republican virtues and the character of the USNLTA player leadership who had popularized the game in America: Richard Sears, a Boston Brahmin and 1880 Newport champion; Henry Warner Slocum Jr., son of a Union general and reigning national champion; Robert Livingston, born into a dynasty of political leaders and financiers, himself an active member of the New York Stock Exchange at the same time he served the USNLTA; Dr. James Dwight, a scion of the game both in America and during his lengthy holidays in England; Howard Taylor, Harvard graduate and distinguished lawyer; and a dozen other players of tennis talent and equally high social standing who ran the association. Taylor's legal background prompted Hall to solicit a treatise on amateurism from the lawyer, which was reprinted in full in the book. Taylor reminded readers that tennis had grown as a sport with official laws against professionalism and that to loosen the amateur codes by obfuscation or by outright elimination would dilute the purity of tennis to the level of some other sport in the eyes of the public both at home and abroad. If people from his own privileged status faced the temptation of accepting free balls, racquets, or hotel rooms, how, then, could people from middle-class or working-class backgrounds resist such temptations? Keeping tennis reserved for "gentlemen," Taylor suggested, would actually protect "the growing hybrid class" from the corrupting nature of money in sports. The amateur rules—in the eyes of the executive committee, at least—expressed the benevolent paternalism that USNLTA officials believed they exhibited. These men wished to extend the social and class positions they learned and practiced in the business world to that of the tennis world.[25] But competition was inevitable; this was the Gilded Age, after all.

Conflict between the United States and Spain almost killed tennis in America before it began. While the growing popularity of golf had taken some of the wind out of tennis's sails in the mid-1890s, the war fever that followed the sinking of the USS *Maine* on February 15, 1898, led USNLTA membership to shrink from 106 clubs to 44 clubs. Just as internationalism in the form of conflict negatively affected tennis in the United States, so too did internationalism in the form of both cooperation and competition positively affect tennis in the United States at the beginning of the twentieth century.[26] Historians Robert J. Lake, Simon J. Eaves, and Bob Nicholson have pointed out that turn-of-the-century British and American tennis matches took place in evolving "Anglo-American relations" that saw the United States gaining ground on Britain's world-leading economic and political position. That process, Eaves and Lake maintain, helped to allow a wealthy American, rather than the actual "combined efforts of several men," to assume near-total credit for founding the most significant of nation-versus-nation team tennis competitions: the Davis Cup.[27]

The standard account goes like this: The first internationalism in tennis came back in 1885 after the USNLTA leadership approved allowing foreign players to participate in the U.S. National Tournament, yet the important moment did not come until 1897, when the St. Louisan turned Harvard tennis player Dwight Davis first voiced willingness to financially sponsor a visit from England's top players to the United States to compete against America's best. That offer went unaccepted on the part of the LTA, although three British players did travel to the United States on their own after they received an offer to play not in a team match but in the U.S. National Lawn Tennis Championship at Newport, Rhode Island. The international players finished third, fourth, and fifth.[28]

The excitement that private visit caused convinced Davis to redouble his efforts to inaugurate an international team competition between the British and American players. Davis further realized that such private tours would continue by foreign players unabated; better for the USNLTA to sponsor them so that they could control the game and keep hold of what would likely prove a revenue source for the association. To accomplish that objective, in

1900 Davis donated a silver trophy first called the "International Challenge Cup" but later named after its bequest the Davis Cup. The hardware incentivized the LTA to send Arthur Gore, Ernst Black, and Roper Barrett to play the onetime Harvard players Holcombe Ward, Malcolm Whitman, and Davis for the championship. Contested on the lawns of the Longwood Cricket Club in Chestnut Hill, Massachusetts, the Americans swept the British. The real test came not on the court but in the second match between the British Isles and the United States. That tie took place in 1902 at the Crescent Athletic Club in Brooklyn, New York, with the Americans again victorious. Attendance was excellent at both matches, and the second challenge could have gone either way. A rivalry blossomed, with the British winning their first Davis Cup in 1903, a victory that solidified the longevity of the competition. The Davis Cup event single-handedly enlarged the USNLTA's treasury from $271.04 in February 1900 to $2,458.48 in 1904. Association membership likewise climbed to eighty-three clubs and twelve sub-associations by 1900. Attendees at the USNLTA's 1901 annual meeting reached the consensus that the Davis Cup "put lawn tennis on a higher plane and assured its permanency as a sport."[29]

That elevated position seemed constantly under threat, with no foe scarier than the fledgling sporting goods industry. The explosive growth of the first truly national market for consumer goods in the final two decades of the nineteenth century left the USNLTA fearing that "dealers" might get their "crack" players addicted to money in the game. From the colonial period up through the young republic, one made, shared, or bartered for recreational equipment. In the 1850s, for the first time, cricket bats and hunting equipment went on sale in numbers noticeable enough for historians to date the beginnings of a market for sporting goods. In the 1880s and piggybacking off of the growth in baseball after the founding of the National League of Professional Baseball Clubs in 1876, major sporting goods firms such as Albert G. Spalding's company began to make and market bats, gloves, and all sorts of equipment in quantities large enough to help make baseball a $10 million business in 1890. The 1890s also marked the appearance of the nation's first truly mass-manufactured good in the bicycle through its complete interchangeability of parts, which in turn propelled a bicycle bonanza that lasted until about 1900 and netted the sporting goods industry $100 million.[30]

Though never approaching the production levels and the payoff of baseball or bicycling, the game of tennis required equipment of just the right size and at the right price point for the fledgling sporting goods industry. All that was needed were contacts who were familiar with this new and relatively unfamiliar game, but both the LTA and the USNLTA took mixed steps to prevent such partnerships between members and for-profit companies from becoming too strong. For example, in Britain the Slazenger sporting goods company published both the LTA's official periodical, *Lawn Tennis and Badminton*, and employed the AELTC's secretary, Archdale Palmer. Palmer stood down as AELTC secretary, and Slazenger ended its publishing arrangement under LTA scrutiny. While softening its original stricter ban on working for a sporting goods company, the USNLTA did cap a member's tennis goods sales at half or more of his total accounts—an uneasy compromise. Likewise, tournaments could receive no sponsorship from sporting goods firms.[31]

Such a strong-handed move into the livelihoods of USNLTA members, not to mention the material growth of the game itself, was a bold attempt on the part of the association to regain control over the explosive growth of the game in the first two decades of the twentieth century. USNLTA leadership therefore stood somewhat apart from the governance of the game in other parts of the world by initially refusing, along with Canada and Norway, to join the International Lawn Tennis Federation (ILTF)—a global governing association for the game founded in 1913. In reality, the ILTF did not really exercise much control over the game until after World War I with the establishment of the federation's International Rules Board in 1922, the subsequent publication of the "Rules of Tennis" in 1924, and the Americans joining the ILTF in 1923. The USNLTA's decade-long reluctance to join the ILTF initially stemmed from an unwillingness to countenance Wimbledon as the "Championship of the World." From within the ILTF, the USNLTA likely could have done little to stop that, as the LTA exercised a decisive voting strength over other nations in recognition of Great Britain's place as the birthplace of the game. Moreover, the seriousness with which the USNLTA took deciding the specifics of its own amateur rules would come under the purview of the ILTF just as the sporting goods companies pressed the amateur issue. In 1919 a full third of the thirty highest-ranked male players worked for sporting goods companies. Sporting goods companies would, more often than not, grant employee-players long vacations with pay during tournament times, while the amateur rules did little to dissuade sporting goods companies who actively sought the best players to work for them.[32]

The following year the USNLTA changed its name to the United States Lawn Tennis Association (USLTA). This newly named association reexamined amateur rules by devising narrower restrictions. Players soon faced an age restriction of thirty-five and a minimum employment period of ten years at a sporting goods firm if they wanted to maintain USLTA tournament eligibility. A member could also lose USLTA eligibility if he or she availed themselves of any article of sportswear, shoes, or tennis gear outside of racquets and strings. Furthermore, racquets could find their way into an association member's hands only if the member's sectional association certified the racquets as being direct from the manufacturer and restricted the amount of string the player received. The association certified a maximum number of only six racquets when these rules came into effect after World War II, even though a top-caliber player might go through a half dozen racquets during a single match. Instead of taking the view that the growth of the American sporting goods industry could promote the growth of tennis by making sure the best American amateur players came outfitted for every match with new equipment and clothes, USLTA officials prioritized their own control over the marketing opportunities accruable by their sport's biggest personalities.[33]

Association national officials, committed to amateurism in every aspect of tennis, also balked at the rise of the sports press. The penny press papers of the antebellum and postbellum decades made a point to cover boxing and other contests that were popular with the working classes, thus helping to create spectator sports in the fastest-growing cities of the North. The scale and the scope of spectatorship grew dramatically in the 1880s with sporting weeklies for male audiences such as Richard Fox's *National Police Gazette* selling hundreds of thousands of copies for issues that covered highly anticipated fights. On the other side of the class divide, magazines such as *Lippincott's Monthly Magazine*, *Outing*, and *North American Review* ran articles on sports that catered to wealthy and middle-class men. For their part, city newspapers reported the latest schedules and scores on special pages dedicated exclusively to sports.[34] On the pages and behind the lines of these newspapers and magazines, the most prominent American tennis player of the 1920s, William "Big Bill" Tilden, challenged the USLTA's amateur by-laws that barred association members from tennis journalism.[35]

No American tennis player better exemplified the USLTA's amateur ideal than Tilden—that is, until he ran afoul of the rules. The young Tilden was born in 1893 in the Germantown neighborhood of Philadelphia, in a large house just down the road from the Germantown Cricket Club. By 1900 the Germantown Cricket Club had largely abandoned its namesake sport and become one of the most prestigious places to play lawn tennis in the entire United States. Tilden's father had made a name for himself in the elite social circles of Philadelphia, opening doors for the young Tilden to attend Germantown Academy followed by the University of Pennsylvania, where he played varsity tennis. All the while, Tilden's social standing allowed him to play on the tennis lawns of local clubs, where he gradually moved himself to the top of the interclub matches and the number two ranking in Philadelphia by 1917. Tilden followed up those advancements in 1918 by winning his first national singles title on clay courts in Chicago, his first national doubles title at Boston's Longwood Cricket Club, and falling in the final to champion Robert Lindley Murray in the U.S. National Championships held at the West Side Tennis Club in Forest Hills, New York. Tilden had put the tennis world on notice.[36]

The following year Tilden did not meet expectations to win the U.S. Championships, finishing the year rated number two in America. In 1920 he traveled to England, where he became the first American man to win Wimbledon Championships. He went on to sweep his Davis Cup matches and returned to the United Sates, where he beat William "Little Bill" Johnston for his first National Singles Championship. Tilden's stellar 1920 year ended with a Davis Cup Challenge Round victory over a combined New Zealand and Australia team. He essentially repeated his 1920 victories the following year by defending his titles at Wimbledon, in the U.S. Championships, and in the Davis Cup Challenge Round played at Forest Hills. Through his complete game and what a contemporary observer called "rare judgment," by 1921 Tilden had established himself as the player to beat.[37]

Tilden and the USLTA may initially have begun to sour on each other in 1922. In the spring the USLTA announced it would not fund Tilden's trip to England to defend his Wimbledon Championship, claiming budgetary reasons and the need to keep Tilden healthy for Davis Cup play. At about the same time, his book, *The Art of Lawn Tennis*, was reissued in a second edition in the United States. Throughout the first half of 1924, controversy over the so-called player-writer raged across the USLTA with different association member clubs taking sides over the merits of the "Amateur Rule," whether or not Tilden had violated it, and, most consequentially, whether or not that violation should bar him from Davis Cup play. The popular sports press wrote overwhelmingly in support of Tilden as did the editor of *American Lawn Tennis*, Stephen Wallis Merrihew, who published Tilden's writings. With their membership divided, the USLTA Executive Committee decided to punt on the issue until the winter of 1925, paving the way for Tilden to lead the United States to a fifth consecutive Davis Cup with a September victory over Australia at the Germantown Cricket Club. The USLTA went on that winter to rewrite its amateur rules, but the matter remained less than settled, with the USLTA threatening to ban Tilden from tennis if he refused to stop writing about his matches. The opposing sides reached an uneasy compromise not long after, in which a player could receive some monetary compensation for an article as long as he or she did not play in the tournament they planned to report on and did not promote their own tennis skills in their journalism and media productions. Despite his apology letter kowtowing to the association, Tilden had no intention of giving up his syndicated columns in outlets such as the *San Francisco Chronicle* and *New York World*.[38]

The USLTA Executive Committee continued to warn Tilden until his match reporting as player-captain of the 1928 Davis Cup team embarrassed the USLTA to the degree that leaders of the organization felt they had no recourse but to suspend him on July 19, just days before the upcoming semifinal tie against Italy "because of [Tilden's] having exploited for pecuniary gain his position as a tennis player, or because of having acted in a way detrimental to the welfare of the game." The USLTA Amateur Rule Committee and Executive Committee may have congratulated themselves on the fairness of their ruling, but the fact that they issued a six-page press release detailing the string of events leading up to Tilden's Davis Cup suspension revealed just how much they realized a significant number of American sports fans might find the association's amateur principle absurd if its enforcement actually meant sidelining the country's top tennis talent from the most important international competition. The USLTA viewed Tilden's defiance as an internal membership issue. The outcry raised by sportswriters made the issue much more public than the USLTA wanted.[39]

The rising popularity of tennis quickly escalated Tilden's case from an internal issue to a national and international brouhaha. After defeating Italy on July 22, 1928, the U.S. Davis Cup team prepared to face off against the French champions in the Davis Cup Finals beginning on the 29th. The Fédéderation Française de Lawn Tennis (FFT) knew Tilden's popularity and lobbied Myron T. Herrick, the U.S. ambassador to France, to confront the USLTA about Tilden's ban. Herrick agreed with the FFT's argument that the ban on players as paid writers amounted to a self-serving position apart from the thirty-two other nations that played in the Davis Cup. Herrick worked to convince

USLTA president Samuel H. Collom to permit Tilden to participate in the match against France. With such controversy swirling, the United States lost pathetically to France, and the USLTA promptly re-suspended Tilden from association-sanctioned tournaments. Howls of protests from within USLTA member clubs and from sports fans reached the association's national offices in the form of letters supporting Tilden and urging the USLTA to reconsider its ban. Tilden appealed his suspension while he served it, returned to amateur tennis in February 1929, and continued to write and spar with the USLTA before turning professional at the end of 1930. In a later irony indicative of the 1928 suspension and the sources of support he did and did not receive, Tilden continued to garner more succor from the tennis federations of other nations than from his own country's governing body. This signaled that competing personalities as much as policies were at play given that USLTA rules fit squarely within ILTF articles 12 and 23 governing amateurism, compared to, for example, the LTA, which actually went further in restricting writing and competition tennis.[40]

The significance of the 1928 Tilden controversy was twofold. Concretely, the USLTA wanted financial control over the tennis talent in America, but the 1928 Davis Cup ban also highlighted another serious threat to amateur standards in a sport whose international footprint had grown to the point that the best players spent much of their time not only playing tennis but also competing in other countries. USLTA officials could not regulate players representing the association abroad to the degree that they could in the United States, because in America all of the clubs that hosted tournaments belonged to the USLTA. That belonging gave the Amateur Rule Committee and the National Executive Committee eyes and ears at every match. Understanding the impossibility of enforcing a ban against accepting money in other countries governed by different tennis associations, the USLTA enacted an "eight tournament rule," in which a player would have to pay their own way in all but eight tennis events a year. Given that the U.S. tournament calendar alone totaled dozens of matches, the rule essentially meant that any foreign tournament a player traveled to could not provide the player with travel, lodging, or meal expenses, because the player would have already exhausted his or her tournament expense quota domestically. The committee members congratulated themselves on another compromise between the pecuniary temptations facing players and the necessity of maintaining the integrity of amateur sports. USLTA officers suggested that the absence of specific penalties and the discretion the executive committee could exercise in not punishing certain players from extending their season at certain tournaments would stave off flagrant violations of the amateur by-laws, but in reality, violations proliferated with such selective enforcement. For example, in 1948 the United States' best doubles team, William "Billy" Talbert and Gardnar Mulloy, asked the USLTA to grant special permission for the payment of expenses related to the Rio de la Plata Championship in Buenos Aires, despite the fact that the tournament not only took place outside the normal tournament calendar for which the USLTA authorized expenses but also exceeded the number of eight events for which Talbert and Mulloy had already received expenses paid. Members of the Amateur Rule Committee griped about Talbert and Mulloy "living off the game" but allowed the players to take the money.[41]

One of the principal ways that tournament players lived off the game was by instructing players who were less capable. In late nineteenth- and early twentieth-century Britain, tennis club members viewed Anglo teaching professionals—Harry Cowdrey, George Kerr, and Charles Hierons, among others—as essentially members of the laboring class and destined to serve. Club members, by contrast, tried to emphasize how little effort it took to learn to play a good game of tennis. That leisure-class identity conflicted with the work life of the British teaching professionals to the degree that some of the most prominent paid coaches chose to move to France, where they could teach tennis in less hierarchical clubs.[42]

In America the class divide was not quite as rigid. Teaching and coaching could keep a top player on the court in order to keep their own game in shape while at the same time creating relationships with wealthy members of private clubs who were all too eager to hit a few balls with the country's best "racketeers." The USLTA did not allow members to earn income from teaching tennis—whether at a university, in a physical education class, park district, or private club—until the 1950s. Officially, there were no paid tennis teachers in America before 1910. Through the 1910s and mid-'20s, some players accepted money, club dues, and travel expenses under the table in exchange for teaching wealthy club members. That pay-for-instruction arrangement became official in 1927, when the Professional Lawn Tennis Association (PLTA) formed after a meeting in New York. USLTA officials so abhorred the idea that anyone should get paid to play tennis, even if payment was made to members of a different organization whose sole purpose existed to promote the livelihood of tennis instructors and thus grow the game, that the association's executive committee banned any competition between USLTA amateurs and PLTA teaching professionals. As with all of their "no money in the game" rules, the Amateur Rules Committee enforced the disassociation between PLTA and USLTA members selectively so that when the U.S. military asked USLTA president Lawrence Baker for his approval of interservice matches involving both professionals and amateurs, the Amateur Rule Committee gave the military the association's blessing.[43]

Such lax enforcement had less to do with USLTA benevolence and more to do with the reality of how tennis had worked in America from the very beginning. Many clubs essentially sponsored top players whose association with the club brought prestige and potentially new members. Since the turn of the century, many clubs had ignored a player's class background as long as the player delivered on the courts. Local clubs preferred flexibility; the national association preferred policy. As the profile of the game increased, clubs poured more resources into the practice time and travel expenses of their top players while forgetting to mention this support to the USLTA. These omissions flew in the face of USLTA rules that since the 1880s had strived for a complete accounting of players' tournament expenses. USLTA officials had floated a ban against all player expenses without success and thus found themselves constantly checking in with private clubs about members' expense accounts. Unreliable assistance in enforcing player expense accounts exemplified the executive committee's and the Amateur Rule Committee's heavy reliance on private sports clubs enforcing rules that often hurt the member clubs' bottom lines despite the national office's claims to the contrary. Counting a famous player as a club member was more important to most club managers than keeping a USLTA official in the national New York offices happy. The association's top amateur tennis talent felt the game "owed them a living," and all but the most genteel of club members were prepared to provide them with that living, albeit with a nod and a wink, while simultaneously espousing the "high ideals of sportsmanship and amateurism" that the association stood for, wrote Holcombe Ward at the conclusion of his decade as USLTA president.[44]

The USNLTA's commitment to amateurism created more opportunities for tennis players who were willing to play by the association's rules. By 1908 the USNLTA sanctioned ninety tournaments in the summer season alone. Leaders in the USNLTA national office formed a committee that strenuously advocated junior development by pressuring reluctant private clubs to host junior tournaments and matches. The association also advocated for the creation of an intercollegiate tennis league, which many universities embraced. For instance, by 1908 Harvard claimed a forty-court facility at Soldiers Field in Boston. A dozen years later, Charles S. Garland of Yale won the first Intercollegiate Championship endorsed by the association. The USNLTA also encouraged new players both abroad and at home. On May 1, 1908, the Mexico City Country Club hosted the first lawn tennis championship in Mexican history, with a dozen or so of America's best players traveling south of the border for the tournament—thanks in large part to the USNLTA's encouragement and financial assistance. Unlike opportunities found in many team sports, women could find tennis matches and tournaments endorsed by the association and covered by the USNLTA's official publication. "These women can play tennis, tennis such as the novice would marvel at, swift and accurate and, indeed, far superior to the game that the ordinary man who thinks that he can play some, is capable of," said one such report on a 1908 women's indoor tournament in New York City. Players in most parts of the country could also find a tournament to test themselves from rural California to the Northeast.[45] (For hosts of the most prestigious USLTA tournaments before the Open Era, see map 1.[46])

Such opportunities came with a cost for participants. Players needed to submit to the association's desire for control over every aspect of tennis. Nowhere did that exercise of control appear in starker terms than within the Eastern Lawn Tennis Association (ELTA), which dominated the national course of amateur tennis from the start. While the ELTA officially formed in 1922, tennis officials from around New York City first organized themselves in the Metropolitan Lawn Tennis League on March 15, 1904. That organization consisted of the West Side Tennis Club, the New York Lawn Tennis Club, Kings County Tennis Club, Montclair Athletic Club, New York Athletic Club, Crescent Athletic Club, and the Englewood Field Club, with the league functioning until 1912 as an arbiter of tournaments and matches between the clubs' teams and players. A similar league named the Metropolitan Association appeared four years later and organized a round-robin tournament among metropolitan tennis clubs. In 1914 the West Side Tennis Club found a "permanent home" in Forest Hills, New York, and that same year the club hosted the Davis Cup Challenge Round between the United States and Australia. The financial success of that match prompted the relocation of the national championships from the Newport Casino to Forest Hills for the 1915 tournament.[47]

The money made at popular events seldom reached far beyond a narrow orbit of clubs clustered along the Atlantic seaboard. The few officers and per-

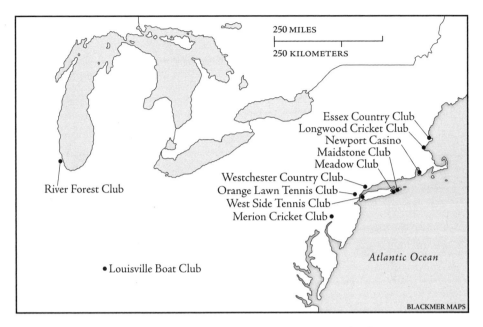

Map 1. Hosts of the most prestigious USLTA tournaments before the Open Era

manent employees such as Field Secretary Paul B. Williams originated from those parts of the country and preferred to funnel dollars back to the clubs to which they belonged. At about the time of the 1915 Forest Hills championship, the ELTA began a junior development program for players within its section funded by a combination of national and sectional monies. The advantage of hosting the big tournaments and running the association's day-to-day business mattered a great deal when combined with its refusal to grant proxy voters from clubs who—because of their location far afield from New York City (the Midwest, for example)—could not send representatives to association meetings. A general pattern of setting agenda business at the annual meeting itself, rather than informing member clubs ahead of time via the organization's official publication, became commonplace. Those policies allowed New York City clubs to exercise disproportional control over the national organization and ensured that the tournaments that offered the highest rating points, and thus attracted the best players, who in turn brought in the most paying spectators, stayed in the New York metropolitan area and kept the coffers of the host clubs full when compared to clubs in other regions of the country.[48]

World War I disrupted that pattern. The association's "Patriotic Tournaments" earned money that did not go directly to the host clubs but instead went to a general fund for the War Department. Nonetheless, at the end of World War I, the USLTA Eastern Section regained more than its former strength by meeting on March 12, 1921, where thirty-four clubs passed a constitution and by-laws that chartered the New York Lawn Tennis Association. Less than a year later, on February 4, 1922, the USLTA's membership accepted that body into the national association at the annual meeting. While not officially called the "Eastern" Lawn Tennis Association until February 5, 1927, the New York clubs effectively controlled their sectional association, the national association, and, by extension, the game of tennis for the entire nation through the 1920s.[49] Cooperation between close-knit clubs would not go unchallenged, however, as tennis gained popularity in California.

CHAPTER 2

The West Coast Game

The real challenge to the USLTA's early control over amateur tennis in America came more from inside rather than outside the amateur game. In the capable hands of amateur officials who were more concerned with growing the game of tennis in their local area rather than in following the amateur precepts laid down in the USLTA's or the International Lawn Tennis Federation's (ILTF's) distant offices, those amateur tournaments could actually turn tennis into a commercial sport that called the stated commitment of amateurism into question. Competition between different factions within the USLTA helped popularize tennis and pave the way for professionalism to enter the sport. In this the American West Coast would lead the way.

Since the 1880s, wealth and youth had moved into California. Tennis grew alongside this migration of people with capital. The game first came to Southern California around 1880 when a Canadian man by the name of William H. Young settled in Santa Monica after having attended Oxford University. Young befriended the Allen family, who—on their own holiday travels—returned to their home with one of Maj. Walter Wingfield's lawn tennis kits. Two years after Young and the Allens's first match, tennis enthusiasts started the San Gabriel Lawn Tennis Club, the earliest effort to organize California tennis along the lines of the cricket clubs on the East Coast. Mainly women, the club sponsored their first tournament in June 1882. Over the next five years, several other clubs sprouted, including the Boyle Heights Club, the first tennis facility in urban Los Angeles. The three most important clubs in the area, Casa Blanca Tennis Club of Riverside, the San Gabriel Tennis Club, and the Pasadena Club, chartered the Southern California Tennis Association in March of 1887. The following year, the California Lawn Tennis Club of San Francisco put on the Pacific Coast Championship tournament on the grounds of the Hotel Del Monte in Monterey, California, marking the first time local tennis clubs hosted a tournament sanctioned by the USNLTA. The California clubs mirrored their East Coast contemporaries by hosting more small tournaments and standardizing play on their uniquely year-round courts. In the words of the association's annals, "tennis had officially crossed the continent."[1]

One of the earliest organizations for lawn tennis on the West Coast began on July 3, 1890, when a group of Bay Area tennis clubs formed the Pacific States Lawn Tennis Association (PSLTA). Much like on the East Coast, the PSLTA formed with a primary purpose of standardizing the rules of the game among different member clubs, but the PSLTA differed in the geographic scope in which it sought to standardize the game. "Any Lawn Tennis Club in the States of California, Oregon, Washington, Nevada, the Territories of Utah and Arizona and British Columbia, shall be considered eligible to membership," read the PSLTA's constitution. The association's treasurer collected five dollars a year in dues for clubs whose membership fell below fifty players and another five dollars a year for each additional fifty members of a club's membership. Monies collected supplemented the various clubs' hosting of tournaments and interclub matches as on the East Coast.[2]

The PSLTA's by-laws detailed essentially the same definition of amateurism in force on the opposite side of the country. Players could not compete in a PSLTA-sponsored event unless they belonged to a PSLTA club, and they could not belong to a PSLTA club if they had ever "taught any sport as one of [their] ordinary means of livelihood." Following much the same rules as clubs on the East Coast did not stop clubs in the American West from expressing pride in their region in other ways. They held an annual championship attended by hundreds who paid fifty cents for day pass admittance. PSLTA member clubs partnered with local sporting good firms such as F.M.L. Peters & Co. of San Francisco to manufacture racquets "expressly for the Pacific Coast trade." Racquets with names such as the "Pacific" featured "Oriental Gut" strings, touted as the best string for both playability and the economy of Pacific Rim trade. Taken as a whole, throughout the first two decades of the game, California tennis associations exercised a far greater tolerance of money in tennis in their game than did the associations on the East Coast, even going so far as to allow some competition between teaching professionals and amateur champions, such as when professional Joe Daily defeated Sumner Hardy 7–5, 8–6 on the courts of San Francisco's California Club. Growth of the game of tennis on the West Coast went hand in hand with the economic growth of places like the Bay Area.[3]

The westward migration of the sport of tennis gained further momentum around 1900 and reflected larger social migrations of people to places like Southern California. During the first decade of the twentieth century, Los Angeles's population tripled from 102,479 to just over 300,000. The beautiful climate, an agriculturally productive landscape, and a budding urban economy provided city boosters with plenty of enticements to dangle in front of potential settlers.[4] The physical environment in particular impacted the materiality of the tennis courts in the West, where a Mediterranean climate made smooth lawns of green grass scarce. After the first games on dirt lots, private clubs and, later, municipalities started to build courts with a concrete surface because year-round warm weather prohibited lawn courts.[5]

Beyond the steeper up-front cost, hard courts were a better investment because they required less maintenance, lasted longer, and could be built on ground that was unsuitable for grass courts. The materiality of the concrete courts produced a higher bounce of the ball, allowing players to adopt a style of play that was different from what worked on the lawns of the East Coast. Rather than the popular underspin shots common on grass, hard-court players favored flat or topspin shots—that is, shots that either moved the ball across the net relatively parallel to the ground or lifted the ball high over the net before the spin brought it quickly down on the opponent's side of the court. To best accomplish the desired ball flight, players shifted their grip over to the fourth, fifth, or even sixth racquet bevel. The revolutionary hand placement became so popular with the hard-court players of Southern California that champions and tennis writers like Bill Tilden came to call it the "Western grip." A Philadelphia native, Tilden advocated the Eastern grip because of his own success in winning the East Coast lawn court tournaments with a grip better suited to the low skidding shots that were common on grass courts.[6] In short, the material conditions of the court established the styles of players hailing from different regions of the country.

What Tilden failed to note was that Eastern USLTA sections tried to hold on to their control over the game through the surface of their courts. Through a stranglehold on the grass-court summer tournament schedule, where players earned the most ranking points, the USLTA leadership kept themselves relevant long after the rise of California tennis as the world's epicenter of competitive players.[7]

California also held an abundance of open space for the construction of parks and tennis courts when compared to the more densely populated Eastern Seaboard. While San Francisco likely suffered the same parsimoniousness on some public improvements and wastefulness on others that characterized the budgets of cities in Progressive Era America, the Bay Area nonetheless got big parks built for their citizenry that afforded recreation for everyone who visited. In the late nineteenth century, the San Francisco Recreation and Parks Department operated a dozen or more courts in Golden Gate Park alone that allowed players of any income level to hit a tennis ball. By the 1910s, tennis courts even appeared 4,213 feet up the side of Mount Hamilton near San Jose in Santa Clara County, where astronomers played the sport when not gazing at the stars through their telescopes at the Lick Observatory. Far from widespread when compared to the tennis court–building boom of the late 1930s, the abundance of California courts before the Great Depression nonetheless set the West Coast apart from the East Coast and the Midwest in the first few decades of tennis in America.[8]

Similar to the evolution of the game on the East Coast, private universities played a role in growing tennis in Southern California. One such institution was the University of Southern California (USC) in Los Angeles, whose most famous early twentieth-century tennis star was Ellsworth Vines. Vines was born in Los Angeles in September 1911 to tennis parents who enjoyed both the readily available courts in Southern California and the blissful weather as compared to the East Coast. Between 1877, the first year the U.S. Weather Bureau measured annual temperature and seasonal rainfall, and 1930, the average daily temperature in Los Angeles hovered between sixty and sixty-five degrees. In the same fifty-year period, rainfall exceeded twenty inches of rain only five times. This remarkable weather made Southern California a veritable Eden for outdoor activity, of which the Vineses and thousands of others took full advantage. Ellsworth's father gave the boy his first racquet at the age of five. Over the next dozen years, Vines played in many of the local tournaments for students in Southern California. His success in high school tennis secured him an offer to play for the USC Trojans, where he excelled during his freshman and sophomore seasons. Toward the end of his second year,

Vines had played so dominantly that he attracted the backing of the Southern California Tennis Association director, Perry T. Jones, who endorsed Vines for a spot on the roster of the 1932 Davis Cup team. Vines accepted. He left the collegiate tennis that had helped make him match-tough in order to begin international competition.[9]

Another important institution that developed tennis players in California was Occidental College, which later produced California singles champion and millionaire East Los Angeles real estate mogul Alphonzo E. Bell.[10] While exceptional male champions like Bell existed and went out East to play in the major grass court events, most Californians and Americans still considered tennis "a woman's game" before the turn of the century.[11] The gendering of the sport began to change with cross-continental competition between Eastern Ivy League men and their hosts on the Pacific Coast. Dwight F. Davis, one the Harvard University players who made the California trip, was particularly impressed with the stimulating competition between players from different sectionals. Returning to the East during the middle of the America's Cup sailing races, Davis realized the potential for starting a transnational tennis competition along the same lines as the sectional matches in which he had participated. Back in Boston, he met with USNLTA president Dr. James Dwight. His interest piqued, Dwight contacted his British counterpart. A year later, in 1900, an American team and an English team played each other for the claim to a sterling silver cup that Davis had commissioned for the match. The personal and national pride of the male-dominated USNLTA Executive Board soon elevated the Davis Cup to the pedestal of primary focus for the organization's competitive player development efforts. More than two decades passed before the dominant ladies' champion, Hazel Hotchkiss Wightman, convinced the USLTA and LTA leadership of the need for an international match for women. In 1923 British and American players competed for bragging rights and Wightman's sterling vase.[12]

The Wightman Cup resembled the Davis Cup in a number of ways without ever gaining the emphasis given to each by the USLTA and the LTA. The Wightman Cup followed the challenge-round format with five singles matches and two doubles matches of best two out of three sets. The USLTA encouraged other nations to participate, but "practical obstacles" meant the contest always involved the United States versus Great Britain. Forest Hills and Wimbledon hosted the tie from year to year. All told, the twenty-three years separating the start of the two competitions shifted the USLTA's earliest focus away from developing tennis as a leisurely game equally enjoyed by women and men toward a new and more masculine sport defined by increasingly structured competition.[13]

Competition often took the form of city versus city in events such as the intercity Church Cup, founded in 1918. Victories on the tennis court for teams made up of hometown champions were a way for local business elites—who supported the teams financially, often captained the teams, and sometimes played on the squads—to mimic victories in the capital markets. Philadelphia, New York, and Boston fielded teams that competed for the first Church Cup in a multiday contest. Teams traveled with substantial entourages, and the contests became opportunities for visitors to the host club to critique and measure the local hospitality and, by extension, the economic growth of the host city. While the courts where the matches took place were privately owned by the members of the host club, the all-hometown composition of the squads and the fact that they were amateur players not beholden to play for whatever side paid them the most money gave these matches higher status than many professional contests during the 1920s—more on par with university football during this halcyon decade of amateur athletics.[14]

West Coast and East Coast also met in major team competitions in 1915 when ranking players met in San Francisco. That battle of the sections repeated in Los Angeles in 1917 and again in the Bay Area in the spring of 1922. The latter contest began with a tune-up exhibition before two thousand fans in Los Angeles in which Bill Tilden, the number one player in America, and his partner, Vincent Richards, took on the Los Angeles champion Harvey Snodgrass and the ranking player in California, William "Little Bill" Johnston. Tilden, Richards, and Johnston then traveled to the Berkeley Tennis Club in Oakland, where John Strachan partnered with Johnston in a narrow defeat for the California team.[15]

Nowhere was intercity and intra-regional rivalry more explicit than in fights over Davis Cup hosting rights. Having the greatest percentage of wealthy members, the USLTA's East Coast section controlled American tennis before 1941. Officials from the Northeast and the Mid-Atlantic wanted tennis's largest international competition played at clubs to which they belonged for reasons of both pride and the publicity their clubs garnered by playing host to such a high-profile sporting event. Club members looked forward to the inquiries made by potential new members after they saw, heard, or read about the Davis Cup matches. Many of the USLTA's East Coast section's most senior members belonged to the West Side Tennis Club, making it no coincidence that those courts traditionally hosted the Davis Cup Challenge Round when the matches took place in the United States. These same officials staunchly opposed letting another club host the tie (match), even when that club made a significantly better financial offer to the association for the rights to hold the competition on their courts. Onetime USLTA president Slew Hester, then a USLTA delegate from the Southern section, remembered casting the tie-breaking vote to accept a one-hundred-thousand-dollar offer from a Cleveland tennis club to host the Davis Cup—twenty-five thousand dollars more than the best deal the West Side Tennis Club offered. Eastern USLTA delegates and West Side Tennis Club members did not forget Hester's vote. "You have pulled the ivy off of West Side walls," they remarked, not long before they informed Hester that he was not welcome to make use of their locker room facilities during a tournament.[16]

By the second decade of the twentieth century, California made a strong claim as the producer of the greatest number of talented tennis players in the country. Whereas in the late 1880s through the mid-1890s, tennis in the American West had suffered from geography that placed lawn tennis clubs too far apart for the best players from different cities to compete against one another on a regular basis, by 1900 improvement in transportation infra-structure allowed for not just greater competition among players in the West but also yearly trips between "Pacific Coast stars" and their peers along the Atlantic Coast. By 1908 the USNLTA's national office and Eastern section sent their best players to compete in the Pacific Championship only to lose in the early rounds to middling players by California's standards. Female play-ers from California fared even better overall than their male counterparts. In 1899 Marion Jones won the U.S. National Championship and retained her singles title in 1902. After having won all the major tournaments in the United States, in 1905 May Sutton, who had learned tennis on a court built by her father on their Pasadena ranch, traveled to England and became the first American to win the Wimbledon Championships—man or woman. California women dominated the next decade of American tennis, with Hazel Hotchkiss of San Francisco, Florence Sutton of Pasadena, and Mary Browne of Los Angeles beating all comers. Champions certainly came from other USLTA sections, but by the early 1920s the most competitive tennis matches in America often involved players from Southern California versus players from the Bay Area.[17]

Those players both benefited from the organization of the California tennis associations and improved the ability of those associations to function by enhancing the prestige of the clubs that made up those associations. The most important of these associations in terms of money, players, and power was the Southern California Tennis Association (SCTA). A weak version of the SCTA had existed in an unincorporated form since 1887, but the SCTA came into its own as an influential tennis body on May 14, 1919, when tennis enthusiasts from Los Angeles, San Bernardino, Riverside, San Diego, Imperial, Santa Barbara, San Luis Obispo, Kern, and Ventura counties met to elect directors for their newly incorporated nonprofit. These men had found relying on numerous tennis clubs and local groups unwieldy in scheduling tournaments and matches; avoiding "conflicting dates" thus proved a primary impetus in the formation of the SCTA. [18]

A more important reason for forming and strengthening the SCTA soon became apparent with the shifting character of social clubs in America. In the late nineteenth century and early twentieth century, private groups such as the Pacific Coast Sportsmen's Club featured a full spectrum of athletics, games, and hobbies to attract members of high social standing regardless of their personal interests. By the early 1910s, and thanks to antebellum economic prosperity, there existed a class of nouveau riche without the same degree of deference to genteel tradition associated with older sports clubs. Clubs no longer operated simply as a place for the leisured to meet and develop solidarity among their class, because competition had grown fierce between different clubs competing for members and their money. Newer clubs thus tended to offer a more limited range of athletics and activities—albeit in a more specialized and focused way so as to attract people who were passionate about a certain activity. That focus meant tennis-specific clubs—rather than sporting clubs that happened to offer tennis—sprouted all over the country. For example, tennis clubs formed from Azusa, to Balboa, to Santa Monica in Southern California. Even with clubs that primarily focused on offering tennis to their members, a degree of diversity of purpose existed. Whereas the Azusa Tennis Association helped members organize social tennis matches, the Santa Monica Club Company tried to operate as a for-profit real estate development corporation whose subscribers wanted to see the game of tennis grow in Southern California for the mixed reasons of pecuniary gain and the pleasures found in playing the game. In either case, older clubs, such as the Pacific Coast Sportsmen's Club, that did not adapt to the new needs of newer potential members closed their doors by the mid-1920s.[19]

The SCTA succeeded in increasing its memberships where many other sporting and tennis clubs failed because of the overlap in that organization and the Los Angeles Tennis Club (LATC), founded by some of the leaders of the SCTA. A. C. Way, who helped start the LATC, chaired the meeting that formed the Southern California Tennis Association. Roland Reinke likewise served as a founding director of both organizations, and the rest of the SCTA's nine founding directors all frequented the LATC's courts. The LATC got its start in October 1920 when, with eyes toward attracting the Davis Cup tie to Southern California, a half dozen community leaders and past tennis champions purchased five and a half square acres of unsurveyed land just south of what would become Santa Monica Boulevard. The club's first directors— Thomas Bundy, Nat Browne, Trowbridge Hendrick, Chester Lyday, Roland Reinke, Simpson Sinsabaugh, and Claude Wayne—were moneyed men of great influence in the national tennis scene. Bundy, for example, had made the finals of the U.S. Singles Championship in 1910; won the U.S. National Doubles title in 1912, 1913, and 1914; competed in the Davis Cup; and married May Sutton—the most successful player of her cohort. Nat Browne, himself a fine player, and Mary Browne, America's first real professional player, who lost to Suzanne Lenglen in the first professional tennis tour in 1926 and 1927, were siblings. As president of the SCTA in 1920, Browne saw the necessity for a grand tennis club rather than several smaller ones, so he coaxed his six fellow investors into paying eleven thousand dollars for the land, out of which, three years later, they sold a third for seventy thousand dollars. With those earnings the group built two courts along Melrose Avenue and invited roughly forty local players in chartering the club in 1925. From the beginning, members envisioned the LATC as a place where the game's best players would compete. Before they built a clubhouse, locker rooms, or more courts, the club constructed bleachers capable of seating 530 people along Melrose Avenue. That was the intention of the club's founding directors, who thought of the LATC as both a place for themselves and their friends to play tennis but also as a place to enhance their social reputation and conduct business deals.[20]

Mixing pleasure, work, and profitable entertainment created the problem of money and taxes, which explained why the LATC affiliated with the SCTA. In 1926 the LATC lost an average of more than $500 a month in addition to carrying a $30,000 mortgage, a $3,100 bank note, and $1,500 in renovation costs. The club opened itself to new members to address these financial liabilities, and the increased revenue that came from ninety-six new members in 1927 stopped the club from losing money—although the large debt remained. Hosting tennis tournaments was one strategy the LATC board took to service that debt, and in 1927 the club's seven-court expansion, donated lighting system, improved heating and plumbing systems, Panatrope radio system, expanded locker room, and wood-fenced perimeter all helped to hold tennis tournaments that made rather than lost money. The LATC directors had incorporated their club as a nonprofit, but in beginning to operate very popular tennis and social events, they in fact began to turn a "pecuniary profit." The money they collected that went beyond what they could use for improving their property could thus move into the SCTA's coffers. That organization kept some and filtered the rest back into the LATC, bearing the more secure not-for-profit imprimatur of the SCTA, whose charter explicitly championed the growth of tennis in Southern California independent of the movement of money into the game in that part of the country. That arrangement gave the leaders of tennis in Southern California secure finances and a great degree of flexibility in moving money around to do the maximum amount of good for the game in their territory. The LATC could stay a "social club" and avoid California franchise tax, while the SCTA had a sugar tree to shake any time their funds ran low.[21]

SCTA directors did not personally profit from money in the game of tennis, but while they railed against the appearance of touring professionals such as Suzanne Lenglen, Vincent Richards, Bill Tilden, and, later, Donald Budge, they did want their tournaments to turn profits. In a quorum held at the California Club in Los Angeles, board members explicitly reaffirmed their commitment to amateur tennis by way of controlling the sport in ten Southern California counties. That amendment expanded their official influence over tennis by only one county from their initial chartering fifteen years earlier; however, the effect would prove far greater because, with the forthcoming construction of so many tennis courts in Southern California, the supervision they asserted essentially amounted to "control of the game of tennis," not just up the West Coast but to an increasing degree throughout the country as a whole. SCTA directors reinforced their regulatory capacity by lobbying the USLTA national office for not only district but also sectional status, by which the SCTA could exercise greater autonomy throughout the year and marshal more votes for the national association's annual meeting. By the mid-1930s, the SCTA had grown into the most robust tennis corporation—either for profit or nonprofit—in the country short of the national office of the USLTA.[22]

That growth did not mean that everyone was welcome. Patricia Henry Yeomans, a longtime LATC and SCTA member, noted that G. Allan Hancock, Thomas Bundy, Alphonzo Bell, Harold Braly, William Garland, and Simpson Sinsabaugh—all of them important early members of the LATC and SCTA—had developed some of the most important real estate throughout Los Angeles County, places like the "Miracle Mile" and Bel Air Estates. These men well understood that exclusivity and status made money in both real estate and in social club memberships. They made sure only the right kind of people played on the LATC's courts. Members barred Jews from joining and ostracized Jewish players who occasionally competed in SCTA tournaments hosted by the club. The courts, and especially the reputation of the club's prestigious tournaments—which attracted important players, officials, and promoters from the East Coast—could not be sullied by people from outside the "proper sort," maintained the 260 voting members in 1929, who were all wealthy, white, male, and Protestants or Catholic.[23]

Members and club policies across the country discriminated against African Americans in even more explicit ways. A case garnering international press coverage came in 1929 when USLTA officials barred Gerald L. Norman Jr. and the African American junior champion Reginald Weir from participating in the National Junior Indoor Championships held at the New York City Seventh Regiment Armory. Under pressure from Arthur E. Francis of the New York Tennis Association, the USLTA revealed they excluded the two players because of race, citing a need for separate tournaments administered by the USLTA for white players and the American Tennis Association for African American competitors. At first the response left NAACP directors confused, as both Weir and Norman had competed in USLTA-sanctioned matches before. What they quickly realized was that the December tournament the players tried to enter had national visibility at a time when the USLTA looked to increase the popularity of the game in the South. "Jim Crow Tournaments are not National," the NAACP stated in a press release that essentially said the USLTA were un-American, class snobs, and scared that an African American player might win the tournament. Despite the protests, the USLTA continued to rely upon its by-laws, allowing only players belonging to designated clubs to enter the national tournaments. The local enforcement of race and class kept African Americans out of the biggest tournaments during the 1920s, '30s, and

'40s at the very same time that women continued to participate fully as tennis players if not as directors of the amateur associations and private clubs.[24]

A West Coast woman, in fact, pioneered the first true commercial tennis tournament. Elizabeth "Bunny" Ryan grew up in Anaheim, California, but spent most of her playing career living in England, where she partnered with Suzanne Lenglen for five Wimbledon doubles titles between 1919 and 1925. At her Southern California home in 1925, Ryan met with *Los Angeles Express* publisher Edward Dickson about organizing a tennis tournament in the area to rival that of the major championships in Europe and the eastern coast of the United States. Dickson thought the idea could boost the reputation of Los Angeles both in America and abroad if he convinced top international talent to attend. A dozen men agreed with him. Thus was born the Tennis Patrons Association of Southern California (TPASC), whose purpose was "to bring Southern California national recognition as a tennis center." The association's directors explicitly saw the running of a highly profitable tennis tournament with international-caliber players as the means to achieve that end. The money such an event earned would then go entirely back into Southern California tennis rather than get spread around to other parts of the country, and focusing funds on junior development in and around Los Angeles would repay the initial investment of their own money and their own time by increasing the number of talented players in the area, thus giving the SCTA more pull at the national level. With the help of the top player in the country and the bane of existence for the USLTA national office, Bill Tilden, who attended the TPASC's first formal meeting at the Los Angeles Tennis Club in late 1926, the directors planned the first Pacific Southwest tournament.[25]

In designing its stadium, the LATC had one model example. In August 1923 the West Side Tennis Club in Forest Hills, New York, completed its horseshoe-shaped stadium court designed to host the U.S. National Singles Championship. That event had moved from its first venue at the Newport Casino to the West Side Tennis Club in 1915. Even with World War I, the thousands who attended the tournament far outstripped available seating and required the construction of temporary bleachers for every year's event. By 1920 the event had proven successful enough to require either a change of venue or an expansion. Club directors and USLTA officials chose the latter course of action and temporarily moved the national championships while construction of the fourteen-thousand-seat stadium and renovation of the West Side Tennis Club grounds took place until they were completed in 1924. The club sold five- to ten-year subscriptions priced at $110 per seat with a goal of filling fifteen hundred of the stadium's box seats on a presale basis. The USLTA and the West Side Tennis Club entered into an agreement that designated the club as the host for the Men's National Singles Championship, the Men's National Doubles Championships, and the Davis Cup Final matches. That contract facilitated the West Side Tennis Club's successful capital campaign to raise $150,000 for improving the facility's amenities. West Side became the first tennis club in the United States to earn a profit from a two-week tournament alone as opposed to an auditorium filled with activities the rest of the year.[26]

The same directors in the SCTA served as officers in the TPASC in addition to belonging to the LATC. Those intersecting relationships meant that the Pacific Southwest Championship received the royal treatment from the host venue but also remained insulated from the direction of the USLTA national office, which looked to secure a sizable portion of the tournament revenue for itself. Autonomy came with the cost of less financial support from other parts of the country when raising capital to get the tournament off the ground, but the LATC members and its partners solved that problem by selling box seats as the West Side Tennis Club had done. Given that the incentive for people to buy tickets in advance at Forest Hills existed because patrons knew they were guaranteed to see the top events on the tennis calendar there, what could the Pacific Southwest offer that no other tournament could? LATC president William Henry decided that people would buy expensive tournament boxes if he attracted the top players in the world. He suspected correctly that a combination of Southern California's beautiful weather and beautiful people could convince the international stars to participate if they received free travel. Henry personally visited France to gain assurance from the FFT that three of the famous "Four Musketeers"—Jacques Brugnon, Henri Cochet, Jean Borotra, and René Lacoste—would play in the Pacific Southwest event. The LATC president also brought top international players from England, Italy, and Australia in addition to America's best. To lure all of these players, the TPASC agreed to spare no expense during the players' stay in Los Angeles. Members housed some players in their own homes, they hired cars to drive players around Hollywood, they bestowed lavish banquets and dances, and they put some players and their families up in fine accommodations such as the Ambassador Hotel. The hospitality blatantly violated the USLTA's amateur by-laws and stance against money in the game, an uncomfortable reality to which the SCTA leadership reconciled themselves.[27]

Keeping top players happy helped fill the stands, however. More importantly, it made for a successful tournament. The pricey Championship Court renovation that expanded the Grandstand to "800 seats with backs" came off well thanks to the presale of the courtside boxes. Standard bleacher seats sold out at $2.20 for weekdays and $3.30 for the weekend matches. The club's proximity to Hollywood studios added a further element of glamour, because the TPASC went above and beyond to make sure top movie talent attended. What better place to put the stars than in the dozen or so private boxes LATC directors shared courtside? In the late 1920s and throughout the 1930s, anyone who came to the grounds of the LATC during the last week of September would find the best amateur tennis players in the world watched by the biggest movie stars in the world. British champion Fred Perry fondly recalled watching actors and actresses show up in the stands at the Beverly Hills–located courts wearing set makeup before returning to the nearby studios to shoot a new scene.[28]

The movie and sports entertainment worlds blended further when film stars reciprocated the favor. They often brought tennis players to backstage sets and glamorous postproduction parties. Top players like Perry played social matches with top actors such as Ben Lyon, Charlie Farrell, Fredric March, and Robert Montgomery. On occasion Hollywood talent like Theodore von Eltz even entered the Pacific Southwest Championships. All of that intermingling of entertainment talent further enhanced the regional, national, and international reputation of the West Coast's great tennis venue.[29]

Tennis fun in the California sun made a lot of money for the LATC, the TPASC, and the SCTA. Perry T. Jones and Edward Dickson, variously the treasurers and secretaries of all three of those organizations at different times, kept meticulous notes on the interaction between these organizations. Some of the records that survive are a complete accounting of the TPASC and the Pacific Southwest tournament interspersed with partial records for both the SCTA and the LATC between January 19, 1931, and December 21, 1937: disbursements routinely found their way to top players such as Don Budge and Gene Mako; accounts receivable revealed the tens of thousands of dollars in profit the Pacific Southwest made even during the Great Depression; and audits proportioned half of those profits to the SCTA, a quarter to the TPASC, and a quarter to the LATC, with seemingly not much left over for the USLTA national office. Just as important as the total amount of money raised by the Pacific Southwest tournament, if not more so, was the amount of money that remained in Southern California to develop tennis players there. The coordination among these different organizations shielded most of that money from finding its way back to the USLTA in the form of assessments the national office required of district and sectional associations. Tennis in Southern California during the '30s thus undercut the authority of the USLTA national office in terms of making amateur policy and functioning as the central banker of tennis in the United States.[30]

Without access to the United States Tennis Association (the USLTA became the USTA in 1975) national office's financial records, the exact amount of those actions is difficult to measure. One historian who was granted special permission to access the USTA archive did note that during the Great Depression "the Association's own finances were surprisingly secure."[31] Such a conclusion suggests that for poorer district and sectional associations, particularly in the South, Midwest, and West, the money sent to New York every year was not insignificant. Pointing that out is not to suggest that the USLTA national office squandered what it received from district and sectional associations; however, a close look at the historical record, at least in the case of Southern California, produced dollar-for-dollar better results in terms of the total number of new players to the game and the total number of top performing tournament players than a more centralized pooling of resources. Local control and lots of competition were crucial.

The success of the SCTA and TPASC sparked imitators across the state and the nation. In addition to the names of the directors, the incorporation records of the Tennis Patrons Association of San Diego and the Tennis Patrons Association of Santa Monica shared the same desire to "promote tennis" and much of the same language with the SCTA's, TPASC's, and LATC's articles. What these other organizations lacked was the coordination between the amateur association and a host club, and that separation initially cost the Tennis Patrons Association of San Diego the California tax-exempt status they wanted. The State of California based their tax policy rulings in part on the federal tax code, which differentiated between "activities more recreational than educational" when a corporation sought nonprofit status as an educational institution. More specifically, a prior tax law case had ruled against the West Side Tennis Club of Forest Hills, New York, which sought tax exemption without success because in hosting the U.S. National Championship, the club made a great deal more income from nonmembers than from assessments and monthly dues from members. With a few changes in language and accounting but without any substantive changes to their incorporation records, the State of California's tax board reversed their earlier decision and classed the Tennis Patrons Association of San Diego "exclusively as a recreational club" and thus qualified for tax exemptions. The willingness of the State of California to forgo taxing tennis clubs, compared to states like New York that did, created a climate for tennis in Southern California that was better than the sunny weather. Tennis clubs that did not have a special tax arrangement faced a far greater chance of financial ruin than those that did.[32]

Along with able leadership who understood how to maximize the favorable tax climate and idyllic actual climate, West Coast tennis had an even more important factor working in its favor to produce so much topflight tennis talent: the concentration of premiere tennis facilities that allowed more people to take up the game. Most cities across America counted a single grouping of public park courts along with one or two private tennis clubs. By contrast, Los Angeles had twenty first-class tennis facilities with a dozen or so more scattered throughout Southern California. Moreover, New Deal agencies found local partners in Southern California who wanted public parks with tennis courts built during the Great Depression. These efforts gave Los Angeles the highest concentration of municipal tennis courts in the country by the start of the Second World War. Talented junior players eventually found their way to private clubs, thanks to subsidies given by the TPASC, but the vast majority of players first learned the game on public park courts in the area.[33]

Nationally ranked players such as Bob Rogers, Mike Franks, Noel Brown, Dick Skeen, and Carl Earn all trained and taught on the storied La Cienega courts, whose bucolic setting and locker room facilities rivaled that of any private club. Ellsworth Vines and Lester Stoefen learned their tennis at Griffith Park. Thanks to Pancho Gonzales's fame, the former black sheep of Los Angeles's tennis parks, Exposition Park, became the citywide focal point for municipal players, with Willis Anderson, Jimmy McDaniels, Gilbert Shea, Herb Flam, Hugh Stewart, and Jacque Virgil forming a regular training group on those courts. A reputation as a fine player was enough earn invitations to play at private clubs throughout Southern California, whereas in other parts of the country, particularly the East Coast, a focus on enforcing club regulations on members and their guests acted as an impenetrable class barrier that never existed to the same degree in Southern California. Players generally expected invitations to play at the North Hollywood courts, the Westside Tennis Club, the courts at Poinsettia Park, the Beverly Wilshire Hotel courts, the city courts at 25th Street and Santa Monica Boulevard, the Hillcrest Country Club, the Altadena Country Club, and, the most important of them all, the Los Angeles Tennis Club. Ted Schroeder, Don Budge, Jack Kramer, Beverly Baker Fleitz, and scores of other topflight talent all played at the clubs in addition to occasional park play. Players-turned-administrators like Perry T. Jones ran leagues such as the Perry Jones All-Stars, which pitted top junior talent against university players at the UCLA and USC tennis courts. During the year, Southern California held tournaments that amounted to fifty-two weeks of the calendar, including the famed Winter Tennis League that kept players competing when the rest of the country took the season off. Climate did allow for that league, but, again, without the players and the organization, Southern California would have had a lot of tennis players, not necessarily a lot of world-class tennis players.[34]

Previous work examining amateur tennis in America in the first half of the twentieth century celebrated the "code of honor" that led these men under the direction of their national association to create a "golden age" for lawn tennis.[35] Looking from a West Coast vantage point and at some previously neglected sources has made for a different story. Competition among rather than harmony between the USLTA sections and regional associations attracted large sums of money into the game at the same time these same groups claimed loyalty to amateurism. Opening that spigot watered seeds that later sprouted into a robust crop of professional players who tipped the balance away from amateurism and toward professionalism. Tennis officials and amateur associations from California stimulated that process in that they presented the strongest challenge to the Northeast and Mid-Atlantic tennis establishment. By synergizing the nonprofit organizations of the SCTA, the TPASC, and the LATC, by 1940 men like Perry T. Jones laid the groundwork for what would become the most important place for tennis excellence in the world. Ironically, to make that happen, men who preached amateurism through and through practiced professionalism in their tennis dealings when they effectively paid top players to attend the Pacific Southwest Championship. The big crowds those players drew made that event into a highly profitable venture whose funds Jones, in his positions as the treasurer-secretary/tournament director of the SCTA, TPASC, and LATC, disbursed throughout the interlocked organizations. Southern California thus developed the most robust player development program in the world, thanks in no small part to monetizing the amateur game.

CHAPTER 3

The Cause Célèbre of the
Pioneering Professional

From the 1880s through the 1920s, women played tennis in numbers that rivaled those of men and surpassed female participation in any other spectator sport. Women headlined the most publicized competitive matches in the world during the same decades, but men ran the private clubs and tennis associations that controlled the game. In America the exercise of that control formed what amounted to a tennis establishment guided by an almost absolute commitment to a precept of amateurism in the game that prohibited money in most forms from finding its way to the players—be they women or men.[1] These dyed-in-the-wool men of various genteel tennis clubs could not separate their love of the game from their love of near-total control over the game. They were the principal foes of Suzanne Lenglen, C. C. Pyle, and the players who staged the pioneering professional tours that brought tennis to the masses. The men of the USLTA outlasted the early professional challenges and kept firm control of the game through the 1930s. Maintenance of that control, however, came at the cost of their willfully allowing more money into the amateur sport at the same time that they attacked professionalism of the game in all its guises.

From the earliest days of the sport as a game for ladies, play, fashion, and gender fused, and the evolution of this relationship revealed the increased sexualization of women in the American public sphere during the decades that birthed mass culture. That 1920s sexualization did not establish professional tennis in its present form, but it did nudge the sport in that direction. Forty years later a new group of women players would complete the professionalization of the game. What mattered in the meantime to tennis followers was that the game had always welcomed women even while it shunned playing the game for money. More than anyone else, women disrupted that balance and thus brought the innocent infancy of the game to a swift end.

Tennis player Suzanne Lenglen became a worldwide sensation during the first half of the twentieth century. Through her style of play, choices of fashion, and indelible charisma, the French champion was the game's first sex symbol. Other women athletes such as the Bostonian Eleanora Randolph Sears and Texan Mildred "Babe" Didrikson Zaharias competed hard as athletes in the late 1910s and '20s—Sears in polo, tennis, and squash; Didrikson in track and field and seemingly every other sport.[2] Yet neither held quite the charm and force of personality that Lenglen emanated to audiences. Lenglen garnered a transnational following by winning five consecutive Wimbledon titles between 1919 and 1923. Despite dominating the amateur game, Lenglen cared little for the all-male officials of the Fédération Française de Lawn Tennis (FFT) and International Lawn Tennis Federation (ILTF), headquartered in London, who dictated who could play and when, and even went so far as to equate her newly realized freedom as a professional with "an escape from bondage and slavery." Lenglen's European reputation informed her 1926 American tour— the first professional tennis tour—where fans and the press alike welcomed her as the most cosmopolitan of athletes. Such a high profile lent special weight to Lenglen's every word and deed. In an interview with the *New York Times*, she stressed the importance of "control" if a young tennis player were to succeed in the increasingly competitive game.[3] Her intended emphasis was on a player's shot selection; however, her remarks implied a broader definition of the individual's command of self that was constitutive of the groundswell of social and cultural changes associated with the "new woman."[4] As the first tennis player and the first woman to unashamedly make money off the game in the most public of ways, Lenglen's decision to turn professional both symbolized the greater role women assumed in the public sphere and posed a competitive challenge to the anti-professional precepts governing the game of tennis in America and abroad.

Lenglen was born on May 24, 1899, the only child of a cycling-crazed French father and an unathletic French mother. While accounts differ in designating her birthplace—Paris or Compiègne, France—Lenglen's real home was the French Riviera, where she lived for much of her childhood and teen-age years. Her family had money, but not the kind of money gambled every evening at the fashionable Casino de Monte-Carlo, where the wealthiest of Europe's wealthy gathered every winter and early spring during the late nineteenth and early twentieth centuries. Charles "Papa" Lenglen both doted on and drove his daughter to live an active lifestyle with gymnastics, outdoor play, bicycling, and dance. Living in Nice, Lenglen drew crowds of tourists and passers-by who watched her play the juggling game *diabolo* along the Promenade des Anglais, performances her father encouraged. She enrolled in the Institute Massena to study classical languages and dance. In 1910 Papa gave his daughter a toy tennis racquet that she batted about with in the family backyard. The father wanted to see great potential in his eleven-year-old, however, and soon gave her a full-size racquet, which she swung with such great fluidity that by her third month of playing she earned second prize at a local ladies' single tournament in Chantilly.[5]

Most tournaments during the late nineteenth and early twentieth centuries provided a tournament umpire who handicapped different players based on their records, experience, and a quick observation of their play in order to facilitate greater competitiveness between two unequally matched players. For example, in playing against women over twice her age, the young Len-glen might begin a match with a 30-love advantage in every game against her more seasoned opponent. Within two years, the handicapping swung in the opposite direction, with the now fourteen-year-old Lenglen beginning most of her matches down love-30 each and every game, after having assembled an impressive spate of wins that included regional championships in Picardy and the South of France Championships played in Nice. On the insistence of her father, the Nice Lawn Tennis Club granted Lenglen an exception to the no-children rule, which subsequently allowed Lenglen to practice on courts frequented by many of the world's best players who wintered in the Riviera.[6]

Many of the top tennis players in the late nineteenth century played on the French Riviera because most players of any standing at that time came from enough wealth to make the trip to France's Mediterranean Coast in order to live the lifestyle of the world's elite. The French Rivera ran from Cannes east to the Italian border and included Cannes, Nice, Monaco, Monte Carlo, and Menton. Prince Rainier and Princess Grace of Monaco took the first step in making this area into a gaming destination, and François Blanc, the man responsible for building Hamburg's gambling reputation, planned and built the casino on the Monte Carlo plateau that opened on June 1, 1866. This spurred Cannes, Nice, and other Riviera cities to build their own casinos. Luxury hotels sprang up with the casinos along the Riviera coastline, making the Riviera home to the highest concentration of exclusive accommodations and playgrounds for the wealthy in the world. Not known as a gambler, Britain's Queen Victoria also helped to popularize the French Rivera as a destination with British elite and with royals across Europe. Those same English and Continental Europeans of aristocratic backgrounds also enjoyed lawn tennis in the same years in the late nineteenth century, but the strongly seasonal and wet weather in their home countries meant they could only play the game with any regularity for at most five months out of the year.[7]

English revelers built the first French lawn tennis courts in the South of France at the Hotel Beau Site in Cannes in the mid-1880s. Within the decade the popular Renshaw brothers, Ernest and William, who had done so much to popularize lawn tennis in the United Kingdom, had traveled regularly to Southern France to show spectators there what the pinnacle of tennis play looked like. Around 1890 those in the American monied class would travel to the French Riviera to mingle with European aristocrats, and top American tennis talent would accompany this migration. Both the good and the bad played on manicured courts baked year-round by the warm Mediterranean sun, situated in groves of trees and flowers, and scented by the mistral winds that blew herbs and lavender across Provence.[8]

In 1912 many of those talented players took a train to Paris to compete in the first World Hard Court Championships under the auspices of the embryonic ILTF. Representatives from twelve of the thirteen founding nations waited to meet at the Union des Sociétés Françaises de Sports Athlétiques to officially form the first international governing body of the sport of lawn tennis on March 1, 1913. The communication among different national tennis societies and the exploratory committee for the first World Hard Court Championships in 1912 led directly to the formation of the ILTF. The French Championships had existed for men since 1891 and for women since 1896, with matches played at either the Club Stade Français, the Cercle des Sports de l'Île de Puteaux, or the Racing Club de France. From the 1880s through the 1900s, the All England Championships, the French Championships, and the U.S. Championships were the main tournaments for the best players within a particular nation. While the occasional foreign national competed in these championships, the 1912 World Hard Court Championships—played, confusingly given the "Hard [asphalt] Court" title, on the red clay courts of the Stade Français in Saint-Cloud, Paris—was the first grand tournament that encouraged international competition among the best amateur players throughout the world. The series took place on grass, clay, and covered (indoor) courts. Alternating the location and the surface of the tournaments fostered a feeling of congenial competition and internationalism among amateurs. The rotation continued until 1923, when, in a successful effort to attract the USLTA to join their organization, the ILTF made the U.S. Championships a "major" tennis tournament.[9] With the acceptance of the Australasian Championships as the fourth so-called major tournament in 1924, the ILTF had established the prime amateur competitions in the sport—competitions whose specifics changed but whose fundamentals did not until 1968.

From its first years, however, the World Hard Court Championships invited women to compete against their peers from across the globe. At age fifteen, Lenglen entered the 1914 tournament and won handily over her twenty-seven-year-old countrywoman Germaine Golding. Lenglen seemed primed to rise, but the coming of the Great War halted tournament play in Western Europe and put tennis far from most people's minds. Top male amateurs entered military service, and top female amateurs assumed jobs that aided in their respective nations' war efforts—though Lenglen spent her war years practicing on the Riviera's courts.[10] Wimbledon, meanwhile, went uncontested for four summers. Ironically, one of the few people with tennis on their mind in 1918 and 1919 was one who was most responsible for the outcome of the war. Vice Admiral Sir David Beatty of the Grand Fleet and the second in command of the British ships in their defeat of the German navy at the Battle of Jutland—the largest naval battle as measured by vessel tonnage in world history—was a major tennis enthusiast who did not let time on the high seas or war prevent him from practicing. With the fleet stationed at Scapa Flow and the Firth of Forth in Scotland, Beatty constructed lawn courts for himself. When American sailors joined the Grand Fleet in 1918, Beatty sought out American shipmen with tennis talent, eschewing the traditional boundaries between officers and enlistees. Ensign Francis Townshend Hunter, fresh from a successful tennis career at Cornell University, thus found himself taking a water taxi from his battleship to the admiral's tennis court for daily doubles matches.[11]

For practically everyone besides the ensign and the admiral, play resumed after a five-year pause. In the first Wimbledon event after the war, the defending champion, Dorothea Lambert Chambers, faced off against the young Lenglen, twenty-one years her junior. The two were a study in contrasts. Chambers had won Wimbledon a handful of times; Lenglen was competing in her first Championships. Chambers also held the Olympic gold medal, while Lenglen had never played a match outside of France. Lambert was married with a family; Lenglen was essentially still a teenager. These differences were not lost on fans and fellow competitors alike, but simply noting obvious differences belied the very real overlaps between the experienced Chambers and the youthful Lenglen.[12] Chambers herself developed these linkages in her best-selling 1910 book, *Lawn Tennis for Ladies,* in which she skewered claims that young women should avoid athletics. She flatly dismissed the first argument—that women need pass on athletics as a health precaution—as nonsense without merit. Addressing the claim that athletic participation made a woman less of a woman, Chambers admitted that the idea may be so if frailty constituted the essence of "womanliness." Citing a heroic example of the participation of women in battle, she threw out the simple gender binary of strong men and weak women in favor of a simpler complementary relationship rooted not in fundamental difference but in what she saw as, at least, a kernel of equality. With this belief in mind, Chambers brushed away the last major claim against lawn tennis for women—that is, that athletics made women less sexually attractive. The instant of a camera flash often caught both male and female athletes in a moment of unflattering concentration, yet attendees in sporting events seemed to enjoy the play of women as much as the play of men. Rather than shying away from competing hard, Chambers emphasized that viewers might find "real pleasure" in watching women play not a dainty game but with "signs of excitement," lean "muscles," and "her face set."[13]

The riveting 1919 final match certainly gave spectators much to feel good about. Chambers held two match points, which the youthful Lenglen fought off, eventually overcoming Chambers 8–10, 6–4, 7–9 in the longest Wimbledon title match in the tournament's history. The back-and-forth of the match was only part of the drama, however, as Lenglen's bold fashion departure turned heads and moved sports fashion in a bold new direction in line with that of the new woman.[14] For her part, Chambers bristled at primped outfits that restricted movement, instead stressing modesty and functionality in dress. Lenglen, by contrast, preferred outfits that accentuated the movement of her body on the court rather than cloaking it. The debut of her "half-calf" dress at Wimbledon tolled the death knell of the traditional ankle-length tennis dress. And like her career itself, the ability to push sartorial boundaries arose from the European-wide reorientation of gender boundaries following World War I. With the major European nations mustering between 15.4 and 22 percent of their male populations, millions of women took up war industries work in factories. Such labor required that many women literally wear pants for the first time. The trouser became a legacy of the war for women, who entered the postwar period with a new horizon for work, in no small part due to the roughly 9.3 million soldiers killed during the war (or between 20 and 40 percent of the military-eligible male population killed, leaving roughly a third of Western European women widows), and a new fusion of form and functionality in their dress.[15]

Over the next seven years, Lenglen dominated tennis in Europe and carved a name for herself as the first continental superstar in women's sports. Spectators, the media, and fellow competitors often likened her movement on the court to that of a ballerina. In so doing, they projected their own assumptions of French national identity onto the Frenchwoman Lenglen. Fellow players like Kathleen McKane Godfree, comparing her to other ladies on the tour, noted Lenglen's "nice figure" accentuated by her revealing mid-calf dresses. Her focused gray eyes were said to haunt opponents and bedazzle fans close to the courts where she strode. She always wore white dresses and tops, occasionally a cardigan sweater, and the vibrant blue, orange, or red chiffon scarf that held back her hair and punctuated her otherwise white attire, which became her fashion staple. Remarkably, her popularity and sex appeal existed despite her widely discussed plainness in terms of facial features. What actually enhanced her charm was the combination of her athletic movement and her confident personality. Technically, she could play every shot in what decades later professionals came to call an all-court game. "You never knew what's coming next," remarked one opponent, discussing a match against Lenglen. This variety of shot-making enthralled spectators, who felt they were watching a graceful and new creation every time Lenglen stepped onto the court and moved to hit the ball. But that same thrill of the new also cut in a different direction, as American audiences were quick to accuse Lenglen of French fickleness. In 1921 the FFT pressured Lenglen to travel to the United States to compete against Molla Mallory in the American championships.[16]

Mallory, born Anna Margrethe Bjurstedt in Mosvik, Norway, on March 6, 1884, took up tennis on the indoor but poorly lit courts of Christiania (Oslo). During her teenage years she quickly established herself as the best player in Norway, woman or man, and played regularly throughout Scandinavia, including with the dignitary and tennis enthusiast Prince Gustav Adolf of Sweden. Like many women in the Nordic countries, Mallory trained "as a masseuse," after which she went to London to give massages at private lawn tennis clubs while working on her game. She also played tournaments in Germany before moving back to Norway and competing as that country's lone entry in the 1912 Olympics. In October 1914 Mallory immigrated to the United States and worked as a masseuse. Living in New York City, Mallory watched the players compete in the Men's National Tennis Indoor Championships held at the Seventh Regiment Armory and told herself that she belonged on the tennis court again. She entered the 1915 Women's National Tennis Championships, the most important women's tournament in the United States, hosted every year since the event's inception in 1887 by the Philadelphia Cricket Club. In the finals, Mallory defeated Hazel Hotchkiss Wightman—a three-time event champion, the most dominant American player up to that point, and an outspoken advocate for the presence of women in competitive public sports. Mallory built on her national title in the coming years by winning tournament after tournament across the United States. Since she had not played in Europe since 1914, though, questions remained on both sides of the Atlantic who the best player in the world was after the end of World War I.[17]

Having won Wimbledon in 1919, 1920, and 1921, and the Olympics held in Antwerp in 1920, Lenglen still had not answered that question to the satisfaction of American spectators when she undertook her first trip to play tennis in the United States in the late summer of 1921. Her visit caused more confusion for herself and for tennis enthusiasts than it clarified, because the seemingly unbeatable champion in London, in Paris, and on the Riviera lost in the most embarrassing of ways to Mallory. With seven thousand New Yorkers filling the West Side Tennis Club stadium court beyond capacity on August 16, 1921, for the Frenchwoman's second-round match against Mallory, Lenglen swooned illness and quit not long into the match as the disgusted crowd howled "cough and quit" to the shocked champion. Lenglen's belief that her play stood in for all the French was turned on its head with her default. Her refusal to play on buoyed the American stereotype of French athletes and, by extension, French people who surrendered to defeat when confronted with the slightest challenge rather than persevere in the face of adversity. British audiences likewise struggled to move past hackneyed opinions of the Frenchwoman Lenglen. In a particularly galling case, a Wimbledon referee scheduled Lenglen to play a cakewalk singles match in the 1926 Championships immediately before a competitive doubles match. Lenglen sent a message from the locker room that she would play the doubles first and the singles after or would need more rest between the matches. When she arrived early for her doubles match, she found an irate official, an angry crowd, and a disappointed monarch in Queen Mary, who had not received Lenglen's request for a postponement of her singles match. The hissing crowd forced Lenglen to retreat to the locker room, where she broke down in tears and decided not to play Wimbledon ever again.[18] As an international amateur champion, Lenglen still answered to the nationalistic perceptions that people expected her to fulfill.

Lenglen proved far more successful in challenging the prevailing parameters of the female breadwinner in the West during the 1920s. Her 1926 American tour marked a turning point in both professional tennis and the history of women in sports. The tour opened on Saturday, October 9, 1926, at 8:30 p.m. at New York City's Madison Square Garden—just three short months after Lenglen had sworn off the grandest amateur tournament, Wimbledon. People thought she was a beauty, aside from her buckteeth. Photographs of Lenglen had long found their way to America, to the delight of fans in the United States. Seeing her live, with her body in motion, was even better. While Lenglen's talent made sure people paid for a ticket, Charles C. Pyle made sure that Lenglen and her five fellow players had a stadium to fill.[19]

Working in the entertainment business as a theater proprietor in the 1910s and '20s in Champaign, Illinois, Pyle used his connections at the University of Illinois to convince the standout running back Harold "Red" Grange of his earnings potential in professional football. In 1925 Pyle steered Grange into a lucrative contract with the Chicago Bears that earned the "Galloping Ghost" and his manager, Pyle, one hundred thousand dollars between the two of them in only four months of professional football. At the same time Grange's career took off, however, Pyle also experienced financial troubles in founding the New York Yankees football team, his unsuccessful bid to bring his franchise into the National Football League, and his subsequent founding of the American Football League, which floundered in its first and only season in 1926.[20]

Pyle's move to professional tennis in the summer of 1926 was an attempt to regain momentum after his football franchise failure. His tennis venture succeeded in that it secured his public perception as a visionary sports promoter who was willing to take on and defeat conservative elements in America's athletic associations. As he had with his Red Grange California tour, Pyle relied on the Hollywood entertainment promoter William "Champ" Pickens to convince Lenglen to agree to tour the United States as a professional. Pickens met with Pyle in Chicago to make clear that they better have at least fifteen thousand dollars—unheard of pay for a single athlete at the time—to persuade Lenglen to turn professional, which Pyle readily accepted. Pickens apprised officials of the USLTA of his and Pyle's plans, only to face a stiff rebuke from secretary Edward Moss, who explained that the association would do what it could to undermine efforts by anyone outside the USLTA to allow Lenglen to play tennis in America. Threats only emboldened Pyle, Pickens, and the press, with newspaper editorials stoking excitement among the American and European public by suggesting that Pyle would pay Lenglen a quarter of a million dollars for her tennis and Pickens would produce another one hundred thousand dollars for movie contracts. In France, Pickens promised Lenglen Broadway roles, ghostwritten newspaper columns, readings for her novel *The Love Game*, and his best efforts for a Hollywood studio contract. The two settled on two hundred thousand dollars for the U.S. tennis tour, with any additional money Lenglen earned from outside entertainments going directly to her. Then the back-and-forth with Lenglen's entourage began, and Pickens needed Pyle to finalize the arrangement.[21]

Pyle quickly regained his reputation for flair, which he had lost during the failed American Football League plan, by pioneering the public contract signing of star athletes. He did this by traveling to France in July 1926, where he signed the agreement with Lenglen. Newsreel crews and print journalists surrounded Lenglen and Pyle sitting in a Pourville, France, garden as the athlete and her new promoter painstakingly read over the contract point by point. For Pyle, the signing presented him to the world as the diligent manager more akin to a business executive than the less scrupulous entertainment promoters associated with prizefight gambling, seedy theater reviews, and jazz nightclubs. As a player forsaking the popular amateur tournaments for an upstart professional circuit, Lenglen's image did not come across as favorable during the signing, primarily because many people thought that with her turn to the heretofore unknown professional competition, they would not get to see her perform on the court. Pyle's outsider status as an American who planned for most of the tennis to take place in the United States further stoked the anxieties of Europe's tennis society. On an unspoken level, Lenglen's paragraph-by-paragraph study of her professional contract projected an image of her as a capable breadwinner who was more than able to earn a living from her trade and look after her own finances rather than rely on the patronage of wealthy tennis fans. By signing the contract, Lenglen announced in the most public of ways her willingness to compete not on someone else's terms but on her own.[22]

Lenglen opined forcefully that financial remuneration was her primary motivation for giving up amateur competition to play on Pyle's professional tour. She complained that having dominated her fellow opponents while at the same time having commanded the public's attention when it came to tennis for the last dozen years, she deserved some of the "millions of francs" that the FFT, the ILTF, the LTA, and the USLTA all collected from the sweat off her back. That labor helped Wimbledon bring in $150,000 in gate receipts alone for the 1926 Championships while the Riviera tournaments that Lenglen headlined leaned on her star appeal even more heavily to get people into the stands. She also paid fees to play tournaments for which she received no prizewinning compensation. While she had certainly accepted more money by covert means than the $5,000 lifetime earnings she admitted, Lenglen undoubtedly would have earned a great deal more had amateurism not prohibited competitive tennis from meeting a player's fiduciary duty to themselves. Lenglen argued that tournament and association officials were the ones who broke their responsibility to tennis by charging high ticket prices for tournaments in order to subsidize their private clubs. She suggested they put the money back into growing the game for everyone rather than for a select few who had the money or the connections to belong to those clubs. With Pyle's help, the Frenchwoman appealed to Americans' deep-seated distrust of inherited wealth, a shared heritage of democratic "revolution," and a belief in the "equality" of opportunity in order to justify professional tennis where it had previously not existed. Spurned by the European tennis establishment at the 1926 Wimbledon Championships, Lenglen expected America to reward her talent and industriousness as Europe had not.[23]

The reality of the professional tour quickly confronted her with the challenges of holding a primary stake in a fledgling sports enterprise. As the headliner of the event, her performance mattered more for the bottom line of the tour than that of her fellow professionals—Californian Mary Browne, New Yorker Vincent Richards, Frenchman Paul Féret, Californian Harvey Snodgrass, and Californian Howard Kinsey—who rounded out the tour. The match format varied somewhat across the dozens of cities the troupe barnstormed across, but the general program pattern featured Richards versus Féret in an opening singles match, followed by Lenglen versus Browne in the main event singles match, then a men's doubles of Richards and Snodgrass versus Kinsey and Féret, and a mixed doubles finale pairing Lenglen and Richards versus Browne and Kinsey. Such a schedule, if the matches went to a third set of play, could mean more than four hours of tennis for spectators who paid between $2.00 and $5.50 to watch the professionals compete in an indoor and rowdy environment far removed from the gentility of the private clubs that hosted the USLTA's amateur lawn tennis tournaments. Association officials would not countenance Pyle's tour and did what they could to hamstring it by encouraging their members not to attend and by forbidding their own chair umpires and linesmen from calling the matches. Pyle solved the logistical problem of finding venues that allowed his group to play by coming up with a homemade transportable canvas court that workers could lay on the floor of any municipal auditorium or city armory; nevertheless, he often had to scramble at the last minute to find officials capable of keeping the tennis on track.[24]

Lenglen's talent and temperament posed the bigger problem for the tour promoter Pyle. Night after night she simply proved not just better than but much better than Mary Browne. With steady and sensationalized coverage from the newspaper sportswriters, the professionals moved across North America from New York to Canada, back stateside along the East Coast, in the Midwest, down the West Coast, from Vancouver to Los Angeles, into Texas, across the South to Florida, and even Havana, before the tour's final engagement at Providence, Rhode Island, on February 14, 1927. But that same coverage meant that as Lenglen won every completed match against Browne (two of the thirty-eight went unfinished)—and with notable exceptions, such as Los Angeles, where around seven thousand fans crowded the Grand Olympic Auditorium for the December 28 match—Lenglen's brutalizing of Browne contributed to the steady decline of attendance and gate receipts as the tour progressed. As the tour began in the South and Florida, Richards, the second draw card for the tour, fell ill and began sitting out most of his matches; Lenglen followed suit as the barnstormers entered their final Mid-Atlantic and Northeast leg. While past champions helped fill the seats in amateur tournaments, a professional tour that paired the same players against one another night after night meant less drama than the more wide-open tournament draws. That fans continued to show up in the thousands even though the results of the night's matches had become a forgone conclusion exemplified that people agreed to pay not to see competitive tennis but to be entertained by the bodies on what amounted to a stage. In giving that sort of

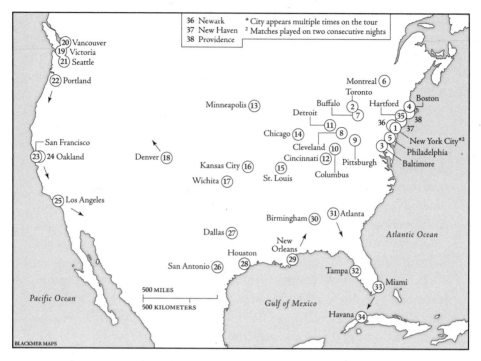

36 Newark   * City appears multiple times on the tour
37 New Haven ² Matches played on two consecutive nights
38 Providence

20 Vancouver
19 Victoria
21 Seattle

22 Portland

Minneapolis 13

Montreal 6
Toronto

Buffalo 2   Hartford 4   Boston
Detroit   35
       7   36   38
       11   1 37
San Francisco   Chicago 14   8   9   5
23) 24 Oakland   Denver 18   Cleveland 10   3   New York City*²
                 Cincinnati 12   Philadelphia
       Kansas City 16   15   Pittsburgh   Baltimore
       Wichita 17   St. Louis   Columbus

25 Los Angeles

Birmingham 30   31 Atlanta

Dallas 27   Atlantic Ocean

New
Orleans
Houston
San Antonio 26   28   29
                 Tampa 32
                          33 Miami
Pacific Ocean   500 MILES
                 500 KILOMETERS   Gulf of Mexico
                                  Havana 34

BLACKMER MAPS

Map 2. Cities played on C. C. Pyle Presents Suzanne Lenglen North American
Professional Tennis Tour, October 9, 1926, to February 14, 1927

performance, Lenglen was truly unrivaled.[25] (For cities played on the Suzanne Lenglen Professional Tennis Tour, see map 2.[26])

Newsreels showed Lenglen moving like a dancer when she played on the tennis court. A BBC newsreel put Lenglen's accomplishments as a sportswoman and sports-growing influence in society on par with the work done by women reforming gender practices in work, health care, education, and politics. One spectator at Lenglen's matches also hinted that fans enjoyed seeing Lenglen's body in motion because her strides often produced unclothed views of her *je ne sais quoi*, to the delight of those seated courtside. Having observed most of Lenglen's matches, Ted Tinling recalled that glimpses of Lenglen's breasts appeared with such regularity that male spectators had given them the nicknames "Mary" and "Jane."[27]

Lenglen's cavalier approach to a predominantly conservative sport and her blasé attitude toward conventional dress and codes of conduct on and off the court set an example that few of her contemporary competitors emulated. Far less flashy but a far better embodiment of the prevailing notion of amateurism was the famed American champion May Sutton Bundy, who won her first Southern California Championship in 1900 at the age of fourteen. Twenty-eight years later, at the age of forty-two, Sutton won her last Southern California Championship. Over the course of her three-decade-long career, she won the U.S. Championship in singles and doubles as well as lifting the Wimbledon singles trophy twice. She never thought about turning professional, and outside of a little teaching, which she despised, Sutton never accepted any direct money for her tennis skills. With financial support from her family, a career as an amateur worked fine. Moreover, like all the very top American amateurs, Sutton accepted the USLTA's travel funding for competition in Wimbledon and on the Wightman and Davis Cup teams. In the USLTA, experience meant as much as or more than compensation, because it offered cultural vistas otherwise closed to teenagers or players in their early twenties. Sutton recalled, with fondness, the ocean liner cabin for the Atlantic crossing, a hotel room for several weeks in London, meals covered, and the possibility for additional European destinations if the match schedule aligned—on balance, a real degree of encouragement for women athletes that was not found in other sports at the time. In 1905 it all seemed like a pretty sweet deal for the teenager from Southern California. In a related vein, Sutton agreed that the ankle-length dresses worn by the ladies into the 1920s seemed a bit silly but were not worth fussing over, because they did not affect her ability to move on the court. This more traditional approach to women in tennis and tennis in general would encounter resistance from those who followed Lenglen's example, but it would remain more or less intact for the next two decades.[28]

Thanks to Lenglen, elements of the stodgy paternalism in the administration of the game came under increasing fire in the early 1930s while traditionalists tried with greater difficulty to remain resolute. Women and on-court fashion again became one of the chief areas of contention when reports came from across Europe in 1930 that Lenglen had designed what the newspapers called "Suzanne Shorts" that sat about an inch higher than the kneecap.[29] American National Champion Helen Hull Jacobs abandoned the tennis dress and courted controversy when she embraced these Bermuda shorts in the 1933 U.S. Championship at Forest Hills. That same season, English Wightman Cup team captain, Tim Horn, refused to allow his female players to wear shorts despite Jacob's insistence that "they're so comfortable and eliminated the not-infrequent occurrence of skirts blown up head-high on windy days."

If modesty mattered, shorts proved the preferred sartorial statement. That reasoning did not persuade the English Wightman Cup handlers, and the British women wore dresses in 1933. A year later, though, this time playing in London, the English team wore shorts. Needless to say, these shorts were far from the Lycra form-fitting styles popularized in the 1970s and worn by female athletes the world over since then. What came later, however, in no way diminishes the sex appeal of the Wightman Cup players' Bermuda-style shorts to contemporary audiences in the mid-1930s and '40s. From then on, women players from across the world often opted for comfortable shorts over the more restrictive dresses.[30]

Pushing fashion boundaries was just one of the ways women players expressed their solidarity across national and against the traditional paternalistic elements of the national tennis establishments. Another important way they did so was through the informal mentor and mentee relationships they made outside of official tennis federation channels. Here as elsewhere, Lenglen set the trend. During her years of competitive play, Lenglen pummeled players so mercilessly that her opponents bragged among themselves about how many points rather than how many games, sets, or matches they had won against the Frenchwoman. But after her retirement from professional tennis, Lenglen proved far less self-absorbed and more nurturing of fellow tennis players than sportswriters and spectators had given her credit for. Helen Hull Jacobs recalled with fondness endless hours of rallying in Paris with a retired Lenglen, who helped Jacobs reach top form. Even in practice, Lenglen "was really an experience," Jacobs said. In the minds of ILTF, FFT, and USLTA officials, once a professional always a professional, meaning these practices flagrantly violated their rules prohibiting the mixing of amateurs and professionals. For Lenglen and Jacobs, these practices were nothing of the kind; rather, they were simply sharing the wisdom of the revered retired champion with the heir apparent—sisterhood and solidarity among sportswomen.[31]

Lenglen looked to share her tennis expertise with an even wider audience when she partnered with the print division of the world's leading sporting goods manufacture—A. G. Spalding & Bros. In 1920 American Sports Publishing Company distributed *Lawn Tennis for Girls*, featuring an inside cover photo of Lenglen, with piercing eyes and bedecked in jewelry, dressed glamorously and provocatively with her bandeau and wrapped in a fur cloak. The firm that Albert Goodwill Spalding founded in Chicago in 1876 continued to grow after his 1915 death by extending their women's athletic market share by converting sections of their flagship department store on Fifth Avenue in New York City into ladies' athletics. They also built "beautiful women's sports specialty" stores on 211 South State Street in Chicago as well as throughout the Midwest, Mid-Atlantic, New England, and Pacific Coast. Lenglen became an important poster child for Spalding's push into women's sports, although when it came to athletic wear, the company recommended ladies dress more conservatively than what Lenglen actually wore on the court. Women should follow her advice, though, on the game itself, urged Spalding. In fact, the preface to the American edition of *Lawn Tennis for Girls* claimed that Lenglen knew more about tennis than any man, praise supported by the convenient omission—from the book's introductory biography—of the male teaching pros Lenglen regularly trained with on the Riviera courts. Her dad had taught her a little tennis, and she taught herself the rest, the personal history read. The remainder of the book described Lenglen's playing philosophy, stroke mechanics, and match strategy. All of that was orthodox for the time except for the particular stress Lenglen placed on movement—a far more forward-looking emphasis that future champions took to heart.[32]

Lenglen also conveyed her accumulated tennis wisdom to men. The subordination of the conventional male realm of athletics by a woman champion elucidated the femininity of tennis in reciprocity to the genesis of most other organized sports. Widely considered the greatest student of top players' technique and tactics, French champion René Lacoste warmly recollected that he in fact benefited from the tutelage of Lenglen when it came to confronting challenging opponents. Lacoste enjoyed a storied transatlantic rivalry with the American Bill Tilden throughout the 1920s in part because Lenglen herself had grown familiar with Tilden's game from her professional tour through the States in 1926. Afterward she shared ways to exploit Tilden's weaknesses with her compatriot. Lacoste took her advice to heart and gained better results against the American before the French "Musketeer"—so called by contemporaries—retired from competitive play in 1930 following his French Championship victory. He went on to control a multinational sportswear company after having created the iconic alligator logo that adorned the ubiquitous polo shirts bearing his name.[33]

Male players even decided to forsake their own amateur careers in favor of professional tennis because they believed that their own financial situations could benefit from Lenglen's appeal, which was raising the profile of professional tennis. Vincent Richards, Paul Féret, Harvey Snodgrass, and Howard

Kinsey all felt that way enough to tour with her, but in that decision they failed to calculate what would happen to them when Lenglen decided she no longer wanted to travel across America. From the beginning of the tour, in October 1926, Pyle had promised that his players would travel across the Atlantic to bring professional tennis to Europeans. By the start of 1927, however, that pledge had become impossible to fulfill because of mistrust between Pyle and Lenglen. Lenglen was more than ready to return to Europe, but not necessarily to play tennis for Pyle. However, Pyle had grown tired of Lenglen's personal demands and the growing number of followers drawn into her inner circle, each with an opinion on what was best for her. So on February 16, 1927, Pyle simply announced that he would not take his players for a European tour and that he would no longer promote professional tennis in any capacity. Whether or not he had taken any concrete steps to make a European tour a reality did not seem to matter to Lenglen, who took the one hundred thousand dollars she had made on the tour and left for France less than a week after the conclusion of the tour. Richards earned around thirty-five thousand dollars, Browne around thirty thousand dollars, Snodgrass and Kinsey likely much less—at least certainly when compared to the one hundred thousand dollars Pyle cleared for himself on the tour. The first professional tennis tour in the world had grossed around five hundred thousand dollars, but that came at a big cost for all the players, who could never go back and play the amateur tournaments or compete for their country in the Davis Cup.[34] Lenglen's departure left American professional tennis in disarray.

CHAPTER 4

Depression–Era Developments in Amateur and Professional Tennis

Competition in both domestic and international tennis intensified during the 1930s in the run-up to World War II. Defections of amateurs to the professional ranks appeared as a political act when nations needed to field the best squads for global competitions. At the same time, the financial realities of the Great Depression spurred a host of talented tennis players to look for ways of making money apart from the game. Competition among amateurs, between amateurs and professionals, and among professionals all increased before World War II stymied the sport of tennis along with the rest of the world.

In the late nineteenth century, Britain led the world in having produced the most imitated players and the most influential coaches. That position existed despite the classist undertones in the LTA's mixed commitment to player development, a stance that actually helped diffuse tennis know-how abroad. Top British professional coaches, including Tom Burke, Tom Fleming, and George Kerr, played money matches along the Riviera and coached in France and Austria-Hungary rather than stay in Britain. Wilberforce Vaughan Eaves showcased his playing talents in both America and Australia along with coaching a cadre of Australian tennis players that included Australia's first Wimbledon winner, Norman Brookes. By World War I, however, Britain had ceded pole position for player development to the United States, particularly Southern California.[1]

Dick Skeen was one of the influential early California coaches. He grew up in Winnsboro, a little hamlet in East Texas, in the second decade of the twentieth century. His father was very prosperous by small-town standards; he owned a large share in the county bank, a small five-and-dime store, and various tenant farms. After Skeen's mother's death, his father married a woman who despised the young Skeen and physically abused him. Skeen spent his summers away from his stepmother's beatings working on one of his father's farms with little in the way of recreational sports prospects. Tennis certainly was too "sissy" a sport for a Texas boy to take up. In 1918, however, Skeen's father moved the family to Southern California, bought a large house and lot for $14,500, and by 1919 had flipped the house for a $100,000 profit. Skeen began school at the Selma Avenue Grammar School and failed miserably at physical education. Down the street from his school along Hollywood Boulevard sat the Hollywood Hotel, where, before Beverly Hills grew into the home for the nation's screen actors, the biggest names in silent film lived. Skeen bummed around the court behind the hotel more to catch sight of the stars than for the tennis. He would also collect tennis balls hit over the fence, and on one occasion he was given a racquet by Bert Lytell after the comedian cracked the wood frame during play. Skeen liked swinging his broken racquet, and when he earned enough money from his *Los Angeles Times* paper route, he bought a new racquet and tennis shoes.[2]

Skeen had a difficult time finding a place to play, though. In the early 1920s, all of Los Angeles had only four courts open to anyone, and the town of Hollywood had only three. Fortunately for Skeen, Hollywood High School, where he began attending, made two of those courts available. Before school and during his lunch hour, Skeen hit on the school's courts, hardly noticing the decrepit condition of the concrete he treaded over. What Skeen had noticed, however, was that next to no one in burgeoning Los Angeles County taught tennis for money. So in 1931 he convinced the parents of thirteen preteen and teenagers to let him try teaching their children tennis lessons on the weekend. Skeen's success with those kids led him to a ten-dollar-per-month salary as a tennis professional, instructing the five members of the Pasadena Tennis Club. While he helped increase the club's membership to fifty in short order, Skeen still faced the difficult reality that the metropolitan area had relatively few public or semipublic courts. He therefore spent most of his time teaching juniors at Bart Wade's private court and instructing Beverly Hills and Santa Monica resident movie stars—including Bing Crosby, Gary Cooper,

Cary Grant, Fred Astaire, Joseph Cotten, Johnny Weissmuller, Merle Oberon, Norma Shearer, Dolores del Rio, Hugh O'Brian, and Cornel Wilde—on the movie stars' private courts.[3]

By the late 1930s, with the proliferation of public tennis courts across the country, the popularity of the game had risen to the point that Skeen joined a tennis professional exhibition tour in 1939 across the United States and Canada. During the war years, he taught for a time in Palm Beach, Florida; with the conclusion of the fighting he went to France and Italy to teach; and in 1946 through 1948 he instructed the Mexican Davis Cup team. He returned to teaching in Southern California that same year and over the next two decades taught at and managed a variety of clubs up and down the Golden State.[4]

Mercer Beasley was an even more influential American tennis coach because of his ability to locate and develop juniors who were capable of promising professional careers. Beasley first played tennis in 1893 on a grass court built by his father at the family's New Jersey home. He struggled because his poor distance vision made spotting the ball difficult, but he seemed to grasp the technicalities of proper stroke production. Over the next few decades, Beasley honed his skills for communicating the best way to hit the ball to college players at Princeton, Tulane, and the University of Miami. His real talent was spotting potential in young players that no one else saw, as was the case of the eleven-year-old Frank "Frankie" Parker, whom Beasley first noticed at Milwaukee's Town Club in 1925 and, who, under Beasley's instruction, went on to win top junior tournaments, two major men's single titles, and join the professional tour in 1949. In 1925 Beasley happened across an even more promising talent in Southern California. Having assumed the coaching position at Pasadena High School, Beasley needed one more player to complete his squad. Someone mentioned he should go by the local bakery, where he found a long and limber teenager named Ellsworth Vines.[5]

Born in Los Angeles in 1911 meant that when Vines began playing tennis in the mid-1920s, courts were in far shorter supply than they would be a decade later. Fortunately for Vines, Beasley had some pull at the Los Angeles Tennis Club, which offered talented junior players like Vines discounted junior or association memberships at two or three dollars per month, sometimes without a twenty-five-dollar joining fee. Such a subsidy put the club's sixteen courts within reach for youngsters like Vines, who now had access to the best practice partners in the city along with the biggest tournaments in Southern California, which the LATC routinely held. After only a few years of routine instruction from Beasley, weekly practice on the club's courts, and periodic competition in smaller tournaments, Vines established himself as one of the top Southern California players. The USLTA national office even took notice in 1930 when Vines became the number one player in Southern California and climbed into the top ten in the association's national rankings. Over the next two years, Vines continued to dominate both Southern California tennis and tennis throughout the United States, winning all the big tournaments in his home state as well as the U.S. Nationals at Forest Hills in 1931 and 1932. After traveling to play tennis overseas for the first time in 1933, where he reached the quarterfinals of the Australian Championship and won the title at Wimbledon, Vines believed no one in the amateur ranks could rival him, so he accepted an offer to compete against Bill Tilden on the professional tour.[6]

Tilden remained a consummate entertainer and continued to draw fans as a professional just as he had as an amateur. He won the 1931 World Professional Championship and the 1932 U.S. professional tour victory. He played frequently against European professionals, doing his best to keep professional tennis in front of the public until an exciting new American challenger arrived. The West Coast Vines completely overpowered the East Coast Tilden during their 1934 U.S. tour. Vines was simply younger, and, thanks to the discipline he received from Beasley and Perry T. Jones in the junior development program in Southern California, he came to the professional tour with a great degree of personal discipline that had never existed in Tilden and certainly had faded a quarter of a century into Tilden's playing career. Vines did not drink or smoke, he socialized but did not chase the girls at the parties put on for the professional players, and he saved his money; while Tilden always seemed short on cash despite the adequacy of their gate receipts when divided among only four professionals. "I can remember traveling in the spring and the summer of 1934 when we played sixteen nights out of seventeen days, and must have covered two or three thousand miles," said Vines.[7]

Entering his prime, Vines was prepared for such a grueling schedule but the over-forty-year-old Tilden was not; nonetheless, Tilden promoted the tour, along with his business partner Bill O'Brien, and helped draw the fans into the stands based on his historic reputation as an entertaining player. At the end of 1934 they added a national doubles exhibition, with Tilden and Vines beating the Frenchmen Henri Cochet and Martin Plaa along with Lester Stoefen and Bruce Barnes. Without the return of the Frenchmen the following year, Tilden modified the tour into a more decentralized format that resembled short exhibition tours and round-robin play. Separating Vines from Tilden made business sense for "Big Bill," who could pair himself with a capable but less strong player like George Lott. Vines toured separately against Lester Stoefen and a few other professionals, and then the tour exhibitions would meet for a round-robin event. Tilden won both of his individual tours in 1935 and '36, as did Vines, the latter winning the final round-robins for both of those years. Clearly the better player, Vines relied on Tilden's promotional abilities until a player came along who could challenge the Californian on a competitive tour. At that point they would not need Tilden's organizational skills, reputation for theatrics, and pedigree as a past champion but could draw a crowd on the quality of the tennis alone.[8]

The challenger who came along was Fred Perry, who remarked that "like most players" in England before 1935, he had grown up playing tennis in the private clubs with the "white company of tennis stars." Perry attended Ealing County School, where the boys played cricket and soccer but no tennis, because the game did not arrive in British schools until around 1933. But Perry found an old racquet at around fourteen years of age and took it to play at the Brentham Garden Suburb Club, the Middlesex Championships contested at the Herga Club in Harrow, and the United Kingdom's top junior tournament at the Queen's Club in London. His big break came when the Herga Club began subsidizing its most promising youngsters. This assistance was far less formal than the better-organized amateur sectional associations and patrons organizations like the SCTA and TPASC in the United States. Perry particularly benefited from the help of A. R. "Pops" Summers, who helped the junior work his way into the Chiswick Park Club starting in 1928. There Perry played against many of the best adults in England, and the quality of his game rose swiftly. The following year he qualified for Wimbledon—the draw still dominated by English club players—where he lost in the early rounds. He fared far better in his 1930 season, however, with late tournament finishes in both Wimbledon and the British Hard Court Championships played at Bournemouth, securing him the backing of the LTA, who sponsored him on a tour of the United States, Brazil, Argentina, Chile, and Uruguay.[9]

Perry excelled in this international competition and began a lifelong love affair with the United States. He traveled with fellow players Leslie Godfree, John Olliff, Harold Lee, Ermyntrude Harvey, and Phoebe Holcroft Watson on a coed team, which was remarkable for its gender progressiveness when compared to tours other sports took in the 1930s. The players traveled aboard the finest ocean liners; stayed at some of the United States' finest homes, such as the Beacon House owned by Commodore Arthur Curtiss James of Newport, Rhode Island; and yachted with some of the wealthiest men and women in the Americas. In terms of tennis, the English ladies outclassed their American competition, while the American men did better than Englishmen, with Perry, the best of the British bunch, making only the fourth round of the national singles at Forest Hills. The British men had a round of excuses, such as the "poor thin quality" of the grass growing on the American courts when compared to English lawns, but Perry put it more accurately that by the mid-1930s the "standards of American lawn tennis [are] the highest in the world." Britain and France could field a fine Davis Cup squad of four to six players, but only America could put dozens of topflight competitors in a draw. That competition and the LTA's money pushed Perry to return to play the American amateur circuit year after year.[10]

By the 1933 to 1934 seasons, Perry realized that the best players in the world were not the amateurs like himself playing for the Davis Cup but the "Tilden Troupe" of Bill Tilden, Vincent Richards, Karel Koželuh, Hans Nüsslein, and most recently Ellsworth Vines. Perry respected not only the game of these men but also their grit, in that they subsisted on their own ability rather than on the "underground sources" of money and "shamateur" practices that amateur players and amateur associations routinely practiced. At that time he defended the practice not only because he took such money himself on which to live but also because he believed subsidizing players from outside of "the moneyed and leisured" was the only way to reach "world pre-eminence in the game." Of his contemporaries ranked in the top twenty in the world, only the Frenchman Jean Borotra had made a business career for himself outside of family inheritance and allowances from amateur associations whose own businesslike approach to collecting cash from their member clubs meant more than enough money to distribute to a half dozen of their country's top competitors. Perhaps because "open tennis" seemed like a real possibility at that time, widely discussed in the press, Perry decided to remain an amateur, thinking the ILTF would resolve his dilemma for him. When that governing body's members decided to continue the prohibition between amateur and professional competition, Perry decided the time was not right to turn professional despite his observations.[11]

Two years later was the right time for Perry. He decided to turn professional because he felt he had nothing left to prove in the amateur ranks and had never received the respect he deserved from the LTA authorities. Where one came from mattered in England, as it did in America, and even though Perry's family had some money, his roots were "the North Country rather than the old-school-tie country" of Sir Samuel Hoare and the other leaders of the LTA. He gave those men four Davis Cup titles and was British singles champion of Wimbledon three times by 1936, and they never batted an eye at the personal and psychological toll that managing such high national expectations for his country had had on the North Country lad. Turning professional was a way for Perry to make tennis personal again—and get paid for doing so.[12]

On November 6, 1936, at the Wall Street offices of the firm Donovan, Leisure, Newton & Lombard, Perry accepted Bill Tilden's one-hundred-thousand-dollar guarantee to play tennis against Ellsworth Vines in a twenty-two-week tour. That agreement took Vines by surprise because he had recently traveled to Japan for a series of international tennis exhibitions. The professional champion Vines and the amateur champion challenger Perry finally connected over the phone, with Perry making the pitch to Vines: "Listen, Ellie, would you like to make some money?" They both did, as did Tilden and the other professional players, but so too did the group of investors Tilden put together to front the cash to guarantee Perry the one hundred thousand dollars necessary to lure him from the amateur ranks. Given the peripateticism of the professional tennis tour during the '30s, these backers did not expect a return on their investment. "If we make any money out of this, I'll give you a horse's ass in diamonds," said one. However, Perry brought with him not only a top reputation as a player but also international connections to well-established lines of credit in London. In particular, he secured coverage from the famous insurance syndicate Lloyd's of London to mitigate the risk of match cancelations from the exacting toll the grueling schedule placed on the players' bodies.[13]

Over the next two years, Perry and Vines played each other approximately 350 times and forged a friendship that lasted a lifetime: they reinvested sizable sums of their individual incomes in their tour, where Vines managed the finances in America and Perry managed their accounts overseas; they mutually owned and ran the Beverly Hills Tennis Club in Southern California; and they entered into various other joint ventures, all without a contract when it came to each other. All the while, they competed hard against each other on the court. Their 1937 tour opened at Madison Square Garden on January 6 to the unfurling of the Union Jack for Perry and Old Glory for Vines as dueling musicians struck up "God Save the King" and "The Star-Spangled Banner" to the eighteen thousand fans in attendance. They made fifty-two thousand dollars that opening night, and the nationalism narrative played well with the spectators who came out in droves night after night.[14]

That public interest, along with the money that came with it, kept the professionals to their vagabond schedule. Each evening's play featured a warm-up match between two undercard professionals, a two-out-of-three or three-out-of-five (depending on the size of the city) main event between Perry and Vines, and a two-out-of-three doubles rubber match to conclude the evening. The players then rushed to catch a midnight train, still wearing their sweats, and rode the four or five hundred miles they usually traveled between matches. The morning schedule consisted of breakfast, press conferences, and local promotional duties before the players finally took some solid hours of sleep at their hotel before waking up in the late afternoon, eating again, pitching the match one more time, usually over radio, and then heading for the arena or gymnasium to warm up for the prime-time match. Sometimes the matches went late and the players drove themselves through the night to the next tour stop, often on the brink of exhaustion. On one occasion, Vines and Perry got pulled over on the Illinois and Wisconsin border when, traveling at 85 miles an hour, Vines ran a stop sign. A search of the car produced dozens of tennis racquets and balls that, along with a small cash gift to the local policemen's benevolence fund, secured the players' release. Traveling through the Southwest, Tilden once flipped his car and decided to leave it, hitching a ride with Perry and Vines so he would not miss the start of their match that evening. Itinerancy bred solidarity among the players, all of whom shared ownership stakes and some logistical duties on the tour. The onus in 1937 fell hardest on Perry, because as the challenger to the champion Vines, people came primarily to watch those two gentlemen play, having been unable to see their rivalry since late 1933, when Vines transitioned into the professional ranks. Vines's periodic ailments and injuries meant that Perry sometimes found himself playing ten nights without a rest.[15]

As a foreigner, Perry also shouldered additional challenges that Vines, Tilden, and the other American players avoided. Chief among those problems was taxes. Players from the United States who kept a permanent residence there simply reported their income and filed their returns as any other worker would, but Perry needed constant monitoring for fear he would flee the United States without paying taxes on his earnings. Given that the 1937 and '38 professional tours flitted across the Canadian and Mexican borders several times, stopped off at a number of Caribbean countries, and ended with an extended tour of Europe, it's little wonder that the Bureau of Internal Revenue assigned an agent to accompany Perry on his different tour stops, where, after the distribution of that night's gate receipts among the players, in the locker room the auditor would report Perry's income for each match.[16]

The European leg of the tour also gave Perry a headache. The tension there came not from taxes but from the logistical challenges he faced as the organizer of the group's schedule overseas. Although the LTA had lionized its champion while he won Wimbledon titles and Davis Cup crowns, his turn to professional tennis led them to pressure affiliated clubs, such as the All England Lawn Tennis and Croquet Club, to revoke all of his privileges, which had included membership at whatever private sporting club he sought to play at in the United Kingdom. That move essentially closed most venues to the professional troupe in England—a country with far fewer armories and municipal arenas than the United States. The players frequently played in town halls or on soccer pitches such as the Liverpool club's Anfield grounds, although they also received invitations to play at grand venues like the newly constructed Empire Pool and Sports Arena in Wembley Park. That stadium and the twenty-seven thousand fans who watched them play over a three-night stay rivaled, if not bettered, any experience the professionals had had in the United States. The canvas travel court the players put down for most matches allowed them to play on almost any surface; because ice rinks, wooden basketball courts, and dance hall floors were all commonplace, they did this often. When they played outdoors, they sometimes struggled to find anchor points to tie down their court, or they competed on two different surfaces, as was the case when they marked out a tennis court in Yankee Stadium between the outfield and along the infield diamond.[17]

Perry, Vines, and all the professionals touring in the 1930s remained out in the cold because of the more adversarial relationship players and sports promoters had maintained with the amateur stewards of the game. Those stewards who organized in the USLTA monopolized most of the tennis venues suitable for hosting a large enough crowd to earn a hefty return on the matches. For example, the 1937 professional tour between Perry and Vines consisted of close to sixty matches between the two professionals in the United States, virtually none of which took place on courts run by clubs that belonged to the USLTA. When combined with a European tour leg and additional matches against other top professionals in substitute matches, both seemed to have done well financially, with Vines purported to have earned thirty-four thousand dollars while Perry received ninety thousand dollars. The large financial discrepancy was due to Perry's position as the recently turned-professional challenger to Vines, who was defending the professional title he had won against Bill Tilden in 1934 as well as in 1935 and 1936, when he beat Lester Stoefen. From the players' perspective, the financial success of their barnstorming also stemmed from how close the players' ability levels stayed throughout the entirety of the tour, with Vines narrowly edging Perry to retain the professional title. That success, however, came at a high cost to the players in energy and time, as they spent a full six months out of their year competing night after night at different venues across the country because appropriate tournament venues were closed to them due to their professionalism.[18] (For cities played on Fred Perry vs. Ellsworth Vines North American Professional Tennis Tour, January 6, 1937, to May 12, 1937, see map 3.[19])

Those difficulties aside, Perry and professional tennis seemed to fit. He endorsed Slazenger tennis racquets and other sporting goods and went on to follow the lead of French champion René Lacoste in founding the successful Fred Perry clothing line. Glamour also appealed to him. While the reality of the professional tour was far from glamorous, the public at least thought of the professionals in much the same way as other celebrities. Perry himself liked that association to the point that he and Vines purchased the Beverly Hills Tennis Club in late 1937, required a minimum income of seventy-eight thousand dollars a year to join, and restricted membership to a total of 125 members, preferably from the movie industry. Such exclusivity worked, with their club counting some of the biggest studio executives and film stars as members. Perry dated German actress Marlene Dietrich and was engaged to English actress Mary Lawson in Europe. While in America he met and married actress Helen Vinson. Their marriage fell apart after a few years, but Perry had no trouble finding other actresses and models to date through the 1940s. The Englishman even found himself cast as a tennis player in a few American pictures produced by Metro-Goldwyn-Mayer Studios, although his talent behind the camera lagged far behind his talent on the court.[20]

Distraction and age took a toll on Perry's game. From the 1938 professional tour on, he was not the same player. Vines and Perry's full ownership stake in that tour also meant that the two top-billing players managed the schedule of the players, accounts receivable, payroll, and everything else that went into

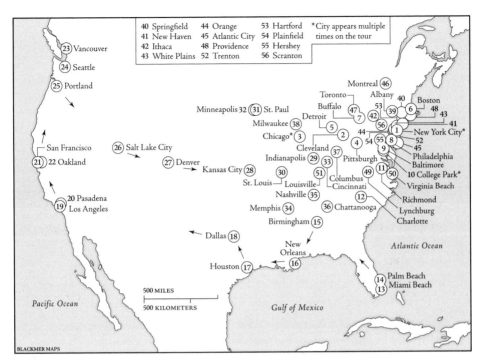

Map 3. Cities played on Fred Perry vs. Ellsworth Vines North American
Professional Tennis Tour, January 6, 1937, to May 12, 1937

running an entertainment enterprise. Those added responsibilities came at the same time that both Vines and Perry seemed more interested in golf than tennis. At most stops the players tried to play a round before their evening matches. In the summer of 1938, the players toured the Catskills, Adirondack, and Pocono Mountain hotels frequented by wealthy New Yorkers and Northeasterners. On what came to be called the "Borsch Circuit," the players raked in the money while still finding time to squeeze in some golf on the resorts' courses. That summer they drove their own vehicles, which signaled the independence that Richards, Koželuh, Tilden, Perry, and Vines began to exercise from one another. For his part, Perry also had trouble at home when Helen Vinson served him divorce papers. That separation prompted him to seek U.S. citizenship in November 1938, not long before war seemed ready to break out between Britain and Germany. Perry's settlement left him financially vulnerable just when a third-year tour headlining Vines versus Perry seemed a hard sell to a Depression-weary public who had grown accustomed to that rivalry.

Fortunately for Perry and for professional tennis, a new amateur champion had agreed to join the professional ranks, and he brought with him more buzz for the sport than any player since Suzanne Lenglen.[21]

The first Grand Slam popularized tennis in much the same way that the thoroughbred War Admiral galvanized public interest in horse racing. In 1937 the horse won the Kentucky Derby, Preakness Stakes, and Belmont Stakes—the Triple Crown. That same year, Californian Don Budge so thoroughly dominated the tennis events he played that he finally received the funding needed to travel to Australia to try for what later came to be called the Grand Slam—the Australian Championship, the French Championship, Wimbledon, and the U.S. National Championships. In that campaign he succeeded in complete fashion with convincing straight-set wins in the final matches over John Bromwich in Australia, Roderich Menzel in France, Bunny Austin at Wimbledon, and a four-set win over Gene Mako at the U.S. Championships. Sportswriter Al Laney recalled that Budge's success led the *New York Herald Tribune* editor to give him "two-and-a half, three columns of space" for his tennis coverage—space greater than that of even more popular team sports.[22]

The public followed Budge's transition into professional tennis with great interest, just as they had followed his quick ascendance in the amateur ranks, where Budge had always stood out as a prodigy. His parents did not play tennis, but his older brother Lloyd, who played for the University of California at Berkeley, encouraged the young Donald to steer clear of football, basketball, and baseball, and instead put his energy into tennis. The pattern of an older sibling taking up the game and playing with a younger brother or sister who goes on to a bigger career did not begin or end with Don Budge, but he certainly fit that mold. A bigger and stronger older brother to play with very much mattered to Budge, because his parents could not afford much instruction in the late 1920s and early 1930s. John Budge managed the Crystal Laundry in Oakland while his mother worked as a type operator for an East Bay newspaper. In 1931 the fifteen-year-old Budge won the California State Championship, the first tournament he ever entered. Such promising early results piqued the interest of his brother's coach at the University of California, Tom Stowe, who instructed the younger Budge in stroke technique and tactics.[23]

Budge first traveled east in 1934 to play in the most prestigious lawn tournaments. He performed so well there that when he returned the following year, he secured the number one ranking in the country, although he had to wait until 1937 for the USLTA to sponsor him to travel to Wimbledon, where he won his first of six consecutive major tournament titles, halted only by his decision to turn professional. In the offices of his Davis Cup captain, Walter Pate, on November 10, 1938, Budge inked a contract with a seventy-five-thousand-dollar guarantee to play Ellsworth Vines in a tour promoted by Jack Harris. Unfortunately for all of those involved in the 1939 and 1940 tours, war in Europe canceled those tours.[24]

Budge came to be remembered as one of only two players in men's tennis history to win all four major tournaments in a calendar year. The Grand Slam became the stuff of sporting legend even though contemporaries within the tennis establishment remembered Budge for something far less grand at the time. USLTA officials despised him for turning professional, because that decision made the world's best player unavailable to them at a time when nationalism reached a fever pitch. In the minds of these men, Budge's professional move made him a traitor to his country and his class. The editor of *American Lawn Tennis* magazine likened Budge's decision to that of Judas Iscariot betraying Jesus for fifty pieces of silver. What these enflamed contemporaries missed was the very real significance that Budge himself noted later in life about his own tennis career and his place in the larger transition from amateur to professional tennis:

> In the Tilden era, it was mostly a wealthy man's game, and you had to belong to the good clubs and have the tennis lessons and so forth to be heard of in the tennis field, but since, I would say, starting with Ellsworth Vines and Mako and myself and many of the other players like Jack Kramer and so on. Gonzales is another one. We all came from the public parks. Eventually, we got to the point where we could play at the clubs. They would like us to play, but initially it stemmed from the public parks.[25]

Those words came from the perspective of a player who lived with tennis rather than that of the amateur association officials who simply lived around tennis.

Budge's doubles partner and champion in his own right, Gene Mako, also grew up playing tennis in public parks and then in the private clubs of Southern California. His path to tennis stardom was far more circuitous, however. Mako's father was a soldier fighting for the Austria-Hungarian Empire at the outbreak of World War I. After the birth of his son Gene in January 1916, the senior Mako approached his superior officer about a brief shore leave. With weekend pass in hand, Mako gathered his family and fled to Trieste, where they hid out for half a year before crossing the Atlantic to Buenos Aires. After three years in the Argentinian capital, Mako again moved his family, this time to Los Angeles in July 1923. The wonderful weather in Southern California afforded the seven-year-old Gene the opportunity to spend day after day playing outside. And that he did, enjoying bat-and-ball games such as softball and baseball, team sports such as soccer and football, running and field events—everything except tennis. He took to athletics naturally, as his father had excelled at soccer, sprinting, and distance running in Europe, along with holding the middleweight wrestling title in Hungary before the outbreak of the Great War. The senior Mako was a cosmopolitan continental in every respect. In addition to playing soccer for club and national teams, Mako's paintings passed jury reviews and were hung in art galleries in Budapest, Prague, and Vienna. In the United States, Mako put his artistic talents to work in the growing movie industry, helping to adorn movie theaters with sculptures and ornaments as Fox West Coast expanded up along the Pacific from Hollywood to Seattle. But for all of his refinement, the senior Mako did not play tennis. Gene did not pick up the game until he was twelve years old, getting ready to enter his freshman year at Glendale High School in 1928.[26]

The summer before enrollment, one of Mako's friends approached him about playing on the poorly built court at Harvard Park near the boys' homes. Mako agreed and fell hard for the game. Later that evening he convinced his parents to buy him a tennis racquet. Gene then began playing with his classmates, hoping to make the high school team the following spring. The boys played often and took to training by running the mile and a half between their school and the park where they practiced. Mako entered his first tournament in both the thirteen-and-under and fifteen-and-under divisions after having played the game for only half a year. Financed and owned by the railroad baron Henry Huntington, the luxurious Huntington Hotel in Pasadena hosted the prestigious Southern California Tennis Association's Boys Championship in December 1928—a setting far removed from the hardscrabble park court where Mako and his friends played. The tournament experience primed Mako to make an immediate impact; he played in the number one position on his squad as a freshman.[27]

Mako also found quick success in the tournaments put on by the SCTA. In the early 1920s, the USLTA had facilitated the expansion of competitive junior tennis through the association's regionally based organizations. The Southern California Section with the TPASC was particularly robust in the number and quality of the junior players produced by the late '20s. The SCTA offered girls' and boys' divisions for thirteen-and-under, fifteen-and-under, and eighteen-and-under play. Each division had a cutoff date, and Mako's birthday gave him an advantage that he made the most of. When he began SCTA competition in 1929, playing in the fifteen-and-under division, Mako did not lose a match or even a set over the next six years in which he played SCTA-sanctioned singles and doubles tournaments.[28]

Mako's undefeated junior career in regional tournaments certainly piqued the interest of college coaches in Southern California. In the 1920s colleges did not recruit players with much vigor; certainly no national or international recruiting network existed.[29] Mako liked his adopted hometown of Pasadena and was thrilled to get the chance to play, ostensibly in his backyard, at the University of Southern California in Los Angeles. As a college freshman, the eighteen-year-old Mako won the intercollegiate national singles and doubles titles in 1934, the first time a Trojan had captured the crown. Mako's tennis career continued to ascend when he hitched his star to the national bandwagon in Davis Cup play. Like Ellsworth Vines had done a few years before, Mako left USC to accept his spot on the 1935 team.[30]

Over the next four years, Mako proved himself to be one of two integral players in the United States' resurgence in international tennis. Don Budge rounded out the doubles team. The two first played together in a 1934 exhibition match in the Bay Area in an event coordinated by Perry T. Jones, the executive secretary of the SCTA and the de facto power broker of tennis up and down the West Coast. Roscoe Maples, a tennis contact in the Bay Area, played matchmaker, and in the late winter of 1934, Mako came to San Francisco. The exhibition took place in the Martina District at the Palace of Fine Arts, one of only a handful of structures that remained from the Panama-Pacific Exposition of 1915. Mako and Budge first locked horns in singles, each winning a set. After a short respite, the main event followed, which pitted Jerry Stratford and Phil Near, two top doubles players from the Northern California Tennis Association, against Budge and Mako, who partnered together for the first time. Budge and Mako flogged their opponents 6–0, 6–1, one game away from the recherché double-bagel match score. Budge, with his fiery red hair and stretched frame, and Mako, with his chiseled facial features and strong movements on the court, whipped the crowd into enough of a frenzy that tennis officials from Northern and Southern California had little choice but to recommend Budge and Mako pair together on the U.S. Davis Cup team.[31]

Three years later, in 1937, Mako and Budge found themselves playing at the AELTC against the Baron Gottfried von Cramm and Henner Henkel in the most politically significant Davis Cup match of the twentieth century. The ascendance of the Nazi Party in Germany during the 1930s in no small part was a result of the arguments of Aryan racial superiority that Hitler and Reich officers shouted breath after breath. The six-foot-tall blond-haired and blue-eyed Cramm presented the ideal image for Nazi propaganda. His world rankings, usually around numbers one or two during the mid-1930s, mattered too. But Cramm never toed the party line. A likely apocryphal story went that he had called himself as having struck an out ball before it bounced out of play in order to deliberately lose a Davis Cup tie against the American Don Budge in a form of protest against the Nazi Party's crackdown against perceived political threats. The questionable veracity of this story notwithstanding, the fact that contemporaries believed it revealed a great deal about the high regard his supporters held for Cramm's sportsmanship and integrity, not to mention the frustrations the Nazi Party had in deploying its most visible worldwide sportsman to meet political ends. Retaliation came first in a refusal to support Cramm in a 1937 return bid to defend his French Championships title of the previous year. More severe measures came in 1938 when the Nazis incarcerated Cramm on spurious charges of homosexuality. He served about half a year in prison, returning to competitive tennis at the start of the summer season in 1939.[32]

Fresh from his March occupation of Czechoslovakia, Hitler eyed further expansion in the summer of 1939. The German players—and everyone else, for that matter—attended the 1939 Wimbledon events with the pall of war ready to fall over all of Europe. When Cramm and Henkel met Americans John Van Ryn and Wilmer Allison in the men's semifinals, national politics intervened directly on the court. On match point for the Germans, Henkel approached the net and called on his partner to translate.

"We default," said Cramm.

"Just say that again. We didn't hear you loudly. What did you say?" replied Van Ryn and Allison.

"All German nationals have been demanded to leave England tonight on the night boat, and we can't play the Finals tomorrow, so that if we should win the next point, we couldn't play. So we default to you," said Cramm.

With that the Germans left the court and England in order to prepare for war. The German military drafted Cramm not long after, in early 1940, and the great champion lost his peak playing years to the fighting. With the prelude to the war, international sport completely broke down.[33]

The Davis Cup match between Budge and Cramm three years before the war later came to symbolize the battle between the Axis and the Allies. Following closely on a doubles win for the United States in which Mako and Budge beat Cramm and Henkel, Budge and Cramm faced off in a decisive reverse-singles match. Cramm blitzkrieged to a two-set-to-love lead before Budge dug in, weathered, and then battled back the German onslaught in the third and fourth sets. Cramm attacked again in the fourth set and seemed poised to punch through, up four games to one in the fifth and deciding set. Budge surged, leveling the game score and eventually besting Cramm 8–6 in the final set to claim the match and the overall victory for the United States. Outside of the political and military significance of the United States' victory over Germany on British soil, which observers would soon come to realize, the 1937 match proved significant in another important respect: Bill Tilden, the famous American amateur-champion-turned-professional, had gone over to Germany to train with the German squad in preparation for his own European professional matches—a move that subjected him to withering scorn from the USLTA and the American press.[34]

Different in degree, Tilden's sexuality became a target for USLTA officials. These efforts came to a head just over a decade later when Tilden sat before a magistrate in a Los Angeles County court on January 17, 1947, facing charges of sex with a minor. Tilden was arrested two months earlier when Beverly Hills police pulled over his Packard Clipper after tailing the vehicle on Sunset Boulevard. A teenage boy—whom Tilden had met the previous week at the Los Angeles Tennis Club—sat behind the wheel with the fly of his pants unbuttoned, and Tilden had had his arm around him just before the pullover. The police took Tilden to the station, where they booked him and forced him to make a confession. Tilden later claimed the police had coerced him into signing the statement and presented false information to him as, being without his glasses, he could not read it. In any case, Tilden soon sought counsel in lawyer Richard Maddox in order to prepare for the coming hearing presided over by Los Angeles Superior Court Judge Alfonso Aloysius Scott, made famous for his rulings protecting the rights of adolescent film actors and for hearing the murder trial against Bugsy Siegel.[35]

Professionally, the hearings could not have come at a worse time for Tilden. He was the primary organizer in the middle of preparing for an upcoming professional tennis tour. To this end, Tilden received letters of support from throughout the sports media and tennis community, with the glaring but unsurprising absence of any support from the USLTA—which seemed glad to see a man face charges who had so chapped their control and commitment to amateurism for so long. Politically, Tilden's legal troubles also came at a difficult time. While the second "red scare" was still several years from finding a voice in U.S. senator Joseph McCarthy, many already thought of Hollywood as a haven for radicals. Tilden's close friendships with actors like Charlie Chaplin, themselves accused of communist sympathies, meant the imaginations of the public, judge, and potential jurors would not need to stretch far in order to associate Tilden with the degeneracy assumed of all communists. The psychiatrists who were ordered to examine Tilden reached essentially these conclusions, going so far as to diagnose him with the degenerate insanity that, coincidentally enough, afflicted all communists and homosexuals in the minds of the postwar mental health profession.[36]

Tilden likely took some of this to heart when he ignored the advice of his lawyer to seek a jury trial and decided to plead guilty with the expectation that the judge would grant him counseling rather than jail time. That was a mistake. After making statements on the particular incident and expressing deep remorse for the incident in the Packard, Tilden then refused to give detailed answers to Judge Scott's questions about his previous homosexual encounters. Fed up, the judge sentenced Tilden to a year of detention, mostly served at the Castaic Honor Farm; to psychiatric counseling following his release; and to prohibition from coming into any contact with minors in the future. Tilden served close to eight months of this sentence before his release.[37] A competitor seldom defeated on the tennis court emerged a thoroughly beaten man. He was dead five years later at the age of sixty.

Most contemporaries knew nothing about Tilden's ignominious personal life. The public preferred to view him as a champion of his class rather than a disreputable derelict. He, along with Ellsworth Vines, Gene Mako, Don Budge, and the adopted Californian Fred Perry, had done the most to keep tennis in the public eye during the difficult decade of the 1930s. That job would soon pass to two more Southern Californians—one of them the game's most notorious professional; the other the sport's most consequential professional.

William Renshaw and Ernest Renshaw, two of the world's leading tennis players in the late nineteenth century, play the 1883 Wimbledon Championships on Worple Road. (©AELTC/WLTM)

The Newport Casino in Rhode Island hosted the first decades of the U.S. National Championships, such as this August 26, 1891, final between Oliver Campbell and Clarence Hobart. (Courtesy of ITHF)

The first tennis meet of the Southern California Tennis Club took place on Colonel Purcell's Las Tunas Rancho on July 12, 1884. (Courtesy of University of Southern California Libraries. California Historical Society Collection)

Harvey Snodgrass and Walter Wesbrook shaking hands on the Midwick Country Club tennis courts in Alhambra, California, in 1925. (Courtesy of *Los Angeles Times* Photographic Archives [Collection 1429], Library Special Collections, Charles E. Young Research Library, UCLA)

By the 1920s, the LATC had become the most important place to play tennis in America. (Courtesy of University of Southern California Digital Library. "Dick" Whittington Photography Collection)

Henri Cochet, French tennis champion, playing at the Pacific Southwest Championships in 1928. (Courtesy of *Los Angeles Times* Photographic Archives [Collection 1429], Library Special Collections, Charles E. Young Research Library, UCLA)

Frenchman Jean Borotra was one of the so-called Four Musketeers, here pictured around the time of his mid-1920s Wimbledon successes. (©AELTC/WLTM)

French champion René Lacoste at the AELTC clubhouse in the 1920s. (©AELTC/WLTM)

May Sutton Bundy playing tennis at the Midwick Country Club in Alhambra, California, in 1925. (Courtesy of *Los Angeles Times* Photographic Archives [Collection 1429], Library Special Collections, Charles E. Young Research Library, UCLA)

Elizabeth Bunny Ryan at the Chamber of Commerce's Celebrities Dinner 1935. (Courtesy of *Los Angeles Times* Photographic Archives [Collection 1429], Library Special Collections, Charles E. Young Research Library, UCLA)

Watching Suzanne Lenglen play tennis was an unforgettable experience for the many spectators watching on the AELTC Centre Court in 1922. (©AELTC/WLTM)

Norwegian Molla Mallory moved to America and became a top champion as seen here in 1910. (Courtesy of University of Southern California Libraries, California Historical Society Collection)

"The Goddess" Suzanne Lenglen poses in Los Angeles in 1927 during her professional tennis tour. (Courtesy of *Herald Examiner* Collection, Los Angeles Public Library)

Helen Jacobs playing at Los Angeles Tennis Club in 1928. (Courtesy of *Los Angeles Times* Photographic Archives [Collection 1429], Library Special Collections, Charles E. Young Research Library, UCLA)

Helen Wills Moody and Frederick Moody return from a cruise in 1928. (Courtesy of *Los Angeles Times* Photographic Archives [Collection 1429], Library Special Collections, Charles E. Young Research Library, UCLA)

Tennis professionals Vincent Richards (left) and Karel Koželuh (right) pose at the Longwood Cricket Club in July 1931. (Courtesy of the Boston Public Library, Leslie Jones Collection)

Vincent Richards, Fred Perry, Ellsworth Vines, and Bill Tilden prepare for a professional tennis match during the Great Depression. (Courtesy of Walter P. Reuther Library, Archives of Labor and Urban Affairs, Wayne State University)

Catherine Rose, tennis champion on the Griffith Park tennis team, playing on a court in 1933. (Courtesy of *Los Angeles Times* Photographic Archives [Collection 1429], Library Special Collections, Charles E. Young Research Library, UCLA)

Don Budge on a court in Los Angeles. (Courtesy of *Los Angeles Daily News* Negatives [Collection 1387], Library Special Collections, Charles E. Young Research Library, UCLA)

To establish himself as the preeminent American amateur in the mid-1930s, Californian Don Budge traveled east to play tournaments like those of the Longwood Cricket Club Tennis in Boston's suburbs. (Courtesy of the Boston Public Library, Leslie Jones Collection)

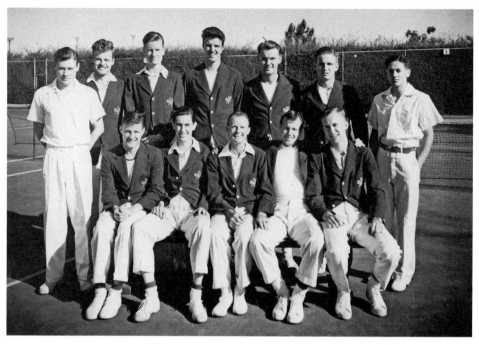

Ted Schroeder was the ultimate all-American amateur, seen here (front row on left) with his Stanford University teammates, around 1942. (Courtesy of Special Collections and University Archives, Stanford University)

Bobby Riggs and his wife, Kay Riggs, worked together to promote the 1949–1950 professional tennis tour. (Courtesy of *Herald Examiner* Collection, Los Angeles Public Library)

Louise Brough enjoyed a long and distinguished playing career as an amateur during the 1940s and '50s. (Courtesy of University of Southern California Digital Library, *Los Angeles Examiner* Photograph Collection)

Hazel Hotchkiss Wightman (right) helped develop a number of women champions, such as Sarah Palfrey Cooke (left), pictured here on February 1, 1930, seventeen years prior to Cooke turning professional. (Courtesy of the Boston Public Library, Leslie Jones Collection)

Gussie Moran was infamous for her sartorial sections as seen here around 1950. (Courtesy of *Herald Examiner* Collection, Los Angeles Public Library)

Alice Marble was one of the most influential tennis personalities via both her pen and her professional play in the mid-twentieth century. (©AELTC/WLTM)

Karol Fageros came to be known as "the girl with the golden panties," as seen here in 1958, before turning professional the following year. (Courtesy of University of Southern California Digital Library, *Los Angeles Examiner* Photograph Collection)

The great Cold War tennis champion Althea Gibson battled racial discrimination throughout her career along with the later stigma that came with becoming a touring professional. (Courtesy of Thelner Hoover, *Herald Examiner* Collection, Los Angeles Public Library)

CHAPTER 5

Wartime Southern California Professionals

That westward movement of tennis literally coincided with the direction toward professionalism the sport had moved during the 1930s and early '40s. One of the most lasting consequences of the Great Depression and World War II was that Americans became more mobile than ever before. Between 1940 and 1945, sixteen million Americans served in uniform in some capacity, and one out of every five citizens of the United States moved to a new city, state, or region of the country. The deeply cherished physical and emotional degree of mobility most Americans enjoyed when compared to their European peers exploded altogether anew in the heady economic times that followed the Second World War.[1]

At war's end, tennis clubs in the United States numbered in excess of eight hundred and covered the entire country. The game that began at a Welsh garden party in 1873, came to America via Bermuda in 1874, and had its rules standardized in a New York City hotel in 1881 had grown, during the first three decades of the twentieth century, to the point that the national office of the USLTA struggled to exercise authority over its member clubs, let alone its player members. The dozen sectional associations that reported to the national association may have held the organization together and helped the game of tennis grow, but at the same time those regionally based sub-associations had their own agendas that often clashed with both one another and the national office. The agendas of the amateur associations also contrasted with those of the amateur champions who had become touring professionals. Onetime insiders Suzanne Lenglen, William "Big Bill" Tilden, and Don Budge became outsiders the moment they publicly played tennis for money. Without the organizational support the amateur associations provided, the touring professionals formed their own subculture on the road that kept them apart from and primed to upend what amounted to the tennis establishment, still based largely in East Coast private clubs.[2] Conflicts between different associations and between the highly visible touring professionals and the heavily cloistered amateur clubs chipped away at the authority exercised by the USLTA and, in so doing, hastened the rise of the postwar professional tennis tour led first by Bobby Riggs and then by Jack Kramer.

From his amateur days through his 1973 Battle of the Sexes match against Billie Jean King, Riggs was the most notorious tennis professional to ever play. Born in Los Angeles on February 25, 1918, to a preacher father and homemaker mother, Riggs cultivated his later reputation as the "happy hustler" at an early age. Adolescence in the Great Depression meant making the most of the outdoors for young Bobby, his siblings, and their friends. Riggs recalled he learned about winning and losing by playing marbles for keeps with his neighbor. After beating a friend soundly enough to collect all of his marbles, Riggs then won the boy's sister's tennis racquet, which had been staked as collateral in a double-or-nothing game. Racquet in hand, Riggs did not immediately focus on tennis; instead, he tossed footballs, caught baseballs, kicked soccer balls, batted, tackled, boxed, sprinted, jumped, swam, dove, and played in all sorts of games as long as winning and losing remained integral. Riggs, the runt of the family, competed so fervently because he sought approval from his older, bigger, and stronger siblings. This need led Bobby to take up tennis for the first time in 1930 at the age of twelve when he discovered that the game masked some of the athletic disadvantages due to his diminutive size.[3]

Without formal training Riggs did remarkably well in his first year of junior tennis competition. Three months into the game, he won his first tournament and attracted the attention of junior tennis power broker Perry T. Jones, who was based at the Los Angeles Tennis Club. Jones recognized Bobby's desire to win and helped to convince the small-framed Riggs that tennis afforded a small athlete with certain opportunities that were unavailable in contact sports. Impressed by Jones's success in producing world-class players like Ellsworth Vines and Don Budge, Riggs agreed with the proven Jones's formula: start young; supervise the youngsters to make sure they learn proper technique; compete, always competition; secure proper fitting and quality equipment for every player; keep the players out of trouble both on and off the court by emphasizing activity over idleness; enter every tournament; play hard every tournament match; pair younger players with players up an age group and ability level so that the mimicry and imitation so crucial to adolescent learning can take place in a natural rather than a forced setting. Combining Jones's system with a cutthroat mentality with the game of tennis, as played in the '30s, became, in Riggs's estimation, "the one game where the large man doesn't necessarily have a big edge on the little fella." In this Riggs spoke from experience. He won thirteen-and-under, fifteen-and-under, and eighteen-and-under junior championships, including the 1933 National Boy's Doubles Championships and the 1935 National Junior Singles Championships. The next year he entered senior competition and won both the singles and doubles titles in the 1936 National Clay Court Men's Championships.[4]

Riggs's quick ascendance to adult competition rankled Jones. The SCTA secretary treated his junior players as investments; while he could not make their value as players move up or down in the competitive tournament environment, he fiercely defended his authority to keep or divest players at the time he considered opportune. Jones wanted to keep Riggs because at age eighteen Bobby maintained his eligibility to defend the National Junior Championships. As the head of the SCTA and director of their Junior Tennis Program, wins from eighteen-and-under players reflected highly on Jones and promoted the national standing of the SCTA section to a degree that adult tournaments did not, because adult players often played out on their own, not beholden to any particular regional tennis association. Tradition mattered to the blue-blooded Jones. His junior players had always followed his orders to defend their titles. Riggs, however, refused to follow the example of earlier junior players, because his ambition, spurred by his modest economic background compared with the tennis champions from past decades, preponderated his physical stature. Faced with insubordination, Jones tried to dissuade Riggs by arguing that the men in the adult competition hit too hard, ran too fast, and competed too hard for an immature player. When words failed to persuade, money talked as Jones pulled SCTA financial sponsorship, a move that forced Riggs to hustle for the first time in convincing patrons at the LATC to fund a trip out east to compete in the national tournaments outside of the channels of the SCTA.[5]

His break with Jones made his 1936 season into a year of ups and downs. Riggs traveled east, won big tournaments, and finished the year ranked fourth in the nation. In fact, he fared well against the other top players, notching straight-set wins over Frankie Parker and Bryan "Bitsy" Grant. Don Budge dominated tennis that year, but the next best player behind him was a toss-up. With several players near equally matched, the selection of the 1937 Davis Cup team came down to amicability rather than ability. Jones had the real say in the selection, and he said no to Riggs, replacing him with a lower-ranked player named Joe Hunt, who, in an irony not lost on Riggs, attracted Jones's attention because of his strength, size, and "stature." Once again on the wrong side of the SCTA, Riggs found help from friends at the Los Angeles Tennis Club who agreed to pass the hat for a trip to compete at Wimbledon. When Jones exited his office at the club and found Riggs soliciting donations, he said, "Bobby, if the Davis Cup Committee don't feel that it wants you on the team, I have a responsibility to Southern California Tennis, I don't feel like you should represent us [at Wimbledon] either." Undeterred, Riggs managed to collect several thousand dollars for the trip to the AELTC, only to hear from Jones that the Davis Cup team captain, Walter Pate, needed Riggs as a practice partner to prepare Don Budge, Gene Mako, Frankie Parker, and Bitsy Grant for their inter-zonal match against Germany. Riggs played the piñata, the funding for his trip to Europe never materialized, and he found himself playing summer matches in Salt Lake City rather than on Centre Court in Wimbledon.[6]

By 1938 Jones and Riggs finally agreed that American tennis needed Bobby Riggs. Joe Hunt and Parker had not contributed to the 1937 team victory to the degree Jones and Pate expected. Don Budge and Bitsy Grant played tremendous tennis, but for how much longer? Budge's dominance worried the amateur tennis establishment that an opportunistic promoter might convince the best in the world to start playing for pay, and Grant's tournament wins simply did not match up to those Riggs had accumulated early in 1938. As the defending champion, the United States would host the Davis Cup Challenge Round after the U.S. Championships, giving the Davis Cup selection committee and captain until late August to make final selections. With Gene Mako's spot secure as a doubles specialist and Don Budge's partner, the second singles spot was ripe for the taking, and Riggs's consistent wins throughout the year earned him the spot. Riggs beat Australian Adrian Quist on September 3, at the Germantown Cricket Club in Philadelphia in the first singles rubber of the Davis Cup Final. Budge made the team score 2–0 with his singles win over John Bromwich, Australia answered back by winning the doubles rubber, before Budge secured the tie for the United States by besting Quist in straight sets in the reverse singles. Riggs had contributed to the international prestige of tennis in a big way, and the U.S. tennis establishment awarded him accordingly.[7]

In 1939 Riggs finally got the financial backing to play in Wimbledon. Needless to say, he made the most of it. Stepping off the Atlantic liner, he beelined for a London bookie who agreed to take a $500 (roughly £100) bet to win the Wimbledon singles title at three-to-one odds. The odds maker, thinking the deal done, sat astonished when Riggs placed an extended wager, taking the presumed winnings from the singles bet and putting them on a doubles championship with partner Elwood Cook. Riggs proposed odds at twenty to one for such a feat, which, given the magnitude of such an accomplishment, actually would have been a suitable stake for the bookie to take. Betting on tennis was uncommon in general and foreign to this particular bookie, to say the least, so he must have sensed Riggs's eagerness rather than focusing on the numbers in proposing counter odds at six to one. Riggs wanted none of that and chose to raise the stakes by proposing, "What if I win the triple crown, the hat trick, it's never been done by anybody up to this time, the youngster to come over on the first visit, nobody's ever won all three, but I'm going to try to do it. . . . I'm going to put it all on the mixed doubles." The preposterousness of Riggs's braggadocio must have convinced the bookie to take the bet at twelve-to-one odds that put $108,000 on the line. Raising the championship trophy at Wimbledon in 1939 meant winning six rounds in men's singles, five rounds in doubles, and four matches in mixed doubles.[8]

Riggs obviously liked his odds to place such a wild bet, but more sober analysis suggests recklessness and hubris. While he had competed well on the world stage in Davis Cup play and raised the trophy at many quality tournaments, Riggs had never won one of the three largest international tournaments—the French Championships, Wimbledon, and the U.S. Championships. He had made it to the final at the French Championship, but the American Don McNeill soundly defeated him in straight sets. With Don Budge's move into professional tennis and therefore barred from the amateur championships like Wimbledon, Riggs was confident that now was his time. But Riggs could not count on the same buoyancy from his doubles partner Elwood Cook and mixed doubles partner Alice Marble, who might bring the effort to a halt either through poor performance or injury withdrawal. Remarkably, he won: first the singles title; then the doubles the following day; and with fading light on the final Sunday, he and Alice Marble raised the mixed doubles trophy. Riggs was rich and on top of the world—so it seemed.[9]

Major world events directed the influence that athletes, like everyone else, could make on history. In 1939 that direction moved for the second time to world war. After Wimbledon, Riggs won the 1939 U.S. Championships contested at Forest Hills, New York. He entered the apogee of his career just as World War II plunged the importance of international athletes to a point lower than that of World War I. Battling German bombers in the Blitz, England did not host Wimbledon in 1940—a pattern that continued until the 1946 championships. While not as long-standing, as it was first played in 1925, the French Championships also went uncontested between 1940 and 1945. Essentially an all-Australian affair from its inception in 1905 until the 1930s, when the tournament received a few more international players, the Australian Championship remained the least cosmopolitan and most regionally focused of the big international amateur tennis championships. Despite this isolation, the Lawn Tennis Association of Australia (LTAA, known as the Lawn Tennis Association of Australasia until 1922) also suspended the tournament between 1941 and 1946. That left the U.S. Championships as the only international tournament played during World War II. Interestingly enough, the U.S. Championships never missed a year between 1881—when the tournament began—and 1968, when the game allowed professionals in for the first time, even playing through World War I when the other tournaments halted for the conflict. This gave Riggs a chance to defend his ranking as the best in tennis, which he more or less did, making the finals of the 1940 U.S. Championships, where he lost to Don McNeill, but bouncing back the next year by defeating Frank Kovacs to claim the September 1941 title at Forest Hills.[10]

Fresh from their final, Riggs and Kovacs joined Don Budge and Englishman Fred Perry on the professional tour. Lex Thompson, the owner of the Philadelphia Eagles gridiron squad, swayed Riggs to forgo amateurism with a twenty-five-thousand-dollar one-year contract that Bobby was only too happy to accept. Kovacs had a reputation as a comedian on and off the court, and he too did not need much sweet-talking to start playing tennis for money—officially. Riggs recalled in his memoirs that in one of their previous meetings Kovacs appeared on the court dressed in the classic long-sleeved shirt and flannel trousers worn by players at the turn of the century. Throughout the match he mocked the skimpy legs Riggs's shorts revealed, only to grab scissors toward the end of the match and slash his own pants into thigh-high shorts right on the court. Fellow players may have hated playing Kovacs, but a promoter like Thompson recognized the crowd appeal that the bad-boy inculcated. Every Kovacs antic, from stalling between points and games, to lying down on the court and refusing to play on because of a questionable ruling by a tournament official, the "Clown Prince of Tennis," as contemporaries called Kovacs, would balance out a tour of the finest tennis players and four of the most recognizable international athletes in the world at the start of World War II.[11]

Their tour began on December 26, 1941, at Madison Square Garden in New York City. Three weeks earlier the Japanese had attacked Pearl Harbor, and in the weeks leading up to the opening night, next to no one wanted a ticket. Thompson simply gave away seats to anyone off the streets in a desperate attempt to create some atmosphere for the players and the media, who were shooting newsreels for distribution. The tennis also disappointed spectators. In particular, the match between Fred Perry and Bobby Riggs proved disastrous when Perry moved for a ball, went down hard, and injured his elbow. The English champion defaulted the match, sought medical attention at a hospital, and withdrew from the tour to return to England. Thompson scrambled to replace Perry with players like Gene Mako and Lester Stoefen, but neither American drew the crowds that a major international celebrity like Perry inveigled. Logistically, the tour also suffered. Government rationing of tires and gasoline made a barnstorming sports tour that depended on daily travel unfeasible during wartime. Thompson cut his losses, called the tour off, and paid the players the little that he could.[12] Athletes like Riggs were out of work.

Two decades of military drawdown and comparative isolation in world affairs compared to that of Western European nations resulted in an American military of smaller size than seventeen other countries along with a military budget of only 2 percent of the United States' entire gross national product in 1940, which rose only slightly above that in 1941. The following year, American workers made more military equipment than all of the Axis powers put together, a gap that widened as the war progressed. By the time of the treaty signing on the battleship USS *Missouri* in 1945, American manufacturing accounted for two out of three planes, ships, tanks, trucks, guns, uniforms, and supplies produced for the Allies' cause. Traditional manufacturers such as General Motors ran at capacity throughout the war, entrepreneurs like Henry Kaiser rolled out new plans for more efficient production, and five hundred thousand new businesses opened their doors between 1941 and 1945. The war increased employment in America from forty-five million people in 1940 to fifty-five million people in 1945 and decreased unemployment from eight million people in 1940 to under one million people by 1945. Those sixty-five million American workers produced one out of every two manufactured goods in the world at war's end. By 1945 twelve and a half million Americans also served in the military.[13]

The last major war had encouraged Americans to think more seriously about organized recreation. In the 1920s politicians from both sides of the aisles stressed policies that purportedly prioritized physical fitness, but World War II was what boosted American fitness. As commandant of West Point, Douglas MacArthur revamped the educational requirements of cadets, making physical training through individual and team sports a critical part of the professionalization of army officers. Fellow generals such as Omar Bradley and Dwight Eisenhower all agreed that sports could help win the war, and they commissioned athletic officers to build company morale over what many believed would be a protracted conflict requiring long tours of duty. From naval stations, to airfields, to forward operating bases, baseball diamonds were part of the daily routines of men in uniform. Soldiers read sporting magazines, played ball against other companies, and attended exhibition games headlined by the biggest Major League phenoms. Both inside and outside the military's ranks, the triumph of American athletics came to symbolize both the supremacy of the American war machine and the eventual push to Allied victory.[14]

Tennis stars were no different from Major Leaguers in that World War II halted their normal routines and forced them to either serve the war effort directly or find a new avenue in which to ply their trade. In Britain the long-standing AELTC professional Dan Maskell organized exhibitions that intermingled amateurs and professionals. In the United States the fifty-year-old Bill Tilden combined theatrics with a new tennis tour featuring some of the finest female talent from the amateur ranks. Just prior to the war, Tilden had embarked on a brief theatrical career, acting in the stage plays *The Nice Harmons*, *The Fighting Littles*, and *The Children's Hour*—receiving some positive reviews from the *Los Angeles Times* for the last of these. At around the same time, Tilden also appeared in war bond drives and benefit events across the country. Buoyed by his popularity in these ventures, and aware of the massive influx of GIs and war workers to Southern California where he made his home, Tilden put together a tennis production for young men in uniform. Tilden partnered with Walter Wesbrook, a Pasadena tennis professional, but the real draw for the soldiers were the widely popular and young amateur champions Gertrude "Gorgeous Gussie" Moran and Gloria Butler. Tilden and Wesbrook would hit a few shots before quickly showing themselves off the court so the soldiers could watch Moran and Butler play. Tilden would add some provocative commentary over a public address system before returning to the court with Wesbrook, both of whom were now dressed in drag. After a few games of Tilden and Wesbrook versus Moran and Butler, the men would throw off their costumes and pair up with women for a mixed-doubles match—basically the only real tennis of the whole show. Needless to say, such a spectacle ran afoul of the USLTA. Tennis officials certainly continued to bristle at the thought of Tilden involved in the game in any way, and the cross-dressing certainly did not bring them on board. What ground their gears, though, was not the intermixing of the sexes. It was the presence of amateur players and professional players on the same court that proved insufferable.[15]

Moran and Butler built on the legacy of women such as Lizzie Stroud and Alta Weiss, who for decades had blazed trails for women to earn money from their athletics. World War II meant increased opportunities for women athletes, most visibly the All-American Girls Professional Baseball League, which ran between 1943 and 1945.[16] Beginning in 1943, the military extended the draft further—Congress had first authorized the draft in 1940 and expanded it after Pearl Harbor—to conscript groups such as fathers previously deferred from service.[17] That move bolstered the ranks of the military with new recruits. The young father Bobby Riggs was one of those recruits when he entered the basic training program at the Great Lakes Naval Training Station.[18]

Riggs and most other athletes soon found themselves sent to Bainbridge, Maryland, where they joined the U.S. Navy Physical Training Section commanded by Gene Tunney.[19] During World War I, Tunney had served in the U.S. Expeditionary Force, where he made a name for himself as a boxer. In the 1920s Tunney won bout after bout and established himself as world heavyweight titleholder with an attendance-setting victory over then champion and celebrity Jack Dempsey. Tunney went on to defeat Dempsey in the infamous 1927 "Long Count" rematch, retaining his title until his retirement in 1928. He remained a prominent public figure in retirement through the serialization of his autobiography in *Collier's Magazine*, which became a best-selling 1932 book titled *A Man Must Fight*.[20] That book's title brilliantly captured Tunney's own experiences as an athlete who was willing to answer his country's call, and military leaders found Tunney a good fit to lead a new generation of soldier-athletes—people such as Major League slugger Johnny Mize, Dodgers shortstop Harold Peter Henry "Pee Wee" Reese, and Chicago White Sox ace Johnny Rigney—in World War II.[21]

In some respects athletes simply continued doing what they normally did: they played games to entertain others. What differed during wartime was who they were entertaining, where they were entertaining, and who was paying for the entertainment. Before the draft began, professional athletes primarily played benefit exhibitions for suitable causes like war bond drives or aid rallies for the Allies. For example, as the World's Professional Champion in 1941, Bobby Riggs joined Warner Brothers movie stars George Brent and Errol Flynn for tennis exhibitions in Los Angeles and San Francisco to raise money for the British War Relief Society. When the draft began in earnest and the country's best athletes found themselves in uniform, the entertainment changed to focus on the fellow men in uniform rather than the public at large, with competitions between different branches of the service being one of the more common formulations. Riggs and Wayne Sabin played for the navy against army officers Don Budge and Frankie Parker. Major Leaguers like Buddy Blattner, Skeets Dickey, and Johnny Lucadello likewise formed intra-service baseball squads to entertain troops. The soldiers gambled incessantly.[22]

Entertainment for troops reciprocated the grand strategy priorities of Allied politicians and war planners. Prioritized operations in the North African and European theaters of battle meant that American troops marshalling in the Pacific—but not yet engaged in heavy combat—were recreated with greater regularity than their European counterparts. In the Pacific, troop entertainment centered on Hawaii because Navy bases like Pearl Harbor massed the most troops. As the intensity of the U.S. military's island-hopping strategy intensified in 1943, physical instruction brigadiers accompanied combat troops battling Japanese troops on Pacific archipelagos. Riggs and Sabin played Budge and Parker in both singles and doubles on Saipan, Tinian, Iwo Jima, and Guam after American troops captured these islands from the Japanese. On Guam, under the direction of the avid tennis player Vice Admiral John Hoover, the ever-busy servicemen of the Naval Construction Forces, popularly called the "Seabees," built a tennis court for the naval brass and physical training soldiers to compete on between war making.[23]

Troops stationed in the United States were also entertained by athletes in and out of uniform. After a tour of duty as the captain of a tank-landing ship for the Allied invasion of Europe, the American Davis Cupper Gardnar Mulloy was sent back stateside by the navy to train for action in the Pacific. In the interim, Mulloy convinced his superiors at the Little Creek Naval Base in Camp Bradford to allow him to organize exhibition and fund-raising matches. Mulloy recognized the draw lady players had for American GIs, so he first recruited Alice Marble and Dorothy "Dodo" Bundy before filling out the roster with big names such as Bill Tilden, Vincent Richards, and the Irish champion George Littleton Rodgers. As the troop toured different bases, they made the most of fellow players in uniform and incorporated them into the exhibitions. In Norfolk, Virginia, for example, naval aviator and tennis champion Ted Schroeder squared off against Bill Tilden before Mulloy and his group moved on to another base in another state. Opinion surveys completed by men in uniform overwhelmingly approved of these entertainments; most soldiers did not seem to mind that these men and women held a tennis racquet or microphone in their hand rather a rifle.[24]

During the war, private tennis clubs also did their part for the American war effort. Those with money and influence held special events such as fund-raising exhibitions featuring the best players, many on loan from their military units. On the East and West Coasts, clubs like the La Jolla Beach and Tennis Club of La Jolla, California, adhered to the coastal evening blackouts by prohibiting night tennis to avoid giving the German or Japanese air forces suitable targets. And clubs fortunate enough to have talented teaching professionals often bid good-bye to those men without complaint when the draft notice of these healthy young men came up.[25]

The war certainly changed the playing careers of many competitive tennis players. Unlike professionals like Tilden who entertained troops for pay without joining the army, or players like Riggs who were themselves in the military and playing for Uncle Sam, amateur players like Doris Hart still could not receive any form of compensation for winning their matches. Furthermore, with players throughout the world serving their respective countries, any semblance of international competition was deferred until the conclusion of the war. Because large numbers of top male players wore uniforms, Hart and other women players carried the torch of amateur tennis throughout the conflict. In some ways, these women resembled their fellow female athletes who filled the bleachers and swung the bat on the baseball diamond while the boys were away from the field. The resemblance did not go much beyond that, however, mainly because the organizers behind the All-American Girl's

Professional Baseball League had a very different background when it came to the place of money in sports. Phillip K. Wrigley and his management staff at the Chicago Cubs spearheaded the league and held few reservations about making money off the backs of their female players during wartime.[26]

On the tennis side, the USLTA still held its defensive position of no money to any amateur player. That stance presented a problem, though, because the USLTA had previously collected money from its high-attendance tournaments and distributed this money to various sectional tennis divisions after keeping a substantial sum for the organization's administrative duties at the national office in New York City. The tournaments could not run by themselves either, so the USLTA decided to donate all of the proceeds—after subtracting the costs incurred in running the tournament—to charity organizations of stature like the International Red Cross. All in all, many top players did not pick up a racquet during the war, while those who did played in fewer tournaments and faced diminished competition between 1941 and 1945. But with most other sports, leisure activities, and entertainments, tennis survived the war and continued on in the immediate postwar period, albeit in a new direction.[27]

As with so many other parts of life, World War II upended positions of power in the tennis world with the antebellum dominance on the court of Donald Budge giving way to Bobby Riggs, who beat Budge for the first time twenty-three to twenty-one matches in the first professional tennis tour after the war. As with some of the tours in the late 1930s, Jack Harris promoted and managed the 1946–1947 tour, which Riggs won. Riggs secured his position as the touring professional to beat in the coming year only by winning over Budge at the Forest Hills National Professional Tournament in September. There Harris made it perfectly clear to both players that the loser of their final match would not receive a tour contract. The winner could expect to take on the current amateur champion, Jack Kramer, in a tour beginning on December 26, 1947, and going into the spring of 1948.[28]

Riggs's victory earned him a contract of 17.5 percent of the tour gross receipts as compared to 35 percent of the total gross receipts allotted to the amateur-champion-turned-professional challenger. In fact, Harris negotiated Riggs down from 25 percent to 17.5 percent simply by threats of finding other professionals to tour against the amateur-champion-turned-professional challenger, whom Harris maintained was the real draw for spectators anyway. The wily promoter further leveraged the power he held over the few professional players, unable to return to the amateur ranks, by offering the Ecuadorian

Francisco "Pancho" Segura and the Australian Dennis "Dinny" Pails not a percentage fee but a flat weekly rate of $300 to play the tour's undercard match. Both signed quickly because they did not have a choice. Regardless of who won the most matches in the tour, Kramer would earn $86,470, Riggs $43,225, Segura around $5,000, and Pails around $5,000. Kramer's first tour had earned him the largest payday per match of any player in professional tennis history, yet he also realized that by not promoting the tour, he had missed out on the roughly $107,705 Jack Harris had netted as tour promoter and manager.[29]

Like Riggs, Kramer's earliest tennis took place on the public park courts in Los Angeles County built because of the New Deal. La Cienega Park, Boyle Heights Park, and municipal courts in the working-class suburb of Southgate were his regular haunts until, again like Riggs, he attracted the attention of Southern California Tennis's boss, Perry T. Jones, who opened the LATC to the promising junior. Unlike how he felt about Riggs, however, Jones adored the clean-cut and well-behaved Kramer. Jones made sure to arrange matches for his protégé with the best junior players and many of the best onetime professional players who played their retirement tennis at the LATC. Great competition in Southern California meant that, in Kramer's own words, he "was almost automatically the best in the country."[30]

Kramer's cockiness stemmed from the quality of competition he came from and the new style of play he pioneered. Contemporary sportswriters and spectators came to call his style the "Big Game." For the first two-thirds of a century of tennis, nearly all top players—Tilden, Richards, Vines, Bromwich, Quist, Pails, Budge, Parker, Talbert, Riggs, and Mulloy—preferred to play groundstrokes from the baseline with an emphasis on consistency and defense. After Kramer, nearly all top players played a hard serve, well-placed return, or penetrating groundstroke, usually a driving forehand, after which they explosively approached the net looking to end the point quickly with a volley or, should their opponent lob to them, an overhead smash. Kramer did not pioneer the Big Game in a vacuum; rather, the innovation owed to the championship 1946 Davis Cup team. Walter Pate, the squad's captain, picked Kramer, Ted Schroeder, and Gardnar Mulloy precisely because he believed an aggressive style of play to be the only means to victory over the seasoned Australian team of Dinny Pails, John Bromwich, Adrian Quist, and Victor Murphy. In front of a boisterous Melbourne crowd at the Kooyong mega-stadium, the Americans' aggressive serve-and-volley game so thoroughly overwhelmed the Australians that only one match out of five went more than straight sets in the sweep for the United States. The huge popularity of tennis in Australia practically required that the LTAA and their internationally famed Davis Cup captain Harry Hopman adopt the strategy of attack, attack, attack of the Americans. From the first year of competitive tennis after the war, the two tennis nations that all other countries looked to as an example espoused the big game.[31]

Kramer continued to popularize and refine the Big Game in his final year as an amateur. In his stellar 1947 season, he increasingly played opponents in the final rounds of the big tournaments who had also begun to serve and volley, chip and charge on the service return, and look for a short ball to hit an approach shot to follow into the net. The 1947 Davis Cup again pitted the United States against Australia, with both teams playing more of the Big Game—though the Americans played it slightly better to defend their title. Having won the Wimbledon title, the U.S. Championship, and helping the United States hold on to the Davis Cup, Kramer turned professional to take his Big Game on tour with the reigning world's professional champion, Bobby Riggs.[32]

Riggs, a highly adaptable, thoughtful, and strategic player, enjoyed early success against Kramer. The defending champion won the December 26 opener at Madison Square Garden in front of a record-setting crowd despite a blizzard outside. Rather than getting drawn into Riggs's gamesmanship, however, Kramer refined his aggressive game in order to maximize what he called a "percentage attack." This meant the likelihood of winning a point based on Kramer's having hit a certain shot in a certain situation. Kramer was bigger and stronger than Riggs, but the real key to Kramer's tour victory came from the realization that he could control his percentages with regularity only if he consistently took the initiative to set up scenarios of shots when the percentages would fall in his favor. If Kramer allowed his opponent to dictate what sort of rallies they entered, then his likelihood of having to play statistically un-advantageous exchanges increased, and too large an increase in such exchanges would result in a lost match and eventually a lost tour. The challenger thoroughly routed Riggs sixty-nine to twenty matches in their 1947–1948 tour.[33]

That summer Kramer again bested Riggs in the twenty-first year of the national professional tournament hosted by the West Side Tennis Club in Forest Hills, New York, and thus assured himself a place on the tour for the following year to take on the top amateur player who could be coaxed to join the professional ranks. Getting to tour mattered so much to the finances of the professional player because of the limited tournament schedule of events for professional players and the small payout each event offered. The highest profile, largest grossing, and best paying professional tournament in 1948, for example, collected gross receipts of $25,856.00. After liabilities, the tournament netted $17,095.17, of which 60 percent (i.e., $8,057.10) was distributed to the roughly thirty players who competed. A first-round loser thus received $50, a round sixteen loser $100, a quarterfinalist $322, and a semifinalist about $500. For his second-place finish, Riggs earned $966.85 while Kramer's win secured 18 percent of the tournament purse—$1,450.20 in winnings for singles, with an additional $825.14 of winnings in doubles. That modest amount when combined with the infrequency of professional tournaments meant that a professional player could not make it financially without a tour unless they were willing to spend most days of the year teaching the game to people willing to pay for the instruction.[34]

The vast majority of people called "tennis professionals" earned their bread coaching rather than playing tennis. In Britain, Queen's Club and AELTC teaching professional Dan Maskell lobbied and eventually convinced the LTA to sponsor a series of professional matches open to anyone whose livelihood depended on tennis. Nearly all who participated were club coaches who belonged to the Maskell-led Professional Coaches' Association, folded into the LTA's Coaching Professional Committee in 1934, whose members held little sway over LTA policy making.[35] In the United States, the moment a tennis amateur earned their first dollar from the game in any capacity, outside of the sanctioned expenses the USLTA approved, they became a professional regardless of the origin of that money. The majority of tennis professionals were simply tennis amateurs who the USLTA caught teaching tennis, stringing racquets, or selling apparel to earn their living. Outside the USLTA's structure, these teaching professionals thus formed their own association in the Professional Lawn Tennis Association (PLTA), which primarily served the teaching professionals rather than the handful of playing professionals. As a tennis professional in 1931, Bill Tilden organized the Professional Player's Association for the handful of top players touring for a living. While never strong, that organization existed apart from the PLTA in functioning essentially as a way for the few top tennis players to discourage competition from other professionals who might think of starting a rival tour.[36]

Division among those labeled as "professional" tennis players reached a boiling point on June 12, 1948, when the PLTA announced that only full members of their organization were allowed to play in the national professional championship sponsored by the PLTA and hosted by the West Side Tennis Club at Forest Hills. That excluded Kramer, Riggs, Pails, Segura, and Budge; however, without those players, who fans across the country most associated with professional tennis, the tournament's draw underwhelmed. Both teaching professionals and playing professionals recognized this, and in final negotiations tour players agreed to forsake their own professional organization in favor of the tennis teacher–focused PLTA if the latter organization would not interfere with the best players' efforts to tour when the PLTA-sponsored championship was not going on. The PLTA would continue to devote the majority of its time and resources to helping their few hundred members receive better contracts for their instruction at different clubs and sporting goods stores while the half dozen touring professionals continued to play tennis for money.[37]

In the late 1940s such distinctions did not really matter that much to Kramer because his on-court dominance assured his place on the professional tour. He continued to test the effectiveness of his percentage play on the grueling 1949 to 1950 professional tour against a bigger and stronger opponent in Richard "Pancho" Gonzales. A fellow Los Angeles public parks player, the Latino Gonzales was far less welcome at the LATC than either Jack Kramer or Bobby Riggs, but the big-serving and hard-hitting Gonzales proved his mettle two years in a row with pressure wins over Ted Schroeder in the finals of the U.S. Championships at Forest Hills. The ability to handle big-match pressure did not beat the percentages, however. Kramer thoroughly defeated the strong-striking Gonzales on the indoor canvas courts of their 1949–1950 tour, with the two having played seemingly every major city in America. For his part, Gonzales learned from his defeat and developed his own percentage attack game that, when combined with Gonzales's physical gifts and mental toughness, thoroughly dominated tennis for a decade beginning in 1953.[38] (For cities played on Bobby Riggs Presents Jack Kramer vs. Pancho Gonzales World Championship Tennis Tour, October 25, 1949 to May 21, 1950, see map 4.[39])

In the meantime, Kramer beat Eduardo "Little Pancho" Segura—whose two-handed forehand and counterpunch hustling style were as far away from

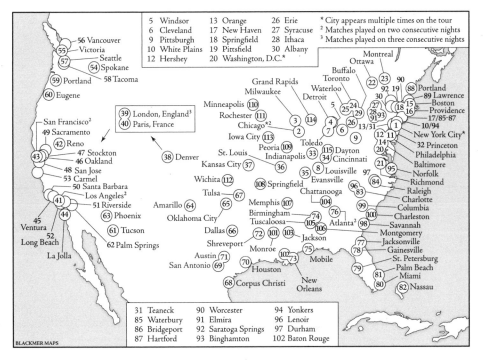

Map 4. Cities played on Bobby Riggs Presents Jack Kramer vs. Pancho Gonzales
World Championship Tennis Tour, October 25, 1949, to May 21, 1950

the Big Game as a player could get—in the 1950–1951 professional tour before defeating Frank Sedgman fifty-four to forty-one matches in a 1953 professional tour. The Big Game, however, had taken a toll on Kramer's body, and after only half of a decade of professional touring, he retired from full-time play to focus on minding the percentages of his promoting.[40]

Professional tennis suited both Bobby Riggs and Jack Kramer from the beginning. They had learned the game of tennis not far from one another in Southern California only to find themselves touring as the best professionals in the world after the Second World War. Their time together would continue into the 1950s, but just as they had competed on the court, they soon would compete for control over the professional game itself.

97

CHAPTER 6

The Cultural Contexts of
Mid-Century Women's Tennis

The first professional player of international renown was the French champion Suzanne Lenglen, who electrified the game in the 1920s. But in the early postwar years, the coast-to-coast tours of the all-American boy Jack Kramer and the ostentatious Bobby Riggs had eroded some of the game's feminine origins in the minds of American sports fans. Women players generally fared far worse financially than their male peers because the career options of women in the 1950s and '60s did not compare to the opportunities men enjoyed. That decline meant that women athletes in particular struggled until the opening of tennis to professionals in 1968. In the highly visualized world of sport during the Cold War, however, competition in both amateur and professional women's tennis intensified in new directions.

Since the game's infancy in the late nineteenth century, women played tennis in such large numbers, with such frequency, and with such visibility that popular culture long talked and thought of tennis as a women's game. The most talked about female sportswoman around the world in the early 1950s was tennis player Maureen "Little Mo" Connolly. As a teenager the San Diegan won the U.S. Nationals in 1951—the youngest player to do so at that point. Yet that same year, the seventeen-year-old found herself working as a copy girl for managing editor Richard Pourade at the Union Tribune Publishing Company in San Diego. In 1953 Connolly won all four major tournaments to become the first tennis player to earn the Grand Slam since Don Budge.

She had brought a fifty-match winning streak in major tournaments into the summer of her 1954 season when a horse-riding accident effectively ended her career while she was still a teenager. She had planned to turn professional after that season, but injury forced her to retire and forgo Jack Kramer's one-hundred-thousand-dollar guarantee for two years on his professional tour. Connolly's short career exemplified just how important it was for topflight women tennis players to consider turning professional and trying to earn money. Even without an injury, if they played only as amateurs, they would still never earn much more than living expenses with no savings to fall back on. Then came the limited prospect of low-wage menial work after their amateur careers inevitably ended when they were still young women.[1]

All of this took place during a postwar period when Americans had renewed emphasis on women's place in the domestic sphere only to see the baby boom generation in part reject that formulation in favor of more public expressions of sexuality and consumer culture.[2] Putting athletics into that context meant youth mattered for more reasons than just the athlete's ability to compete on the court. Spectators wanted vitality in their athletes and held women players to a higher standard in that regard. The popularity with the public that women tennis players always enjoyed was a devil's bargain that was due, to a considerable degree, to both the graceful movement of their bodies on the court and their willingness to push the acceptable boundaries of fashion.[3]

The most important fashion designer of sportswear in the twentieth century cited Lenglen's play and public life as the inspiration behind his aesthetic, which fused athleticism and sexuality. English born in 1911, Ted Tinling grew up around tennis and embraced the game to such a degree that he moved to France to serve as one of the inaugural chair umpires for the first French Championships. Influenced by Parisian fashion, Tinling returned to England to set up his own label while also working as an official at the AELTC. To help heighten sex appeal, Tinling studied the movement of women tennis players. Between 1932 and 1969 he watched them compete in tournaments and on the practice courts, where he took notes in order to design clothes that both functioned as athletic wear and captured the attention of fans watching those women play. His photographs captured classic matches and how champions such as Helen Wills Moody, Dorothy Round, Helen Jacobs, and Joyce Willing moved on the court. Suzanne Lenglen appeared in more of Tinling's photographs than any other player, a testament to the first worldwide professional tennis player's impact on modern sports fashion. The challenge of drawing on professional athletes for the design of sportswear was not one of inspiration but rather of applicability and scalability. What worked for the athletic body did not easily translate to the everyday body. Tinling and designers compensated for that discrepancy by covering rather than revealing. A more conservative approach to his leisurewear for women matched the very functional and practical polo tops, track jackets, shorts, and high-waist chinos Tinling designed for men. But designing practical clothing for men and looser-fitting clothing for mature women held little excitement for Tinling, who produced only a few collections not inspired by and directed toward young, vivacious women. By removing material and revealing a little skin, Tinling announced the bolder position of women's bodies in both the public's space and in people's imaginations. None of his outfits did that more infamously than the décolleté he produced for the 1949 Wimbledon Championships.[4]

The Californian Gertrude "Gorgeous Gussie" Moran turned heads whether she had a tennis racquet in hand or not. Her good looks and gregarious personality led to brief movie roles, regular photo shoots, and numerous product endorsements that she leveraged off of her most sensational moment at the 1949 Wimbledon Championships. A finalist in the women's title match at the end of the tournament, Moran's fortnight at the AELTC broke tradition and protocol with her bold fashion choice. For the club that hosted the first lawn tennis tournament and most prized tradition, Moran's sartorial selection of a short skirt and white lace panties flew in the face of over sixty years of tennis history. The typical stretches and lunges of a competitive match with legs on full display revealed a tennis garment that had never before been treated as appropriate for stylizing. Pilloried in the press for her titillating fashion, the crowds could literally not get enough of Moran, further stoking the controversy.[5]

Moran defended her attire with a practical assessment of the connection between competitive tennis and women's fashion: "After all, jumping and dancing about the court, people see your underwear anyway, so they might as well see something with lace on it." A tournament spectator, A. Steward of London, England, agreed, remarking on the fine play and good looks of the American players while also singling out Moran's underwear for keeping the "female flag flying high."[6] Moran's intimates even attracted the attention of members of Parliament, who denounced the "panties worn by 'Gorgeous Gussie'" along with the media outlets that were zealously covering her lack of coverage.[7] The player Moran, the spectator Steward, and the government officials understood that the tournament crowds looked at female players with more on the mind than the spin of the forehand or the power of their serve.

Gazers expected style, grace, and celebrity as defined by a balance between the old and the new. Tinling thought any woman in the ladies' events could and should wear the panties and short skirt he designed. He went so far as to take his prototype into the locker room, where he propositioned players who met his prodding with mixed reactions. Pauline Betz seemed to show some interest, while Louise Brough stridently resisted, labeling the clothes a "distraction"—prophetic words, as the heavily favored Moran lost on Wimbledon's Centre Court to a relatively unknown Chinese player. What Brough did not realize was the entertainment power the panties possessed. Spectators cared more for the sizzle of the players than their strokes and strategies. As a sport, tennis was entertainment, and by dressing just a little differently, Moran made a name for herself that would help to pay the bills in the decade to come while the great champion Brough scraped by, teaching tennis lessons to beginners.[8]

Bobby Riggs and Jack Kramer saw opportunity in the panties' notoriety. After a grueling 1949–1950 tour between two masculine stylists, Kramer and Pancho Gonzales, both the promoter Riggs and the professional champion Kramer were looking for a change of pace on the 1950–1951 tour. Many fans had tired of Kramer's predictable bruising of challenger after challenger. The fast-paced serve-and-volley power game of the dominant male players in the late 1940s and early 1950s had turned people off because of the predictable one-off serve, return, volley, point over. Fans wanted less predictability and more variety. They wanted the longer rallies that were more in line with the women's game. Riggs thus invited Francisco "Little Pancho" Segura, Moran, and Betz to tour in what proved to be a mixed venture.[9]

The foursome played a typical stop on February 1 at the Oakland Civic Auditorium. Attendees paid $1.80 for a gallery spot, $2.40 for a balcony view, $3.60 for a position in the dress circle, and $3.60 for main floor seats. The tour promoted "the California boys who have made good" to the East Bay audience, even though Kramer came from Southern California, Segura hailed from Ecuador, and Moran and Betz made up half of the tennis tour without even being acknowledged on the tour's promotional materials. Failing to mention the so-called better half of the tour was a lost marketing opportunity, as neither Betz nor Moran were strangers to the sexualized gaze of onlookers. Moran had embraced that attention with her sartorial selections, while *Life* magazine's coverage of the 1946 U.S. Women's Singles Championship featured that year's winner, Betz, flat on the ground with a view looking up the back of her legs to her rear end. The interest of arousal proved fleeting for many fans, however, as Betz bested Moran night after night on the court.

The one-sidedness of the tour became so bad that Kramer and Riggs each approached Betz about withdrawing from the remainder of their matches, because people decided to forgo attending if they could guess the outcome ahead of time. In trying to force Betz out and then offering to buy her a car as a quid pro quo for her withdrawal from the tour, both Riggs and Kramer earned themselves reputations for sexism that continued to cling to them throughout their later careers. Kramer never disclosed how much Betz got paid, but given that she had toured previously as a professional in the late 1940s, the number he and Riggs agreed to pay her likely fell more in line with the one thousand dollars a week they offered Segura compared to the thirty-five-thousand-dollar guarantee plus 25 percent over thirty-five thousand that both Moran and Kramer accepted.[10]

Betz grew up playing tennis in Southern California, first on the Queens Playground public park courts near Los Angeles High School and later on the courts of the Los Angeles Tennis Club after she became California's high school state champion. Throughout her junior career, she learned the game from Dick Skeen, one of the country's most successful professionals at developing youngsters. At the LATC she had matches against other top players like Louise Brough, arranged for her by Perry T. Jones. Jones took an even greater interest in Gertrude Moran and actress/model Jinx Falkenburg, who also began playing there in 1938. As he did with so many players, he paid for their lessons, secured practice partners for them, and even bought their tennis balls. That support figured prominently in cresting the wave of Southern California female players that thoroughly dominated women's tennis in the middle third of the twentieth century. Those women won thirteen National Singles Championships between 1935 and 1950; they held seven national eighteen-and-under championships between 1940 and 1950; they raised the Wimbledon singles trophy five times in a row between 1945 and 1950; and the Southern California female players likely would have won more tournaments had World War II not limited the amateur tournaments available to them in the prime of their careers.[11]

The USLTA male directors grew so accustomed to the dominance of the association's women players that they balked at any hint that one of their amateur champions might consider playing tennis for money on a professional tour. Since Suzanne Lenglen and Mary K. Browne's 1926 tour, the few notable women to play professionally were Californian Alice Marble and English champion Mary Hardwick, who joined Don Budge and Bill Tilden

in an ill-fated 1941 professional tour promoted by Jack Harris. Women players continued to play with their male professional peers in fund-raising until
after World War II, when those matches stopped. The excitement of matches
on the road outside of the control of the USLTA inspired Betz and a handful of other women champions to consider playing some exhibition matches
of their own outside the auspices of the association. The USLTA leadership
treated that curiosity as a complete betrayal of the financial support they
had given Betz and New Englander Sarah Palfrey Cooke during their prewar
amateur careers. Those same male directors thus helped to make Betz's and
Cooke's decisions to turn professional when they suspended the champions'
amateur status. Shortly thereafter Betz and Cooke announced they would play
a professional tour in the summer of 1947, with former player Elwood Cooke,
Cooke's husband, managing their tour. Women now had a professional tour
of their own.[12]

Betz and Cooke tuned up their games in a series of exhibitions before they
played what they billed as their first official professional match in front of fifteen hundred fans in Los Angeles on June 8, 1947, after a signing ceremony
at the Beverly Wilshire Hotel. Their opener certainly showcased the fine on-
court ability of both players, but spectators noted the contest as more of a
splendid spectacle than a serious competition, because, in addition to the
singles match, Cooke paired with actor Mickey Rooney and Betz partnered
with the fine tennis player and coach Carl Earn for a mixed doubles match.
Over the coming months, the two women played match after match from the
West Coast, to the Midwest, and on to the Atlantic Coast with crowds that
averaged one thousand spectators. Betz beat Cooke most of the time, but the
matches remained competitive and the competitors remained on good terms
throughout.[13]

Finishing their solo tour in America, Betz and Cooke then jumped the pond
with Bobby Riggs and Don Budge for matches in Europe. After two final nights
at the Belfast Boat Club in Northern Ireland, the female pros arrived back
stateside on August 27, having spent six weeks abroad with the boys. Cooke's
husband, Elwood, met them in New York City to inform his wife and Betz
that he had scheduled them to play the Colony Surf Club in New Jersey. The
Cookes and Betz discussed a lengthy tour around the United States and abroad
in Europe in 1948, but their touring together had more or less run its course.
Rumors circulated that Jack Harris, the promoter of the 1948 Riggs-versus-
Kramer professional tour set to begin in late December 1947, would look to

Betz, Cooke, or Alice Marble to fill out the long North American tour. That did not happen, as Harris went with Dinny Pails and Pancho Segura instead. Betz and Cooke drifted apart as Elwood Cooke struggled to book matches for the pair. Betz spent much of 1948 playing coed table tennis exhibitions against the Hungarian table tennis champion Sándor Glancz, mostly headlining trade shows in industrial exhibit halls.[14]

Betz and Cooke had nonetheless proven very popular with spectators by combining highly competitive tennis and on-court comedy. In a match in Chicago, for example, the players parodied the teaching professional and amateur student dynamic when Cooke dressed as a tennis coach preparing to give a lesson to a costumed newbie Betz. The wit of both players shined through as well. Betz joked that the linespeople—usually local volunteers who struggled to make correct calls—were familial relations of hers after they would miss an out-ball call in her favor. Cooke put her distinctive Boston accent to great effect, carping for the amused crowd whenever she missed a put-away volley. They competed hard, but viewers wanted something more. The Associated Press ran a photograph of the women in their bathing suits playing tennis along with the suggestive text that, more so than their male peers, the women professionals made tennis "an attractive spectator sport."[15] The image of the tennis player mattered, but what mattered differed in whether or not that player was a woman or a man.

Tradition-bound amateur tennis associations like the USLTA struggled to keep their depictions of tennis players relevant in the context of the Cold War. In the summer of 1956, the ILTF accepted the Soviet Union into membership just as the USLTA began a U.S. sports publicity campaign in coordination with President Dwight Eisenhower's Youth Fitness Program. The association hired Larry Fairhall, son-in-law of an emeritus USLTA president, to mark the association's seventy-five-year anniversary with $20,000 for a comic book that then USLTA president Renville McMann said would sell millions of copies, a book written by Parke Cummings, and a "Miss Tennis of 1956" contest. All went nowhere in promoting tennis, and the costs spiraled to around $100,000 with little to show for it except the individual USLTA sections, which were forced to pony up $20,000 in un-recouped fees. Long-serving USLTA treasurer Ellsworth Davenport offered his resignation over the debacle, but the association's executive committee demanded he stay and stonewalled anyone who inquired about nepotism in the anniversary mess that saw the association's treasury fall from $66,000 in 1954 to $1,000 at the start of 1958 before Wilson Sporting Goods came to the rescue and purchased $15,000 worth of comic books.[16]

The comic book medium fit with the USLTA's message that the Davis Cup remained the association's top priority in the postwar period. The men who sat on the USLTA's Executive Committee hindered their own sway over the future direction the game would take, because they ignored the impact that women already had in cultivating the game. Since the early twentieth century, efforts to promote amateur tennis in America relied primarily on subscriptions to *American Lawn Tennis* magazine, published monthly by Stephen Wallis Merrihew—periodically under the auspices of the USLTA. One reason the association agreed to bless Merrihew's magazine was that the editorial staff only had room for men. That bias existed because the USLTA itself did not want women in any authoritative position over the game of tennis except playing on the court, where they could be controlled. With Merrihew and the USLTA's break following Merrihew's 1924 support of Bill Tilden in the face of the USLTA's assaults on Tilden's character as the tennis-player-turned-tennis-correspondent, the association's ties with *American Lawn Tennis* were severed irrevocably.[17]

Voices that readers never tired of hearing were those of the players themselves. As with Bill Tilden's outspoken views, women players had long expressed their opinions on their sport in the press. Unlike in other sports, where women's opinions were reported by male sportswriters, the opinions of women tennis players routinely took the form of their own columns.[18] After Bill Tilden's sexual proclivities alienated him from many former supporters, the amateur-champion-turned-professional Alice Marble assumed the duties of providing the player perspective in *American Lawn Tennis*. In her monthly column, "As I See It," she spoke out on a host of issues that ranged from mismanagement of association resources on the part of the USLTA to how professional players such as Don Budge and Fred Perry received invitations from various city chambers of commerce to provide youth with athletic clinics as a means to "combat child delinquency." The photograph of Marble that accompanied her columns showed to all of her readers a knowledgeable, erudite, and athletic woman capable of challenging the old-guard men who still made the most important decisions in her sport. And challenge them she did, both in her writing and on citywide playing and lecture circuits, where she not only entertained but also instructed on technical tennis issues that ranged from the proper grip to use for the overhead stroke to more serious issues such as urban recreational policy and sexism in sports.[19]

Marble had one of the more remarkable life stories of any professional athlete in the middle part of the twentieth century. Like so many top tennis players, she came from California, but far from the sunshine and the starlets of Los Angeles. The fourth child of farmers in Plumas County, Marble spent as much time as a preteen milking cows in the Sierra Foothills as she did swinging a tennis racquet. The young Marble also met an assortment of strangers, unusual for such an isolated location, who traveled through her father's land to bathe in the sulfur springs on the family farm. Although she learned a work ethic there that served her later in her career, Marble never could have developed as a player had her father and mother not decided to move the family to San Francisco when Marble was still a preteen.[20]

In 1919 sadness struck Marble's family when an automobile accident incapacitated her father at the same time that most of the family—and much of the city, for that matter—fell ill with influenza. Most of Marble's relatives pulled through, but her father died from his sickness. His death required Marble's mother to work long hours cleaning offices in addition to her homemaking to keep the family fed, and that hardship meant that Marble spent a great deal of time under the supervision of her adolescent brothers. The boys relished playing in city parks, and Marble had little choice in accompanying them to the Golden Gate Park baseball fields. Marble quickly gained a reputation as a tomboy and an athlete, more interested in ball games during recess than in her schoolwork or chores. On one occasion she even made the *San Francisco Examiner* when the Pacific Coast League Seals were a player short and, in desperation to field a full side, mistook Marble watching the game for a teenage boy they could use on the diamond. She earned the spot. For the rest of her teenage years, she could usually count on an invitation to play with the males, no matter their caliber.[21]

Athletic ability soon took Marble in a different direction. Right after their father died, her oldest brother, Dan, dropped out of school to help support his mother and siblings by working in the lumber business. He always played handball to unwind after a long day of work, and by his late teenage years he was the number one ranked player in Northern California. That success, along with respectable work in the lumber trade, led Dan to frequent "fashionable clubs" in San Francisco that offered facilities for tennis and other individual sports. Dan's position as the de facto head of household led him to exercise a great deal of influence over his younger siblings, and he had grown tired of hearing about his younger sister playing all afternoon with boys in San Francisco's Recreation Park in the Mission District. Marble had grown from a little girl to an athletically built young woman of five feet, seven inches and

150 pounds, and Dan expected her to start acting like the young adult she had become.[22]

However, Dan also recognized the athleticism of his sister. He soon settled on tennis as the right sport for a young woman. Marble wrote that her "heart was broken" when he gave her a tennis racquet with the warning that her baseball and basketball days were over. She claimed to endure teasing from her old friends, but with encouragement from her history teacher, she went to the Golden Gate Park courts, where she made new friends, including a coterie of athletic young women not altogether different than herself in the junior tennis club. After only four months of playing the game, Marble won her first tournament, and within a year's time she rose to the top of the junior players in the San Francisco public parks. At sixteen she was invited to play at the Berkeley Tennis Club in the California State Championship against the top females throughout California. Unaccustomed to losing, Marble lost in the finals and almost quit the sport. Her brother Dan, however, purchased a forty-five-dollar junior membership for her to San Francisco's California Tennis Club, where she confronted the best competition in the Bay Area. Marble still preferred to play in the more free-wheeling environment of the public parks, where she routinely competed against people from all backgrounds, including Chinese, Japanese, and Filipino men. As she rose in the rankings, she credited the diversity of the people she played against as a major factor for her fast success.[23]

By 1932 Marble was the top player in California after having won the state women's championship. She relied upon the well-funded California amateur tennis associations to provide her with travel expenses to play on the East Coast. She also benefited from the collected wisdom of California coaches like Eleanor "Teach" Tennant and the retinue of fellow California players who formed a clique on the East Coast amateur circuit. That solidarity proved important for Marble when the West Side Tennis Club lost her entry into the 1933 U.S. National Championships at Forest Hills and refused to remake the draw. Had the famous San Francisco champion "Little Bill" Johnston not intervened on his compatriot's behalf, Marble would have missed her first major tournament because of a miscommunication and potential prejudice on the part of the Eastern USLTA section. Johnston's support of Marble exemplified the tendency of sectional differences to matter more than class and gender differences when it came to the tennis players themselves. A West Coast player would support a fellow West Coast player, a Southern player a Southern player. Likewise, compared to other sports, the amateur tennis associations funded top women players to much the same degree that they funded top men's players. That support and camaraderie was most visible at the national level in the form of the Wightman Cup team, which pitted the best women players in the United States against the best women players in England, with the USLTA paying all related expenses for the American athletes. Marble first earned a spot on the squad in 1933, and she played her last Wightman Cup match in 1939. That experience helped her grow close to the handful of other top women players in the country, and the chance to develop her game with those players led to her first U.S. National Singles Championship in 1936. That victory gained her the financial support necessary to travel to England for Wimbledon, where she won the singles championship in 1938 and '39 before World War II halted that competition.[24]

Yet the financial support that the USLTA provided could also sow seeds of discord between players and the directors of the association. Earlier in her amateur career, when Marble required hospitalization during the middle of the Wightman Cup team's tour of Paris, not only did the USLTA leadership not console the hurting player, but also, upon her return to the United States and her subsequent medical treatment there, Wightman Cup chairman Julian Myrick went so far as to tell Marble and her coach, Tennant, that the association wanted nothing more to do with Marble, because she had already "cost them a great deal of money" and proved to be a "bad investment." Tennant remained loyal to Marble, however, and provided room, board, and round-the-clock care to her player over the next year as Marble recovered. Feeling strong enough to play again, Southern California Tennis Association secretary Perry T. Jones, acting on behalf of the USLTA national office, notified Marble that the association had refused her entry to tournaments in the East Coast lawn tennis circuit. After much pleading, she eventually received a hearing in front of a selection committee, which took the form of a four-day tryout under the gaze of five men who begrudgingly admitted she seemed fit enough to play in their tournaments. That audition galvanized Marble to think more seriously about turning professional despite her renewed success in amateur tournaments in 1940. Wartime service entertaining troops as part of the Bill Tilden, Don Budge, and Mary Hardwick Hare tour in the States and purported clandestine activities in Europe delayed that professional career.[25]

Marble's decision to turn professional infuriated the USLTA directors. They ignored her and forgot how they abandoned her during her health struggles, only remembering their sponsorship of Marble's 1938 and '39 European ama-teur trips, which they believed deserved the debt of gratitude that she would remain an amateur throughout her playing career. Instead she diversified her money-making activities to include professional tennis tours, paid consultant-ships with firms like Wilson Sporting Goods, and clothing design lines. Her willingness to tour professionally with men especially galled the male leaders of the USLTA. Marble set an example of strength for women in her own work life; she also advocated for women in her writing. While most of her writing presented straightforward arguments in favor of women tennis players, on occasion she waded into more controversial waters, as when she served as an early editor of DC's *Wonder Woman* comic and wrote "The Wonder Women of History" series, which earned her fifty thousand dollars. Her personal letters too, like those to Doris Jane Hart, encouraged talented young women players to stick with the game in the face of the uphill challenges they faced.[26]

No player benefited more from Marble's help than African American cham-pion Althea Gibson, who faced more discrimination than any other topflight player. Gibson's parents were South Carolina sharecroppers who migrated to Harlem in 1930, three years after she was born. In this vibrant urban neighbor-hood, Gibson benefited from a law enforcement and community organizing program called the Police Athletic League, in which law enforcement officers provided urban youths with sporting goods and coaching. Gibson took to paddle tennis and quickly excelled. Of the league's programs across major U.S. cities in the mid-twentieth century, Gibson remarked that they "set up these play streets to keep the kids or the youths on the courts instead of in the courts." Community leaders also came around and befriended the young people. In Gibson's case, the big band leader and tenor saxophonist Buddy Walker looked after her block in Harlem. He quickly noticed Gibson's racquet skills, her tall and lanky physique, and her athleticism. He encouraged her to practice and practice. Despite these interactions with authority figures, the games Gibson grew up with in Harlem were more informal and unstructured than recreational officials would admit. The games were both of and on the street. Gibson zealously guarded the concrete paddle tennis court where she had taken to playing a modified game of lawn tennis. The winner stayed on the court. Gibson never lost and did not see any reason to give up the spot she had earned by winning so that someone else could get a turn.[27]

After about two years of playing on paddleball and handball courts, Walker introduced Gibson to friends at the leading New York City athletic club. The

Cosmopolitan Tennis Club allowed Gibson honorary membership so that she could train for the New York State Championships sanctioned by the American Tennis Association (ATA). Upwardly mobile African Americans founded the ATA in 1916 out of necessity because the USNLTA sanctioned a de facto color line by allowing member clubs in the organizations to exercise their own discretion in who they did and did not admit to membership at their clubs. African Americans exercised far greater racial tolerance in their own tennis organizations. In her first ATA New York State Championship, the girl whom Gibson defeated in the finals was white.[28]

In 1947 Gibson won her first ATA National Championship. She continued to hold that title for the next decade. In the meantime, ATA officials lobbied the USLTA for Gibson's inclusion in USLTA events. Progress proved slow, but with a little help from Alice Marble, who penned an open letter of support for Gibson's cause, USLTA officials relented and allowed the young African American champion to participate in USLTA-sanctioned events. Gibson's first tournament took place at the 369th Regiment Armory, located just off of Fifth Avenue on 143rd Street in New York City. She won that Eastern Indoor Championship, which secured her entrance into the National Indoor Championships, held at another military drill pavilion—the 66th Street Armory on Park Avenue. Gibson did not lift that crown, but through her performance on the court and the tireless behind-the-scenes efforts of her supporters at the Cosmopolitan Tennis Club and in the ATA, she found most tennis tournaments open to her in the following years.[29]

Marble helped make sure of that. She forcefully spoke out in favor of desegregating tennis competition by allowing Althea Gibson to compete openly in USLTA-sanctioned tournaments over the objections voiced by the individual clubs that hosted these tournaments. In the same July 1950 issue of *American Lawn Tennis* that told readers about Gibson's New York public parks background, her schooling at Florida A & M University, and her dominance of the ATA tournament circuit, Marble made a persuasive case for Gibson's entrance into the draw of the 1950 U.S. Championships, despite objections from some members of the West Side Tennis Club. Before Marble's letter of support, Gibson's chance of playing on those lawn tennis courts seemed unlikely to happen in 1950, because the other East Coast elite clubs, where a player earned the necessary qualifying points to secure a spot in Forest Hills, used their "invitational" discretion with regularity to tailor-make their tournament to the liking of their membership. Marble's rhetoric appealed to the vanity of those club members, who from the beginning of the game in America had viewed themselves as the stewards of the game. She convinced enough of them that a refusal to allow Gibson to compete with the best players in the country undermined the competitive spirit of tennis, where the best players rose to the top of the rankings regardless of their social standing. That such top players were now African American, Marble argued, made sense because African Americans had already broken through as top athletes in "baseball, in football, or in boxing." The editorial concluded with Marble going beyond supporting Gibson with her words by imparting her accumulated wisdom on the tennis court from years of playing in topflight tournaments. Gibson had a practice partner and mentor in Marble almost everywhere she played, because Marble herself also had had to prove herself to the USLTA's leadership a dozen years before.[30]

Gibson proved up to that challenge. Throughout the 1950s she made the most of what competitive amateur tennis had to offer. International travel was first and foremost. In addition to Wimbledon, Gibson traveled to Great Britain and the Continent for Wightman Cup matches, where she helped the U.S. team capture that hardware in 1957 and '58. She also became a player in the United States' global struggle against the Soviet Union when in 1955 State Department officials requested that she join Karol Fageros, Bob Perry, and Hamilton Richardson on a goodwill tennis tour throughout Southeast Asia. Gibson agreed, and soon she found herself playing her first match as a representative of the U.S. government in Rangoon, Burma. Over the next six months, Gibson and her teammates played exhibition matches, visited schools to instruct children, competed against local champions, and spread the message of freedom, as President Eisenhower and his foreign policy team feared the region was poised to tip over to communism like dominos. Gibson's teammates were all white: one from the South, one from Florida, and one from California via the Midwest. Richardson was an NCAA champion and a Rhodes Scholar. The popular press and spectators alike pined for the buxom and blonde Fageros, attention she was happy to encourage when she donned her signature gold lamé panties underneath her short tennis skirt. Gibson certainly stood apart from the rest of the team and understood that her selection carried no small amount of politics as baggage. Pushing this aside, however, she made the most of her time by winning the All Asian Championship in Calcutta, India, demolishing Fageros and all other local competition. She did not lose a match until coming to Europe for the French Championship the following year, in 1956.[31]

Althea Gibson's tennis was just one of the many varieties of popular entertainments that became propaganda in the Cold War. Historians have paid particular attention to dance, music, theater, literature, radio, television, and film, in addition to sports. In the countries of Western Europe bordering the Soviet Union, for example, the United States Information Agency broadcast sports reporting, the U.S. Army ran athletic events, and American Houses and Information Centers sprouted where European youth could use complimentary sports equipment. In German-speaking countries, the United States' occupation changed hearts and minds by introducing both the actions of and the words for joggers and bodybuilders. The triumvirate of American team sports—most notably collegiate football, professional baseball, and Harlem Globetrotters basketball—projected American power and values to the rest of the world.[32]

The Olympics were the most significant but only one of the important international sporting events in which the United States and the Soviet Union competed against one another.[33] As a sport whose global popularity grew at the same time as tension between communism and capitalism increased, tennis matches—every month, year after year, played between players of different countries—assumed tremendous political significance that rivaled if not eclipsed earlier politicized matches like the 1937 Davis Cup tie between Germany and the United States. What had changed after World War II was that in the postwar world, tournaments between players of all nationalities assumed the political and diplomatic symbolism previously reserved for Davis Cup matches that pitted the best of one country against the best of another in team competition.[34]

Tennis players in the Soviet bloc suffered tougher times compared to their fellow competitors from Western Europe and the United States. A European correspondent reporting on the Davis Cup squads of Yugoslavia and Hungary identified two types of communist players: "those who have gotten out and, alas!, those who haven't." What was known of the latter came largely from what the former said, and therefore generalizations should be advanced with caution. Some sensational stories of tennis families executed or sent to gulags for listening to Wimbledon on pirated BBC radio stations lack credibility, but the fact that, given the opportunity, most top Yugoslav and Hungarian players defected to the West suggests draconian treatment of Soviet athletes compared to their international peers. Franjo Punčec left Yugoslavia for Egypt in 1948. Pursued by communist enforcers, Vinicius "Vinny" and

Magda Rurac escaped from Romania using fake names, claiming they left because, after a few years barred by the Communist Party from competing in Western Europe, their government finally acquiesced to their traveling to the West, where they promptly realized life was better outside the Iron Curtain. They eventually found their way to the United States. Helena Straubeova fled Czechoslovakia for Italy, and Władysław Skonecki left Poland under the threat of execution. In 1949 Jaroslav Drobný and Vladimir Cernik, Czechoslovakia's two best male players, chose exile when Cernik left his family behind to play and live in Western Europe, while Drobný asked Switzerland for asylum before becoming an Egyptian citizen married to the English player Rita Jarvis Anderson. Dragutin Mitić's flight from Yugoslavia was far more heartbreaking, as he left with his wife and son but had to leave his daughter behind. The Hungarian champion András Ádám-Stolpa related how the regime preferred players with dependent children because officials thought them less of a flight risk. Despite his having won the French Championships in 1947, authorities barred Ádám-Stolpa from competing in the tournament between 1949 and 1954, fearing he might defect.[35]

Soviet players who continued to play for their countries in international competitions did so under the watchful eyes of party chaperones. The Hungarian men's team was captained by a man whose tennis aptitude was questionable but whose party loyalty was above reproach. Zsuzsa "Suzy" Körmöczy, the top Hungarian woman in the late 1940s, reappeared on the international tennis scene at the Monte Carlo tournament in 1952 after having been kept back from competition outside the Soviet Union in the late 1940s and early 1950s. When the American player Gloria Butler saw Körmöczy, she found the Hungarian cold, a shadow of her former self. Only in the women's locker room, clear of earshot from the Hungarian player chaperone and party hardliner, did Körmöczy open up to Butler about her life since they had last played. Davis Cup competition, more than individuals traveling to tournaments in other countries, raised the seriousness with which Soviet bloc countries took their tennis. In 1949 Hungary hosted the Belgium Davis Cup squad in Budapest. Soldiers ushered spectators to their seats underneath flowing standards of Hungarian leader Mátyás Rákosi. Except on the tennis court, the Belgian players could not interact with the Hungarian players; guards kept the teams separated in the locker room, and at the after-match dinner, each squad had a table kept at such a distance apart that conversation proved impossible. "It is a sad thing to consider that in this world where sportsmen are again getting together to compete against each other in a spirit of friendly rivalry, that there should still be fine talents that are being wasted, and still places where men are not free to take part in the world of sport, how, when, and where they choose," remarked an American player.[36] But what that player missed was that the United States' own record on inclusivity and sensitivity in tennis also could have used improvement.

Proper projections of gender relations and racial balance were foremost on the minds of Washington power brokers fighting the cultural cold war.[37] That context meant that while amateur tennis offered opportunities for international travel to exotic places and prestigious sporting clubs, players also faced drawbacks. Money was the biggest concern. In Gibson's case, she supplemented her income by teaching gym class in the Department of Health and Physical Education at Lincoln University in Jefferson City, Missouri. Gibson felt that such instruction as an untenured assistant instructor was clearly below her status as a national champion. She needed the money, however, as well as income out of the prying eyes of USLTA officials, who patrolled the boundaries of amateurism with an iron fist in a velvet glove. Having won the French Championships, Wimbledon twice, and the U.S. Championships twice in singles, in addition to several doubles titles, by 1959 Gibson had nowhere left to go in the amateur ranks.[38]

Needing money, she signed a contract with Abe Saperstein, the owner of the Harlem Globetrotters. Gibson and Fageros agreed to play warm-up matches before the Globetrotters took the court against the Washington Generals. In a year of barnstorming, Gibson won more than one hundred matches to Fageros's four, a feat that exemplified the Washington Generals' team logo, featuring a tall and long-limbed Globetrotters star towering over a squat and ineffectual Generals player. Such dominance did not mean financial security, though. After the end of the barnstorming tour, Gibson entered the Professional Indoor Championship in Cleveland in 1960, where she won against Pauline Betz and established herself as the best of the best. But once again she had nowhere to go, as the money for a professional tennis player was to be made in the barnstorming tours. Promoters did not think Gibson would draw the crowds. With few options left to her in tennis, Gibson made the remarkable switch to professional golf, which may have had small purses in 1960 but was the only contest in the world of sports where an athletic African American woman could support herself.[39]

Women's professional tennis had a "long way" to go in the pre-1968 years.[40]

CHAPTER 7

The "Kramer Karavan"

The first international sports tour took place in 1859 when a dozen professional English cricketers traveled to Montreal, Quebec, and Rochester, New York, to compete against Canadian and American batsmen. With only a few stops, minimal promotion, and poor turnout, the 1859 tour nevertheless prompted imitation from other national sporting associations and private clubs.[1] In 1861 an English cricket team toured Australia, and seven years later the Australians reciprocated and toured England. The first Tour de France did not involve bicycles but baseball teams, who barnstormed France in 1903. International test matches and world championships were in place for nearly all sports by the first third of the twentieth century, but in the United States, at least according to a British sports historian, what would become the triad of post–World War II American spectacle sports—baseball, football, and basketball—preferred domestic tours if the teams and clubs toured at all. In fact, most professionals in the three major team sports in America had found comfortable city homes by the mid-1950s.[2]

The sport of tennis had likewise embraced the idea of touring in the first half of the twentieth century. In the late nineteenth century, Wilberforce Vaughan Eaves pioneered transatlantic tennis competition between Britain and the United States; in the early twentieth century the Davis Cup popularized it.[3] Over the next several decades, the tournament-to-tournament travel of players for USLTA-sanctioned events, LTA-sanctioned matches, FFT tournaments, LTAA matches, and any other country that belonged to the ILTF all constituted what a few contemporaries called the "amateur tennis circuits." But what people meant and thought of when they spoke or read about tennis tours were the professional barnstorming matches of Suzanne Lenglen, Bill Tilden, Ellsworth Vines, Fred Perry, Don Budge, and Bobby Riggs, among other players and promoters.[4]

A fresh-faced challenger taking on a seasoned professional champion constituted the core attraction of nearly all the tours in the prewar years, and that drama remained at the center of the postwar professional tours led first by Bobby Riggs and then by Jack Kramer. Whereas fresh faces in terms of players helped the tours, a high turnover in terms of tour managers and tour promoters hurt professional tennis. Kramer's constant presence as the head of the postwar professional tennis tour during the next decade began to corporatize professional tennis, which, in terms of a business enterprise, had come across as scattered and at times sloppy. The consistent entertainment product that Kramer put before the U.S. public and people around the world on his international tennis tours popularized the sport in the postwar years at the same time that his constant presence in seemingly all aspects of the game unnerved the directors of the USLTA and amateur tennis abroad. Kramer thus became an impediment to the arrival of open tennis competition between amateurs and professionals because he did so much to grow the game. The "Kramer Karavan" was professional tennis in the '50s, for better and for worse.[5]

Kramer thought he understood what earlier professional tennis promoters from C. C. Pyle to Bobby Riggs did not: the USLTA would countenance professional tennis if it received part of the action. Better to make the amateur association the ally of professional tennis rather than its antagonist. So at the same time the SCTA, acting on authority from the USLTA national office, labored to make sure even a truck driver working for Jack Kramer's World Professional Tennis Incorporated (association member Hugh Stewart, who wanted to maintain his amateur status to play tournaments) could not pick up a racquet and hit around for fun with the professionals and could only receive compensation "no greater than those ordinary payable to a truck driver," the directors of the SCTA agreed to split profits from the Los Angeles professional tennis tournaments Kramer and his players sponsored. Such an arrangement between amateur tennis and the professional tour happened because of Kramer's special relationship with Perry T. Jones, the leader of Southern California tennis. Jones believed in amateur tennis, but more than anything he wanted Southern California to lead the world in grooming tennis champions. Forty-five percent of the gate receipts for the professional exhibitions introduced innumerable young players to tennis if that money found its way into the SCTA and the TPASC. The alliance could also happen because Jones always considered Kramer his favorite player to come out of the junior development system at the LATC. In Jones's mind, professional tennis did not look so bad if it looked like the blond and muscular Jack Kramer.[6]

In particular, the potential for television contracts that Kramer dangled excited the SCTA, TPASC, and USLTA board members. They liked Kramer so much they even went so far as to ask him to scoop up a dozen of the best junior players after the national juniors in Kalamazoo, Michigan, to go train with him and his professional players. That flew in the face of the USLTA leadership's normal paternalism, amateur code, and the ethics statements they drafted at around the same time, which sought to prohibit contact between amateur players and association members with professional tennis players and promoters at all costs. The TPASC leadership wanted the money they expected to make from the televised professional tournament, so the USLTA sanctioned Kramer to hold his event. Jones and his peers at the association's national office always fancied professional tennis as a windfall-profit generator for the players and promoters, both Kramer and his predecessors, but the limited receipts that came in from the first major association of the professional tennis troupe with a major amateur-owned and -operated venue in the LATC revealed to anyone who cared to count the money that the life of a touring tennis professional and their promoter was filled with risk but little financial reward.[7] As the player professional to beat in the early 1950s, an ambitious sports promoter, and the spokesperson for professional tennis, Kramer saw the opportunities and challenges better than anyone.

Kramer could have made close to the same amount of money not playing as he did playing because he retained his key source of income long after he stopped competing on the court. Since the 1920s, sporting goods companies had tried to establish endorsement deals with the best amateur players of a more robust sort than the few gratis racquets. Every time such deals were attempted, the USLTA had nixed these attempts through the enforcement of its "sporting goods rule," which not only prevented an association player from having their likeness attached to a racquet but also prohibited any amateur player from working for a sporting goods company in any capacity. Once again, the primacy of the Davis Cup in the thinking of the USLTA Executive Committee raised the tolerance of the association's voters for amateurism when, after having held the Davis Cup for four years in a row, the Americans lost to the Australians in the 1950–1953 ties. USLTA Executive Committee members correctly attributed at least part of the Australians' newfound dominance to the LTAA's acceptance of its top amateur talent working for Australian sporting goods firms. In fact, the LTAA's position on amateur tennis players working for sporting goods firms went beyond forbearance to active encouragement of the practice, whereby senior LTAA members secured lucrative consultant-ships for the most talented young Australian players, who no longer had to worry about actually clocking in and could spend all of their days improving their game and traveling for tournaments. Those actions seemed to violate both the spirit and the letter of ILTF rule number 28, which stated that even an indirect "pecuniary advantage by the playing, teaching, demonstrating or [other] pursuit of the game" of tennis forfeited one's amateur status regard-less of the source of the money. LTAA head Sir Norman Brookes disagreed and convinced the Dutch ILTF president, David Croll, that Australian tennis had done no harm. The USLTA bristled at that action by the Australians until 1954, when the hundreds of delegates and their proxies met at the association's annual meeting and overwhelmingly ended the sporting goods rule with only one dissenting vote. Tony Trabert, the United States' top amateur player in 1954, went to work for the Wilson Sporting Goods Company; that December he led the American Davis Cup team to victory over the Australians.[8]

The USLTA 1954 vote was supposed to go only so far. Delegates did not countenance the so-called givesmen of sporting goods companies, which outfitted amateur players with free racquets, strings, and apparel, as well as the association of a player's likeness to a racquet, sneaker, or tennis ball in exchange for a small percentage of each good sold. In a satire published in *World Tennis* magazine that same year, player Art Larsen and editor Gladys Heldman gave a comical but highly accurate portrait of the absurdity of the USLTA's Amateur Rules Committee's obsession with policing gratis sporting goods and product endorsements from amateur players. Sporting goods firms in the early 1950s simply did not have that much free stuff to give away, because they did not op-erate on big margins themselves. Firms such as Spalding, Dunlop, Wilson, and Cortland preferred to use their extra equipment not for giveaways to amateur tournament players but in free junior tennis clinics sponsored across public park courts. The players they partnered with for endorsements had to play professionally, because the players' likeness or signature that came to literally appear on the neck of the endorsed racquets in those days made plain to the USLTA who got paid to play with that racquet. Hiding such an affiliation so that players could keep their amateur status made no sense from the point of view of the sporting goods firms, who wanted the association of their product with the best players in the most visible of ways. The dual strategy of big play-day-in-the-public-parks and professional product endorsements paid off for the big four sporting goods firms, who in 1958 reported that over the past decade they had increased sales of tennis equipment and apparel by 60 percent. That increase came about because of an innovative marketing partnership between the Wilson sports equipment company and Jack Kramer.[9]

Sporting goods firms liked tennis because the game required a lot of equipment. Whereas late nineteenth-century outdoor sports sellers, like Peck & Snyder of New York City, as well as early twentieth-century racquet makers, like the A. J. Reach Company of Philadelphia; string manufacturers, such as Armour and Company of Chicago; and sporting apparel clothiers, such as Brooks Brothers, all marketed and advertised without a prominent player associated with their firm, by the mid-1930s professional tennis players had toured enough that profitable sporting goods manufacturers thought the time was right to pay professionals to associate themselves with the company's products. At first those associations took the form of a company like Dunlop Sport claiming that Bill Tilden, Vincent Richards, and other professionals "designed," "tested," and "played" with a racquet with a generic name such as "Maxplay." During the war years, marketing in the sporting goods industry tapped into patriotism to sell more products and used their professional player spokespersons for campaigns like "Yes Tennis Will Help Keep the Nation Fit in 1943." If a professional player served in the military or directly aided the war effort, his or her image might appear alongside a product such as Don Budge's, Bobby Riggs's, Alice Marble's, and Ellsworth Vines's, all having a head shot in Wilson's "New Wartime 'Championship' Tennis Ball" campaign. During wartime and in the first few years afterward, sporting goods manufacturers stopped short of a complete association between one of their racquets, balls, strings, or apparel, and a professional player. Wilson's early advertising in the prewar and war years did not feature a player endorsing the product; to pay a professional player a flat fee or percentage would have made little financial sense, since little tennis touring was taking place in the early 1940. As the war continued into the mid-'40s, professional and amateur players alike entered military service and put on exhibitions for troops and war bond fund-raisers;

however, patriotic advertising placed limits on the individual professional making money during a time of national sacrifice. In a major campaign immediately after the war, Wilson emphasized the technology of their "Strata-Bow" racquet frame by equating it to the jet airplanes of the present and future.[10]

Wilson soon recognized, however, that features could take a product only so far, even at a peak time of technological vogue. The firm needed people to help sell their products, and no tennis person appeared more visible than the popular professional champion Jack Kramer. His full partnership with Wilson began in early 1948 right after Kramer signed a contract with Jack Harris to play Bobby Riggs on a professional tour. Wilson wanted everyone to know that no matter who won the "World's Tennis Championship" in 1948, either Riggs or Kramer, both men "have used Wilson rackets since their early amateur days . . . and still play Wilson exclusively." The key innovation came after Kramer secured the World's Professional Champion title and Wilson recognized that Kramer would dominate the game both on the court and in the court of public opinion for the foreseeable future.[11]

In December 1948 Wilson announced the company's new partnership with Kramer to present the "Jack Kramer Autograph" racquet. Advertisements to the contrary, the racquet had the same specifications as Wilson's standard Strata-Bow racquet except it came in two different weights and displayed Kramer's cursive handwriting on the stick's neck. "I'm as proud of this racket as I was of my first championship trophy. It's the finest racket I've ever played with," said Kramer about his new equipment. While the Kramer Autograph was not the first signature racquet—Ellsworth Vines and Don Budge, for example, each had racquets designated as their very own by Wilson in the late 1930s and early '40s—the Jack Kramer Autograph was the first tennis racquet to come out during a heady time for the sale of sporting goods. In a meeting at Wilson's Chicago offices, Kramer wisely accepted an offer from Wilson president L. B. Iceley and the company's sales executive Bill King's to receive 2.5 percent earnings on units sold compared to the 3 percent Riggs, Vines, and Budge collected. Wilson pushed the Kramer racquet on wholesalers and retailers harder than they did all their other racquets, and Kramer's royalties rose from $13,000 in the early years for the Kramer Autograph, to $50,000 in the late 1960s, and $160,000 a year in 1975. The tennis boom of the mid-1970s ensured that the Jack Kramer Autograph became the best-selling tennis racquet of all time and paved the way for a host of athlete signature sporting goods endorsements in other individual and team sports.[12]

Playing style and product endorsements alone did not make much change to a tennis professional's bank account if the athlete behind the endorsement did not back up their action on the court. In that regard Kramer made good. He overwhelmed Bobby Riggs in their late 1947–1948 tour; he soundly beat Pancho Gonzales in the 1949–1950 tour; he remained the all-American champion, widely popular across the country after besting Pancho Segura in their 1950–1951 tour; and he defeated Frank Sedgman in their 1953 tour. Four tours in a row, Kramer, called "Big Jake" by his friends, had retained the title World's Professional Champion. On the thirty-fourth match of the last tour, Kramer met the one-hundred-thousand-dollar guarantee that he had offered Sedgman and Ken McGregor to lure the Australian champions out of the amateur ranks and to his professional troupe, which was rounded out by Pancho Segura. In the United States alone, the four players reported eight hundred thousand dollars in gate receipts, eclipsing the next closest professional tennis tour by three hundred thousand dollars. Kramer thus understood that people wanted to pay to watch him defend his title.[13]

Kramer, however, refused to risk losing to Gonzales. Although he did not play night after night on the tour, Gonzales still had established himself as the man to beat in professional tennis both by fellow professionals like the Irishman George Lyttleton Rogers, who ranked both Gonzales and Pancho Segura in front of Kramer, and through his on-court play by having won titles as the World's Professional Champion through the yearly tournament contested in Cleveland, Ohio. He was playing against the strongest professionals across the globe. Kramer compensated for his own absence on the court by instituting a new mini-tournament format that replaced the standard "exhibition" event, which had always paired an undercard match before a main event match. Now players scrambled against one another during the first night of a tour stop, with the two winners playing each other on the second night for a prize-money incentive. This two-night format led Kramer to institute a new tennis scoring system called the "pro set," which replaced the standard tennis scoring system of first player to win two out of three sets or three out of five sets, with a single set played to eight games. These reforms did not address the real issue, though, of having the director, manager, accountant, and promoter of the tour also being a part-time player, which brought a great degree of emotional baggage to the enterprise of professional tennis in the 1950s. That baggage weighed down the financial prospects of the players as they readied to travel across the country for another season.[14]

Along with Kramer, the person who most made the tennis tour successful and exciting to the audience was the last person to come on board. In
the Lenglen and Tilden tours, people paid to see the grace and dominance
of the champion. But after the Depression tours of Vines, Perry, and Budge,
promoters believed people paid to see conflict between the upstart amateur
challenger and the established touring professional. They therefore prioritized luring the most attractive amateur champion, no matter the cost. The
David-versus-Goliath narrative continued to resonate with Americans into
the '50s for several reasons. First, differences notwithstanding, the conclusion of World War II had brought American Jews and American Christians,
both Catholics and Protestants, into common cause to a greater degree than
at any other time in the nation's history. With the onset of the Cold War and
the godlessness of the new enemy, it was little wonder people of different faiths
found the emerging popularity of the Judeo-Christian tradition settling and
righteous warriors from the Old Testament beating insurmountable odds
inspiring. Second, the Gilded Age and Progressive Era middle class built a
foundation for the American Dream in the twentieth century supported by
a plank of professionalism. At the same moment when doctors, lawyers, and
accountants, to name a few of the upstart career trajectories, all grew in the
rigor of their training and standardized in their methods and results, so too
spectator sports grew and modernized, with the athletes dedicated to full-
time training and specialization for the first time in any real numbers. Third,
ever since the explosion of modern consumer culture and leisure in the late
nineteenth and early twentieth centuries, Americans obsessed over what historian William Leach has called "the cult of the new"—that is, finding happi-
ness in the next good to buy, the next spectacle to see, the next experience to
experience.[15] Kramer intuited all of this. With his tennis tours in the 1950s,
he reaped respectable gate receipts with minimal advertising expenses. But
it was not just Kramer who was bearing the cost of the tour. That burden fell
on the players.[16]

The start of the 1954 tour revealed just how touch-and-go professional tennis in the '50s was. The Australian professional arrived in the United States
from the Melbourne-hosted Davis Cup tie on January 2, 1954—the day before
the professional tour began. Jack Kramer had spent the last couple weeks of
1953 not preparing to play but in promoting the tour across newspapers, radio, and television. Big Jake made more than a hundred phone calls a day on
subjects that ranged from renting a truck large enough to move their canvas

court, securing a driver for the truck, insurance policies should one of his four touring players injure themselves, and printed programs for each tournament venue. The tour opened at Madison Square Garden on January 3, 1954, and featured a pre-card match of Don Budge versus Pancho Segura, a main attraction of Frank Sedgman versus Pancho Gonzales, and a doubles pro set of Segura and Gonzales versus Sedgman and Kramer. At their second night at the Garden, Gonzales and Segura faced off, as each had won the night before, with Gonzales serving ace after ace to win the match and secure the fifteen-hundred-dollar bonus for the event's winner. On January 5 the troupe left New York City for their city-to-city tour with plans to play the same format at most stops—that is, two-night engagements with winners from the first night's matches squaring off against one another for the second night with an additional prize-money bonus on the line.[17]

As they set off, a sports reporter asked the competitors who they expected to win the tour. Segura thought Gonzales, Gonzales named himself, neither Budge nor Sedgman offered a definitive pick, and Kramer picked Sedgman, thinking Gonzales was out of shape, ill-focused, and weak in spirit. The players had one hundred engagements to bear these predictions out. In the next month, for example, the tour played the Onondaga Memorial in Syracuse, New York, before moving on to Rochester, Albany, and Boston Gardens, and then departing the next day for Montreal for the Forum. The Canadian leg concluded with matches in Quebec City and the Auditorium in Ottawa. Cornell University, Duquesne Gardens in Pittsburgh, and the Fort Wayne, Indiana, Arena followed. The players then planned to go on to play Kansas City, Los Angeles, Pebble Beach, Sacramento, Oakland, and Palm Springs before the end of February, despite Kramer's not having secured final venues for any of the California matches. Such fly-by-night scheduling exemplified just how underdeveloped barnstorming professional tennis remained in the 1950s.[18]

The play of the professionals was far from underdeveloped, however. During the tour's first month, Pancho Gonzales proved his own prediction of his success true with a singles record of 15 wins and 6 losses as compared to Segura's win-loss record of 13–9, Sedgman's of 10–10, and Budge's winless record of 0–15. Kramer's prediction that no player could win more than 45 percent of their matches was certainly a marketing strategy on behalf of the tour promoter to gin up media interest. Claiming that no player had an edge over another player made for more intrigue over the day-after-day, months-long tour, which, as past experience had shown, dwindled if one player became too dominant. Kramer's unwillingness to recognize how thoroughly Gonzales dominated the matches also stemmed from an unwillingness to move past his own playing prime as Big Jake. He practiced with the players on a regular basis and played some doubles matches in select cities, but on the court Kramer was only a shadow of his former self. His domination of tennis in the late 1940s and the first few years of the 1950s was near complete.[19]

But the candle that burns twice as bright burns half as long. Aggressive play meant Kramer developed nagging pains that turned into career-ending injuries after what amounted to less than a decade of combined topflight amateur and professional play. Compared to other players of his generation, along with prior and subsequent generations of players, for that matter, Kramer's dominance was short-lived—so much so that at times he disparaged the very professional players he needed to promote and market. The ego of Kramer the athlete was not the reason professional tennis only scraped by in the '50s, but it certainly did not help Kramer's touring company, World Professional Tennis Incorporated (WPTI). What did help was the fine entertainment value the players themselves provided. Crowds loved Segura's unorthodox two-handed strokes and never-quit hustle across the court. They respected Budge's place in tennis history as a two-time Grand Slam amateur champion despite the nightly shellacking he took on the court. With Sedgman, and especially with Gonzales, the crowds sat in awe of the talent and the power of the play. Even while filming Gonzales practice serves and overheads, a television crew remarked that he hit with such power that "TV viewers would have a mass heart attack if this were in 3-D."[20]

After a season of nightly matches, Gonzales emerged above Sedgman, Segura, and Budge in match wins. Having watched seventy-five nights of play, and even umpiring a few matches, sportswriter Hugh Stewart remarked that Gonzales beat out the other players simply because of "his big serve" and his "complete all-court game" without mentioning his determination and willingness to work hard to capitalize on his second chance at professional tennis. In fact, in writing short summaries of Sedgman, Segura, Budge, and Kramer, all of whom Gonzales soundly defeated on the doubles court and the singles court, Stewart considered all of them superior in "fighting spirit" and "concentration" to Gonzales, but "Big Pancho" simply had more physical strength to draw from than any other tennis player in the world. Such observations seemed difficult to justify when Stewart himself umpired matches where Gonzales "caught fire" and ground his way back from major score deficits to win a match, or, in the case of a Fort Wayne, Indiana, match where Gonzales held the nerves at bay to win twenty-eight to twenty-six games when the match could have ended at eight to six games.[21]

Stewart's opinions of Gonzales revealed a deep dislike on the part of sportswriters for Gonzales the man, not the player. His game stood above reproach, but his personality came under frequent attack. The harsh commentaries came, at least in part, because of Gonzales's outspokenness about his financial compensation for his performance on the tennis court. Having won the tour handily with victories in 85 of 126 singles matches played over sixteen weeks, Gonzales secured $39,425, for the 1954 tour—$35,000 less than he earned for losing badly to Kramer on the 1949–1950 tour.[22]

Modest attendance for the 1954 tour partly explained why Gonzales earned half as much for playing twice as well. Gate receipts from the most recent tour gave Kramer less money to move around compared to the first professional tour Gonzales participated in and the early '50s tours that Kramer forced Gonzales to sit out. But differences in compensation had more to do with how Kramer structured the tour now that his skill was diminished. The round-robin mini-tournament format was supposed to reward the player with the most match victories, but Kramer distributed prize-money bonuses based on his own whims rather than on the actual wins of the players. For example, in April 1954 the tour swung down into Texas with Gonzales maintaining a healthy match lead, Sedgman second, Segura third, and Budge fourth, despite Segura sitting atop the prize-money standings at $25,525; Gonzales second at $25,240; Sedgman third at $20,025; and Budge, having won only one match on the entire tour, with $10,900. While Big Pancho did end up with $4,000 more than Little Pancho and a few thousand dollars more than Sedgman by the tour's final accounting, the percentages Kramer paid to the players did not accurately reflect their win-loss record on the tour.[23]

Big Jake also took a more whimsical approach to his promotional duties than in previous tours. In the years where he both played and promoted, conventional wisdom would have suggested an underpromoted tour when compared to the 1954 tour, where he essentially just promoted. The opposite actually happened. When the tour played New Haven, Connecticut, on February 4, 1954, Jerome Scheur recalled how much fuller the arena had been in Boston the year before when he saw Kramer play Sedgman. Scheur's sister-in-law lived in New Haven and had not even heard that the tour planned to visit. At the matches she had no other explanation for the "third full" gymnasium than the "lack of advance publicity." Whereas in previous years the troupe had always come close to selling out Madison Square Garden for the tour opener, the January 1954 Garden matches set an underwhelming tone, soon followed by five hundred people at the Teaneck Armory matches in New Jersey, when, only the year before, four thousand people had filled that venue. Kramer missed basic details he had never before missed, such as securing ball boys in advance for the matches. He spent a lot of time playing golf at the different cities where the troupe stopped rather than looking ahead to make sure the marketing was set for future stops on the tour. Kramer put on tennis clinics for promising junior players with the blessing of the USLTA and the underwriting done by corporate friends such as the publisher of *Holiday* magazine. He partnered with Perry T. Jones and the SCTA to hold a professional tennis tournament in Los Angeles. In short, the promoter Jack Kramer realized that he could still make the money he wanted—even with skimping on marketing and contracting out what publicity took place to Frank O'Gara—because the players had no recourse to challenge the compensation Kramer decided for them.[24]

WPTI was the only game in town for the world's best professional players who had been shut out from returning to play amateur tournaments. It owned the professional players, body and soul. The meritocracy of professional tennis, where the best player got paid the best, was as much fiction as fact on the professional tour. Whereas professional tennis tournaments like the 1953 Wembley Professional Tournament attracted record crowds of up to fifteen thousand paying spectators a night and paid the players based on how they finished in the tournament, enough of those events simply did not exist for a professional player to earn a living in the 1950s. If people like Gonzales wanted to make it through the year just by playing tennis, they needed Jack Kramer as much as if not more than Kramer needed them.[25]

Kramer's influence over the professional players even extended to when the players were not officially under contract with him. In February 1954 Kramer sat down with Jack March, who ran the World Professional Championship in Cleveland, at the Sutton Restaurant in New York City—the preferred venue among sports promoters for tennis deals. The two signed an agreement that required all professionals in Kramer's troupe to play the Cleveland event after Kramer's tour ended. The details of the enforcement mechanism for such a deal do not survive in the written record, but Kramer likely threatened his players with refusal to renew their tour contracts if they did not play March's tournament, from which Kramer drew what amounted to a finder's fee. While they did not care for getting told what to do, the professional players certainly wanted to play in the World Professional Championship tournament, because March ran a good event. The Pilsener Brewing Company supplied ten thousand dollars in prize money for the sixteen-person tournament, with the winner after four days of play receiving two thousand dollars. A tournament-approved betting pool assured gambling action on the tournament and stoked excitement among bookies barred from the grounds of amateur tennis tournaments.[26]

After four months on tour, Gonzales and Sedgman entered the main tournament in peak form and played each other in the Sunday afternoon final on May 2, 1954, after having demolished the rest of the field. While March certainly had every incentive to hype the talent of the players in his event, he also spoke truthfully when he remarked that what fans saw in the final was "the finest tennis" the world had ever seen. Night after night of playing on the tour had perfected Gonzales's serve to a point where he literally threw down two aces a service game against one of the strongest service returners around. He lost his own serve in only one game to take the match 6–3, 9–7, 3–6, 6–2 for a repeat as the World's Professional Champion. Sedgman played his best tennis, committing next to no unforced errors and missing only one overhead lob the entire tournament. "Not since the days of Tilden has a top player so completely overshadowed the field," remarked March. Such dominance actually posed a real problem for the champion's future in professional tennis, because Gonzales had already established his dominance over the best professional players, and what amateur wanted to turn professional only to get embarrassed on the court and forfeit the financial assistance they received from their amateur tennis association? March was glad that Gonzales planned to return to Cleveland in 1955 to try to defend his title, but the tournament director couldn't help but wonder if Pancho had "dug his own financial grave."[27]

Gonzales proved himself to be the most consistent winner of all tennis professionals for the next decade. His dominance, however, was incomplete. Segura bested Big Pancho and six others in the Pacific Coast Professional Championships on August 22, 1954. These professional tournaments were often slapdash combinations of tennis, movie stars, comic entertainment, and last-minute funding from a business executive with a fondness for tennis. On the Copa Club courts on the grounds of the Beverly Wilshire Hotel in Los Angeles, for example, actors Walter Pidgeon, Mark Stevens, and Howard Duff umpired the matches, while actress Ida Lupino handed out the prizes, and Rosemary Clooney, Spike Jones, Jose Ferrer, and the Ritz Brothers sat in the stands and attended the post-match cocktail hour. Outside of a few household names, including the two Panchos, less-well-known teaching professionals like the Irishman Freddie "The Fox" Houghton would fill out the draw and willingly subject themselves to embarrassingly one-sided losses for the few hundred dollars of a twenty-five-hundred-dollar total purse awarded to first-round losers as a thanks-for-playing incentive. That Gonzales, Segura, and a handful of other top professionals demolished their competition so systematically certainly did not help Frank Feltrop and other tournament promoters put fans in the stands, but a champion winning convincingly against weaker opponents, as people expected champions to do, did not hurt attendance nearly as much as naysayers had predicted. If anything, people paid a little to see their expectations met and then were willing to pay more to see a contest with a less certain outcome in a tournament semifinal or final, where the best players would meet.[28]

Beyond the results on the court, the basic logistics of the professional tour posed another big problem to the sports promoter. Small and medium towns had few venues suitable to hold a tennis match where enough spectators could attend to make a decent amount in gate receipts and also provided enough lines of sight so that those spectators would not howl in protest over paying so much for so little viewable action. The ambitious schedule WPTI maintained made rain an ever-present fear in the promoter's mind, which in turn led Kramer to favor indoor over outdoor venues. The players might have despised playing on armory and gymnasium floors in front of a howling crowd that raised temperatures indoors to stifling temperatures, but they wanted to get paid.[29] Professional tour veteran Barry MacKay remarked, "I have played tennis in 42 countries throughout the world—traveled around the world five times and played in matches on every surface from burned clay courts in Moscow to dried-out cow dung in Hybrabad [Hyderabad], India." In the adversity the barnstorming players faced daily lay one of the sport's greatest profit generators, because difficulty meant drama. Furthermore, the fact that difficulty played out in locations exotic to and far flung from the American viewing public meant that if television could be brought to lay the struggles of those players bare, then tennis stood a good chance of growing in the future as the world became more globally connected.[30] That same drama also cut the opposite direction from the players' point of view, and that different perspective helped to explain why so few chose to join the professional tour during the '50s

Professional prospects gave a number of other reasons why they often chose to remain amateurs. They cited the physical and emotional toll of a barnstorming tour. For example, player-turned-promoter Bobby Riggs courted Richard Savitt in 1951 in the midst of Savitt's remarkable season. Winning the Australian and Wimbledon titles, Savitt seemed the heavy favorite to win the U.S. Championship at Forest Hills and the heir apparent to replace Pancho Gonzales as the challenger to world professional champion Jack Kramer. Savitt's semifinal exit at Forest Hills made the picture of who was the best amateur player a little less clear, but it also gave Riggs more flexibility in negotiating a better contract for the tour and a worse contract for the player, because Savitt's domination in 1951 proved less sure. Without a truly sweet contract, Savitt had an easy time putting the thought of playing as a professional out of his mind. Matches in armories and night after night on the road simply made for "a difficult life" from Savitt's perspective. But forgoing the professional circuit in no way meant that Savitt removed tennis from his life. Instead, he continued to play in the U.S. Championships for the next decade and even won the U.S. Indoor Singles Championships, all the while making a name for himself in financial services on Wall Street. Savitt simply thought professional tennis in the '50s was a bad investment.[31]

Amateurs did, however, admire and seek to emulate the independence from the USLTA that professionals exercised, even though most tennis players at the time were unwilling to forgo the limited financial support and network of tournaments the association provided. For example, in 1954, during the peak tennis tournament months of June through September, the USLTA's various sections sanctioned three hundred tournaments across a few dozen categories that ranged from under-ten-year-old players to super-senior age divisions and father-daughter events. The problem from the amateur player's point of view was not with the number or variety of tournaments but with how the tournaments were run. In an anonymous short story titled "The Rich Man's Game," the player-author, presumably Gardnar Mulloy, lambasted sportswriter Bob Considine, who had written an article claiming that "big-time tennis was now monopolized by poor sandlotters and public parks players." Mulloy goes on to rebuff the sportswriter by conjuring a satirical Associated Press story that listed number one ranked player "Gardnar Mullard" (Gardnar Mulloy) as the seventh-wealthiest person on the planet and reported that tennis champion "Smudge Patty" (John "Budge" Patty) kept full households of servants at his American and European mansions, and that top lady player "Patricia Podd"

(Patricia Canning Todd) did not attend a tournament without a dozen luggage bags and her personal assistant. Given their ostentatious display of wealth, Mulloy observed, did organizers of events such as the Overhampton grass-court tournament really expect a player who drove up to the match with his 1926 Rolls Royce and who played with six 24-carat gold racquets to sleep six players to a room in the club's servants' annex? Did tournament organizer, Harrison Pringle, need to give the players their twenty-five dollars in expenses with such secrecy and beam with such pride when the tournament champion received a piece of used luggage as first prize? Did such a wealthy Long Island Club need to plan a special player menu of sardines and bread rather than the club's normal turtle soup, foie gras, and soufflé? The satire was not subtle, but it was consistent with a growing middle class looking to make their own way when it came to sports.[32]

Mulloy's opinions rallied fellow players because his views were based on their actual experiences. At Southampton, New York, for example, members of the Meadow Club literally put their player guests on army military personnel cots stacked side by side on a squash court. They served the players "special tennis meals," which was code for innutritious and cheap food rather than the normal delicacies enjoyed in the dining room. These slights aside, the biggest problem from the players' point of view was that members treated the competitors "as if they were the performers solely for the enjoyment of the Meadow Club's exclusive membership" rather than invited guests who happened to play tennis very well. Worse still, players would sometimes show up for a tournament, often after having traveled across the country, only to find an event like the Narragansett tournament canceled for inadequate organization on the part of the host club. At other times, the USLTA tried to overmanage the schedules of players without input from the participants. In the fall of 1953, the USLTA and the LTAA agreed to a quid pro quo whereby Australian players would attend the U.S. Championships at Forest Hills while American players would remain in Australia after the Davis Cup for the Australian Championships. When USLTA committee members told Davis Cup competitor Tony Trabert about the deal, he flatly refused to stay, because he wanted to return stateside to his wife. Such treatment at event after event spurred amateur players to organize the game's first amateur player association in the summer of 1953.[33]

The "Tennis Players' League" made a public announcement in September 1953 that named the organization's nine specific goals. First, give the players a substantive voice on the important USLTA decision-making committees. Second, help create better press for the USLTA and the game of tennis. Third, aid tournament officials in securing players and bringing more money into tennis by running better tournaments through promotions and marketing. Fourth, coordinate the schedule of sanctioned tennis events to avoid tournament overlap. Fifth, convince tournament officials and association leaders to recognize what players brought to the game. Sixth, grow junior tennis, especially through player-run clinics. Seventh, promote public interest in tennis by bringing the rules of the game out of the late nineteenth century and into the postwar world. Eighth, assist in the building of new public courts and the opening of new tennis clubs. Ninth, increase the financial resources of the game.[34]

The players chose Sidney Wood Jr. to lead the league as president. They elected the outspoken Gardnar Mulloy as vice president, with Grant Golden serving as secretary-treasurer. Vic Seixas, Art Larsen, Chauncey Steele, Billy Talbert, Don McNeill, and Tony Trabert also served on the league's first executive committee, which meant that the lion's share of the top-ranking amateur men's players in the country participated in the league. Such solidarity gave the USLTA president, Col. James H. Bishop, little choice but to work with the players toward the mutual purpose of growing amateur tennis.[35]

Wood and his fellow amateur players certainly had statistics and anecdotal evidence on their side to show that the growth of the amateur game had not been well served by the USLTA Executive Committee since the 1930s. In 1935 U.S. sporting goods companies sold 6,250,464 tennis balls and 537,002 tennis racquets. By 1952 those numbers fell to 5,070,288 and 382,600—respective declines of 18.8 percent and 28.6 percent, even as the U.S. population as a whole rose 11 percent from 138,439,069 to 154,233,234. In the early '30s, major grass-court tournaments took place at Wilmington, Delaware; Seabright, New Jersey; Orange, New Jersey; Newport, Rhode Island; Staten Island, New York; Rye, New York; Boston, Massachusetts; Narragansett, Rhode Island; Providence, Rhode Island; Germantown, Pennsylvania; Merion, Pennsylvania; Southampton, New York; Glen Cove, New York; Piping Rock, New York; and Forest Hills, New York. Two decades later, the only substantive lawn tennis tournaments that remained were the Eastern Grass Court Championships played at Orange Lawn Tennis Club, the Pennsylvania Lawn Tennis Championships at the Merion Cricket Club, the Newport Casino Invitational at the Newport Casino, the U.S. National Doubles Championships contested at Longwood Cricket Club, the U.S. National Championships at Forest Hills, and two new but smaller tournaments at the Nassau Country Club and across greater Baltimore. European tournaments attracted much greater crowds than

American tournaments, and "in Australia," one American player noted, "more people watch members of our Davis Cup team practice than attend any tournament final or Davis Cup match in the United States!"[36]

Yet in certain respects the game had actually grown in the United States over the same years. By 1950 thousands more people played the game competitively than ever before, which was due largely to the proliferation of public courts built during the Great Depression. While elite East Coast lawn tennis tournaments suffered and came to occupy only four weeks on the USLTA's national tennis calendar, tournaments in the South, Midwest, and Pacific Northwest boomed along with the long popular Southern California amateur circuit. Initiative to expand the amateur game seemed to come from everywhere except from the USLTA's national office. In July 1953, American sportswriters contacted the USLTA in Manhattan to ask for an interview and some photographs with recent Wimbledon champion Vic Seixas upon his arrival back in the United States. The USLTA had no idea when Seixas would arrive, despite their insistence to the players that they manage all aspects of United States tennis abroad. That paternalism in thought but not in practice contrasted sharply with golf, the game to which sportswriters most often equated tennis. The Professional Golfers' Association and the United States Golf Association were only too happy to help the mayor of New York City coordinate a ticker-tape parade along Broadway for golfer Ben Hogan upon his return stateside after having won the British Open. So the blame for the parts of the tennis that had declined lay not with larger social forces but with the passive mismanagement of the USLTA national officers, or so the players argued. [37]

In selecting Wood to lead them, amateur tennis players picked a capable spokesperson for their interests. Wood established himself as an amateur player who was consistently ranked in the top ten in the nation during the 1930s and '40s; however, he never ranked in the top three, and therefore a career change to professional tennis made no financial sense. Wood also realized that simply accepting the expense payments provided by the USLTA would never give him a stable or satisfactory income. He solved this problem by partnering with professional tennis player Don Budge to establish one of the first celebrity-athlete-owned-and-operated businesses in America in 1940. The Budge-Wood service pressed the laundry, waxed the floors, washed the windows, and shampooed the carpets of New Yorkers on Manhattan's East Side. Headquartered at 306 East 61st Street, by 1953 Budge-Wood Services employed 350 people who serviced clients in Manhattan, Long Island, Westchester, Connecticut, and Rhode Island. Wood then plowed some of this money into a nonprofit tennis club called Town Tennis Club, built on the site of a former brewery at Sutton Place, sandwiched between 55th and 56th Streets. The tennis champion and dry-cleaner kept clean from the stains of professionalism by refusing to accept any money directly from this sporting venture and by using all monies collected from member fees to subsidize player development for competitive juniors. He also ran a public relations business with connections throughout the New York City sports media. That combination led one sportswriter to remark that along with Jack Kramer, "Sidney is tennis's foremost business man."[38]

To a degree not seen before from a player turned promoter, Wood succeeded in softening the hardest edges of the tennis establishment by appealing to USLTA officials' vanity about their own importance. He cajoled players, both amateurs and professionals, to play against each other in exhibitions specifically for USLTA national and sectional officers. At a 1953 event hosted by his Town Tennis Club, Wood convinced mayor-elect Robert Wagner along with many of New York City's first families—the Chryslers, Vanderbilts, Coreys, and Fairchilds—to watch a match between Don Budge, Bobby Riggs, Don McNeill, and Gardnar Mulloy with the far less prominent USLTA officials, all of whom enjoyed an over-the-top champagne brunch. Special treatment dampened association officers' opposition to Wood's proposal for a nationally televised thirty-five-week round-robin tournament played at Wood's Town Tennis Club and complete with corporate sponsorship, Monday evening television coverage by WPIX for thirty-five weeks, and publicity by Wood himself. Play week after week meant amateur players drew their maximum association expenses of fifteen dollars a day on a much more regular basis than the current tournament schedule allowed for—a fact seemingly lost on the notoriously tightfisted USLTA, which at the same meeting voted down a player expense increase per play day from fifteen to twenty dollars. The players' spokespersons had figured out a basic rule of influence: make people feel important and they will go as far as acting against their own financial self-interest and embracing impractical schemes such as a nine-month revolving tennis tournament.[39]

Actually running a successful tennis event was another matter entirely, and Wood did not prove up to the task. On Monday, April 26, 1954, WPIX crews ripped out a fence behind the show court at the Town Tennis Club in order

CHAPTER 7

to secure line-of-sight positions for their television cameras. They brought in special 24,000-watt lights strung atop twenty-four-foot poles that required power cable connections running to the top of a nineteen-story building next door. Logistics aside, WPIX producers had a fundamentally different view of what they were televising from that of Wood and his players. The Tennis Players' League, USLTA officials, and Wood all wanted the broadcast of a sporting competition, while the network wanted to air a television program. That difference of opinion contributed to the poor reception television viewers gave the match between the biggest stars of amateur tennis—Tony Trabert, Vic Seixas, Gardnar Mulloy, and Ham Richardson. Wood wooed the USLTA board members to provide the match with linesmen, umpires, and ball boys by once again providing gratis food and beverages along with a spate of celebrities that included Gene Tunney, Lana Turner, and Igor Cassini. About twice as many guests as were invited turned up for dinner and the open bar, an overflow that pushed back the start time of the match. So much reliance on celebrity service bulletins and publicity from Charlie Einfeld and Martin Michel at 20th Century Studios led Wood and his team to overlook the basics of running a tennis event.[40]

Disorganization reigned with play set to begin. The players did not even have tennis balls with them on the court for the start of the match. Lights made it difficult for players to see the ball, and photographers' flashbulbs further handicapped the players, who put on a less than stellar performance. Eighty letters from viewers found their way to Wood, a full quarter of which complained of the poor event and the larger problem of having turned topflight tennis into a bacchanal. Those epistles, not openly hostile to the round-robin event, offered suggestion after suggestion to improve the experience. To his credit, Wood tried to put some of these suggestions into practice, such as adjusting the position of the cameras so that the entire tennis court fell into the field of view rather than showing only one player at a time. But changes like limiting celebrities' time on camera in favor of keeping the action on tennis did little to solve the fundamental problem with the venture. The round-robin simply demanded too much from America's top amateur players in terms of time away from crucial tournaments in Europe during the late spring and early summer. Without financial remuneration, how could Wood expect the players he supposedly represented to block out substantial parts of their schedules so that he could earn a commission from television networks for promoting a tennis event hosted at his club? Sportswriter Jim Burchard of the *New York World-Telegram* panned the event; his opinion was shared by the sliver of viewers who watched the match and the few players themselves who participated. USLTA officials, their fascination with television and their susceptibility to selective flattery aside, likewise felt underserved by the event and by Wood.[41] Jack Kramer's position outside of the amateur association as the head of the professional tour put him in a much better place to take advantage of the changed economic outlook for sports in the '50s that television had made possible.

Society-wide changes in the postwar period that moved entertainments squarely from the public sphere to squarely inside the home by the early 1950s had brought on what one historian has called "The Great Sports Slump of the 1950s." Between 1947 and 1949, Americans spent about $282 million per year on attendance at sporting events. Over the next decade, that yearly number fell by 30 million to $252 million dollars. Every spectator sport suffered at the same time that the economy hummed along and consumer spending boomed. In addition to where they spent their money and what they spent their money on, *who* spent the money mattered in the '50s. Women exercised increased control over their household incomes, and tasked with raising the largest generation, up to that point, of children in American history, it comes as no surprise that their spending focused on the home. The role of women as primary household consumers became so total by the early 1950s that even when men did spend money on entertainments outside the home—be it movies, concerts, and especially spectator sports, which they previously had attended exclusively with male friends—these men now bought a ticket for themselves and a ticket for their wives. Given the long popularity of tennis with women compared to baseball, football, and boxing, tennis fared proportionately better than the major team sports and prizefighting, whose spectatorship slumped during the '50s.[42]

The rise of television in the home also impacted attendance at sporting events. Home viewership did not, however, toll the death bell for many spectator sports as quickly or as loudly as commonly assumed. Television ownership rose from four million Americans in 1950 to 75 percent of all families by 1956. Families in the United States by the middle of the '50s watched television about five hours per day. At the same time, the popularity of sports programming fell from the high-water mark in the late 1940s and early '50s when teams and sports ranging from the Chicago Cubs and championship prizefighting had sold their broadcast rights to television networks on the cheap, or for nothing at all, because the sports executives believed television boosted their gate sales. Once the novelty wore off, television viewers quickly realized that some of the fun of attending a wrestling match or the incredibly popular roller derbies of the late '40s and early '50s did not translate well into the family room. The technical limitations of the standard camera at the time, popularly known as "Doctor Cyclops," also limited the angles of the action to a degree that the quick and oftentimes decentralized movement of team sports proved too complicated to capture for home viewership. Networks compensated for these shortcomings by doubling down on producing quality programs in other areas such as comedy, drama, and game shows, which most families spent more time watching in the '50s than sports shows.[43]

Whereas football had proven troublesome to televise, tennis had long been made into a camera-friendly sport. The reality of airing a tennis match nonetheless posed a real challenge for broadcasters. Editors could add sound effects and commentary later, but camera operators had difficulty keeping the ball and players in frame, especially as the speed at which the top professionals hit increased. The predictability of the serve-and-volley game helped camera operators pan their cameras immediately up following the serve and frequent charge to the frontcourt, but the different environments in which the matches took place—stadium one afternoon, armory that evening, gymnasium the next—meant that without the purchase and setup of dark matting along the back and sides of the court, players' white outfits, not to mention the white tennis balls, would appear only vaguely on screen if they showed up at all. But they did show up with great regularity during the intermission of double features, where tennis newsreels brought faraway and posh tournaments into the movie palaces that were popular with the less well-to-do. The focused drama of two competitors, one rectangular court, and one ball meant that one camera rather than a troupe of operators could cover a match. The major newsreel series—*The March of Time, Pathé News, Paramount News, Fox Movietone News, Hearst Metrotone News,* and *Universal Newsreel*—all recapped tennis tournaments and ties with dramatic commentary and cheesy tennis-shot sounds. The rapid rise in television ownership and viewership in the late 1950s and early '60s ended those sports newsreels. Television sports programming grew worldwide, as was the case in Australia in 1962 when producers shot thirteen thirty-minute television shows of professional tennis in Sydney and planned another thirteen episodes in Melbourne. The next year, the Riviera Tennis Club in Los Angeles taped matches of Kramer's players and aired those matches on KTTV and other California networks in 1963 and '64.

In 1965 CBS Sports further abbreviated a tennis tournament by interspersing one-hour matches with bowling shows as the popularity of that sport rose steadily in the mid-1960s.[44]

Jack Kramer's tour took partnership between competitive tennis and television to a new level by separating production from the amateur tennis associations and their tightly controlled tournament venues. Without set tournament homes such as Forest Hills, Wimbledon, or Paris's Roland-Garros, the more peripatetic professional tour could attach itself to venues whose owners and operators seemed amenable to sharing revenues generated by televised coverage of the tennis. Kramer's abbreviated round-robin match format between just four players made for a night of interesting television without locking the network into paying a steep price to secure two weeks of tennis tournament coverage where they were likely to use only a small fraction of what they had paid for.[45]

The players embraced television. Kramer secured short-term broadcast contracts that stipulated cameras would not adversely affect play by being poorly placed around the court. With television, Kramer and his troupe expected a positive impact on their pocketbooks. They did not do as well as they hoped. At the cusp of the Open Era in 1968, tennis remained, in the words of former-tennis-champion-turned-longtime-broadcaster Barry MacKay, "wide open as far as television goes." It took the next generation of sports managers to create multiyear contracts worth multimillion dollars, but by getting media outlets like the BBC to agree to televise dramatic tennis matches at London's Wembley Stadium, for example, Kramer's barnstorming tennis tour demonstrated to sports promoters and marketers the realizable future, especially after 1968, when the problems between professionals and amateurs became less apparent.[46]

A great number of problems remained, though, with the sport of tennis and the place of the professional player in that sport prior to 1968. Australian champion Frank Sedgman, who toured with the Kramer troupe beginning in 1953, captured the essence of the professional tennis tour in the 1950s and '60s when he said, "With professional tennis in those days, you'd just have to get out there and play, and not complain about it, because you were there to make a buck. And you had to put on a good show."[47] But a good show in the '50s was a heavy burden to carry. On no one's shoulders did that burden fall more heavily than on the longtime World's Professional Champion, Richard "Pancho" Gonzales.

CHAPTER 8

The World Champion from "The Wrong Side of the Tracks"

Richard "Pancho" Gonzales was born to Mexican immigrant parents in Los Angeles on May 9, 1928. The hustling world of the public parks and streets were a far cry from the clubhouses and manicured lawn courts of Philadelphia, Boston, and New York City. The personal refinement and self-control with which the game instilled amateurs—according to ILTF and USLTA officials—did not stop the adolescent Gonzales from running afoul of the law. His life of struggle on the streets almost ended his tennis career before it began. The game he learned to play in the public parks resembled the sport played by East Coast elites and the country club caste in name only. The circuitous path he followed to become the U.S. amateur champion was part of a broader renegotiation and disintegration of a half century of sports tradition devoted to amateurism. In tennis it took Gonzales, someone pilloried as from "the wrong side of the tracks," to make that accommodation happen. But even among the touring professionals, a veritable band of outsiders, Pancho lived his life on the outside.[1]

Gonzales's mother, Carmen, encouraged the competitive youngster to enjoy wholesome play. A longtime admirer of the sport of tennis as played by the wealthy in Mexico, Carmen bought Richard a hardware store racquet as a Christmas gift. Richard hit the ball against the garage doors for the first half a year until a trip to the movies opened his eyes to the world-class play of Britain's Fred Perry—an amateur-champion-turned-touring-professional who at that time made his home in Southern California. Walking out of the theater, Richard told his mother, "I'm going to be just like him." An avid marbles player, Richard regularly journeyed a mile north and half a mile west of his home to Exposition Park for games and the National Marbles Championship. Starting in 1935, the grounds surrounding the Memorial Coliseum, which had been the site of the 1932 Olympics, would be where Gonzales learned the game of tennis. While tennis was not an Olympic sport in the 1932 Games, the facility master plan had called for courts on the southeast side of the park.[2]

The shortage of recreational spaces in Gonzales's neighborhood compared to the citywide average was offset by the quality of supervised leisure that Exposition Park afforded the community. However, it was unlikely that members of the coordinating council actually understood the type of tennis played there. Frank Poulain, a washed-up and ostracized teaching professional, managed the tennis shop, and a ragtag assortment of players helped maintain the courts. African Americans, Mexicans, and people with physical disabilities hung around the shop, where betting on marbles and poker occurred nearly every day. The confidence games of the street played out on the hard concrete of the municipal tennis courts. Gonzales himself recalled trash-talking and hustling. He also looked to the courts as a "sanctuary" from the truant officer. Without proper adult supervision, Exposition Park tennis fell far short of the transformative vision that reformers had in mind when renewing the city's recreational space.[3]

On the other hand, the park courts were truer to real life than the cloistered world of the private club. Bill Tilden's generation of elite players originated in, and thus remained somewhat ensconced in, what was popularly called at the time the "country club set." The clubs provided players with club professionals, the only people who knew and could teach the proper stroke mechanics and tactical patterns. The clubs were the likeliest places to secure the funds necessary to travel and compete in the growing number of tournaments; early on they were the only places to find tennis courts. That began to change in the 1920s and accelerated in the 1930s, with new court construction that ushered in a fresh cohort of players centered in California. Ellsworth Vines, Gene Mako, Bobby Riggs, and Pancho Gonzales, as their West Coast contemporary Don Budge recalled, "all came from the public parks."[4]

After exhibiting promising results in the public parks, Gonzales and his generation of recreational revolution players might find some acceptance by USLTA authorities. That attention could mean financial support to improve one's game. It certainly meant subjecting oneself to a great deal of paternalism that was not dissimilar to the control exercised by recreational reformers more broadly at the same time. As executive secretary and president of the SCTA, Perry T. Jones directed the warm-weather USLTA Western section's evolution from a fine place to play to the epicenter of championship tennis. Born forty-five miles east of Los Angeles in Etiwanda, California, on June 22, 1890, Jones was scarcely older than tennis in America and one of the first Californians to take up the game. His father, a bookkeeper, moved the family to San Bernardino by 1900, where Jones started playing tennis around the age of ten. During his teens and twenties, few tournaments existed west of the Mississippi River. A player but only a onetime champion—holding the Los Angeles Metropolitan singles title in 1918—Jones worked as a salesman and began officiating and promoting small tournaments before directing the major Pacific Southwest tournament during its inaugural year, in 1924. That same year Jones secured the position of junior development chairman for the SCTA.[5]

The responsibility of supervising training, setting up tournaments, and chaperoning juniors on away tournaments fell to Jones. He was tasked by the LATC members making up the newly formed TPASC to develop both world-class tennis and well-behaved juniors. Beyond his basic responsibility of helping boys hit better backhands, Jones emphasized proper social behavior in his interactions with Southern California's young tennis players. Jones himself was a bit of a dandy, usually sporting a bow tie, tinted glasses, and a double-breasted suit. He often took afternoon tea at the club. The stress Jones placed on etiquette in his own life informed his efforts to refine his junior players both on and off the court. After returning from a tournament and a homestay, Jones always required his players to write thank-you notes to their host family. Likewise, if he could not travel with the players, he arranged a chaperone to make sure the youngsters used their silverware properly. For Jones, tennis was still an elite sport, where manners and gentility mattered a great deal. He emphasized proper dress and "all white attire" on page one of his guide to junior tennis, linking confidence on the court to the right clothes, ethics, and sportsmanship.[6]

In considering the moral uplift of tennis, Jones was far from alone. The game's history bespoke a strong tradition of refinement and gentility designed to uplift the elite player above the suspect leisure pursuits of the middle and working class. Will Levington Comfort understood as much, opining in the *Los Angeles Times* that tennis served as the best antidote to temptations confronting youths between the "dangerous age[s]" of twelve and seventeen.

Moreover, Comfort pointed out the popularity of the game among the working class and the importance of growing the game on the public courts where the "less favored" boys could compete. Likewise, the Presbyterian minister, college president, and USLTA Tennis Clinic Committee chairman, William Plumer Jacobs, believed tennis to be the best sport for increasing the "moral stamina" of America's youth. Plumer thought tennis was not just for the well-to-do. He called on every city across America to provide public courts and instruction in a game that bred self-reliance, persistence, and wholesome competition. Plumer also saw the potential for "spiritual development" in the sportsmanship required to play the game. Echoing Teddy Roosevelt's call for a "strenuous life," Plumer argued that primarily as a game for the young and impressionable, tennis played a more important role in "citizenship building" than any other sport.[7] High-minded to be sure, Plumer and Comfort failed to address the specific hurdles facing a working-class youth trying to become a competitive player.

Tennis's unique blend of mental and physical match play fused the cerebral challenges of golf with the corporeal demands of one-on-one boxing sans violence. As a sport that demanded complex biomechanical moves in order to progress beyond the most rudimentary level of play, tennis required the watchful eyes of a seasoned instructor who corrected and guided the newcomer on the proper stroke mechanics, playing tactics, and match strategy. On one level, then, becoming a competitive tennis player resembled an apprenticeship, where the master shared direct experience and gave direct feedback to the journeyman. This mode of training meant a challenge for any outsider trying to break into the cloistered world of competitive tennis, because the traditionally elite champions felt most comfortable training new players who resembled themselves. By excluding working-class players from private club courts while simultaneously holding tennis up as a wholesome activity for all people, elites limited the ability of the "wrong" players to break into the top echelons of the game.[8] In the sport of tennis, where one played often dictated not only how one played but how good they could become.

California clubs did care about who played on their courts, but classicism and racism were less overt there than on the East Coast. When asked about three African Americans competing in the Southern California Tennis Championships held at the Los Angeles Tennis Club, Perry T. Jones told his East Coast superiors that the SCTA had always encouraged talented players from outside the club to participate in the tournament. Feeling the pressure to take a harder line toward unwelcome players, Jones became more selective in inviting juniors to the courts of the LATC. Regardless of efforts to police play, the strength of competition and subsequent number of champions produced on the courts set the LATC apart from competitive tennis found anywhere else in the country. By 1940, Californians held nine of ten national championship titles, and the SCTA had burgeoned into the largest USLTA section, with more than fifty public and semiprivate clubs paying dues. The junior development program Jones invented was so rigorous it earned the nickname the "Factory System" from the national media because of the consistent champions Southern California tennis produced. Consistency, however, extended down to include the background, appearance, and attitude of players. All the players knew that "Mister Jones" kept a list of favorites who looked, dressed, and acted the part.[9]

The most significant tension to ever surface between Jones and a player involved not Bobby Riggs but Pancho Gonzales. While not explicitly about Gonzales's class and racial background, Jones's decision to ban Gonzales from sanctioned tournaments was bolstered by the young player's refusal to attend school about the time he entered seventh grade. Although the association had a policy in place requiring schooling if a junior planned to play tournament tennis, they enforced the rule inconsistently. The talented Jack Kramer was a few years further along in development than Gonzales. Jones granted him court time at the LATC that fell during the normal school day. With this comparison, it is hard not to read Gonzales's ban as directed at his working-class, Mexican, and, potentially, delinquent background. While not from the worst part of town, Gonzales did live in a neighborhood that had a slightly higher than average number of cases of juvenile delinquency. Moreover, the long hours Gonzales's parents worked and the aggressive discipline his father imposed made Richard particularly prone to delinquency in the eyes of reformers. But most damning was the association Jones could make between Gonzales and the Mexican subculture known as the Pachucos. Big for his age, Gonzales seemed a potential leader of the Mexican youth gangs roaming the city in the 1940s. He also had a prominent scar on his face that resembled the type of cut one received in a knife fight. While the fears were not completely unfounded, as Gonzales did choose to drop out of school and hang out with hustlers before his ban from competitive tennis, the SCTA's decision to sanction him removed his most important recreational outlet.[10]

Jones's strict instructional methods and unrivaled successes in producing so many top-class players set him apart from any other tennis coach and official in the United States. He was not alone, however, in espousing regimented training. The second most successful nation at producing world-class tennis players in the late 1940s and '50s was Australia. The Australians had their own Jones in Melbourne-based coach Harry Hopman. When Australian Davis Cup winner Frank Sedgman referred to Hopman as a "very strict disciplinarian," he greatly understated Hopman's approach to the game. While Jones sought to help youngsters gain self-discipline over their minds through the manipulation of their bodies in terms of proper tennis technique, proper dress, and proper sportsmanship, Hopman more straightforwardly strove to have his players master their bodies through unprecedented physical conditioning. "Physical fitness," remarked Hopman, was his "philosophy" and his "whole theory." He introduced weight training to tennis players at a young age, placing prospects in gymnasiums when they turned thirteen. He made his players run mile after mile, for both distance and speed work. His signature conditioning move, the kangaroo jump, where an athlete squatted down and then exploded upward and brought their knees up to their chest and their elbows down to their knees, became the bane of every youngster baking underneath the Australian sun.[11]

Those who survived Hopman's training and developed the right stroke mechanics went on to successful careers. The regime secured Australia's international reputation for the fittest players in world tennis competition. But as long as they remained amateurs—even playing at the highest level, as demonstrated by winning the Davis Cup—Australians remained under the control of coach Hopman and the LTAA just as the American amateurs remained under Perry T. Jones's and the USLTA's control. In fact, the better a player became, the more tennis officials tightened their handling of a player. Players competing abroad in major tournaments and Davis Cup play, in particular, garnered unwanted scrutiny from their respective federations, which feverishly promoted and policed the international reputations of their countries' games. Hopman flatly told his players, "I don't want you talking to the press, I want to do all the talking to the press."[12] In words and actions, Hopman was far from the only tennis official who protected the purity of the amateur ideal and safeguarded the sanctity of the national tennis federations over the basic freedoms of speech and property, which were earned but not enjoyed by players whose on-court labor was what actually put those national organizations on the world map.

As a youth Gonzales had none of those thoughts and actions on his mind when he once again ran afoul of both Jones and Los Angeles legal officers.

Gonzales encountered the truant officer one too many times, stole toys from local stores, and even burglarized homes in 1942. A 1943 juvenile court ruling removed Pancho from his neighborhood and put him in the custody of the California Youth Authority (CYA), which operated a series of reform schools throughout the state. The CYA first placed Gonzales in the Preston School of Industry in Ione, California, forty miles east of Sacramento and thirty miles south of Folsom State Prison along the Sierra Foothills. The foreboding "Preston Castle" was a place of woe for Gonzales and his fellow wards. Opened in the summer of 1894 to a handful of youths transferred there from adult penitentiaries, by the 1920s the school had earned a reputation for cruelty toward wards and recidivism among those released. Superintendents routinely flogged boys and used solitary confinement to coerce certain behavior. Nine out of ten boys sent to Preston found themselves back in the CYA or in adult corrections not long after their discharge from the reform school, compared to estimates of only 2 percent reformed to the satisfaction of CYA officials.[13]

President Harry Truman's willingness to continue to project U.S. military power after the defeat of Germany and Japan gave Gonzales an opportunity to get out of the custody of the CYA by joining the military in 1946. Like many veterans who returned to Southern California after the war, he became enamored with drag racing. The appeal stemmed from three factors: young men had spent months, if not years, working around and fixing vehicles and other machines; former airfields and roads along landing strips proliferated in Southern California, which allowed for flat and safe driving; combat culture became speed culture for returning veterans. Gonzales built vehicles and drove them with his brother Manuel and other veterans on abandoned airfields and salt flats across Southern California, racing on top courses like the Saugus Drag Strip against the fastest dragsters in the world at that time. Gonzales's affinity for time in and around cars attracted him to the traveling lifestyle of the professional tennis tour, which existed as a road show of sorts. But in the meantime, his military service encompassed none of the fun of playing tennis exhibition matches that Don Budge, Bobby Riggs, and other more established players had enjoyed on exotic courts built by the U.S. military as it hopped from Pacific island to Pacific island.[14]

Gonzales's return to competitive tennis in late 1947 marked the most significant comeback in the history of the sport. He had spent almost four years without touching a tennis racquet. Fresh off a troop transport ship moored off the California coast, the nineteen-year-old Gonzales arrived back in Los

Angeles and told his parents he now planned to dedicate his life to tennis. The news shocked Gonzales's parents, whose strained relationship with their son had further deteriorated during his long absence from home after the juvenile division of the Superior Court of Los Angeles removed the delinquent Gonzales from their care. He had not picked up a racquet in so long, his parents thought, how could he ever regain lost ground? With determination to show everyone he was now his own man, Gonzales started on the path to become a professional tennis player.[15]

Gonzales went back to the Exposition Park courts on which he grew up. He began to practice six to seven hours a day against anyone willing to play. He worked on his forehand, his backhand, his volleys, and his overhead. The weight he carried around as a child was gone. He had grown into a six-foot, three-inch slender frame. Long legs and a wide reach made his court coverage tremendous. To combat years off the court, Gonzales emphasized conditioning, going on long runs and training relentlessly to increase his foot speed.[16]

The quickness took a while to return, but his longtime flawless serve only improved. Fully extended, Gonzales's arm stretched just beyond the 114-inch height of tennis's longtime dominant server, William "Big Bill" Tilden. Along with its height, the brilliance of the Gonzales serve came from the unteachable timing of his motion, which, at the perfect moment, transferred the energy coiled from his body into the ball. A kinetic chain of physics began when his legs pushed off from the ground, up through the rotation of his hips, which pivoted the trunk, chest, and shoulders up toward the ball. The once opened chest and shoulders facing the sky now closed and moved parallel to the ground in a movement that whipped his serving arm up into the ball with tremendous force just as the ball floated in the air at the top of the toss. The racquet was simply an extension of his body that moved where and how his body did, naturally decelerating at a pronated angle after the ball left the sweet spot of the racquet's string bed. Gonzales's body now followed the stroke naturally into the court, giving him an aggressive position to exploit a weak return of serve with either a forehand drive or a well-placed volley. More than most players, Gonzales understood that winning in tennis meant playing to one's strengths. In so doing, Gonzales, along with Jack Kramer, initiated and popularized the new seize-the-initiative style of play.[17]

Gonzales's fast return to winning in topflight tennis happened because he badly wanted it. The early losses never discouraged him. The confidence of losing a match but knowing he would win the next one had a great deal to do with his success after such a long layoff. Contested in October 1947 on the LATC courts, his dominant wins over Czechoslovakian champion Jaroslav Drobný, intercollegiate title holder Bob Falkenberg, and two-time U.S. amateur champion Frankie Parker in the Pacific Southwest Championship propelled him to national attention. After only a year of practice and minimal tournament play, Gonzales established enough winning potential to force the SCTA officials—men like Jones, who previously harbored significant reservations about Gonzales—to reexamine their opinions of him.[18]

The ban Jones imposed on Gonzales for not attending school expired upon his return from the military service. Jones, however, could have continued to keep Gonzales out of tournaments by refusing to fund the young amateur. Long obsessed with "What is an amateur in tennis?" Jones and his fellow USLTA officials diligently protected the purity of their players from the corrupting influence of money in sports. The enforcement of what they called the "amateur ideal" had a great deal to do with the USLTA's charge to field the best Davis Cup team possible—an international competition that allowed only amateur players. At the same time, the zealousness of the USLTA's Amateur Rule Committee in imposing sanctions on players for the slightest infractions smacked of bureaucrats looking to maintain whatever measure of control they could over the game's future. Sometimes fickle in enforcement, in Gonzales's case the SCTA and the USLTA were more frank. A poor kid from urban Los Angeles with Mexican parents and a delinquency record was hardly the representative Jones wanted to send east to play in the summer grass-court circuit and national championship. That same young man representing the United States against other nations had seemed equally unthinkable just a year earlier.[19]

As historian Robert J. Lake has made clear, "social exclusion" in tennis was hardly an American phenomenon. For decades British tennis clubs followed a strict class divide that gradually weakened with the upswing in new clubs in the twenty years after the Great War and slackened further after the Second World War when the LTA made a genuine push for democratizing the game.[20] The USLTA moved alongside this trend in general and particularly when it came to their topflight talent. By the spring of 1948, the USLTA could no longer afford to keep the gifted Gonzales on the sidelines. Not contested during the war, the Davis Cup returned to the United States in both 1946 and 1947 with the Angeleno and world number one Jack Kramer leading the squad to victory both times. Winning more than forty matches in a row, including the 1947 U.S. Championships, Kramer turned professional in the fall of 1947, leaving the Davis Cup Selection Committee scrambling to find fresh faces to continue American dominance on the world stage. As Gonzales related, "The Emperor Jones" himself decided to stake the still unproven talent on his first extended trip east to play in all the matches leading up to the U.S. Championships at Forest Hills.[21]

Jones's reversal also had a lot to do with Gonzales's newfound maturity. While far from a decorated soldier, Gonzales did serve in the military, and on March 23, 1948, he married his first wife, Henrietta. For the conservative Jones and the entire USLTA establishment, Gonzales the serviceman and Gonzales the husband and soon-to-be father were necessary steps for the young man to take in order to potentially represent the United States abroad. And beyond the symbolism of a patriotic family man, Gonzales also made the actual choice to remain eligible to play for the United States. In February, the Bank of Mexico—on behalf of the Mexican government—offered the nineteen-year-old Gonzales financial security for life, a nice beachfront home, and a lifetime appointment at the Mexican consulate in Los Angeles if he agreed to accept Mexican citizenship and compete for Mexico in all international tennis competitions. Gonzales briefly considered the offer before turning it down, saying, "I prize my [American] citizenship above all the benefits." USLTA officials like Jones gave him the necessary funds to compete in the tournaments leading up to the U.S. Nationals at Forest Hills.[22]

Gonzales's record in those tournaments was mixed. He won some important tournaments—most notably the U.S. National Clay Court title contested in River Forest, Illinois. But losses in some smaller events to low-ranked players allowed for many to write him off as too inconsistent to mount a serious challenge for the U.S. Championships in September. The year before, Gonzales had made the trip east for the Nationals but lost in only the second round. People believed him to be soft, a reputation that developed into his nickname of "Gorgo"—that is, the cheese champion. But on Saturday, September 18, 1948, Gonzales dominated South African Eric Sturgess in straight sets for the U.S. Championships singles title. More than ten thousand fans attended the match and shook their heads in disbelief at the "meteoric rise" of the "the scar-faced Pancho"—the second-youngest champion in the history of U.S. tennis.[23]

The press interpreted Gonzales's winning in several ways. Some outlets dismissed it as a fluke. Others stereotyped Pancho as a Pachuco miscreant. More rightly recognized the incredible social upheaval the new champion had just caused in the ranks of elite sports. During the coming year, Gonzales's reputation ebbed and flowed depending a great deal on how he fared in bouts with California rival Ted Schroeder, who exemplified the simon-pure amateur. A crew-cut Anglo from California with a wonderful family and a prosperous refrigerator business, Schroeder played a very limited schedule, often skipping major events in order to spend more time at home. He long refused contracts from professional promoters, preferring to see tennis as a serious hobby rather than a means to make a living. When Gonzales repeated his 1948 win over Schroeder at the 1949 U.S. Championships, many who followed the tournament disbelieved it.[24]

Gonzales's decision to turn professional just days after lifting the amateur trophy again surprised no one. As the youngest player to join the professional ranks, an inner-city kid who grew up gambling and hustling around public park courts could hardly be expected to turn down sixty thousand dollars, tennis followers thought. The press pointed out that a Mexican youth knew no other way to get ahead. Some capitalized on controversy. Bobby Riggs, who would promote the 1949 Kramer-versus-Gonzales professional tour, encouraged such talk among the nation's sports reporters. Riggs's preferred word to describe Pancho to others was "colorful." Sports reporters were not as vague, having long pushed a narrative of Gonzales as the so-called bad boy of tennis.[25]

Gonzales's Forest Hills championship was the biggest story in amateur tennis in 1949. He followed that up with the biggest story in both amateur and professional tennis when he decided to turn professional. Gonzales ended his amateur tennis career a few weeks after his second U.S. National Championships with one final win on the courts of the LATC. On September 18, 1949, in front of Jones, Southern California tennis doyens, and USLTA officials, all of whom despised the Mexican American player until his talent left them little choice but to begrudgingly accept him, Gonzales demolished Ted Schroeder one final time—a symbolic victory over amateur tennis and the men who guarded that ideal.[26]

Upon turning professional, Gonzales quickly found himself facing a different attack—that of his seasoned opponent Jack Kramer. The 1949–1950 tour opened on October 25, 1949, in front of 13,357 fans squeezed into New York City's Madison Square Garden, who paid at least eight dollars apiece to see the professionals. Francisco "Little Pancho" Segura and the recently turned professional Frankie Parker warmed up the crowd with Segura's unorthodox two-handed forehand electrifying onlookers. Most everyone, however, came to see how well Gonzales would hold up against the champion. As the main event got under way, many people thought he would fare quite well. The two matched each other power for power, hitting harder than any tennis player, professional or amateur, ever had up to that point. The canvas court that had been rolled over the arena's floor increased the pace of their blistering serves and shocked spectators who had seen the speed of amateur tennis played only outdoors on slower courts. In the end, Kramer's experience on the fast court and the big stage propelled him past Gonzales in four sets—the last set the most one-sided of the four. "He's not as tough as I thought he'd be," said Gonzales after the match. "I figure it will take eight or nine matches before I hit my stride against Jake. But don't worry, I'll hit it."[27]

Riggs certainly was not worried. A veteran barnstormer, first as a player and then as a promoter, Riggs knew how much the opener set the tone for the rest of the professional tour. A gate of over one hundred thousand dollars from night one meant that Riggs would far exceed the minimum guarantees he had made to the players, and that neither of the singles matches were blowouts boded well for the continued interest of his players with fans as play continued over the next one hundred matches. Alice Marble, herself a former amateur-champion-turned-touring-professional and therefore no stranger to what made tennis profitable, advanced another reason why the Kramer-versus-Gonzales tour would pay dividends to the promoter and the players: Pancho intrinsically knew how to whip fans into a frenzy either with his big shots, long stretches, or his on-court behavior. "The spectators automatically enthuse when they see his handsome dark face, his splendid physique and his many delightful mannerisms," Marble said after watching the Madison Square Garden match. She linked Gonzales's crowd appeal to his troubled background, which had not only produced some of the young professional's more appealing physical features, such as his muscular legs, shoulder, and core, but also packaged Pancho in a ready-made narrative of Mexican American machismo that contrasted sharply with Kramer's all-American backstory and those of most topflight tennis players in the past. From his fast serve to his fondness for fast cars, from his spurning of the amateur authorities to his wide smile, what Pancho did both on and off the court titillated the public. He was both the good player and the bad boy of tennis at the same time. Riggs promoted Gonzales as the "people's choice" on the lookout for "new worlds to conquer."[28]

But the tour quickly went from good to bad for Gonzales as the grind continued into the winter of 1950. Whereas the USLTA's prohibitions against accepting money had sheltered players during their amateur careers, upon turning professional, Gonzales and Parker found themselves constantly at the beck and call of companies that wanted them for everything from cigarette advertisements to tennis racquet designs. Part of succeeding as a professional meant balancing off-court moneymaking opportunities with on-court commitments. More so than his fellow professionals, Gonzales faced the greatest degree of media scrutiny for two reasons: first, because so many sportswriters clung desperately to the mistaken belief that the best amateur tennis players could beat the professionals, and, second, because of his Mexican American heritage. Gonzales had ended the year 1949 ranked number one while Parker ended it ranked fourth, but the hollowness of world rankings that included only amateurs but not professionals rang true night after night as the more experienced professionals Kramer and Segura consistently beat their young colleagues. To help explain those losses, sports reporters once again used the Mexican American narrative, this time stereotyping the challenger Gonzales as lazy and tired, unfit for the day-in and day-out work of professional touring. The reason Gonzales trailed Kramer by thirty matches through January 1950 had less to do with the former's effort and more to do with the latter's experience—although such a straightforward explanation hardly made for good copy. In fact, when the barnstormers made it to the West Coast in February, Gonzales began winning matches more consistently than Kramer, even notching an 80 percent winning percentage over a California stretch of matches. Gonzales was far from lazy. Most of their matches consisted of hard-fought tennis, point after point. For example, on February 2, the first set alone of their Seattle, Washington, match went fifty-four games—hardly an uninspired effort halfway into a tour of night-after-night play. Yet at the midway point in the tour, the ball rested firmly in Kramer's court, with Gonzales behind eighteen matches to fifty-nine.[29]

By that point Gonzales simply did not have enough dates on the schedule left to claim the professional tour. He nonetheless continued to fight on, because he knew he was improving and believed that if he finished the tour strong, he would secure himself a place on the next professional tour. Entering the spring of 1950, the current tour had no fixed end date. Riggs played his players as long as people continued to pay to see them. The promoter also made his troupe play the *Philadelphia Inquirer*'s professional tournament the week of March 20. Gonzales beat his fellow touring professionals along with a few dozen non-touring professionals to earn $2,376 in prize money and claim the title of the best player in the City of Brotherly Love. There was no love lost between Kramer and Gonzales, however, as the two continued to battle through New England during the month of April. When the tour finally ended a month later, Kramer had thoroughly vanquished Gonzales. As anyone who had attended understood, however, the series score did not do justice to the quality of the tennis they saw. But professional tennis was about getting paid, not about justice. Kramer, Riggs, and Gonzales all got their fair share of the money, pay far exceeding the guarantees the players retained. Kramer and Riggs then tried to end Gonzales's professional career as their tour concluded.[30]

In May 1950, Kramer and Riggs began feeding the Associated Press rumors that Gonzales himself wanted a year respite from the tour in order to rest and recuperate. The veracity of such a claim seemed questionable, given that Gonzales had started to play stronger tennis when compared to his earlier play on the tour. The casual follower of the sport, however, accepted the rumor because it fit with the lazy Mexican American stereotype. Gonzales did himself no favors in that regard when he posed for beer advertisements that made their way into popular glossy magazines like *Life*. There he was lounging on a chair and swigging beer—"a natural alliance if we ever saw one," remarked one sports commentator.[31]

Such images served the purposes of Kramer and Riggs. They waited until their tour ended on May 21, 1950, in Dayton, Ohio, after over one hundred events on the road, and then quickly dismissed a bewildered Gonzales. Pancho believed that the four hundred thousand dollars in gate receipts he had helped earn would have secured him at least a place as the undercard match for the forthcoming fall 1950 to spring 1951 tour, especially given that Ted Schroeder and other eligible amateur champions had turned down Riggs's offers to tour against the professional champion Kramer. Sports commentators shared that view, editorializing how much "the crowds loved him," how they "lustily" rooted him on, and "how heartening for a kid from the other side of the tracks" to make a living in such an elite sport. Unbeknownst to Gonzales, though, Riggs had already started working to entice Gertrude Moran to turn professional with a first offer of one hundred thousand dollars to play on the tour. The two agreed to seventy-five thousand dollars for "a 100 match barnstorming tour" four months later.[32]

Gonzales returned to Southern California embittered. He began to drink heavily, and a few weeks later San Diego police arrested him on charges of disorderly conduct. Law enforcement put Gonzales in jail before releasing him on a twenty-five-dollar fine and requiring him to make an apology to the women to whom he and his friends had made inappropriate remarks. Feeling deflated, Gonzales decided to sit out some of the summer tournaments that filled out the professional players' schedule in between the touring months, even though those tournaments were some of the only events he could play now. That absence gave other players like Segura an opportunity to shine, and "Little Pancho" took full advantage, winning Jack March's first big professional tournament in Cleveland, leveraging that win along with his entertaining personality to make a case for his spot on the forthcoming professional tour, and sealing the deal with his willingness to play on the tour for less money than any other challenger. Even the champion Kramer realized his precarious position in that the promoter could replace him at will, so he re-signed with Riggs for the same percentage that had earned him one hundred thousand dollars from the previous year. For his part, Riggs especially wanted to pinch every penny because he was in the middle of a messy divorce proceeding with his wife, Kay, who had also acted as an unpaid accountant and manager for the tour. The Riggses' separation left Bobby flailing to get his tour organized—and only days before he planned to open. Riggs even considered letting Gonzales play the undercard, only to revoke that offer at the last minute.[33]

Gonzales did get to spend more time with his family when Riggs and Kramer sidelined him—impractical when a player barnstormed. Shortly after turning professional in the fall of 1949, Pancho and Henrietta used twelve thousand dollars of his guarantee to buy a two-bedroom ranch house at 5838 South Arlington Avenue in the low-income neighborhood of Park Mesa Heights in South-Central Los Angeles. There most of the child-rearing fell to Henrietta, who looked after six-year-old Richard Jr., five-year-old Mike, and four-year-old Danny. A few nights a week, "Henry" and Pancho drove their Mercury sedan to the neighborhood bowling alley for league night, where Gonzales averaged a 183. Pancho spent a significant amount of his time away from home building and racing hot rods on a strip forty miles away at Saugus, California. The mechanical side of building cars drew Gonzales to racing, but the danger also thrilled him. That personality trait also led him to dog breeding, and he kept a kennel of boxers in his backyard. Mostly, though, the player widely regarded as the best in the world at that time hit tennis balls much as he had as a kid, before anyone who mattered had ever heard of him. At his house that meant hitting against his garage door at all hours of the day, much to the frustration of his neighbors.[34]

The Exposition Park courts he had learned to play on as a junior, however, provided a more favorable place for Pancho to practice. On any given day, kids and local hustlers might find themselves across the net from the two-time U.S. National Champion and holder of professional tournament victories, because he did not hold the U.S. professional tour title. A fifteen-minute car ride from his house to those courts spurred Gonzales to purchase the pro shop next to the Exposition Park courts. He would string racquets and teach the occasional lesson; his heart never went into retail or instruction. Fiduciaries upon his professional debut had encouraged Gonzales to buy annuities and other structured investments that would look after him and his family when his playing career inevitably came to an end, but that financial counsel pre-supposed that Pancho would play as a professional full-time for at least half a decade rather than finding himself all but shut out after only one full year of touring. Not a pauper, he nonetheless needed cash more than the least talented of professional athletes in other sports. Every day he was looking more like a teaching professional than a touring professional. "Richard Alonzo Gonzales is a troubled man," said Pancho's friends in the early 1950s.[35]

The question on the minds of everyone who followed tennis after the 1952 U.S. professional tour never materialized was "Where's Pancho?" Through all the trials, Gonzales kept his game remarkably sharp while not barnstorming on tour. He practiced against University of Southern California players and the best amateurs and teaching professionals in the area. He belonged to the LATC, which always worked hard to get one of its own a match. More frequently, Gonzales's professional matches took place overseas, where other countries paid better than what the limited professional tournament circuit paid in the United States. Four months of exhibitions across Southeast Asia from Japan to the Philippines netted Gonzales thirty-thousand dollars, where in cities like Seoul, Korea, fifteen thousand fans might queue for hours at a time to watch him play. Tennis-mad Australia offered even handsomer remuneration. Four-man tournaments in Melbourne, Perth, Adelaide, and Newcastle averaged ten thousand fans who paid about sixty-six thousand dollars per event. Gonzales swept through the competition, winning twenty-eight hundred dollars per event for his first place and doing a great deal to promote professional tennis in the process.[36]

Gonzales's success abroad explained sportswriter Arthur Marx's answer to Pancho's whereabouts on America's professional tour—that is, "They're all afraid of Gonzales." Kramer had said so, at least, admitting that Gonzales's consistent wins in the tournaments that featured all the best players made him the player to beat even though he was not touring with Big Jake, Frank Sedgman, Pancho Segura, and Ken McGregor in the winter and spring of 1953. That fear, along with grudges each one held for the other, hurt the bottom line of the tour when Sedgman versus Kramer failed to compel fans to pay as had past matchups. Kramer intensified their mistrust by spreading rumors that he had made an offer that the greedy Gonzales turned down—scuttlebutt that Gonzales and most sportswriters denied but some Kramer fans believed. In driving that wedge between himself and the future of professional tennis, Kramer set back the cause of professional tennis a few years and may have inadvertently pushed back open tennis by at least a few years.[37]

Unable to reconcile with Kramer, Gonzales began a comeback in the United States that would rival his earlier return to championship tennis in 1947 and '48. On June 21, 1953, Pancho won the World Professional Tennis Championship contested on the Lakewood Park courts of suburban Cleveland. The preeminent professional tournament in the world was a study in contrasts with the most prestigious amateur tournament in the world. Pancho competed against 15 other professionals over four evenings, while the 1953 Wimbledon draw included 128 men's singles entries reduced down to one champion over two weeks of play. Every player in the World Professional Championship came from the United States, while Wimbledon focused attention on players from more than two dozen countries in the men's singles draw. The women's professional contest contrasted even more with the women amateurs. Pauline Betz defeated the only other entry, Mary Hardwick, for the professional title—the first contested in four years—while the Wimbledon's ladies' draw presented 128 entries. For his first-place finish in singles, doubles, and mixed doubles, Pancho earned sixteen hundred dollars in prize money out of a total prize pool of a mere eight thousand dollars. Those earnings should have dwarfed the zero dollars Wimbledon players were supposed to have received, but the top players from most countries attending Wimbledon secured stipends and honorariums in excess of Pancho's winnings. The AELTC made more selling strawberries and cream in one day than the total purse of the World Professional Tennis Championship offered in 1953.[38]

Gonzales nonetheless accepted the engraved P.O.C. (Pilsener of Cleveland) trophy from Sam Benjamin and Mrs. George Carter with a big smile. He had established himself as the best player in the world despite the amateur and professional divides. Moreover, as a whole the professionals could view 1953 as a major success in popularizing their sport, because for the first time, their championship aired on prime-time television. When the Empire Oil Company had their WXEL broadcast four nights of professional tennis coverage, viewers who tuned in would have watched both the highest-level tennis in the world and a poorly run event when compared to the major amateur tournaments like Wimbledon. For example, the professional players planned to give their own commentary rather than have a separate announcer narrate the matches. Don Budge had been both playing and broadcasting, but when he won in an upset, he could no longer broadcast. Carl Earn was just playing, but after Budge won and Earn lost, Earn took over broadcasting duties. In the tournament's final order of business, the players elected Cleveland's Robert Trenkamp as the professional tennis commissioner. That move did little to gain respectability for professional tennis, which continued into 1954 without open competition between amateurs and professionals.[39]

Kramer fretted that year about whether or not to step back from professional play, because he knew the high likelihood of losing to a man he loathed in Gonzales. He knew his pocketbook would take a hit, but he also hated the idea of losing his first professional tour. Kramer reached a compromise with himself by announcing that because of health complications he would play doubles on the tour but not singles. Yet he offered no explanation about how bending down for low volleys and rotating one's trunk for the American twist serve—the biomechanics that put the most stress on the players' spine—did not aggravate his back in doubles play while the same actions did on the singles court. The simple reality was that Kramer wanted to maintain his legacy as a player at all costs. His ego, a personality characteristic of many great competitors, actually worked against the financial success of the tour even after Kramer mostly retired from singles, played doubles sparingly, and focused almost exclusively on promotion just before the start of the 1954 tour.[40]

Gonzales took full advantage of that opening. He soundly beat all of his challengers in a 1954 tour that more resembled a round-robin than the undercard and prime-time format Kramer had used for himself when he played. Gonzales won a total of eighty-five matches compared to Segura's seventy-four and Sedgman's sixty-five. Budge, Riggs, and Earn won only two singles matches between themselves. The tournament format made for a mixed picture in that one player might lose in the stop's semifinal match one night and at the next stop win two matches in a row over two different opponents. The games of some players might match up well against all the competitors save one who would consistently beat that player. Kramer did his best to run the tour with a seasoned hand to try to prevent one professional from consistently dominating the others to a degree that the gate receipts might suffer.[41]

The tour format also kept the players' finances in check, because they were paid only if they won the two matches at each stop as opposed to a contract guarantee or option of a percentage of the gate receipt that the promoter had to meet. Whereas the professional champion may previously have secured upward of $70,000 for winning the tour, the round-robin tournament meant that after seventy two-night tournaments—in effect more matches than had ever taken place on a professional tour before—the champion Gonzales, who won twenty-nine of those seventy events, took home $39,425, a little more than half of what he had earned when he went down in defeat four years earlier in the 1949–1950 tour. Moreover, more players on the tour meant more professionals in the spotlight and more confusion among sponsors about who to endorse. From Kramer's standpoint, that was all to the better because he could hide behind having won the last tour in which he had fully competed and keep his contracts with Wilson Sporting Goods and other companies intact. The new round-robin format did not give the same conclusiveness of results that the previous challenger-versus-champion format had. The lesser professionals did not seem to mind the round-robin format, because the previous challenger champion had allowed for only two prime-time players paid on guarantees or gate percentages and two undercard players paid on weekly salaries. All players could now compete for the dollars, and the prize-money results showed a more equitable distribution than any previous tour: $1,550 for Earn; $2,125 for Riggs; $3,170 for Kramer; $12,050 for Budge; $31,025 for Sedgman; $31,025 for Segura; and $39,425 for Gonzales. Given that even the tour's last-place finisher, Earn, made $1,550 more than he would have as an amateur tennis player, the round-robin format was attractive—attractive, that is, to everyone except the winner, Gonzales, who in rising to the top now wanted a chance to show his dominance and be paid accordingly.[42]

The professional tour of late 1955–1956 would more closely resemble Gonzales's first professional tour in 1949–1950 in that the world's number one amateur-turned-professional to challenge the World's Professional Champion. This time Gonzales was the champion and Tony Trabert was the challenger. Along with Trabert, Kramer had convinced the Australian amateur doubles champion, Rex Hartwig, to turn professional in order to compete against the most entertaining of all the professionals, Segura, in the preliminary match. Kramer tried to adapt the format of each tour to suit the particular players competing that year. For example, in the 1955–1956 tour he knew that Segura would soundly defeat Hartwig, so he kept their match short, at only one set. He expected a close series between Gonzales and Trabert, so the main-event match would be best three out of five sets. Hartwig's doubles skills would feature in the doubles contest, which he increased from previous years to the best two out of three sets.[43]

Kramer also justified why he had again decided to skip playing in the tour. It came down to the stamina that Kramer lacked to play the "100 match series." When the players practiced, Big Jake laced up the boots, strung the racquets, and hit with them should an injury ever force him to "step in and fill the breech," but laying out a second season made clear to everyone who followed competitive tennis that Kramer's playing career had come to an end. He had won four tours, the same number as Don Budge and two fewer than Ellsworth Vines, but over those four years Kramer had played four hundred tour matches in addition to the selected tournaments and random exhibitions the professionals played. His body was breaking down, and the baton passed to Pancho Gonzales. Yet Gonzales still had something to prove to everyone despite his past results: he had won fourteen out of the past eighteen "major pro titles," which included the Nationals at Cleveland, the Internationals at Cleveland, the Miami Beach Professional Championships, the Los Angeles Professional Championships, the International Professional Championships at Wembley Stadium, the National Indoor Championships at Philadelphia, and the National Hard Court Championships in Beverly Hills. He won the 1954 world's professional tour against the world's six best professionals with the most lethal shot in the sport, a 112-mile-per-hour serve—the fastest in recorded history.[44]

Kramer and Gonzales needed each other, so the promoter went looking for the best players to compete against his new professional champion. Early headhunting did not go well when on October 17, 1955, the Australian amateur champions Ken Rosewall and Lew Hoad publicly walked back their decision to turn professional. While competing in the United States for the defense of the Davis Cup, Rosewall and Hoad agreed to a behind-closed-doors offer from Kramer for a guaranteed twenty thousand pounds apiece for a professional tour against Big Jake and Tony Trabert. Once back in Australia, however, LTAA officers applied pressure to the Slazenger and Dunlop sporting goods companies, which employed Rosewall and Hoad, to increase the players' compensation to a level Kramer could not match. Slazenger went on to promise Rosewall the job security that professional tennis did not give with a five-year contract, an employee option to cancel the contract without penalty, and an executive position with the firm following his full-time playing days. To persuade Hoad against professionalism, the LTAA dangled what amounted to a blank check for tennis-related travel to Hoad; his wife, Jenny; and his family.[45]

Kramer considered legal action. He produced contracts Hoad and Rosewall had signed for the professional tour. The LTAA produced contracts the players had signed prohibiting them from professional tennis. But Kramer realized the difficulty of litigation against popular athletes from another country, especially when the sporting goods companies also held employment contracts for each player that predated Kramer's contract. In addition, both players had been minors when they signed his contract without the binding signatures of their legal guardians. Kramer instead decided to try a carrot of his own with a red-eye flight to Sydney in order to sweeten the pot. When Dunlop stepped in again to offer more compensation to their player consultants, Kramer packed his bags and returned empty-handed. Rosewall and Hoad decided to stay away from the grueling reality of the professional tour until they were more prepared than Gonzales had been back in 1949.[46]

Kramer succeeded where other promoters failed because as a player-turned-promoter he knew his sport and knew how to manage his professionals. Two decades in the game had helped him refine the player contract that served as the principal mechanism he used to manage the strong-minded Gonzales and his fellow players. Whereas he had previously offered guarantees for a minimum income to entice players to join his tour, by the fall of 1953 Kramer felt self-assured enough to court globally known professional players such as the Czechoslovakian-turned-Egyptian and onetime world's best amateur, Jaroslav Drobný, to whom he offered a contract without a minimum compensation figure.[47] Contractual terms with the tour promoter mattered just as much if not more than match attendance, because without good terms for the player, any additional gate receipts could go right into the hands of the promoter. Donald Dell, a former amateur tennis champion, friend of Kramer, and a sports agent who managed professional athletes, nicknamed Kramer "the czar of tennis" because the long experience Kramer had in professional tennis would give him influence to wield over the future of the game as tennis opened in 1968.[48]

Kramer certainly used his player contracts first and foremost to benefit himself, but he did do some good by the players in helping to found the International Professional Tennis Players' Association (IPTPA) in Los Angeles during June 1960. Kramer realized that after his retirement from play at the end of 1953 and his sole focus on managing and promoting the top four professional players for his WPTI tours, he had created some antagonism with the players, who believed they drew the fans and therefore were entitled to a greater split of the gates than manager Kramer offered. His solution was to make the players greater stakeholders in their tennis enterprise. Kramer invited Butch Buchholz, Andrés Gimeno, Rod Laver, Kenneth Rosewall, and Tony Trabert to join the IPTPA.[49] The association's by-laws and constitution stated a greater goal of mutual cooperation with the ILTF in bringing about open tennis competition between amateurs and professionals throughout the world. Two years after its founding, the organization claimed twenty-three members across a half dozen countries, in effect the best tennis players on the planet.[50]

Those players could now run the professional tennis tour themselves. This suited Kramer just fine, because by the spring of 1962 he was tired of promoting the sport. In March he shuttered his Los Angeles offices—a quick process given that the only payroll he had to meet consisted of himself and his immediate family members who had kept his accounts. The option clause in the players' contracts allowed Kramer to step away in quick order without having to meet any further financial obligations to the Australian professionals Lew Hoad, Frank Sedgman, Ashley Cooper, and Mal Anderson. All effectively entered free agency, while Pancho Segura relocated to Los Angeles to run the tennis program at the Beverly Hills Country Club. Pancho Gonzales likewise retired from touring to direct the tennis program at Paradise Island Bahamas. The former amateur champion and professional touring player Tony Trabert tried to organize a professional tour. Without any top-card American players to recruit from amateur ranks or within the professionals themselves, Trabert decided to work with the four Australian free agents; sign Australian professional Ken Rosewall, who had spent a good deal of 1961 retired from touring; and attempt to draw more top Australian players, who had dominated amateur tennis in the early 1960s, into the professional ranks. Both Neale Fraser and Roy Emerson declined professional contract offers, but the IPTPA landed the biggest name in world tennis in December 1962 when fresh off of a fourth consecutive Davis Cup win, Grand Slam champion Rod Laver joined the professionals.[51]

The recruitment of Laver brought the first player since Don Budge to have won the Grand Slam to the tour at a time when professional tennis desperately needed a fresh face. Everyone expected a positive impact on professional tennis because of Laver's talent. Less apparent, however, to anyone except those on the inside was the discord among the players at that time. Trabert's deep dislike of Gonzales made his choice to work with the Australian players as much a personal decision as a business one. Trabert considered the Australians agreeable and the future of tennis; he thought Pancho was surly and the past. While Gonzales had made his own decision to enter retirement with Kramer's retirement, he did so expecting that the professional tour would go away with Kramer. Trabert's resumption of the tour without giving Gonzales, the reigning professional champion, a chance to join on favorable terms prompted Pancho to channel his anger into a lawsuit that found its way to a federal court in Southern California.[52]

That 1963 case laid bare the fragility of professional tennis in the pre-1968 era as the players squabbled among themselves for the little bit of money in the game. Unfortunately for the petitioner Pancho, his counsel did not adequately explain to the judge just how little money there was in playing tennis professionally. The lawyer failed to reveal that a small clique of players (about half a dozen) in a larger group of three hundred tennis professionals actually earned income from playing matches. More importantly, they monopolized that revenue source. He further failed to demonstrate that Gonzales's fellow professionals were guilty of envy if not discrimination. They deeply resented the position Pancho had held as the tour champion from 1954 to his first retirement in 1961. Along with his 1954 and 1955–1956 wins, Gonzales defeated Ken Rosewall fifty to twenty-six matches in 1957; Lew Hoad fifty-one to thirty-six matches in 1958; Mal Anderson, Ashley Cooper, and Lew Hoad in a 1959 round-robin; Ken Rosewall, Alex Olmedo, and Pancho Segura in a 1960 round-robin; as well as a half dozen challengers in 1961 to retain his supremacy as the world's best professional tennis player. Yet here he was, seemingly at the end of his career, suing competitors he had bested on the court for scraps.[53]

Near the conclusion of Pancho's suit against his fellow professionals, the judge spoke. "My judgement of Mr. Gonzales is he is a pretty good business man. I don't know how good a tennis player he is but he is an excellent business man," explained Judge Charles Carr.[54] In that decision, at least, the judge was completely wrong. Gonzales played a great game of tennis, but in the business of professional sport he failed miserably. He beat all the best players in the world throughout most of the 1950s and into the early '60s, a decade at the top of the game, yet he fared financially worse than players he crushed on the court. Racism was an important factor. Pancho's income in 1963 was a pittance by the standards of the top handful of athletes in a global sport, but that income accurately reflected the outsider status of professional tennis. He earned twenty-five thousand dollars for four months of seasonal employment at the Paradise Island Bahamas resort, where he taught tennis to rich tourists, his principal source of income. He earned fifteen thousand dollars a year from the Spalding company for his Pancho Gonzales Signature racquet and endorsements of other sporting goods products. His status as the top-draw tennis player in the world also netted an additional income of four thousand dollars in media appearances and five thousand dollars in tournament guarantees, which together put his total income in the last year of his real tennis form at forty-nine thousand dollars. He was thirty-five years old.[55]

The reality of Gonzales's money troubles appeared in sharp relief when compared to the generation of players who peaked right after he did. Pancho dominated professional tennis for the better part of a decade, but he did not own the sport. There was not much to own. Few television contracts, limited corporate sponsorships, and inadequate tournament venues kept the best players in the world playing points for pennies. Tour promoter Jack Kramer retained the lion's share of what professional tennis made during that decade. Barred from returning to subsidized amateur competition, Gonzales and his fellow touring professionals had little recourse but to begrudgingly accept a sport that was not yet ready to reach its true potential. That would begin to change in 1968.

CHAPTER 9

Tennis Opens

Pancho Gonzales's on-again-off-again retirement from professional tennis helped propel the sport into the doldrums during the early 1960s. People attended matches to see the familiar champion. Kramer's withdrawal from managing the tour also mattered. He was the only person truly experienced in managing the more than one hundred separate appearances the group made across six continents. The players tried to compensate for both of these absences by creating a tournament circuit with far fewer dates and venues to replace the more peripatetic touring days of WPTI. That changed format seemed especially necessary because the professional players now managed themselves in the IPTPA, which purported to organize prize-money events for any player who belonged to the association and wished to compete. Although real equality never materialized in practice, the IPTPA did have a number of more active professional players competing for prize money than Kramer ever had without any of the carrot-and-stick contracts he deployed to control his players during the 1950s.[1]

Yet the pickings were still small; the professionals remained divided between those who taught the sport for a living and those who played the sport for a living. A slightly larger number than in previous decades but still little more than a handful of professional players toured, playing matches night after night. The balance of the tennis professionals, usually around two hundred people in the United States, mostly taught tennis and hoped for a "professional tournament circuit." Noel Brown, one of the professionals without a place to play, found the situation so discouraging that he appealed to the USLTA for reinstatement of his amateur status, which he received after forswearing professional tennis and serving a two-year probationary period before being granted remittance to the amateur ranks. "The future of professional tennis is dismal, from the point of view of a pro circuit," remarked Brown. "There is always room for the National Champion in an organized four-man pro tour, but the pros offer nothing to the lesser player who is still interested in playing tournaments."[2]

Brown knew. He had tried to make a living as a professional for four years. Beginning in autumn 1946, as one of the top ten players in the country and a collegiate standout for UCLA, Brown decided to make a living as a professional, with ruinous financial consequences. Passed over by Kramer and Riggs for their tour, Brown taught lessons for six dollars an hour on the private Beverly Hills courts of clients such as William Wyler, Robert Parrish, Elia Kazan, Laurence Olivier, Coleen Gray, Jose Ferrer, and Montgomery Clift. He liked the work but missed playing. He knew that he had no job security and no means for promotion in what equated to life as an independent contractor. Three or four lessons a day were the most any freelance professional ever secured in Los Angeles—the tennis capital of the country in the mid-twentieth century. Even in major tennis areas like Southern California and Southeast Florida, only a handful of tennis clubs existed with a membership and grounds to support a professional looking to teach and raise a family: the LATC in Los Angeles, the La Jolla Beach and Tennis Club in La Jolla, California; the Boca Raton Club and Hotel, and the Hollywood Beach Hotel in Florida, as examples. More club professional positions existed along the private tennis, cricket, and athletic clubs and resorts along the Mid-Atlantic and Northeast, but here class privilege often meant that the club professional's treatment and compensation did not rise above that of "hired help." Unless a player had the game of Jack Kramer, Pancho Gonzales, Ken Rosewall, or Rod Laver, with a personality to match, it made more financial sense to remain in the amateur ranks, where small subsidies and allowances appeared with surprising regularity.[3] Even for the best players and their promoters, professional tennis was not that great to them before 1968.

Themselves riven with rivalries, the professional players failed to mount a substantive tour of the United States in 1962. The following year the IPTPA organized a robust "fifty match round robin series" followed by a final round of matches between the top two winners and the consolation finishers. They also returned to the West Side Tennis Club in Forest Hills to play a professional world tournament in 1963. The next year the IPTPA again did not organize a barnstorming series of the United States, but the professionals did play a busy schedule abroad in Australia, New Zealand, Europe, and Africa, in addition to a schedule of seven professional tournaments in America with the addition of an important new competition, the U.S. Professional Grass Court Championship, at Boston's hallowed Longwood Cricket Club. In 1965 the IPTPA organized a series of professional tournaments that carried an average purse of ten thousand dollars divided across a sixteen-player draw. The one thousand dollars the first-place finisher earned for a half week of work barely covered his expenses in many parts of the world. Since the early 1960s, the finances supporting the tournaments had improved somewhat, but most everything else behind the events remained touch-and-go. The promotions of the events, or rather the lack thereof, caused spectators to confuse the 7th Regiment Armory with the 71st Regiment Armory when the troupe played New York City in the early summer of 1965. One professional, Barry MacKay, woke to nightmares of crowds crushing him in the cramped quarters where the players performed, only to find the real nightmare of actually playing in front of only two hundred fans. Lew Hoad and other older professionals continued to draw fans, but they sometimes withdrew from important events, such as a CBS televised tournament in Dallas, at the last moment because their body or mind simply could no longer take the day-to-day grind of life on the road in front of what seemed like dwindling crowds. Such last-minute withdrawals left fellow professionals playing in front of hostile or smaller crowds who were upset that the player they most wanted to see had bailed at the final moments.[4]

The IPTPA only ever counted around 20 players as members. Out of that number, only about 10 participated in exhibitions, tournaments, or tours put on by the organization. The USPLTA, by contrast, counted 268 members in 1963, but these teaching professionals rarely played outside of their lessons and a handful of local or regional tournaments at tennis and country clubs. Not only did the professional players and the professional coaches not really work together, but some of the most important professional players of earlier years—names like Don Budge, Frank Parker, Fred Perry, and Bobby Riggs—did not belong to the IPTPA. On balance, the professionals could not pay nor police themselves let alone negotiate with the USLTA, LTA, and ITHF for open tennis from any sort of position of strength—a competitive weakness that, ironically, helped the case of open tennis.[5]

Frailty and factionalism of the professionals attracted the attention of out-siders who saw opportunities to better organize and promote the players. At the same time, the national amateur associations became so divided over the long-simmering debate of open tennis that the ILTF could no longer punt on that important topic. Disunity among and between both the amateur and professional leaders of the sport had prevailed from Suzanne Lenglen's playing days through those of Bill Tilden, Jack Kramer, and Pancho Gonzales. Those discrepancies would only increase, however, with the unprecedented forth-coming flow of money into the sport.[6] Sports promoters from outside orga-nized tennis saw opportunities to make money in the game, because disunity within and between national amateur associations had reached a degree that open tennis seemed a real possibility by the mid-1960s. Over the next decade, the competition and compromise between insiders and those outsiders made that possibility into modern professional tennis. The Open Era was on the way.

The most tradition-bound of all the national associations actually did the most to bring about open tennis in the years leading up to 1968. Modern sport began in Britain in the eighteenth and nineteenth centuries and then spread throughout the world, thanks to Britain's colonialization efforts and empire building. That geopolitical development assigned to Wimbledon a great deal of symbolic weight for the British and foreigners alike. Before World War II the English crowds at Wimbledon (also known as SW19) had a reputation for restrained applause and general appreciativeness to competitors from any-where in the world. After 1945, however, Wimbledon fans earned a reputation for the reproach of foreign players. Strangely, given that they were allies during the war, British spectators tended to treat American players more harshly than athletes from any other country, as several players made clear: "They would like to see the Americans lose," remarked Indian player Narranda Nah; "Yes, they are anti-American," said Violette Rigollet Alvensleben of Belgium; "I don't think they like the Americans," stated Frenchman Jean-Claude Molinari. In the 1948 doubles final, featuring Gardnar Mulloy and Tom Brown of the United States versus John Bromwich and Frank Sedgman of Australia, the British fans broke all tennis protocol by applauding wildly after service faults by the American team. In that match, along with each match that involved Americans, the Wimbledon fans reenacted the decline of the British Empire and the ascent of the United States as a world power. "It is because of Empire," said English player Gem Hoahing when asked why the British had changed the way they cheered. For a quarter of a century since the Englishman Fred Perry had last won the Wimbledon Championships, in 1936, Britain endured not only the drought of a national champion but also watched while Australia and the United States competed in nearly every Davis Cup Challenge Round in the postwar period. The serious consideration the LTA gave in 1961 to hosting an open tournament without the ILTF's blessing exemplified a willingness on the part of British elites, some of whom also served in positions within the government, to reassert sovereignty over the governance of the game and to take a measure of pride in the face of waning influence.[7]

In the recent past, pride and insecurity had prompted the LTA to thwart attempts by other national associations to bring about open tennis. As far back as 1930 the USLTA had brought the idea of open tennis to the ILTF in the midst of the swirling controversy of the great American Bill Tilden's Davis Cup suspension and decision to turn professional. The resolution stalled until 1934 when USLTA president Louis Carruthers again broached the idea of amateur and professional competition. Once again open tennis went down to defeat. The Depression and World War II kept open tennis off the radar until after 1945, when the aggressive professional touring and promoting of Bobby Riggs and Jack Kramer soured a number of tennis officials on the character of professional tennis. By 1961, however, Kramer had mostly left the picture, and USLTA officials revived Carruthers's 1934 open tennis resolution and presented it to the ILTF. The Fédéderation Française de Lawn Tennis and the Lawn Tennis Association of Great Britain effectively killed the USLTA's push for open tennis, divided the USLTA sections over open tennis, and embittered tennis officials in the United States against their British counterparts. Several years later the British would need the cooperation of the Americans they had not long ago spurned.[8]

At first many members of the ILTF did not believe that the highly conservative AELTC would come out in favor of open tennis. The Wimbledon host retained only between three hundred and four hundred total members and admitted a new member to full status only after a fifteen-year probationary period. The titled nobility who comprised a significant proportion of the club's membership roll certainly favored tradition in most other walks of their lives, while the new-money members likewise valued the tradition of Wimbledon for the prestige that heritage imparted on their own social statuses. Tradition cut both ways, however. Since the mid-1920s, the LTA had allowed, as historian Robert J. Lake has noted, "amateurs and coaching professionals" on court together in doubles competitions. In 1930 the LTA went on record with the ILTF in favor of a very limited schedule of open tennis matches. This support again came from a fairly conservative position of professional coach versus professional player.[9]

In the interwar period and accelerating into the postwar years, many tennis enthusiasts within Britain could not help but wring their hands over how lawn tennis had languished in the land that invented it when compared to the successes of other nations such as America and Australia on the international scene. As Great Britain failed year after year to advance to the Davis Cup Challenge Round, the LTA began to rely almost entirely on the Wimbledon Championships to subsidize all tennis activity in England. Even after some efforts to expand the tournament grounds, by the 1960s capacity crowds of thirty thousand people attended most days of the tournament's fortnight, prompting the AELTC and the LTA, their partners in running the tournament and sharing revenue, to return more than $250,000 in presale tickets to fans who had requested tickets but could not be accommodated during that year's tournament. Total monies collected by the LTA from the tournament approximated $140,000 annually by the 1960s. That number alone outvoted the hundred councilors from across the country who decided the policies of the LTA. With the wishes of the Wimbledon Championships Committee of Management, stacked with AELTC members who were firmly in favor of open tennis, the many members of the LTA who were opposed to open tennis consoled themselves with the history that when cricket began open competition, the sport had still retained much of its heritage while also improving its revenue stream. They hoped for the same with tennis.[10]

The leadership of the LTA understood that Wimbledon was a jewel in its crown that put the organization in a unique position to press for open tennis compared to other national amateur associations making up the ILTF. Most ILTF member nations hosted their own national championships that invited popular foreign players to attend in order to increase the revenue the associations collected at the tournament gates. At the same time, few of these tournaments offered the players much in terms of expenses, while many of the associations ran the tournaments in a sloppy fashion that frustrated the international players to the point of not attending, had the players had a choice in the matter. In fact, they did not have much of a choice, because the real value in the ILTF came in the unity of the amateur associations at the expense of the players within different national associations. For example, players despised the poorly run Italian Championships to the point that the tournament would have folded long before 1965 had the Federazione Italiana Tennis (FIT) not asked the ILTF to direct other member countries to require their own players to attend the tournament. The attendance of the international players, despite their own frustration with the situation, prompted more spectators to attend the Italian Championships than otherwise would have. That in turn put the FIT in a better financial situation, having run a more profitable tournament without investing money in actually improving the experience for the players. That situation was not uncommon among national associations within the ILTF.[11]

Not surprisingly, most of the smaller countries that ran smaller national championships offered little in the way of player expenses. They wanted to see nothing change in how the ILTF conducted business. In the fall of 1965, then, the LTA planned to move slowly in bringing other countries around to open tennis. The first tournament allowing amateurs and professionals to play could take place in the summer of 1966 or perhaps not even until 1967, and then a few more open tournaments would appear on the schedule each year. The British plan of gradualism and compromise proved difficult to execute, primarily because the memberships of other national amateur associations were themselves divided over open tennis.[12]

Such was the case in the United States for years. The USLTA's national office failed to control Kramer's professional tennis players and struggled to keep the association's various sections under its control. Those shortcomings finally cracked the long-standing opposition to open tennis within the USLTA, the ILTF's largest member nation. In 1956 the USLTA celebrated its "Diamond Jubilee" not at the traditional site of the annual meeting in New York City but in San Francisco, in what one meeting attendee called a testament to the "growing power" of the West Coast sections of the association. There, representatives from the 193 California tennis clubs realized that if they joined with clubs from the Pacific Northwest, Southwest, Mountain States, Midwest, and South, they could easily defeat the votes held by the 213 Eastern section clubs. They did so the following winter, sweeping New Yorker Renville McCann out of the top position in the association in favor of Seattle financier Victor Dinny. Dinny replaced the officers from the East Coast and Mid-Atlantic with his own retainers, who ranged from Chicago to Florida. The highest-profile removal that Dinny made concerned the holy-of-holies of amateurism in American tennis: the Davis Cup. Bill Talbert, a former player turned coach, had led the Davis Cup team since 1953. Although the 1954 team defeated Australia, the squad put together by the famous Australian coach Harry Hopman had won seven of the previous eight challenge rounds. By 1958 Dinny decided to make a change. With one phone call he replaced the flabbergasted Talbert with Perry T. Jones, a surprise move, given Talbert's pedigree as both a champion player and a proven match-situation coach compared to Jones's strength as an organizer rather than an on-court tactician. Jones got the job done, though, and the Davis Cup returned to the United States from Australia in 1958. That victory brought Dinny a great deal of goodwill from conservatives within the USLTA in terms of pushing other reforms centered on player expenses and amateurism.[13]

At the annual meeting of the ILTF during the first week of July in 1960, voting members seemed ready to allow open competition between amateur players and professionals for the first time. Perry T. Jones's popularity on the national tennis scene allowed him to convince many reticent USLTA voters that Kramer had no designs to monopolize the sport should the United States back the prospect of open competition. Australia, France, and Great Britain, along with the United States, collectively represented the big four tennis nations. Those countries produced most of the world's top players and had won every Davis Cup competition since the event began in 1900. All agreed and voted in favor of the open tennis resolution, though Britain and France chose not to exercise their sizable influence over other European countries, which would have resulted in a landslide victory for the American-championed open tennis resolution. Other countries saw the matter differently, however. Spain's fear of losing their top player, Andrées Gimeno, to a Kramer contract single-handedly led that country's members to vote against the proposed rule changes. Open tennis in 1960 fell only five votes short of the necessary two-thirds supermajority. That autumn a sportswriter opined that the sport of tennis had reached its "low point," and over the next half decade many USLTA members wrote to the association's leadership with much the same views.[14]

Jack Kramer, for one, certainly agreed with that assessment. He fervently believed that ILTF members had voted more against Jack Kramer than they did against open tennis. Some members of the ILTF admitted as much. Reluctant supporters within the USLTA of the 1960 open tennis legislation returned to their normal tennis activities. Perry T. Jones, for example, began devoting his energy to attracting the U.S. National Championships from Forest Hills to the LATC. USLTA conservatives opposed to open tennis had their biases confirmed with the 1960 no vote, and they redoubled their efforts to keep money out of the game, or at least money they did not control out of the game. Between 1963 and 1966 the USLTA in effect voted for a gag rule on the issue of open tennis when the topic arose at the ILTF annual meeting.[15]

Yet change was on the horizon, with the LTA proposing to the ILTF a semantic change from amateur versus professional to a single category of "players," out of which applications could be made for tournament travel and training expenses in a more transparent and less under-the-table way. Jean Borotra, the former French amateur-champion-turned-FFT-director-and-ILTF-official, urged refining the player designation category. In his formulation, a "Special Committee" would meet to designate a player who was acceptable—in the view of the various national associations and the International Tennis Federation (ITF)—to receive traveling stipends and living expenses throughout the year. Such semantics did not actually solve the "hypocrisy of sham-amateurism" that was constitutive of topflight international tennis for more than half a century, but Borotra's words and the policies that followed gently nudged tennis toward open competition at the same time the vote tallies of ILTF member nations told a different story.[16]

As before, the AELTC considered letting professionals onto their courts only if the tournament committee worked directly with the players and had nothing to do with Kramer. His aggressive recruitment of Australian amateur champions Roy Emerson and Rod Laver further soured the mood for open tennis, because the LTAA felt compelled to pay its players unmatchable expenses to remain amateurs at the same time the ILTF had sought unanimity from national associations in piloting their new player expense structure. By 1960, top Australian players were accustomed to Australian sporting goods companies putting up one hundred thousand pounds per year for player expenses. When decreased Davis Cup revenue from the Australians' near-perpetual hosting of the challenge round dwindled in the mid-1960s, Australian businessman and tennis fan Bob Mitchell bankrolled Australian tennis players at four thousand pounds per player, which, combined with money from the LTAA and other sources, proved enough to keep players like Roy Emerson, Ashley Cooper, and Margaret Smith Court amateurs playing for Australia rather than professionals playing for Jack Kramer. That practice put the differing agendas among different national associations within the ILTF into sharp relief in 1966 and ultimately delayed what many sports commentators thought was inevitable only a year before. Yet at the same time, contemporary officials in the USLTA, other national associations, and the ILTF missed the irony that the apotheosis of amateur tennis in the Davis Cup was the Trojan horse about to let the professional raiders in to sack their amateur stronghold.[17]

George MacCall's Davis Cup captaincy and Robert Kelleher's USLTA presidency during the mid-1960s pushed the USLTA away from the anti–open tennis stance they had maintained between 1963 and 1966 and toward greater amenability to the idea by 1967. For the first time in his life, Perry T. Jones began delegating some of his tennis responsibilities to others as the old SCTA leader started to slow in the early 1960s. Based in Los Angeles and with personal wealth and a flexible schedule from his insurance business, MacCall became one of Jones's protégés, performing some administrative duties for the Pacific Southwest Tournament and the SCTA. The USLTA named former Utah tennis champion David Freed as Davis Cup captain to replace the aging Jones in 1960, thanks to the voting alliance of the Mountain States section and the Pacific State section. Freed, however, proved an ineffective choice. The captaincy then passed to Robert Kelleher until the association believed Kelleher better served U.S. tennis in several vice president positions and as a delegate to the ILTF before his election to the USLTA presidency in 1967. George MacCall assumed the duties of Davis Cup captain in 1965.[18]

MacCall immediately set to bringing more money into amateur tennis by convincing the USLTA to bolster the budget for his handful of players from twenty-six thousand dollars to sixty-four thousand dollars. The investment did not pay off in terms of wresting the cup away from the Australians. In fact, under MacCall, the U.S. Davis Cup team suffered repeated pre–challenge round losses: first to Spain in 1965; then to Brazil in 1966; and, most disastrously for the reputation-conscious USLTA, to Ecuador in the Americas inter-zonal final in 1967. In defending himself from attacks both outside and within the USLTA, MacCall went on offense, stating that "nothing succeeds with the USLTA like failure" when asked by reporters about his records as Davis Cup captain in April 1967. With failure on the courts and finger-pointing in the press, MacCall started the summer with the job still his in all likelihood because he maintained strong relationships with most of his players. Both coach and players defended one another from outside threats, and that common defense created the camaraderie that MacCall soon put to his advantage in deciding to break away from the amateur ranks of the USLTA and forge his own tennis tour.[19]

In the fall of 1967 MacCall was ready to make his move. He signed many of the best players, because his position as the U.S. Davis Cup captain from 1965 to 1967 gave him access to America's and the world's best players at just the right moment. Arthur Ashe, for example, sought the counsel of his coach on whether or not to compete in the 1968 Wimbledon Championships when the ILTF had yet to affirm open tennis and therefore threatened disciplinary actions against any player who bucked the organization's authority. MacCall quickly named Pancho Gonzales coach of the 1965 squad because of Gonzales's successful coaching of the last U.S. Davis Cup squad to win the cup in 1963. MacCall's appointment of Gonzales built a working relationship between the semiretired professional champion and the upstart tennis promoter. Gonzales's regular practice sessions with the Davis Cup squad players at the LATC got the former champion back in playing shape. That led to MacCall's signing Gonzales as one of his first tennis professionals for his newly formed National Tennis League (NTL) and newly formed Tennis Championships Incorporated. A minimum guarantee of forty thousand dollars for a twenty-six-week season was much more money for much less work than Gonzales had earned as the number one player in the world under Kramer's control. MacCall used Kramer's technique of offering substantial guarantees to sign most of the top international players to his troupe at just the right time.[20]

Kramer's heavy-handed and at times underhanded management of his players resulted in myriad conflicts between the professionals and their promoter. In the main, though, Kramer's stern approach kept the big personalities of his players more or less in check, and that meant he could schedule a robust series of international tour dates, actually deliver his players to the events in order to keep sponsors happy, and in turn make sure his players were compensated well enough to keep them touring in the face of many obstacles. The same could not be said for the professionals in 1964, 1965, and 1966, when the players themselves—mainly led by Australians—more or less ran their own international tour, which increasingly focused on tournament tennis in the land down under. Kramer continued to promote a handful of tournaments in the United States and Great Britain that generally did quite well, but the players took the day-to-day management of the tour into their own hands through their shared IPTPA enterprise. In July 1966 that organization passed a code of conduct that stipulated fines for behavior infractions. Self-policing, however, meant individual professionals continued to do as they please.[21]

The year 1967 began in much the same inauspicious way, with the failure of the professionals to recruit top amateurs such as Roy Emerson and Tony Roche into the pay ranks. Emerson, Roche, and other amateurs maintained they could make more under the table than the guarantees they were offered to turn professional. These top amateurs likewise did not believe the professionals could actually deliver on the guarantees they made. Rod Laver, for example, went on record reporting that as a top amateur he earned "between $600 and $700" per week from the LTAA and various other sources. During the year he made around forty thousand dollars of tax-free money in a sport whose amateur bodies purported that no money outside of single figure per day's (and then only during select tournament weeks) expenses made it into players' pockets.[22]

That hypocrisy mattered more than ever to the professionals, because without new challengers to fill their ranks, people failed to turn up to watch the same matchups they saw before. Whereas during the Kramer tours of the 1950s, the professionals mainly toured in a group of four, by 1967 a dozen professionals wanted to play on at least a semiregular basis. Those numbers, combined with a lack of suitable venues to accommodate multiple matches, simultaneously forced the professionals to divide into two groups for the 1967 tours. A reduced schedule for each individual player made few of them happy, and the unwillingness of venues like Madison Square Garden—which professional tennis had been closely associated with since the tours of Suzanne Lenglen, Ellsworth Vines, and Fred Perry—to host the players for their opener further distressed the athletes. To a person they vocalized that distress in screeds against the ILTF, the LTAA, and the USLTA—the latter of which took steps at the start of 1967 toward paying top American amateurs' expenses equivalent to a full-time white-collar job. At the very moment when their tennis touring reached a nadir, the professionals catalyzed the cause of open tennis not through their actions but through their words. The willingness of Laver and other professionals to speak candidly to the sports press, particularly newspapers and magazines in Great Britain, about the secret payments they had received while playing as amateurs galled LTA officials and galvanized them to take action against amateur-shamateurism.[23]

Over the next year, that action culminated in tennis becoming one of the last major world sports—along with track and field and rugby—to allow open competition between amateurs and professionals. In the summer of 1967, the ILTF held its annual meeting at Mondorf-les-Bains, Luxembourg, where open tennis was up for a vote for the first time since 1961. The early tally looked like open tennis would carry with three of the four largest tennis nations—the United States, England, and Australia—in support. The latter defied LTAA president William "Big Bill" Edwards's conspicuous hatred of tennis professionals. All voted in favor of the resolution. The situation changed, however, when France mysteriously abstained from voting, and then smaller nations cast their votes. Every country in South America, Africa, Asia, the Middle East, and Eastern Europe voted no on open tennis. The resolution failed with 139 no votes to 83 in favor. While the LTA had expected solid opposition from the Soviet countries, whose state sponsorship of players amounted to professionalism in all but name, the lack of support from countries such as Italy, France, India, and Brazil had ultimately doomed the measure to defeat.[24]

Further inspired by the professional soccer players on England's 1966 World Cup winning squad, the LTA moved ahead undeterred in staging a speculative professional tournament at the grandest venue in tennis. Since his first year as a professional, Jack Kramer had spoken of his desire to get onto the lawn courts of the AELTC and play a professionals-only version of Wimbledon. Twenty years later, in August 1967, the LTA decided to make that happen in part because Kramer had all but exited the promotional business. The AELTC extended direct invitations to Rod Laver, Ken Rosewall, Andrés Gimeno, Dennis Ralston, Fred Stolle, and Pancho Gonzales, with an additional two spots to be determined by qualification matches. Some of these players had not entered the walled grounds of the AELTC as a spectator, let alone a player, since they had turned professional; all would now play for the largest tournament purse in professional tennis history, at £21,500. The tournament initially underperformed expectations; the short horizon of the preparations, the novelty of the event, and the lack of publicity led to only half of the seats on Centre Court filled on day one. Thirty-nine-year-old Pancho Gonzales and thirty-two-year-old Lew Hoad salvaged the tournament, though, with a spirited 3–6, 11–9, 8–6 match that repeatedly brought the crowd to their feet and left spectators wondering what they had been missing by not getting to see these two professionals on Centre Court, where the caliber of their play clearly evidenced that that was where they belonged. Centre Court remained "standing room only" for the remainder of the tournament as the BBC broadcast the matches in color television around the world. Laver won the singles, while Gonzales and Gimeno partnered to win the doubles. All the professionals walked away from the Wimbledon Professional Championships feeling good about the experience. In fact, the real winners of the Wimbledon Pro were the LTA and the AELTC, who now had the confirmation that an open tournament would prove a commercial success.[25]

That momentum carried into the turning point that made open tennis a reality. On October 4, 1967, the LTA decided to hold an open tournament despite the prohibition against such events by the ILTF. "We have hopes of not going it alone," said LTA president Judge Carl Aarvold, "but we have had no assurances from anyone." The boldness of the LTA action took other ILTF member nations by such surprise that assurances of any kind did not come for what felt like forever. To heighten the anxiety those opponents faced, the IPTPA had recently been restructured into a corporation with an elected board of directors that for the first time included managers from outside tennis. Those directors brought a more aggressive approach to dealing with infighting among the professionals and, more substantially, in terms of shaping the open tennis debate, a more aggressive approach to pressuring top amateur players to turn professional. In addition to the dozen professionals currently touring the world, the IPTPA board pursued the top twenty ranked amateurs so aggressively that amateur officials in countries like Australia expected they would lose at least half of their world-rated players to professionalism. That was enough to prompt leaders such as USLTA president Robert Kelleher to put the idea of open tennis to a USLTA sectional vote after his own executive committee defeated the measure twenty-two opposed to twenty-one in favor. The seventeen USLTA sections unanimously supported the idea, and the USLTA delegates felt free to offer quiet support for the LTA's open tennis agenda. Two years earlier the USLTA Executive Committee had paid private investigators to ferret out expenses paid to players under the table; now the USLTA sections voted unanimously that no open tennis position held by members of that committee was irrelevant.[26]

Most people who spoke up about the open tennis issue supported the LTA in its decision to make the 1968 Wimbledon Championships a tournament that was open to professionals. ILTF president Giorgio de Stefani's position that "a certain hypocrisy" on the part of the ILTF was preferable to the "antidemocratic and illegal action" of the LTA was well outside the mainstream. De Stefani expressed his intention to remove any country from the ILTF if those national associations did not enforce ILTF rules against open tennis on their players. He seemed more or less alone in his opinion that the Open Wimbledon tournament would prove such a financial flop that other countries would not even consider allowing professionals to play their own national championships. USLTA section association presidents from Richard Botsch in Delaware to Robert Kelleher in the national office spoke up in favor of the open Wimbledon. Amateur players, from Tony Roche in Australia, to Pierre Darmon in France, and Allen Fox in the United States, all voiced their intention to play the Open Wimbledon. Even recently retired professionals like

Lew Hoad announced their intention to get back into playing shape so that they could participate. Professional promoters both past and present—Jack Kramer, George MacCall, and David "Dave" Dixon, a recent arrival to the scene—all pledged the participation of the professional players. The only minority opinion that would matter was retired French Davis Cup player Bernard Destremau, who remarked that France "should organize a Roland Garros Open."[27]

That, it turned out, was exactly what happened. French tennis had languished at the world level since the days of Suzanne Lenglen and the glory years of the Four Musketeers. Lenglen had died thirty years earlier, in 1938, but Jean Borotra, Jacques Brugnon, Henri Cochet, and René Lacoste were all still living in 1968. Of the four, Jean Borotra remained the most involved in the administration of tennis in France and in the government of the ILTF. As president of the ILTF in 1961, Borotra put himself out in front of the open tennis debate when he conducted an important press conference on January 19 of that year, remarking that while the ILTF planned to continue to keep professionals away from amateurs, personally he favored open competition. George MacCall remembered those comments made to Chicago sportswriters when he visited Paris in 1965 with the U.S. Davis Cup team. Over the next two years, Borotra redoubled his efforts to push the FFT to lead on open tennis. Those efforts stalled until the LTA announced it would hold an Open Wimbledon in 1968.[28]

As with the Tennis Court Oath of 1789, the French relished a good revolution, and in March 1968 they whipped enough votes from the ILTF Committee of Management to sanction open tennis. The so-called Declaration of Principle stressed the "retention" of "amateurism" as the principle that guided the ILTF, the "right" of "self-determination" among member nations to categorize players as amateurs or professionals as they saw fit, and the tight cap on the number of "open tournaments" allowed by the ILTF. The *digestif* the French proposed that helped other nations swallow such sweeping reforms was the category of the "authorized player"—that is, a player allowed by his or her national association, and thus the ILTF, to accept an unlimited amount of expenses and other remuneration without forfeiting his or her amateur status, thus remaining eligible to play in both open tournaments and those closed to professionals, especially the Davis Cup. What an authorized or registered player compared to a professional would actually mean in practice would take several more years to clarify, but in the meantime French tennis officials felt they could move ahead with holding Roland-Garros as the first important open tournament just weeks before Wimbledon.[29]

The French had less than two months before their big tournament. Borotra's primary contact became MacCall, whom he knew and with whom he knew most of the top professionals remained under contract. The FFT authorized a first offer of twenty thousand dollars in guaranteed prize money. The low figure surprised MacCall and his players, who held long-standing beliefs about how financially lucrative each of the four major championships were for the sponsoring amateur bodies. The professionals failed to take into account that, compared to Wimbledon and the U.S. National Championships, the French Championships seldom recorded a big profit for the FFT. More importantly, the involvement of the professionals reintroduced the key concern of tax liability that shaped the policies of the private clubs that made up the amateur associations. Having no precedent in tennis for the division of taxable prize money to professionals, nontaxable expenses to the authorized players and amateurs, and partially taxable revenue to the FFT, Borotra and his fellow officials preferred conservative accountancies.[30]

Offers and counteroffers between the FFT and MacCall kept an open French Championship an unresolved question days before the May 27, 1968, tournament start. In the interim, a tournament took place in Bournemouth, England, from April 22 to April 27 where professionals and amateurs played against one another in an event sanctioned by a national amateur tennis association. The British Hard Court Championships thus technically became the first open tournament, but the significance of that event is that it catalyzed the professionals and the FFT to work out a deal. MacCall finally gave way on demanding close to the same purse for his professionals that the far more consistently profitable Wimbledon offered the NTL stars. Likewise, the FFT agreed to pay the professionals lavish expenses in addition to prize money—a compensation structure the professionals preferred because it minimized their income taxes.[31]

Upheavals spread around the world in 1968. Major social and political revolutions in the United States, Poland, Mexico, Nigeria, Spain, Israel and Palestine, and Czechoslovakia, among other countries, as well as military interventions, particularly in Vietnam, bucked the stability of nation-states the world over. Roland-Garros was played in the middle of massive riots throughout France and centered in Paris. MacCall's professional players had to fly into Brussels, Belgium, and then travel via bus to Paris. Laver, Emerson, and Stolle received special permission to land at a U.S. Air Force airfield near Paris. Many of the world's top amateurs skipped the French Open to play the far smaller Berlin Championships both as a protest of the presence of the professionals at Roland-Garros and because of the significant logistical challenges of getting to the Parisian red clay courts. The competitors shared towels because the launderers in the city remained on strike, and the tournament did not serve the customary afternoon tea because electric rationing made cooking and hot water unavailable during those hours. Police and demonstrators clashed in the streets. One-fifth of the 128 men in the draw defaulted their first-round matches because gas rationing meant having to walk to the tournament. The smell of food rotting along the avenues wafted through the stadium. Open tennis seemed poised to fail at its beginning.[32]

Yet the fans came in droves to watch the competitors, both amateur and professional, play brilliantly against one another. Perhaps because Parisians had nothing else to do but protest, perhaps because they wanted to watch the professionals play the amateurs, more fans attended Roland-Garros in 1968 than even in the halcyon days of French tennis, when Lenglen danced on the courts and the Four Musketeers won the Davis Cup for all of France. That the crowds came to watch the professionals play in a place of such tennis tradition became clear by the quarterfinals, in which five of the remaining eight players were professionals. Out of retirement, forty-year-old Pancho Gonzales, the literal grandfather of the game, won a five-set grind against the reigning number one amateur in the world, Roy Emerson, a victory that left an overexuberant sportswriter claiming the French viewed Gonzales's effort equal to that of "General [Charles] de Gaulle."[33]

Just as President de Gaulle weathered the strikes of that May to find his political career end in resignation a year later, so too did Gonzales's victory come to a quick end at the hands of Rod Laver after such a stirring victory. Laver then lost a mediocre final to fellow Australian Ken Rosewall, who raised the trophy of the first major Open Championships. All the professionals won, however, because they had finally come back to play the courts where they belonged. The best facilities should have the best players, the professionals had argued for years, and the pocketbooks of the fans who came to watch the 1968 Open Championships validated that claim. During the first five days in 1967, the French Championships reported 13,000 francs in gate receipts. That number increased more than 1,000 percent in 1968 to 142,000 francs. Even a competitor as fierce as Gonzales considered the 50 percent stake in the gate that he and the half dozen other professionals under contract received to be a victory.[34]

Strangely, the professionals' promoter had a different view about winning and losing. Losses on the court rather than in the accounting ledgers were the chief concern MacCall carried with him in the early days of NTL. He knew full well that any new enterprise might incur debt while the concept found its footing with a public willing to pay. But every time one of his contract players lost to an amateur player, he wondered aloud whether or not a spectator would continue to find paying extra to see a professional worth it. Too many defeats of his professionals at the hands of amateurs would embolden the ILTF to reverse its course change to open tennis and ruin MacCall financially. The conservatives who had long balked at money in tennis might be proven right after all. Such fears weighed heavily on MacCall's players every time they took to the court. The history associated with the AELTC setting added pressure to the professionals who competed in the 1968 Wimbledon Championships.[35]

At forty years old, Pancho Gonzales stood no chance to win Wimbledon that year. Memories of him as the best professional player for so many years and the number one player in the world at the time of his effective retirement in the early 1960s, however, led many to hold unrealistic expectations for Gonzales. Fans carried those same expectations for all the professionals. Unlike the predictable grind of consistent tennis on the slow red clay of Roland-Garros, the slick grass courts of the AELTC always produced more uncertainty throughout the tournament fortnight. Players very seldom lost serve. If they did, their opponent more often than not ran out the set. A dark horse with a hot hand could down a champion, because hour-long matches often came down to only a handful of big points. Physicality mattered in a far different way than on red clay, where the fittest player usually won. Early summer in England meant frequent rain delays and sometimes cool conditions that combined to cause not infrequent injuries in even the fittest of athletes. As the oldest seed in the draw, Gonzales competed more against time than against his younger opponents, and his third-round four-set loss to Russia's Alex Metreveli seemed to have surprised him less than it did the fans who were excited to see the old champion play his first Wimbledon since 1949. The bigger surprise was the early exit of both amateur and professional seeds, so that amateurs made up half of the field of the round of sixteen, professionals the other. In the final, veteran professional Rod Laver beat young professional Tony Roche in straight sets to lift the title, but as with the French Championships, the real winner of the first Open Wimbledon was tennis in general. Whereas Roland-Garros proved that open tennis could make money, Wimbledon demonstrated that open tennis could grow without forsaking tradition. Top amateurs might not beat the best professionals in the end, but they could win matches and not get blown off the court. Moreover, the game was bigger than the biggest names, either amateur or professional, and as with all sports, the big names of today would eventually fall to the new names of tomorrow.[36]

Professional promoter George MacCall found that last development more unsettling than most because of the average age of the professionals he kept under contract. His players—Laver, Rosewall, Emerson, Gonzales, Stolle, and Gimeno—won the majority of big professional events. But it came at a high cost and for how long? All in all, the NTL lost $208,403.89 in 1968. The league's tournament earnings were good, but MacCall had promised unrealistically high guarantees in order to secure the signatures of nearly all the top professionals. He never stood a realistic chance of meeting those guarantees in his first full season of operation. While he personally did fairly well, thanks to his side business of selling premium life insurance policies to all of his top players, his investors felt burned by the enterprise. Men like Charlton Heston may very well have wanted to see topflight tennis grow because they thought the game was great entertainment, but more than that, they were investors interested in achieving a return on the capital they had provided to MacCall. They put pressure on MacCall to repay their investments. MacCall responded in the spring of 1970 by first shedding the contracts of a few women professionals he held. Then in July 1970 he admitted defeat, sold the remainder of his player contracts, and saw his enterprise absorbed by Lamar Hunt's World Championship Tennis.[37]

Australia produced many of the finest tennis players in the world by mid–century, with the Davis Cuppers Ken McGregor, Frank Sedgman, and Mervyn Rose (left to right) seen here on September 6, 1951, arriving in Los Angeles to take part in the 25th Annual Pacific Southwest Tennis Championships. (Courtesy of University of Southern California Digital Library, *Los Angeles Examiner* Photograph Collection)

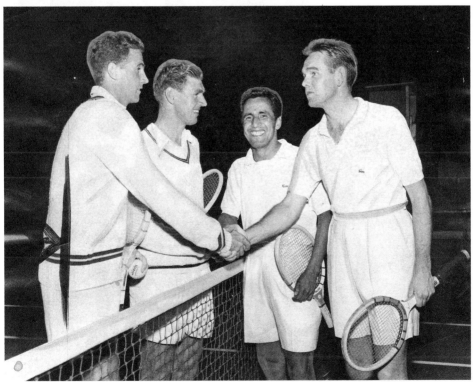

Jack Kramer promoted the 1953 professional tour that featured, from right to left, himself, Pancho Segura, Frank Sedgman, and Ken McGregor. (Courtesy of *Herald Examiner* Collection, Los Angeles Public Library)

Tennis players Tony Trabert (right) and Pancho Gonzales (left) with Beans Reordon (middle) in Los Angeles in 1955. (Courtesy of *Los Angeles Times* Photographic Archives [Collection 1429], Library Special Collections, Charles E. Young Research Library, UCLA)

Pancho Gonzales learned tennis and returned to play on Los Angeles's Exposition Park tennis courts over his long career. (Courtesy of University of Southern California Digital Library, "Dick" Whittington Photography Collection)

Richard Gonzales plays a tennis match. (Courtesy of *Los Angeles Daily News* Negatives [Collection 1387], Library Special Collections, Charles E. Young Research Library, UCLA)

From his headquarters at the LATC, Perry T. Jones (left) was one of the most important figures in directing tennis during the twentieth century. Here he is pictured with Australian champion Ashley Cooper in 1958. (Courtesy of University of Southern California Digital Library, *Los Angeles Examiner* Photograph Collection)

The competitive relationship between Jack Kramer (left) and Pancho Gonzales (right) was a key dynamic in the professional tours of the 1950s and 1960s, as the two discuss here on August 27, 1957. (Courtesy of *Herald Examiner* Collection, Los Angeles Public Library)

The Australian Lew Hoad, seen here in one of his early matches as a tennis professional in February 1958. (Courtesy of University of Southern California Digital Library, *Los Angeles Examiner* Photograph Collection)

Ken Rosewall was a successful professional before and after 1968. (Courtesy of Howard Ballew, *Herald Examiner* Collection, Los Angeles Public Library)

The AELTC moved to its current location along Church Road beginning in 1922. (©AELTC/WLTM)

Rod Laver (left) beat Tony Roche (right) in the 1968 men's final of the first Open Wimbledon Championships. (©AELTC/Michael Cole)

Pancho Gonzales (left) and Charlie Pasarell (right) played for more than five hours over two days during the first-round match of the 1969 Wimbledon Championships. (©AELTC/Michael Cole)

Mike Davies was an important British amateur-turned-professional and very involved in player self-governance related to the move into open tennis. (Courtesy of ITHF)

Lamar Hunt owned and operated WCT, just one of his many sports enterprises. (Courtesy of ITHF)

USC tennis player Dennis Ralston during the final round of the 1964 Southern California Intercollegiate Championship. Ralston would turn professional as one of Lamar Hunt's so-called Handsome Eight group of young professionals. (Courtesy of *Los Angeles Times* Photographic Archives [Collection 1429], Library Special Collections, Charles E. Young Research Library, UCLA)

Slew Hester was the USTA president most responsible for the commercial success of the U.S. Open. (Courtesy of ITHF)

Mark McCormack founded International Management Group, the most influential sports agency in the world. (©AELTC/Michael Cole)

Donald Dell was a fine tennis player who did even more to shape the game through his representation of ATP professionals and the ProServ agency he founded. (Courtesy of ITHF)

Arthur Ashe playing in the Southern California Sectional in Los Angeles on May 4, 1966. Ashe would go on to win tennis championships and to advocate for social causes around the world. (Courtesy of *Los Angeles Daily News Negatives* [Collection 1387], Library Special Collections, Charles E. Young Research Library, UCLA)

Gladys Heldman (right) did as much as anyone to shape women's professional tennis in the twentieth century. Here she is pictured with Frank Sedgman and Margaret Court at the ITHF. (Courtesy of ITHF)

Billie Jean Moffitt King, Pancho Segura, and Stan Smith (left to right) at a tennis clinic in Los Angeles in 1966. Southern California continued to produce top tennis talent in the 1960s. (Courtesy of *Los Angeles Times* Photographic Archives [Collection 1429], Library Special Collections, Charles E. Young Research Library, UCLA)

The so-called Original Nine hold up one-dollar bills to symbolize the contracts they entered into with Gladys Heldman, sitting in for Julie Heldman, front right and holding a contract at the Houston Racquet Club in September 1970. (RGD0006N-1970–2841 [*Houston Post*], Houston Public Library, HMRC)

Years after retiring from professional tennis, Bobby Riggs reemerged for his very public loss to Billie Jean King in the famous 1973 Battle of the Sexes. (Courtesy of *Herald Examiner* Collection, Los Angeles Public Library)

Virginia Wade, seen here in 1975, excelled on the Virginia Slims Circuit. (Courtesy of *Herald Examiner* Collection, Los Angeles Public Library)

Chris Evert was one of the most popular tennis professionals during the 1970s. (Courtesy of *Herald Examiner* Collection, Los Angeles Public Library)

CHAPTER 10

The Rise and Demise of
World Championship Tennis

No promoter and tour owner proved more significant in commercializing competitive tennis in the early Open Era than Lamar Hunt and the World Championship Tennis tour he founded. Hunt made a major name for himself in sports by leveraging family business assets into owning and operating professional sports teams such as the Kansas City Chiefs in football. He took major risks in professional sports as well, helping to found the American Football League (AFL) and starting Major League Soccer in the United States. So when a fellow sports entrepreneur, Dave Dixon—who brought the National Football League's (NFL) Saints franchise to New Orleans to play in the Superdome, which he helped finance—approached Hunt about the potential to make money off a properly promoted professional tennis tour, Hunt expressed the interest that later resulted in WCT.[1]

Tennis was not Hunt's primary focus when it came to professional sports. His first encounter with professional tennis came only a decade before he founded WCT at the Southern Methodist University tennis courts, where he watched Pancho Gonzales, Ken Rosewall, and Rod Laver battle each other in the Texas heat for the modest crowds that Jack Kramer's WPTI and IPTPA matches tended to draw. When Hunt and Dixon met in August 1967 to discuss forming a tennis tour of their own, Dixon sold Hunt on the waste of that talent. "The finest players in the world were playing their biggest tournaments before 150–200 people at little private clubs," Hunt's friend Bob Moore recalled

Dixon saying at the meeting.[2] Hunt and Dixon thought Kramer and George MacCall, both former players-turned-barnstorm-tour-promoters, could never look too far beyond the game of tennis itself to the sport's broader position in the entertainment industry. Hunt and Dixon, on the other hand, thought they knew how to make tennis pay.

The first step was to muster capital. Hunt arranged the financing from some of his other sporting investments—notably the AFL's Kansas City Chiefs—as the AFL and NFL looked to cease competing by merging into a super-league, and he added a business partner named Al Hill Jr.[3] Then they needed players. The difficulty of convincing amateur players to turn professional and forever forgo playing the major amateur tournaments of Wimbledon, the U.S. Championships, the French Championships, and the Australian Championships was one of the crucial factors that kept professional tennis tours of the 1920s through 1950s usually at four players. Hunt and Hill's money convinced double that number of players to join. The top names in the game—Pancho Gonzales, Rod Laver, and Ken Rosewall—already had existing contracts with George MacCall's NTL, so Hunt went after the players of the future. Yugoslavian Nikola "Nikki" Pilić; South African Cliff Drysdale; Frenchman Pierre Barthès; Englishman Roger Taylor; two players from Australia, John Newcombe and Tony Roche; as well as two Americans, Dennis Ralston and Butch Buchholz, formed what Hunt called "The Handsome Eight." The finances made a difficult decision for players more palatable. John Newcombe, the best nonprofessional player in the world, fed his family on fifteen thousand dollars per year. The chance to almost triple that with a three-year guarantee persuaded Newcombe and his fellow amateurs to turn professional.[4]

For the present those players had a chance to play in places not available to players from the past. Those venues began to sprout in what historian Robert C. Trumpbour has summarized as the "third era" of sport stadium construction in the United States, marked by "the geographical expansion of sports teams, acceptance of taxpayer-funded sports facilities, and the construction of large all-purpose stadiums and arenas."[5] The popularity and profitability of football largely propelled sports stadium constructions in the 1950s and '60s. Hunt's position as the owner of a professional football franchise meant he knew firsthand just how much the venue mattered to the bottom line. Hunt made meticulous notes on the suitability of different tournament venues, which he kept in journals for reflection. For example, he noted that the West Side Tennis Club, then the host of the U.S. Championships, had too many courts spread over too far a distance for the small group of WCT professionals to suitably fill the Forest Hills grounds. Financial success in sports entertainment meant taking the specific rules and particularities of each sport and each sporting venue into account.[6]

Hunt's tour officially began in late 1967. The eight up-and-coming WCT professionals competed directly against one another; indirectly they competed against George MacCall's NTL veteran professionals. After MacCall accepted Hunt's summer 1970 buyout, WCT made it on the world scene in 1971 when thirty-two players agreed to play twenty tournaments across the continents of North America, Australia, Europe, and Asia. In cities as different from one another as Sydney, Miami, Rome, Tehran, Louisville, Vancouver, Cologne, Boston, Stockholm, and Dallas, among others, what Hunt called his "Million Dollar Tour" put the "World" in his organization's title.[7] But WCT also needed a home base—a fact Hunt might have realized from his professional football experience when he moved his AFL Dallas Texans to Kansas City in order to avoid direct competition with the upstart NFL franchise Dallas Cowboys.[8] (For cities where WCT held tennis tournaments, see map 5.[9])

Hunt and his partners strove to anchor the tour's year with a season-ending championship held in, of all places, Dallas's Memorial Auditorium in November. To this end they also drew on their experience in football, where a week's worth of hype meant more to a game's bottom line than four quarters' worth of action. Players spoke at press conferences, promoters wore tuxedos at galas with sponsors, and Hunt hosted his own version of Breakfast at Wimbledon on finals morning at his Dallas home. In that famous May 1972 match, two veterans from the Kramer and Gonzales tours of the early 1960s—Australians Ken Rosewall and Rod Laver—played a competitive match after officials paraded the players courtside in colorful outfits, much like boxers and their trunks moving ringside. Rosewall won. He collected fifty thousand dollars in prize money, which was 100 percent more than he had received with one of his earlier professional titles, where a sponsor's bankruptcy meant winning the name of the best tennis player in the world without a dollar to show for it.[10]

Stadiums and stable sponsorship agreements mattered a great deal in making WCT a sustainable professional sports venture. Television contracts mattered even more. WCT had recorded and privately distributed the 1971 Rosewall-Laver final. The popularity of that match with both the national and international media convinced the National Broadcasting Company (NBC), after WCT director Mike Davies and Hunt had approached the net-

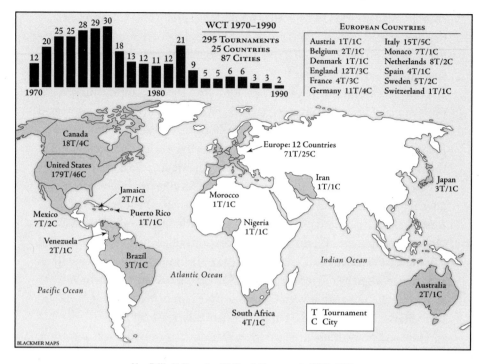

Map 5. World Championship Tennis Tournaments, 1970–1990

work, to accept a broadcast contract with WCT to begin in 1972.[11] Here as elsewhere, Hunt drew on his previous experience founding and growing the AFL, during which he had successfully negotiated a television contract with the American Broadcasting Company (ABC) that had single-handedly kept his upstart football league in business against the more powerful NFL during the early 1960s.[12]

For their part, the players did what they could in 1972 to attract and solidify attention. They competed hard in WCT tournaments held in twenty-three different cities and six different countries. Compared to the farther-flung 1971 season, players played more matches in the United States, Canada, and Western Europe—a decision indicative of the importance Hunt assigned to cultivating his tennis league's fledgling relationship with television. Over the next few years, WCT television ratings ebbed and flowed when competing against other televised tennis events and a host of "live" sports productions competing for network airtime. Hunt tried to solve this problem by owning and operating a television network that, by 1979, taped, sold, and distributed thirty-eight weeks of recorded WCT matches with a market that reached 70 percent of American households. The following year Hunt inked a five-year deal with the upstart Entertainment Sports Programming Network (ESPN) for television coverage of WCT matches played in the United States, Canada, and Europe in the winter and spring. The ABC network carried WCT's most important tournament, the $250,000 Dallas WCT Championships played in May, along with a major $500,000 prize-money Tournament of Championships at the historic Forest Hills Stadium on the grounds of the West Side Tennis Club.[13]

WCT made, was made by, and was ultimately unmade by the popularity of tennis with the public in the mid-1970s. The A. C. Nielsen Company reported that the number of people who played tennis in America increased from 16.5 million people in 1973 to 30 million people in 1976—just 5 percent shy of doubling. In 1974 WCT counted eighty-four professionals, divided into three touring groups, who played matches in twenty-five cities across eleven countries. The following year WCT retained the three-group format and awarded an innovative golden tennis ball to Arthur Ashe, who outperformed his fellow professionals in 1975. The participation of fewer players in the 1976 WCT tour meant a consolidation of three touring groups to one, a foreboding trend that continued in the 1977 season when only twenty-three professionals played WCT. Hunt took this as a sign to compromise with his competitors, who had also grown strong during the years that one observer labeled the "Tennis Bubble."[14]

That bubble would burst for WCT on January 21, 1983, when Hunt initiated a lawsuit against the International Tennis Federation (formerly ILTF until 1977), the Men's International Professional Tennis Council (MIPTC), and the Association of Tennis Professionals (ATP). A decade earlier WCT was on competitive but less acrimonious terms with the ILTF. In 1972 Hunt had agreed to stop signing professionals to exclusive player contracts, and WCT and federation officials had agreed to a 1973 schedule that allowed the sixty-four best players in the world to compete in two tours of thirty-two players on the WCT circuit during the first five months of the year. After the WCT Championships contested in May at the Moody Coliseum on Southern Methodist University's campus, the players' contracts stipulated their freedom to travel to Europe and the United States to compete. The players preferred the freedom to make their own schedule and play the events that paid them the most. A better-organized ITF schedule of Grand Prix tournaments gradually drew players away from WCT tournaments. At the time of Hunt's lawsuit, WCT could count only a few matches that attracted top players, because most big names played Grand Prix tournaments instead. That a businessman of Hunt's caliber in running highly profitable sports franchises like the Kansas City Chiefs and the Chicago Bulls should have WCT succeed at first, only to collapse, owed a great deal to the peculiarities of tennis as a sport with a complicated history of professionalism.[15]

Jack Kramer knew that history better than anyone. In 1972 he leveraged his prior experience managing players as both the head of WPTI and a founder of the IPTPA to form a new player union with Donald Dell and Cliff Drysdale called the Association of Tennis Professionals. The relative weakness of the IPTPA had taught Kramer that for a player union to hold any power, the stakes must be high for any type of pocketbook posturing. With the prominence Wimbledon had assumed during the push for open tennis, no more visible place for a show of player strength presented itself than the grounds of the AELTC during the championship's fortnight. In May 1973 Yugoslavian standout Nikki Pilić had qualified for a high-paying WCT match that made him unavailable for the Yugoslavian Davis Cup tie—that is, a national match he had previously notified the Transylvanian Tennis Federation authorities that in all likelihood he could not play. Rather than thanking Pilić for the heads-up and confirming the reason for his unavailability, the Yugoslavian authorities told Pilić he *had* to play in the Davis Cup. When he replied that he would not, they not only sanctioned Pilić but also coordinated with all ILTF member associations to bar the Yugoslavian from tournament play. The French Open was the next tournament on the calendar and whose chairman, Philippe Chatrier, had long enjoyed a warm friendship with Kramer. Their fondness for each other did not dissuade Kramer from informing Chatrier that the ATP players would not play in the French Open if the tournament refused Pilić entry into the draw. However, their camaraderie did prompt Kramer to offer Chatrier a way out by asking the ILTF to delay any action until the Pilić prohibition could be studied and ruled upon. That ruling took place in the weeks leading up to Wimbledon. When the ILTF president, Alan Heyman, signaled that Pilić would in fact be banned, Kramer and the ATP leadership met to chart a way forward.[16]

Boycotting a major tennis tournament had happened before. Just a year earlier, Lamar Hunt held his players out of the French Open because of a contract dispute with the FFT. The FFT convinced the ILTF and the AELTC to retaliate by locking a number of WCT players, including defending champion John Newcombe, out of the 1972 Wimbledon Championships. In assuming the players had learned their lesson, the ILTF underestimated the players' resolve. Meetings in London, with stakeholders who ranged from the ILTF's Heyman, the AELTC's Herman David, the ATP's Kramer, and British Broadcasting Company (BBC) leadership, went unresolved. The matter moved quickly into the courts, where a British judge ruled that he lacked jurisdiction to rule on the case. Meanwhile, reports in the British press spotlighted the conflict and came to call on the players to not do anything rash. Less than a week before Wimbledon, the entire ATP leadership met and voted 9–0 with one abstention to hold its player members out of the championships. On June 20, 1973, ATP president Cliff Drysdale announced what amounted to a player-led strike at the highest-profile tournament of the year.[17]

The ATP athletes themselves voted unanimously to not play Wimbledon. Enforcement took vigilance in the face of the pressure the ILTF put on national associations to convince their players to play the tournament. ATP leadership realized that players who lived in Soviet bloc countries had to play if their national associations told them to, as resisting a communist government carried higher personal consequences than ignoring a national tennis association located in a democratic country. Likewise, LTA affiliated players faced an especially difficult decision because Wimbledon was played on their home country's soil. The ATP board met a second time to reaffirm their commitment in the face of a waffling membership. They decided to hold strong, and when the tournament came, only two ATP players of truly international significance, Englishman Roger Taylor and Romanian Ilie Năstase, broke with the union and played the 1973 championships—both of whom having felt duress from their national circumstances. The tournament draw was thus filled with second-rate players, American university athletes, and up-and-comers too young to have established themselves enough to join the ATP. The tournament suffered from the weakest draw of the Open Era, a field filled with the fewest notable names in the history of the championships. In the months that followed, the 1973 Wimbledon players' strike began to show why it mattered in the future direction professional tennis would take. The ATP demonstrated to ILTF leadership and member associations that the players themselves were a big enough force in tennis that the path forward was not to compete but to work toward compromise in the future. To make that happen, the ILTF joined with ATP leadership to create a new nine-member governing council, the Men's International Professional Tennis Council, which would grow in strength in the late 1970s and '80s. The MIPTC would come to control the ILTF Grand Prix, which effectively muscled the WCT out.[18]

During its first year of operation, in 1974, one-third of the MIPTC came from the ILTF, one-third from the ATP, and one-third from prominent tournament directors. For a half dozen years, the first and the last of those constituencies proved significantly consequential to the success of the MIPTC not just because of the votes they cast but also because of what they brought with them. Both the history associated with and the physical ground of the four major tournaments continued to hold a significant share of the tennis market that was totally disproportionate to the number of weeks that Wimbledon as well as the Australian, French, and U.S. Opens occupied on the close to yearlong tournament calendar. Everyone on the MIPTC council knew this to the degree that they believed the four majors could anchor a tour that rivaled if not surpassed Hunt's WCT.[19]

Kramer first floated the idea of a Grand Prix tournament circuit back in 1969 after the success of the first open tournaments. The USLTA president, Alastair Martin, and the AELTC chairman, Herman David, supported the idea, but George MacCall's old contracts from the struggling NTL and Lamar Hunt's new contracts from the succeeding WCT combined to thwart the initial push for ILTF approval. Both Hunt's growing power after buying the NTL players from MacCall in 1970 and Hunt's disinterest if not inability to make sure all his contracted athletes played ILTF tournaments in addition to their WCT calendar led the ILTF to reconsider the Grand Prix. Kramer was given the go-ahead to negotiate a sponsorship deal with the Pepsi-Cola Company for what became the Pepsi Grand Prix rights prior to the 1970 Wimbledon events. During the first few years, Pepsi and the former Commercial Union Life Assurance Company provided only moderate prize purses. But with the formation of the MIPTC, the players, the tournaments, and the ILTF leadership were able to better coordinate their efforts to make sure players competed in the Grand Slam tournaments, thus encouraging new tournaments to affiliate themselves with the Grand Prix, with the positive spillover of attracting larger corporate sponsorships. In 1970 Pepsi-Cola put-up $75,000 in bonus money for players who ranked high and won matches in the Grand Prix. By 1979 that figure had grown to $1,500,000 under Colgate's sponsorship and a ninety-tournament yearlong calendar, with $175,000 purses for seven-day tournaments the norm. Hunt put on popular and innovative tennis tournaments with top players, but even his annual year-end WCT championships could not carry the rest of his circuit in the same way the historic majors did with the Grand Prix. Hunt tried to counter by increasing his stable of players and paying higher prize monies than he could sustain. By 1978 he decided to work his WCT events into the larger Grand Prix schedule. That concession happened largely because of the coordination of the different elements of the MIPTC.[20]

With the common threat of WCT neutralized, balance on the MIPTC began to shift. A North Carolina lawyer named Marshall Happer saw an opportunity to increase the power of the MIPTC itself when he assumed an administrative appointment to the council in 1981. Happer used his tiebreaking votes to shift professional play to and away from certain tournaments, to get even more money into the hands of the players, and to put power in administering the tournaments themselves on the MIPTC itself. By the mid-1980s, the MIPTC owned only two tournaments outright; however, they were big ones, with the year-end Masters Singles paying players anywhere between $2 million and $4 million. More significantly, the MIPTC began to assume the officiating of tournaments the council did not actually own, in effect asserting a role of governance over tennis matches that the ILTF had never in its history exercised. In the late 1980s, MIPTC referees officiated three-quarters of the hundred or so Grand Prix tournaments at fees that increased steadily up to estimates of $7.5 million by the start of the 1990 season. The MIPTC grew to thirty-three employees on staff with Happer, some of whom entertained corporate sponsors and potential friends of the sport in tournament-provided luxury boxes at the four Grand Slam events. The established tournaments like Wimbledon could afford to pay the MIPTC $500,000 a year for player bonuses and fees. Lesser tournaments owned or operated by ITF member associations struggled financially, while certain elements of the MIPTC also wrestled with the complicated legacies of their earlier stances toward commercialism in tennis when charting the sport's future.[21]

Those struggles all took place in the context of international sport during an era that one sportswriter has called "bankruptcy, boycotts, and the end of amateurism." Specific to tennis, though, were new players in the game's governance and the long-standing sensitivity to criticism about money in the game dating back to the pre–Open Era. No barbs had dug deeper than top players taking the USLTA to task for money-grubbing tournament ticketing and fees, with simultaneous miserliness when it came to the on-court competitors. Players like Bill Tilden and Ellsworth Vines deserved punishment for the opinions they penned in the popular press, the USLTA leadership maintained. In the case of Vines, the USLTA Executive Committee tried to bar him from entering the broadcast booth at Forest Hills so that he could fulfill his contract with NBC to provide commentary for their radio broadcast of the U.S. National Championships. USLTA leadership thus seemed willing to hurt the bottom line of their showcase tournament and one of their biggest sources of revenue by sidelining the popular commentator and well-known sports personality Vines simply because he had thwarted the control they exercised over him by turning professional. In the mid-1930s, the USLTA had "refused to accept money from a sponsor for the broadcasting of the national events because we did not want the events used for the promotion of business." Whenever journalists in the United States reported on the USLTA barring players for actions deemed professional while simultaneously paying other players' expenses above and beyond the amateur threshold without penalty, association leadership lashed out. As president of the USLTA in the late 1940s, for example, Lawrence Baker wrote to *Life* magazine editor Henry Luce complaining about the latter's June 14, 1948, story highlighting hypocrisy in the USLTA's amateur player expenses. A decade later, in one prominent case, the USLTA Amateur Rule Committee prohibited the request of Gardnar Mulloy, one of the top amateur players in the United States, to appear in a television commercial teaching tennis strokes in exchange for a small honorarium. The USLTA denied Mulloy's request, but had he played in a non-American country, such a request likely would have been granted by the LTAA.[22]

At other times, the USLTA came across as not hypocritical but simply confused and in need of counsel as to their own rules. Such was the case most often for the USLTA Amateur Rule Committee, which, in just one of many available examples, sought legal advice over whether the Wheaties Sports Federation's pursuit of Dennis Ralston's services in an educational tennis series for broadcast turned Ralston into a professional player. Robert Kelleher and Perry T. Jones each thought Ralston could participate. They wanted the best for Southern California tennis after all, but they also sought assurance from USLTA president James Dickey that such participation could proceed without fear of Ralston losing his amateur status. USLTA leadership decided to approve Ralston's participation if Wheaties agreed to remove all mention of professional tennis as played by Jack Kramer and his troupe.[23]

The quality of the tennis the Kramer professionals played throughout the '50s had created a climate of permanent crisis at the USLTA by 1960 at the same time that constant barnstorming had brought tennis to most parts of the country. The latter likely contributed to a steady rise in USLTA membership from 12,555 dues-paying players in 1958 to 27,521 in 1962. Most of that growth came from junior players, because during the leaner finance years of the mid-'60s the USLTA wisely invested heavily in junior tennis as opposed to adult tennis. Between 1962 and 1963, for example, USLTA adult membership actually fell from 9,129 to 9,108—the first time that had happened in the postwar period. Open tennis caused "peak memberships" in 1969 and 1970, with 52,474 dues-paying members belonging to the organization by 1971. The crisis came in part because increased membership rolls had not put the USLTA on a firmer financial footing. Association leaders read with disgust newspapers that printed ten times more lines about golf than tennis despite the United States boasting 1.5 million more tennis players than golfers. They also misread the reasons why golf had become more interesting to report on than tennis. Far from harming golf, professionalism encouraged a cult of personality around certain players. Sports marketers like Mark McCormack used that to secure sponsorship dollars from company executives who were willing to spend their firm's advertising and branding budgets on sports marketing. Managers decided on sports rather than other promotional opportunities in large part because such a decision came with a tee time with Arnold Palmer at Pinehurst, Pebble Beach, or Augusta National. That money made for better golf tournaments. More importantly, the flow of dollars into the professional golf tour helped forge partnerships with television networks. Greater media attention helped make the sport of golf seem more popular to a television-hungry public than it was at the grassroots level. More people played tennis than golf, but a viewer would not see as much tennis on their television screen. Instead of picking up on that disconnect, USLTA leaders scratched their heads at how golf seemed more popular with the press than tennis when the former maintained an even stricter policy of no talking or photographing during play than the latter.[24]

In the run-up to open tennis, Robert Kelleher's Beverly Hills legal background made him the first USLTA president to feel comfortable monetizing the majority of the association's activities through licensing agreements with the Licensing Corporation of America. In the same year, 1967, the USLTA also looked to partner with Madison Square Garden Attractions, which managed the entertainment spectacles at the newly built venue. What Fred Podesta, the president of Madison Square Garden Attractions, offered the USLTA was actually a pittance compared with professional tournaments run a decade earlier. The USLTA received a guarantee of only thirty thousand dollars from Madison Square Garden Attractions with two-thirds of that sum going to player prize money, while the USLTA had to shoulder the burden of securing the best American and international competitors, and Madison Square Garden Attractions kept all television revenue and receipts above the thirty-thousand-dollar guarantee.[25]

Licensing Corporation of America handled other negotiations that went even worse for the USLTA. Wilson Sporting Goods flatly told the association that they would not play ball with them when it came to paying a licensing fee in order to have Wilson balls used in USLTA events. The USLTA under Kelleher took an important step toward professional tennis, but before open tennis, companies simply did not see enough potential in a sport whose international governing body still officially outlawed money from entering the game in a commercial capacity.[26]

That all changed in 1968 with Open Wimbledon. For the first time, sponsors saw real financial potential in sponsoring tennis events, and the USLTA had a bigger incentive than ever before to pursue those sponsors even though such pursuit put American tennis at loggerheads with the ILTF. In his capacity as president of the USLTA in the two years immediately after the beginning of open tennis, Alastair Martin pointed out a number of problems with open tennis and the free-wheeling authority the ILTF exercised. Martin reiterated to his fellow USLTA Executive Committee members that their organization should take their own path on these issues or suffer whatever fate the ILTF Committee of Management decided for them. The most significant area of disagreement toward the beginning of open tennis addressed the "authorized player" idea proposed by committee. Taxes presented the most glaring problem to the USLTA leadership. No stranger to litigation over tax law, the association's counsel advised the executive committee that the Internal Revenue Service would almost certainly require authorized players, despite their technical amateur status under ILTF rules, to pay income tax on their expenses before leaving the United States for a tournament abroad. USLTA officers feared such an arrangement might leave them partly responsible for not providing a fellow ILTF member nation with players on time for the start of a tournament or consider them an accomplice in players' shirking their tax responsibilities. Whether or not the IRS would ever have held up the travel of a player who claimed they were an amateur and did not receive income from their tennis proved a moot point, because the very possibility galvanized the USLTA to look for another way to try to help their sport grow.[27]

The first mechanism for growth they tried was to "sanction" events. Before 1968 the USLTA sanctioned amateur tournaments, but if a professional player competed in an event not sanctioned by the association, he or she would forfeit eligibility to play in USLTA-sanctioned events. That rule reflected the consensus of the ninety-six ILTF member nations infuriated by the fee that professional player promoters demanded of tournament committees and national associations in order "to deliver them to tournaments." The ILTF took the action of "closing all events to players under contract to such promoters." National associations had the blessing of the ILTF to charge appropriate sanction fees to tournaments within their jurisdiction, and the USLTA required a 6 percent cut of the tournament total prize money, along with USLTA travel expenses, in order for a tennis event to receive a sanction. Little wonder, then, that promoters such as George MacCall, Dave Dixon, and Lamar Hunt came to blows with the USLTA and the ILTF, although the sides seemingly reached "an agreement" by the summer of 1972.[28]

The USLTA justification for the sanction fees they assessed in the years immediately after open tennis made sense from the point of view of the men who ran the association. A great amount of sponsorship dollars had entered into tennis, and the sanction fees provided, in the words of association representatives, "an ever increasing source of revenue to the USLTA." The association, in turn, could use that money to keep "the future of tennis in this country . . . better off in the hands of the USLTA than of any other organization." That they certainly meant, as association lawyers prepared suits and countersuits to wrestle as much control of professional tennis as possible from other stakeholders such as World Championship Tennis and the upstart Virginia Slims Women's Tour run by *World Tennis* publisher Gladys Heldman and Philip Morris chairman Joe Cullman. "In complete candor, I suggest that we stop pussyfooting with Gladys Heldman, Joe Cullman, Lamar Hunt, and others whose interests are selfish, short term, and in opposition to ours. Let us go our own way and build our own tournaments and our own players," said USLTA leadership. Their idea of building would mean abandoning the West Side Tennis Club as the host of the U.S. Open Championships and the construction of the most commercial of all tennis venues. Sanction fees gave them the capital to get that project started, and what they needed then was a little luck.[29]

Flushing Meadows Park first came to the serious attention of New York City urban planner Robert Moses as far back as the 1930s, when a torrent of New Deal money for urban recreation made even the grandest of park plans seem possible. Thirty years later, toward the end of Moses's building career, Flushing Meadows remained undeveloped. Moses saw the opportunity to finally get his park built with the New York World's Fair of 1964–1965. His lack of enthusiasm for the fair itself, however, undermined his vision for a grand Flushing Meadows. Buildings were built on the cheap without the usual Moses mustard, and the simultaneous loss of ten of his dozen planning commissionerships during the fair's preparation meant he directed that organization with an even greater degree of heavy-handedness than usual. Employees routinely lost their jobs without cause, and over a year went by before Moses finally listened to the accountants, who reported that the fair had lost around $17,000,000 in 1964. The fair closed the following year having made only $8,600,000 rather than the $29,000,000 Moses expected to have in order to make Flushing Meadows Park grand after the fair left town. Moses took $6,576,000 more from his other remaining post—the chairmanship of the Triborough Bridge and Tunnel Authority—for additional improvements to Flushing Meadows. The park, however, remained full of cleared land with little in the way of development due to the disappointing finances of the fair.[30]

The USLTA saw a great opportunity for American tennis in Moses's failure to remake Flushing Meadows. After declaring irreconcilable differences with the West Side Tennis Club in Forest Hills, the USTA (until 1975 USLTA) withdrew from talks in February 1977 and began to search for a new home for the tournament, which, upon the decline of the Davis Cup in the 1960s, single-handedly made or broke the association's balance sheet. That summer USTA president Slew Hester and association lawyers reached an agreement with the New York City Parks Department to lease some of the Flushing Meadows–Corona Park land that had been the site of New York World's Fair barely more than a year earlier. Property in Queens, the largest in land area of New York City's five boroughs, did not command the potential real estate values of property in midtown Manhattan or much else of the city, for that matter. The USTA also had the makings of a prime-time show court in the Singer Bowl, left over from the 1964 world's fair. Boxing bouts between Floyd Patterson, Vito Antuofermo, Saoul Mamby, and Edwin Viruet, among others, in the 1970s revealed that the odd rectangular-shaped venue could deliver the thrill of one-on-one sports to an audience large enough to justify the pricey location compared to more suburban venues near major freeways and with large parking lots. A functional enough public transportation network already existed, by and large, connecting the Singer Bowl to neighborhoods in Queens and New York City.[31]

Hester was the right person at the right time to help the USTA. His personality disarmed those in the association who were heavily steeped in traditional amateurism and still reeling from the 1968 opening of tennis to professionals managed by the likes of Mark McCormack and Bill Riordan and the tours of Kramer, MacCall, and Hunt. He was perfect to navigate the new frontier of big money for big-time tennis. A World War II officer from the South, Hester wisely noted the commercial opportunities in the broad economic, political, social, and cultural strip that people came to call the "Sunbelt."[32] He first tapped the region's business potential by providing the most essential postwar technology that facilitated the mass demographic shift to this region—cool air on the cheap. He owned and operated a Carrier air-conditioning distributorship after returning from overseas in 1955. The following year, Hester prospected for oil in his home state of Mississippi during the rough-and-tumble wildcat postbellum decades of the Gulf Coast oil boom. The business worked like this: Hester hired geologists who proved the oil reserves of plots; he then purchased leases on lands that held oil and whose owners did not know what they had, at least not enough to demand a better offer; investors gave Hester money to negotiate individual drilling deals worth hundreds of thousands of dollars, agreements he often made on the telephone. He served as the executive vice president and chief operating officer of the Southern States Oil Company until 1962, after which he opened a new office, which he ran until his retirement from the energy industry.[33]

A tournament tennis player since 1925, Hester served the USLTA and then later the USTA at the regional, state, sectional, and national level until the 1980s, all the while playing national-level tournaments from the junior level up through the Men's 65 and Over. USLTA officials looked favorably on Hester's experience in developing new oil lands and negotiating complex and profitable deals on the quick, just as they noted that he had founded and built a successful tennis complex in the River Hills Club of Jackson, Mississippi. The national office admitted a mistake and unanimously reinstated Hester after having ousted him from the board in a five-to-four vote following his refusal to approve a contract negotiation between the USLTA, Hunt and WCT, and the ILTF that would have effectively monopolized control of high-level American tennis. Hester's fellow board members rightly recognized that they needed Hester to ward off the eclipse of the association's relevancy in the tennis boom of the 1970s. A new tennis complex for the new moneyed game was the cornerstone of that effort.[34]

Just fourteen months before the 1978 U.S. Open, Hester, the only person within the USTA who believed construction of the tennis park could hold to a ten-month timeline, and New York City politicians and commissioners signed contracts. The USTA moved quickly to secure bids from contractors to complete a major renovation of Singer Stadium and the construction of other courts and tournament facilities on the surrounding grounds. Engineers first divided Singer Stadium into two tennis courts; workers then installed seats to bring the seating capacity of the newly named Louis Armstrong Stadium (after the famous trumpeter) to 20,600. The smaller court, called simply the Grandstand, sat 6,200 and abutted the prime-time stadium.[35]

What set the Flushing Meadows tennis complex apart from not just any other tennis tournament site in the world but also from every other major sporting venue in the world in the late 1970s and 1980s was the catering. The USTA built nine indoor courts and air-conditioned them—first for serving meals and only a distant second for tennis. Those nine courts accommodated five thousand people at any one time, with spectators in the late August and early September heat availing themselves of the shade, refreshments, and cool air throughout the tournament.[36]

When it came to food, however, the USTA preferred hot over cold. Before the facilities at Flushing Meadows existed, no major sporting venue served sit-down hot meals to spectators. Concessions reflected class conventions and country traditions: duck gillette and smoked salmon at the U.S. Open golf tournament; ploughman's lunches or pâtés with Champagne at Wimbledon; "beef on the barbie" at the Australian Championships; beer and brats at the American baseball park. Hester planned to prevent the complaints from athletes and fans who disliked the smell of large quantities of cooking meat wafting through the grounds on a late summer day. The USTA spent thirty thousand dollars on one smoke washer alone that allowed for the firing of charcoal steaks without forcing the smell of accelerant and burnt flesh across the noses of thousands of people. Another larger smoke washer located in a restaurant situated between the highly trafficked area of the Grandstand

Court and Louis Armstrong Stadium ascended 110 feet up an elevator tower, essentially to the railway line that linked the grounds to the Metropolitan Transit Authority.[37]

Food and drink sales immediately made tennis' U.S. Open more profitable than the far older, more prestigious, and more exclusive championships at Wimbledon. As good as the AELTC's strawberries and cream tasted, Flushing Meadows outsold SW19 three to one. Furthermore, California and Florida growers sold strawberries to the USTA at a price far below that of producers in the United Kingdom, which allowed U.S. Open vendors to turn around and sell the classic tennis tournament fare to attendees at a price 60 percent lower than what Wimbledon vendors charged, while operating at a more favorable margin. The Americans' clotted cream might not rival that of the British, but the U.S. Open tournament operated on a quantity of scale far beyond that of the Wimbledon Championships let alone the biggest tournaments during WCT's best years.[38]

Unlike Wimbledon—and former high-profile tennis tournaments in the United States, for that matter—Flushing Meadows stressed inclusiveness over exclusiveness. Compared to the private tents and the Royal Box, the two most visible VIP areas at Wimbledon, Flushing Meadows brought to the fore an Open Club for anyone willing to pay twenty-five dollars above their ticket price. Outside the player locker room and broadcast booth, only one other room existed on the entire grounds that required preapproval to attend. Called "Slew's Place" after USTA president Hester, the VIP room was actually open to anybody on a first-come, first-served basis who asked the current USTA president for a card to enter. Such openness compared to other major sporting grounds, which by the 1970s had already reached a point of high stratification, set Flushing Meadows apart as a sporting experience. The genesis of that openness lay in Hester's own experience as a player during the Great Depression and the New Deal. Compared to the East Coast during those years, the South had few private tennis clubs. In fact, despite the fine weather for outdoor competition and the rich sporting tradition of the region, few tennis courts existed there before government initiatives built courts throughout the South and the rest of the country in the 1930s and '40s. The speed at which these courts were built inspired Hester. So, too, did the intransigence of the Eastern private clubs in the face of an onslaught of new players to the game and new competition at the highest level. Clubs throughout New England and the Mid-Atlantic doubled down on their exclusivity, some even barring spectators from using the clubs' restrooms, eating at the clubs' restaurants, and drinking at the clubs' bars.[39]

A gamble for openness in a traditionally closed game paid off handsomely for the USTA. In 1976 the USTA's entire budget stood at $800,000. Two years later, when the tournament concluded at Flushing Meadows, owned and operated exclusively by the USTA, the association boasted a budget of more than $8 million. The new National Tennis Center at Flushing Meadows single-handedly increased the USTA's budget more than 100 percent, with the tournament immediately becoming the most profitable year-to-year athletic contest in the world after 1978.[40] Such success did much to enhance the attractiveness of the Grand Prix, whose success came at the expense of WCT.

During the summer of 1970 it had appeared that Lamar Hunt and WCT would rule Open Era tennis, having eliminated their chief rival in George MacCall and absorbed his NTL contract professionals into a robust and a commercially viable tournament circuit. The erstwhile Jack Kramer knew better. Just two months earlier, Kramer had sat for an interview in which he explained that the storied venues of the game's amateur past—clubs such as the West Side Tennis Club, the AELTC, the Longwood Cricket Club, and the Philadelphia Cricket Club—were the trump cards the ILTF and the USLTA held over WCT. While Hunt made the most of television contracts, WCT struggled to find suitable venues that allowed for more than one match to take place at a time. Older tournament grounds affiliated with national tennis associations and under the auspices of the ILTF could stage larger tournaments, with more players, and greater competition. "You can't have a 64-man tournament on one or two courts," Kramer remarked.[41]

The construction of the sixteen-acre and twenty-court National Tennis Center made Kramer's prophecy a reality faster than the old promoter could have known. Even with its innovative use of television, WCT did not surpass the television ratings of Wimbledon or the U.S. Open.[42] By retooling the traditional amateur championships like the U.S. Nationals into the commercial juggernaut of the U.S. Open, the USTA, other ILTF member associations, and their new entertainment agency partners had the linchpin to hold up the Grand Prix circuit. They had out-competed WCT.

CHAPTER 11

The Impact of Sports Agents and Agencies on Professional Tennis

The most profound change to modern entertainment in the second half of the twentieth century was the rise of management and marketing agencies. These organizations managed and marketed every hair on their clients' heads in order to maximize the clients' public exposure and moneymaking potential. The most successful generated solid earnings for the athlete, artist, and actor while ensuring healthy profits for the agency and hefty commissions for the agents. Whereas entertainers like singers and actors had for decades retained counselors and promoters, sports management became a new arena in the 1960s and '70s, thanks in large part to Mark McCormack and his International Management Group (IMG)—the earliest, most successful, and most historically significant agency.

McCormack and the agents who worked for him did not create a new sport; they created a new species of entertainer in the managed athlete. Those athletes who contracted with management agencies and the agencies that followed the trail they blazed struck it rich. Those athletes who did not seek their representation or did not obtain their representation struggled financially in the age of the managed athlete. Pancho Gonzales was in the latter category. His application for IMG representation was denied by IMG sometime prior to the fall of 1965, but McCormack still "admired [him] as one of the truly great professional athletes of all time."[1] McCormack, on the other hand, was named twice by *Sports Illustrated* "the most powerful man in sports," for twenty years was consistently ranked number one in *Sporting News*'s power ranking for the influencers in global sports, and is remembered by his top competitor as a juggernaut whose firm made every other sports marketing firm up until the new millennium resemble little more than a "mom-and-pop operation."[2]

IMG preferred representing athletes in individual sports over athletes who played team sports. From the perspective of the company's history, that preference made sense because the agency's first and most important early clients played golf—not to mention that McCormack liked golf the most. But there were also more hardheaded business motives free of nostalgia. Questionnaires that the firm required potential clients to complete before a meeting about the athlete's suitability for representation revealed differences between how athletes in team sports versus individual sports earned income for themselves and the agency. For example, the agency made clear to professional footballers such as Pat Summerall, Leo Sugar, Buddy Humphrey, and Joe Krupa that endorsements were where athletes from team sports made their money, while exhibitions made up a mainstay of the revenue that individual sport athletes generated. Herding a whole football team together—or two, for that matter—proved expensive, whereas a single golfer or tennis player could play an exhibition for pay at a club and promote the clothing and equipment he or she endorsed at the same time. That difference explained why IMG favored signing clients from elite sports like golf and tennis.[3]

IMG's chronological files of important tennis clients reveal just how the firm operated. Rod Laver peaked as a tennis player during the late 1960s just when traditionally amateur tennis tournaments opened to professionals and IMG expanded its influence—they had major offices in Cleveland, Johannesburg, London, Los Angeles, New York, and Tokyo—over global entertainment. The redheaded Aussie may have earned his "Rocket" nickname back in his home country, but IMG's agents were the ones who transformed Laver into a worldwide personality. He first approached McCormack about representation in 1966, but as with Pancho Gonzales, McCormack turned Laver down. With professional tennis coming off some of the game's most unsuccessful years monetarily in America since professional tours in the United States began in 1926, McCormack simply did not see much potential in making money from a professional athlete who was positioned in a still largely amateur sport even if that player was the best in the world.[4]

Two years later Laver wrote to McCormack again, and that time IMG responded differently because tennis had opened to professionals. The firm's Jay

Lafave met Laver, signed him in short order in September 1968, and then put IMG's resources into gear for their first tennis client.[5] Most of that work began with letters Laver's IMG agents sent to companies that might consider paying the tennis player for the privilege of attaching his likeness to their company's product. Janet A. Horvath's letter to Howard Friedman, who managed Kodacorp's menswear division, typified the usual pitch: "Mr. Laver is one of the hottest properties in the sports world today and we are looking to develop a manufacturing program for him that would be ready for Spring '72."[6]

Letters never made any promises about how much money Laver's image would make for the company. Platitudes and generalities abounded. Companies that themselves operated in industries that did not make a physical product but rather traded in information—financial services, for example—tended to view unsubstantiated pitches with reluctance and passed on paying for endorsements.[7]

Apparel companies proved far more amenable to paying for a player's likeness attached to their products. Those firms continued to seek athlete endorsements without a clear sense of how that endorsement actually affected their sales. The upstart Adidas Apparel Company agreed to pay Laver a 3 percent royalty and a $10,000 guarantee to name a shoe after the tennis player with no market research into the impact his likeness might have on sales. A brief photo shoot for a cover of a product catalog placed Laver between two female models; as far as Adidas was concerned, this small bit of Laver's labor made a difference to their bottom line. Adidas's operations and export department records show a far more complete picture, demonstrating that the company's real profits came from cheaply producing shoes in different countries throughout the world and then selling those same shoes to buyers in countries that could pay more. Arbitrage aside, IMG convinced Adidas and many other companies that a global product in a global economy needed to associate with a global sports figure. Athletes like Laver had few qualms in accepting 3 percent of $302,507.31 generated by the sale of 18,480 pairs of shoes, because they did little direct work for their endorsement check and they earned so many other endorsements through the ceaseless work of IMG's agents.[8]

Those same agents diversified Laver and IMG's other client entertainers into as many different areas as possible. Consulting work at the Palmas del Mar resort in Palm Desert, California; Laver-Emerson tennis magazines distributed throughout Hyatt's twenty-eight thousand U.S. hotel rooms; management positions relating to the tennis programs at places like Hilton Head Island

Resort and the Newport Beach Tennis Club, where pro shops paid to screen the instructional copies of the program titled "Laver Emerson Method"; joint ventures with other tennis players; insurance companies such as Mass Mutual, which thought their products would sell better by putting a young and vigorous athlete in advertisements; the creation of player management companies named after the player and managed by IMG with the intention to manage and move some of the player's assets as needed; and various tennis products that ranged from tennis string to ball machines that claimed to spit out tennis balls in the way that shots came off of the professional's racquet—IMG's agents tried to put Laver into all of it.[9] In those efforts—along with the cattle breeding, ranching, and numerous other investments they found for their clients—the agency largely succeeded.[10] In less than a year, McCormack doubled Laver's off-court income; moved him from a no-name clothing endorsement to the up-and-coming Adidas sportswear brand; segmented the world market for Laver's racquet endorsement into Europe, Australia, and the United States for fifty thousand dollars a year; and negotiated twenty contracts for Laver across a range of fields.[11]

Defending a player license against unwanted infringement from outsiders mattered almost as much as brokering the original sponsorship deal. McCormack practiced law; so too did many of the agents who worked for him. Patrolling the unlicensed usage of an athlete client often meant IMG counselors went after small individuals or companies for petty infringements. One case occurred in 1975 when Rod Laver wrote to IMG's legal department about imposters who produced cassette tapes that purported to teach his and Ken Rosewall's groundstrokes. At fifteen dollars apiece, Dick Bradlee of Dick Bradlee Tennis College planned to get rich off those images of Laver. IMG threatened Bradlee with a lawsuit and dissuaded him from trying to profit from "the highly valued property" that was "Rod's name and likeness."[12]

In the case of female athletes, IMG essentially worked as hard to promote the images of women as it did for those of the men. McCormack's writings revealed some sexism when it came to hiring women and promoting them into senior management positions within his firm. On the occasions that women working for IMG rose above the secretary ranks to positions where negotiations of real weight took place, McCormack gave those employees due credit for rising high in the "traditionally . . . male bastion" of sports while simultaneously hinting that a woman executive or lead attorney was the result of something unusual, such as the impression made by the imposing six-foot height of IMG lawyer Betsy Groff on negotiators looking to make a deal.[13]

As IMG grew, though, McCormack's reluctance to acknowledge the executive capabilities of many women softened, and he promoted women to lead core parts of the firm. For example, Stephanie Tolleson headed the IMG's Women's Tennis Division in the 1990s and grew that area by signing crucial contracts with players like Venus and Serena Williams. Whereas women employees of IMG had an uphill climb to succeed in sports management, the company's account executives bent over backward to please the company's female athlete clients. When it came to representing players such as Evonne Goolagong, Billie Jean King, and Martina Navratilova, McCormack put the business instincts of these women on par with if not exceeding many of IMG's male clients. The chief complaint the agency's account executives leveled against sportswomen pointed not at the athletes but at their entourages, spouses, and partners, who proved much more meddlesome in the financial well-being of the IMG client than did the wives or girlfriends of male players. That perhaps explains why the two women athletes McCormack most admired and most enjoyed managing were Billie Jean King and Martina Navratilova. Both players kept their sexual preferences secret during much of their playing careers and came to IMG unencumbered by male partners who thought they knew sports and sports management.[14]

The most influential female player IMG represented during the first two decades of the firm's tennis representation was Billie Jean King. She agreed to IMG's representation in September 1978, though IMG may have done some work for King as early as 1974. In either case, by June 1980 IMG had generated and was managing nineteen contracts for King with companies ranging from American Express to Yonex Trading, each paying out retainers and annual minimum guarantees of between twenty-five hundred and one hundred thousand dollars, with each guarantee set to rise between 10 percent and more than 100 percent annually over the two to four years of most agreements. In exchange for her retainer, King may or may not have had to make an appearance at a company event such as a photo shoot, conference, or exhibition. The inconsistency of the amount of money the contract awarded for the amount of real work in terms of appearances revealed not only the persuasive powers of IMG agents to make deals for their clients but also how difficult companies found assigning a dollar value to an athlete's likeness. For example, the Nestlé company paid King fifty thousand dollars a year beginning in 1980 to drink their light iced tea but did not require her to make a single appearance or anything else except, on occasion, sip the bottled beverage. Charleston Hosiery, on the other hand, paid King ten thousand dollars in 1980 to wear their athletic socks in all of her matches and attend one of their corporate events for the day. Simply put, the impact an athlete had on an advertising campaign was close to impossible to measure.[15]

King's personal measurements, on the other hand, were essential from IMG's standpoint. On March 15, 1980, IMG prepared detailed measurements of every part of King's body down to the quarter inch. Armed with that information and King's impressive biography, IMG agents approached potential clothing sponsors with much of the information those companies needed to make a decision about whether or not to offer King an endorsement deal. IMG worked on biographies for many of its athlete clients. But in terms of the detailed analysis of athlete's bodies, IMG actually worked harder in generating that information for its female client athletes than its male client athletes—though the fact that a company sought such information points to the importance of sexualization of female athletes when compared to their male counterparts. By June 1980, half of IMG's tennis clients were women. That percentage rose in the 1990s as IMG's tennis division grew compared to that of other agencies with strong positions in tennis recruiting.[16]

When it came to athletes from traditionally marginalized groups, IMG's efforts varied. The company represented only 67 African American athletes out of a total of 2,335 unique clients—though the firm did count as clients the two most famous African American athletes in the world, Muhammad Ali and later Tiger Woods, and the most famous athlete of color outside of the United States, Brazilian striker Pelé. Despite doing a tremendous amount of business in Japan, particularly with Japanese companies obsessed with golf, IMG represented only six Japanese entertainer-athletes: LPGA champion Ayako Okamato, PGA champion Tsuneyuki Nakajima, PGA champion Asao Aoki, poet Karou Maruyama, tennis player Soichi Nakamura, and Japanese American tennis player Ann Kiyomura. The company preferred participating in Japanese sporting events rather than managing Japanese athletes. Religion and ethnicity mattered much less than race: Pope John Paul II and Itzhak Perlman both had IMG representation. IMG also did not mind getting political in representing presidential hopeful Bob Dole and other candidates in their campaigns. Nor did the company refuse to manage easygoing entertainers with audiences far afield from sports—Fred Rogers of *Mister Rogers' Neighborhood*, for example.[17]

Examples of openness notwithstanding, when they had the opportunity to recruit a major African American athlete, IMG agents, at least early in the firm's history, were less aggressive and successful. After a third recruitment meeting, Arthur Ashe described McCormack as "aloof."[18] At the same time, the agency worked with the NFL's lawyers to discourage the formation of a "Negro Union" made up of African American representatives from the league's sixteen franchises authorized to bargain on behalf of African American footballers. Lionel Aldridge, Elijah Pitts, Henry V. Kane, and other black athletes reported that they and "almost all of the other negro athletes in the NFL" had received "nil" in terms of dollars from advertisers, endorsements, and personal appearance fees. Writing on behalf of IMG, Richard R. Alford pointed out that while the tide of a "white only" preference among national advertisers was beginning to change, the proposed union's efforts "of Negroes banning [sic] together partly because they are Negroes is a step in the wrong direction." Alford simply did not see McCormack wanting to lend his influence and offer marketing help to "the Negro nobodies of the NFL."[19] Having said that, to my knowledge, nowhere in McCormack's voluminous correspondence do specific slurs or specific policies of African American exclusion appear. Sometimes silence and inaction, however, speak louder than words and actions.

IMG's traditional stance against athletes who had already peaked likewise seemed more like general guidance than a hard and fast rule when race entered the picture. The agency turned down Pancho Gonzales for representation when he was still the number one tennis player in the world, while at the same time the company looked to sign Jack Kramer, who promoted tennis but had not played the game competitively in more than fifteen years. McCormack himself even considered supervising Kramer's account.[20] Here and elsewhere, IMG's agents made choices about who and what to represent, with race an underlying but not explicitly stated factor in those decisions.

Stepping back from the work they did for individual clients to look at the company as a whole, how did IMG spend the bulk of its resources? An imprecise but instructive inference is revealed by examining the scope of the company's files and counting the frequency with which employees worked to promote clients' interests as those interests related to certain sports. Golf dominated with 8,621 (36.287 percent), followed by tennis with 2,368 actions (17.38 percent), and compared to sports often considered far larger, such as baseball with 158 (1.159 percent), basketball 144 (1.057 percent), and football 487 (3.575 percent).[21] Out of 13,622 specific actions IMG's agents took relating to twenty-eight different sports or categories of sports (e.g., water sports), IMG prioritized individual sports eight-and-a-half to one over team sports, with golf first and tennis second, for a combined eight for every ten sports activities IMG undertook. That prioritization goes far to explain the "tennis boom" of the 1960s and '70s.[22]

Less than a decade after McCormack signed golfer Arnold Palmer as his first client, IMG counted a significant number of the most recognizable "personalities" in sports among the agency's athletes. That rapid ascendance was attributable to how well McCormack ran his agency, to how much demand professional athletes had for professional representation, and, more broadly, to how popular sports—particularly individual sports—were with the broad public. McCormack also put into practice the old adage that it takes money to make money by pioneering—much to the chagrin of ProServ, his closest competitor in the sports management business, which was less than a third the size of IMG—the awarding of guarantees to potential sports clients. An IMG executive would ask an athlete how much money he or she had received for an appearance or product endorsement and guarantee to double that number regardless of whether IMG actually convinced a company to match the stated offer for licensing or appearance fees. The athlete usually agreed to IMG representation, which forced the firm to make good on their promise of increased compensation. They often honored that pledge by simply paying the additional money to their client out of IMG's bank accounts without revealing to the athlete the true source of the money. Making good on its guarantees thus allowed IMG to accumulate far more athletes than it might have otherwise and created for the firm an economy of scale and a stable of clients unmatched by most of its competitors combined.[23]

In a 1974 letter bragging about the "caliber of athlete" they represented, an IMG executive put together something close to a master client list. For team sports, the agency represented only a handful of baseballers, including the talented Frank Robinson. IMG's basketball clients included names like Hank Finkel, and the firm highlighted more football players of high caliber such as Archie Manning. Hockey and soccer clients of the status of Kyle Rote Jr. were also few when compared to the individual sport athletes IMG boasted most about. The agency counted many more team sport athletes as clients, but they liked to brag about their best. The same was true, even more so, for their individual sport athletes: Arnold Palmer and Chi Chi Rodriguez, among dozens of other golfers; tracksters such as Brian Oldfield and Jim Ryan; motor racers like Jackie Stewart, Sam Posey, and Brock Yates; tennis's most elite players such as Bjorn Borg and Martina Navratilova; along with dozens of other athletes at the top of their comparatively minor sports. IMG even counted nonathlete entertainers among the entertainers the firm represented, including fashion model Jean Shrimpton, broadcaster Chris Schenkel, and several classical musicians.[24]

By the year 2000, IMG employed approximately 2,500 people in 81 offices across 31 countries. The firm represented the most profitable events in sports along with major music competitions—including the Winter and Summer Olympics during the 1980s and 1990s—and put Tiger Woods on course to become the first athlete in history to earn more than one billion dollars in pretax income.[25] At the time of McCormack's death in 2013, the agency had represented 2,335 client athletes, entertainers, organizations, and sporting events in a total of 42,937 negotiations.[26] All in all, the agency's influence over professional sports and entertainment more broadly was beyond quantification, but with influence came conflict with the other power brokers in the entertainment market.

The closest competition came from fellow sports agents courting celebrity athletes for representation. On December 30, 1968, McCormack wrote to U.S. Davis Cup captain Donald Dell, via the U.S. embassy in Canberra, and wished Dell luck in the Davis Cup Challenge Round. The real purpose of the letter was to persuade Dell to join McCormack's agency, because, in McCormack's words, "there is an awful lot that we can do together in this area." McCormack meant tennis, and he feared the competition Dell could give IMG if Dell decided to mimic McCormack's success with the greater connections he held with tennis players.[27]

That concern proved warranted because Dell brought a tremendous pedigree to the sports agency business. Dell garnered all-American honors three of the four years he lettered at Yale, and he reached the National Collegiate Athletic Association (NCAA) Men's Tennis Final his junior year. He competed in USLTA and ILTF tournaments during the 1960s as well as playing on the American Davis Cup squad in 1961 and 1963. A year later he earned his law degree from the University of Virginia and entered practice at a firm along the Washington Beltway. Dell worked for powerful politicians such as Bobby Kennedy and Sargent Shriver, whom Dell served as special assistant when Shriver directed President Lyndon Johnson's Office of Economic Opportunity.[28]

After Shriver left that position and accepted an appointment as the U.S. ambassador to France, Dell continued to serve his country both domestically and abroad. That career also satisfied Dell's ambitions to develop his own service-based business marketing professional athletes around the world. In the late 1960s he lived in Georgetown along the Potomac River, giving him ready access to the Beltway power brokers. He talked to and dined with President Johnson. He drank with the Australian prime minister and Australian ambassador to the United States when he captained the U.S. Davis Cup team, just when tennis moved to open competition between amateurs and professionals. He worked for Senator Robert Kennedy, ate lunch and played tennis at the Kennedy compound on Cape Cod, and sat next to the senator in Kennedy's campaign plane when President Johnson announced on May 31, 1968, that he would not accept the Democratic Party's nomination for president.[29] With the White House in Republican hands, Dell still maintained political connections with subsequent administrations as his ProServ agency expanded dynamically in the 1970s, speaking, eating, and praying with President Gerald Ford—himself a former University of Michigan football player and fan of athletics. Throughout his career Dell consistently maintained that his personal record of accomplishment on the tennis court gave him access to people who were powerful in both politics and business.[30]

Like McCormack, Dell recognized the seismic shifts in the American and the global economy in the late '60s and early '70s. When the U.S. Labor Department reported that most American workers earned their living in service rather than in agriculture and industry by the 1980s, Dell saw not an overturned economic sector but an underperforming one. Nonetheless, Dell hesitated to enter the sports agency business, because he believed his career lay in legal practice focused on Washington politics. At the same time, he kept one foot in the tennis world by captaining the U.S. Davis Cup team, and one of his players gave him the push necessary to leave his Washington law firm behind to create a rival agency to McCormack's IMG. In 1968 Arthur Ashe won the first U.S. Open as an amateur; suddenly the U.S. Army officer and champion received offer after offer from sports promoters to turn professional. The best offer came from George MacCall, who guaranteed Ashe four hundred thousand dollars in playing fees over five years—serious cash when compared to the paltry earnings that professionals like Pancho Gonzales had made on tour just a year earlier. Ashe asked his mentor Dell for advice. "Arthur, I'd wait. Your name value is going nowhere but up. You're playing well. You are allowed to win prize money now. You're in the army. You're single. You don't need the contract now. I think the money will be bigger if you wait," replied Dell.[31]

At the same time, Dell arranged a series of meetings between McCormack and Ashe with the belief that IMG could make Ashe into the "Arnold Palmer of tennis," but those talks ultimately foundered. "Why don't you represent me?" a frustrated Ashe asked Dell after leaving another failed meeting with McCormack. Dell spluttered unconvincing responses and waffled when Ashe pressed him late in 1968, until the lawyer abandoned his public service and his firm to open his own practice focused on "representing tennis players." The first player was Ashe, the second Stan Smith, who—in a story right out of McCormack's playbook—agreed to Dell's representation with a shake of the hand. Overnight, Dell had the top two American tennis players on board. And as studies in contrasts, they gave Dell a great deal of flexibility in approaching companies for endorsements: Ashe was African American, a Southerner, a military officer, soft-spoken, with an elegant serve volley and touch game; Smith, by contrast, was blond, from California, brash, with a big game to boot.[32]

Nearly all the agents Dell hired were attorneys. Licensing an athlete's image essentially fell in the realm of intellectual property work, where the strengths of lawyers in argumentation, contractual nuance, and combativeness mattered more than in other business pursuits, where producers and consumers of a good could more easily reach agreement on the essence, utility, and value of a product or service—as well as the transaction from one party to the other of that product or service.[33] Agents with legal backgrounds meant ProServ could move against established stakeholders to set new precedents in professional sports. For example, in 1974 ProServ handled eighteen-year-old basketballer Moses Malone and his direct transition from high school basketball to professional play without the requisite stop in college. In so doing, the agency defied upholders of tradition and threats from the NCAA.[34] Malone immediately excelled in the American Basketball Association (ABA) and then the National Basketball Association (NBA), following the 1976 merger, for twenty years. At the time of his retirement in 1995, another talented high school senior, named Kobe Bryant, prepared to forgo college and head directly to the NBA draft despite the warnings against skipping college that continued and intensified two decades after ProServ's agent-lawyers made that vertical move a reality for players.

During ProServ's first twenty years, Dell and his agents secured "playing contracts" for five hundred athletes and negotiated countless endorsement deals with companies for those athletes and additional clients.[35] The most important of those contracts came in the spring of 1984, when Dell and coworker David Falk met with Michael Jordan and University of North Carolina coach Dean Smith to discuss the upcoming NBA draft in June and Jordan's future in the league. ProServ's agents approached that meeting with a great deal of confidence because the dozens of tennis players they managed and, effectively, turned into sports franchises in and of themselves, had established a reputation in the minds of team sport athletes that the firm could do the same for them despite the presence of four teammates on the court at the same time. "Why don't we use this time for you to ask questions?" Dell suggested to Jordan. Before he even entered the draft, ProServ had made sure Jordan understood himself as a player apart from his teammates, his franchise, the league, and his sport. They launched Jordan not as a player but as a "high-flying sports hero." Dell convinced Nike to agree to make the Air Jordan sneaker even before Jordan played his first professional game. That deal happened because Dell had long cultivated a relationship with Nike founder Phil Knight over bottles of wine with their wives at Dell's private box at the Italian Open tennis tournament in Rome. The actual "Air Jordan" brand name that is synonymous with the most profitable endorsement deal in sports history was simply an afterthought—without any market research or focus grouping—that arose as a throw-away comment at a final meeting between Nike and ProServ. With that contract for the yet unproven Jordan, Falk and Dell created the concept of athlete individuality in leagues and sports crowded with talented players. It became the agency's most powerful recruiting tool. From the mid-'80s and after, ProServ agents wooing a new client had only to present a contract after citing some specifics on the firm's success with "licensing and merchandising" Michael Jordan.[36]

Two major clients who signed contracts with Dell were the communist nations of Russia and China. In 1986 Mikhail Gorbachev publicly announced policies of glasnost and perestroika within the Soviet Union.[37] Three years later ProServ secured a contract with the Russian Tennis Federation for representation, unaware that the Berlin Wall would soon fall. The seeds of that arrangement dated all the way back to 1961 when Dell, along with his Davis Cup teammates, became the first American tennis players to compete behind the Iron Curtain. That international amateur competition gave the Russian Tennis Federation representatives and Dell a place to work from in crafting marketing policies for the international professional tennis that had proliferated in the 1980s.[38] President Richard Nixon's visit to Peking in the spring of

1972 started a dialogue between Chinese and American political leaders.[39] Toward the end of that decade, Dell began reaching out to the Chinese athletic associations as well. ProServ agents did their first deal with Chinese athletes and their political handlers in 1979, and the agency and China continued to do business throughout the 1980s and into the '90s with events like the Asian Games, which China hosted in 1990.[40]

Like IMG, ProServ's pull came to extend over athletic events themselves, because the managers of star athletes could direct a player away from one event and toward another. For example, in tennis tournaments, seeding committees and directors often had discretion in admitting a small number of "wild cards" into the event's draw without regard to the ATP's computer-generated ranking of the player under consideration. With prize money awarded to a player who lost even in the first round, simply making the draw of a tournament meant a payday for the player and the agency that represented him. The possibility of losing several ProServ client athletes or one ProServ client superstar often proved too great a threat for a tournament director to not extend the up-and-coming ProServ-managed athletes an entry into a tournament, regardless of if his or her rankings warranted such an invitation. But the events also did much for Dell's business. Toward the end of his career, he reflected that the single greatest asset he had in closing a deal was his courtside private boxes at the French Open and the U.S. Open, which he received as a thank-you, along with millions of dollars in fees, for representing the FFT and the USTA's television rights to interested networks.[41] McCormack adopted the same approach at the two exclusive tournaments to which he was closest—the Masters Tournament at Augusta National Golf Club and Wimbledon. The founders of the two major entertainment agencies that dominated sports management up until the 1990s understood that the CEOs and upper managers who controlled the budgets of corporations large enough to invest in sports marketing and advertising preferred the perceived exclusivity of golf and tennis events with a glass of champagne, a fine cigar, and strawberries with cream just a finger snap away. Show them a good time, and they would show the money.[42]

McCormack and Dell built their firms focused on individual sport athletes at the same time athletes in team sports wielded new power. For example, sports historian Charles Korr has written about the "enormous leverage" the Major League Baseball Players Association exercised between 1961 and 1980.[43] Baseball players had free agency, but tennis players were free of franchises. That freedom, when combined with the finances new to tennis after

1968, meant that IMG and ProServ made tidy profits from tennis players despite the game's low profile in the United States compared to larger team sports. Furthermore, whereas team sport owners assumed little financial liability over publicly floated bonds for stadium building, sports management agents like McCormack and Dell did not even have to answer to voters, elected representatives, or municipal officials.[44] They built someone else's reputation for winning into sports celebrity, not bonds into buildings. The intellectual and legal sports world in which they moved proved more malleable than concrete. They cared less about local public opinion because they did not deal in specific places and spaces. The images of athletes they created moved across borders and away from local populations who were so fickle with their own tax dollars. In the entertainments that constitute popular culture, levels of abstraction have increased over time. The transnational sporting celebrity became the apotheosis of that transformation in the late twentieth century.

In 1967 McCormack published a promotional tract of his first client that masqueraded as a biography of Arnold Palmer. The second to last chapter of *Arnie* included a selection of letters golf fans had submitted to Palmer. Not one of the letter writers realized how much Palmer's managers, acting on behalf of the golfer, invented and enforced questionable legal practices, practiced creative accounting, and manipulated companies that then passed their extravagant marketing budgets onto consumers in the prices for their products; instead, all the letter writers declared that Arnold was their friend, he inspired them, he played phenomenal golf.[45] That focus on emotional connection and athletic skill rather than on inequality and waste was—and remains—the power of sport in the contemporary capitalist marketplace. The great tennis champion and social activist Arthur Ashe had firsthand experience with that influence as a friend of Dell's and a longtime ProServ client. During a thoughtful speech at Yale University in 1991, Ashe told those assembled, "Sports in America is a $65 billion industry today, and it's still growing. The top ten most watched television shows ever are sports programs with the exception of an episode of 'Dallas.' . . . Sports are an addiction for us."[46]

The media-first tour and the managed athlete were just two expressions of that power. In tennis that power reached its fullest expression in the evolution of the game's greatest tournament. In the winter of 1985, Mark McCormack sent a company memorandum stating, "Wimbledon is our most important client and, therefore, it is your most important assignment as far as I am concerned—I don't have to tell you this either."[47] For a firm whose primary mission was to convince companies that attaching a person's likeness to their products would help sell more goods, such blunt talk about the prioritization of a single sporting event over the dozens of celebrity-athlete clients hints at just how profitable selling the sport of tennis became after 1968. The importance McCormack assigned to Wimbledon was right on the money.

The first Wimbledon Championships dated back to 1877. By the start of the twentieth century, the tournament's popularity had grown to the point that the AELTC made a massive investment in bleachers around the club's Centre Court to accommodate the burgeoning crowds. Detractors believed the club had overreached, but year after year the number of spectators grew and filled the Centre Court stands. Eventually the crowd overflowed the grounds. With a proven track record of peak attendance, the AELTC signed a contract with the LTA to hold the Championships at Wimbledon until 1972, at which point both parties agreed to revisit the suitability of the AELTC as the Championships' host. To players, wrote the revered British champion Fred Perry, "Wimbledon indeed is the Mecca of lawn tennis." Perry went on to note that the tournament was even more than that, however, for the late June and early July event helped promote the best time to visit London and became just one more fashionable reason for people with financial means and influence to visit Britain's capital. Wimbledon established itself during the late nineteenth century just as a host of other major sporting championships diffused from England and across the British Empire. The Championships thus served as a "great missionary," in Perry's words, for tennis and for Britain's athletic legacy more broadly.[48]

Sports historian Robert J. Lake has noted both the desire for and the care AELTC members took to make sure the Wimbledon Championships reflected a legacy of British lawn tennis for the world to see. The precisely manicured grounds, the tastes of British summer strawberries, and the competitors' white playing attire were purposeful decisions made to enhance the tournament's distinctiveness. In McCormack and IMG, the AELTC had found a partner that was willing and able to put those plans into practice beyond the on-grounds and United Kingdom market matters ably handled by the Irishman-led firm Bagenal Harvey Consultants.[49]

The first Wimbledon to allow professionals to compete with amateurs proved a sweeping success for IMG because Rod Laver, the firm's lone tennis client at that point, lifted the trophy on Championship Saturday. The next year proved even better for Laver, IMG, and the AELTC, with Laver again lifting the trophy three-quarters of the way to his second Grand Slam—the first of the Open Era. Here McCormack's plan to develop international offices paid off, because the IMG division World of Sports Ltd., run by Bob Ferrier, was already in place in London. Ferrier worked contacts throughout the United Kingdom to move behind the scenes after McCormack first caught wind that national tennis associations within the ILTF would move to allow open competition between the sport's top professionals and amateurs in the biggest tournament venues.[50]

McCormack directed his Transworld International Division to develop a project to impress the AELTC committee members that could be executed in a few weeks' time. The producers decided on a video to highlight the historic moment when one of the oldest sporting tournaments in the world belatedly entered the contemporary world of commercial sports. Cocktails of nostalgia and excitement flowed in the club's boardrooms as committee members quickly approved the pitch. Six months later, Jay Michaels of IMG's Transworld International screened the film to Herman David, chairman of the AELTC committee, and his fellow board members at Wimbledon. They heartily applauded; good news for Michaels because his real purpose at that meeting was to gather information about how IMG might make Wimbledon into the most profitable sporting event in the world. He knew that international broadcasting held the key.[51]

The previous year's contract between the BBC and the AELTC had the broadcaster pay £15,700 for "worldwide" radio and television rights, while the ITV network paid £10,750 for broadcasting rights throughout the United Kingdom. Michaels thought both networks paid well below a fair price; however, he soon realized just how much power the BBC wielded in Britain. Confusion existed about whether or not he could even ask around in Europe for a better offer for the AELTC without first speaking with the recalcitrant BBC. What the Wimbledon 1968 video bought IMG was the blessing of the club's leadership to pursue interested parties in the United States for Wimbledon broadcast rights. ABC, CBS, and NBC, all showed interest, but here again the BBC frustrated Michaels and IMG by refusing to relinquish any space suitable for a camera broadcasting the tournament in the intimate Centre Court. Without their own cameras and crews, American networks had little control over their sports production, and the sale of an event to a network became untenable from IMG's point of view. The AELTC would have to allow IMG's

Transworld International Division to remove several prime Centre Court seats if they wanted an American network to agree to pay a sizable broadcast fee.[52]

Twenty years later at the 1989 Championships, McCormack sold $19.5 million in television rights across at least fifty-four countries for the AELTC. The club collected an additional $60,995 in radio rights. McCormack understood that a sale was only as good as the seller's ability to collect payment from the buyer. He thus exercised a great deal of flexibility in the price he asked different networks and media companies to pay for Wimbledon broadcast rights. He gave the Honduran-based Canal 5 the lowest asking price, at $600 for exclusive broadcast rights in that Central American country—a deal Canal 5 apparently thought was no good for them, as their money remained outstanding a year later after IMG's repeated attempts to collect. Most companies did pay, however, because the financial stakes were too high for IMG to simply brush off nonpayment. The lion's share of funds payable to the AELTC for the 1989 Wimbledon tournament came from the U.S. market, where NBC paid $9.5 million for exclusive cable broadcast rights and Home Box Office (HBO) paid $3.25 million for pay-per-view coverage rights. The German-based Universum Film AG paid the same amount as HBO for television broadcast rights on the European continent. After IMG deducted its fee, the broadcasting of the 1989 Wimbledon tournament netted the AELTC $18 million. A year later, television and radio rights earned the club $21.5 million. The AELTC's profits from media broadcasts continued to rise at the millennium.[53]

At the same time that the very tennis federations who had belatedly embraced professionalism signed massive television contracts, courted major corporate sponsorships, and built historic tournaments into commercial juggernauts, some of the professional players who made the tennis boom of the late 1960s and '70s possible found themselves out in the cold. Richard Savitt, a contemporary of Pancho Gonzales, looked jadedly at the state of tennis several years into the Open Era. Sure, a player would feel thrilled to play in front of a big stadium-size crowd for a big paycheck, but the growth of the game also came with a cost for the players. The intimacy that competitors enjoyed with their fellow players, with the fans, and with the members of the host clubs found at the likes of the LATC and the Berkeley Tennis Club was absent at the bigger tournaments in the Open Era. "The money wasn't there, but the way of life, who we met, and what we got to see can't be replaced or can't be equated with a dollar amount," Savitt said. Tennis used to foster community and solidarity through physical competition, verbal banter, stewardship of club's facilities, and the mutual pursuit of the beauty of the human body in motion among players as collaborators in a game of ultimate skill. After 1968, at least in the mind of one player who peaked before tennis opened, tennis simply became "like all other professional sports," and that was something to regret.[54]

Players also held certain misgivings when people overidentified them with their former athletic accomplishments even after they had long retired from sports and instead wanted recognition for their new business ventures. Savitt explained that tennis did not directly open doors in the commercial world in the conventional sense of business executives at members and men-only golf clubs hashing out deals over cigars and chip shots on the links. For Savitt, however, tennis did allow him to travel abroad to new places where he met different people he otherwise would not have met. He thus returned to the United States with a more cosmopolitan worldview, which translated into a more competent, comprehensive, and flexible business acumen than Savitt would have developed without the travel afforded by the tennis tours. The rub came when a business associate identified Savitt by something he did on the court thirty years ago rather than what he did for an account yesterday.[55]

In an individual sport like tennis, such an affront was especially common because players' bodies simply could not compete at a high level for very long, which forced them out of the professional game, almost always before their mid-thirties. Before the game began to pay players money enough to save for retirement, in the mid-1970s, the body's decision for early retirement meant most players still had half of their working life ahead of them without the ability or opportunity to work in the sport for which they had trained most of their life. Players like Pancho Gonzales, who competed for more than twenty-five years, were certainly the exceptions to the normal career of players; however, as Gonzales's career and retirement make clear, two decades on or near the top of the game did not set a player up with the financial resources necessary for retirement before the tennis boom of the '70s. But just as missing out on the money that flowed to the new professional was a bitter pill for veterans of the barnstorming tours to swallow, championship tennis after 1968 also afforded a host of new players with a big income during the economic stagflation of the 1970s. McCormack's and Dell's managed athlete was the prime reason.

CHAPTER 12

Women's Professional Tennis in the Early Open Era

At the start of the Open Era in 1968, eight million people played tennis in the United States. Many if not most of these players were women. Such statistics may very well have surprised sports marketing agents like Mark McCormack, who tended to bring a fair amount of macho to their work, but to a steady number of topflight women tennis players, the game was always one of their own making.[1] More than anyone else, three women shaped women's professional tennis in the early Open Era and put the sport on a path to the present: the publisher and founder of the women's professional tour, Gladys Heldman; the player and women's sports leader Billie Jean King; and the physician and pioneering trans athlete, Dr. Renée Richards.

Unlike most figures who helped usher in professional tennis, Gladys Medalic Heldman did not play tennis as a junior. After high school she attended Stanford University, where she graduated magna cum laude with a history major. There she met Julius Heldman, and they married in 1942, the day after he finished his PhD in physical chemistry. The young couple went on to Oak Ridge, Tennessee, where Julius worked to enrich uranium for the U.S. atomic weapons program. After the war, the couple moved to Berkeley, California, with the nearby National Laboratories in Livermore and Berkeley. The Heldmans resided conveniently next to the Berkeley Tennis Club, where the once nationally ranked Julius Heldman began playing again. Gladys Heldman picked up the game there after the birth of their second child. She struggled at first but took lessons with local teaching professional Tom Stowe, who taught her the fundamentals. With her technique then in place, she started playing games with any local woman she could find, as well as frequent sets with her husband. By the time the family moved to Long Beach, Gladys Heldman ranked number twelve in California and improved even faster in Southern California with more frequent tournaments and better competition. By 1949 she felt ready to tour the United States on the amateur tournament circuit and played the U.S. National Mixed Doubles Championship with her husband. That same year, Julius Heldman's work for the Shell Oil Company moved the family to Houston, where they quickly assumed leadership positions in the tennis community—Julius as president of the Houston Tennis Association and Gladys as publisher of the *Houston Tennis News* bulletin, which she multiplied from sixty-two subscribers to more than one thousand. Two years later she received "Tennisdom's Woman of the Year" award at Boston's Longwood Cricket Club, which honored her achievements: putting together a competition pitting Texas tennis players against other players on the U.S. team; publishing a Texas tennis magazine, *The Round-Up*; sponsoring junior clinics; organizing the Houston Junior Tennis Association; keeping the Houston city challenge ladder; chairing the Junior Wightman Cup team; and promoting "Tennis Week" across Southeast Texas.[2] All that experience served Heldman well in the national tennis work she soon assumed: first in publishing and editing the tennis magazine of record she founded, *World Tennis*, and later in helping to found and run what became the forerunner to the contemporary women's professional tour.

Heldman published her first issue of *World Tennis* in June 1953 from offices listed in Houston, Texas. From the beginning, she made sure to keep the control of her magazine in the hands of women. As editor and publisher she retained final copy approval for herself, but she rarely exercised veto prerogative on her writers and her staff, because she employed so many women who knew all too well the specific challenges women athletes faced in the 1950s and '60s. Gloria Butler, for example, covered tennis throughout Europe and in her reporting worked tirelessly to promote women in the sport. Sarah Danzig, who formerly went by the name Sarah Palfrey Cooke when she had played professionally and before she married *New York Times* sportswriter Allison Danzig, did the same from her account executive position in the *World Tennis* publishing office. From a subscription point of view, what changed with Heldman's publishing the top tennis periodical was the number of subscribers, which increased from forty-five hundred readers of *American Lawn Tennis* to sixty-six hundred readers of the first print run of *World Tennis*. By the end of 1953, Heldman counted fifteen thousand subscribers. She replaced an outmoded two-color journal presentation with a glossy full-color magazine. She also emphasized player photographs and advertisements to a degree that drew the ire of the USLTA Amateur Rule Committee, who looked wearily at most anyone's, let alone a woman's, embrace of the commercialization of the game.[3]

That commercialism also made women tennis players increasingly visible on the court. Prior to 1968, women professionals such as Suzanne Lenglen, Mary Browne, Alice Marble, Mary Hardwick, Pauline Betz, and Gertrude Moran occasionally played with the handful of professional men who earned a living by barnstorming across the United States, Australia, and Europe, dueling one another rather than being seeded in an amateur tournament draw. The peripatetic touring lifestyle brought with it real dangers: burnout from hundreds of days on the road; low gate receipts that could halt a tour midstretch or squash a tour the coming year; and the forfeiture of amateur status, effectively limiting one's competitive tennis outside of the very few professional touring opportunities. The dangers of turning professional were more acute for women than for their male colleagues; women received little compensation and prize money for their victories and next to nothing for losing. Limited matches and money explained why women more often than men appealed for reinstatement in the amateur ranks—as Moran did in November 1953. Heldman tried to counter the inequality in her editing of *World Tennis*. More importantly, she put her money and her management skills together in promoting women's professional tennis.[4]

Heldman had a terrific vantage point from which to view the ILTF's and the USLTA's belated experiment with open tennis. She reported on the first Open Wimbledon and the first U.S. Open, quickly learning what worked and what needed improvement. By the fall of 1969, she thought the USLTA was moving in the right direction by appointing Joseph F. Cullman III, Philip Morris chairman of the board, to chair the U.S. Open, but the place of women players on the professional tennis tours needed a complete overhaul. Lamar Hunt and WCT signed only male professionals, and the faltering position of George MacCall's NTL meant the handful of professional women MacCall signed made only a fraction of their guarantees. Most topflight women players thus tried to straddle professional and amateur tennis by way of the dubious "registered player" classification that ILTF had adopted in order to secure enough votes for open tennis. Heldman's voice was one of many opining that any distinction the USLTA, the ILTF, or any tennis organization made that called a person who made money from their tennis game anything other than a professional was unsuitable and unsustainable.[5]

The concept of the association-approved player was a vestige of the amateur federations' long-standing attempts to control the flow of money into and out of the game. Heldman further bristled at that control because she saw how classism fused with racism and misogyny into a capricious cocktail of discrimination. In her playing career, Heldman had once partnered with Althea Gibson during a Florida tournament, only to find that when the pair tried to play together again, in 1952, the Longwood Cricket Club and the Essex Country Club disallowed the partnership because of the color of Gibson's skin. Although Gibson was ranked in the nation's top ten, the USLTA allowed member clubs to bar her entry in tournaments from 1950 to 1954. Gibson's incredible talent and persistence eventually made her too valuable for the association and the U.S. State Department to keep off the court. A dozen years later, however, Heldman still had to call on the USLTA to "throw out" member clubs that continued to discriminate against African Americans and women.[6]

The club that for decades had most placed the on-court ability of a tennis player above all else was the LATC. Those courts served as the setting for an important moment in sports history one final time. Since Pancho Gonzales's regular training at the LATC in the early 1950s, top male talent played there far less than in previous years. Stan Smith and Bob Lutz were the last two players of any international class to come out of the junior development program led there by Perry T. Jones. By 1970 Jones had spent half a century leading Southern California tennis, and his health was failing. The eighty-year-old felt he had no choice but to relinquish his responsibilities in leading the SCTA, the TPASC, and the Pacific Southwest Tournament—all of which he ran out of his LATC office. Always fond of Jack Kramer and rightly aware of Kramer's success running profitable professional tennis, Jones asked Kramer to take over the management of the tournament that brought so much money into the coffers of Southern California tennis. Kramer accepted, and Jones died on September 16, 1970, five days before the forty-fourth start of the tournament he had created. In his last tournament, Jones still required all of the male competitors to wear their hair short.[7]

Heldman never knew Jones, but Billie Jean King did, and she did not shed a tear when he passed. As a junior player she had fulminated at Jones's paternalistic approach to developing players even though she directly benefited from his tutelage, organization, and the funds that his Pacific Southwest Tournament funneled to the SCTA's top young talent. For example, after an afternoon of training at the LATC, Jones gathered the players together for a photograph but kept King out of the picture because she could not afford to wear the white tennis dress he insisted the female players don. King saw classism mix with sexism during Jones's reign at the LATC, noting that Pancho Gonzales, Jack Kramer, and other top professionals in the world who trained at the club when they were not touring went out of their way to develop male players like Dennis Ralston without paying the slightest attention to talented women like King. In the minds of King and other women players, the replacement of Jones with Kramer at the LATC and as the director of the Pacific Southwest simply traded one chauvinist for another.[8]

Kramer confirmed their view when he set the tournament's purses at $12,500 for the men's singles champion compared to just $1,500 for the women's singles winner. According to King, those figures insulted the women and hurt the business of their careers. No stranger to sexism in the commercial world, Gladys Heldman agreed with the women professionals' misgivings. She put her resources to work for them. Through her *World Tennis* company, she offered the so-called Original Nine one-dollar contracts to compete in an event outside the sanction of the USLTA to be played in Houston, where Heldman had recently moved her company's offices. Previously, players like King and Rosemary Casals played matches as contract professionals under George MacCall, only to have their registered player status restored by the USLTA, which allowed for them to enter association-sanctioned tournaments. Initially they expected the same treatment because Jack Kramer told them he did not intend to make a fuss over their withdrawals from the Pacific Southwest Tournament. Heldman and the players then received notice that because of opposition raised by the SCTA (in which Jack Kramer held a leadership position), the USLTA decided not to sanction the Houston tournament, meaning any player who went ahead and played the event would very likely lose a chance to play in any future tournament—including the U.S. Open—under the auspices of the association. Eight players—Peaches Bartkowicz, Rosemary Casals, Judy Tegart Dalton, Billie Jean King, Kerry Melville Reid, Kristy Pigeon, Nancy Richey, and Valerie Ziegenfuss—decided to defy that ruling and play the Houston event. Heldman called on friend and fellow tennis fan Joseph Cullman III to furnish part of the five-thousand-dollar purse for the players. On Wednesday, September 23, 1970, eight women took to the courts of the Houston Racquet Club to, in the words of one participant, play "professional tennis." "This is not a women's liberation movement," said Billie Jean King at the time.[9] That came later.

The Houston Invitational Tournament proved promising for Philip Morris, Heldman, and the women professionals. With the example set that a women-only field of players could make money and garner media attention, Heldman went to work on Cullman. The two knew each other from their days paired as a mixed doubles team. Later Heldman impressed Cullman with her insights into improving the U.S. Nationals when she used the influence *World Tennis* wielded to help secure the post of U.S. Open chair for Cullman. As a business pair they quickly realized the business opportunity lurking in their partnership. Heldman could advance the cause of women's tennis while Cullman found a marketing niche for Philip Morris's women's line of cigarettes. While roughly a hundred women made a living as tennis professionals, Morris targeted the upswing in public interest for tennis during the late 1970s and early '80s. The new women's tennis tour fit like a glove with the tobacco company's larger marketing campaign, which championed the recent achievements in the women's movement in order to exploit women as consumers. A year after Houston, women tennis professionals played fourteen tournaments on the Virginia Slims Circuit. Fourteen years later, Gladys Heldman remarked with great pride that the partnership between women's professional tennis and Virginia Slims amounted to "the most successful sports sponsorship ever."[10]

Heldman tried to put professional women's tennis on the path to profitability by coordinating players in a new organization called the Women's International Tennis Federation (WITF). A typical Virginia Slims event was played in Philadelphia in 1973 with thirty-six professionals in the draw competing for $50,000 in prize money. After two rounds of preliminaries, which paid $270 and $450, respectively, half of the players remained, each of whom earned at least $720 for making the second round of the tournament. From there the pay increased exponentially, with the quarterfinals paying $1,530; the semifinals $3,000; $6,300 for the runner-up; and $10,800 for the champion. Doubles featured a handful of other players in addition to the singles players, with considerably less prize money paid, at only $900 for the winners. Such pay disparity between singles and doubles was a pattern set during the pre–Open

Era professional tournaments by promoters like Jack March, and that prize-money disparity continued during the first decade of open competition. The greater emphasis on singles rather than doubles explains why so many of the top players forgo doubles at tournaments today. Having said that, the structure of the women's professional tour varied somewhat from earlier professional tournaments and the contemporary men's tour in that early-round losers in Virginia Slims events earned a comparatively higher dollar amount than a male player who lost in the first round of their tour event. Well-run tournaments on the women's side, such as the Philadelphia tournament, also featured a back-draw that allowed first-round losers to compete for additional prize money in a consolation bracket. Players on the women's tour competed every bit as hard as players on the men's tour, but after years of limited pay compared to that of their male peers, women professionals and the woman who promoted their tour felt an obligation to give one another at least a livable wage.[11]

Along with moderate equity in prize money, another way Heldman structured women's professional tennis differently from the men's professional tour was in levying a 5 to 10 percent assessment on money that entered the women's professional tour. Those assessments took the form of a 10 percent withdrawal of the tournament purse for women's professional tennis expenses—$4,920 in the case of the $50,000 Philadelphia tournament—and in a 5 percent assessment on WITF members' earnings from tournament purses, endorsements, and appearance fees. WITF financial records show difficulty in collecting endorsement and appearance fees from the individual incomes that players earned as celebrity athletes on their own time, but Heldman managed to get around $20,000 for the prize monies that she pooled in a surplus account for distribution during tight times on the tournament calendar. Often, Heldman and her husband personally fronted cash for everything from car rentals, to telephone calls, to larger expenses such as prize-money advances. More than enough deposits came in to keep the Heldmans in their home, but the novelty of running a women's professional tour meant the WITF boss had to accept frequent cash shortages. Ingratitude from former professional players and from friends who knew her best, wrote Heldman after she retired from managing the professionals, was what saddened her the most during her many years involved in tennis. Different from the pre–Open Era barnstorming tours, when promoter Jack Kramer far outpaced his players in terms of personal income, Heldman's bank balance from her work as tour director tended to sit in the low five figures compared to the six-figure income Kramer earned.[12]

WITF financial records for the 1972–1973 financial year reported 750 members who supported women's professional tennis by paying dues. That remarkably high figure for such a young organization, whose genesis had come just two years earlier, owed not only to the bravery of the players but also to the resonance of Heldman's personal appeal to friends she had cultivated over the years who wanted to see tennis grow. The low dues the WITF collected helped too. Membership came in two varieties: full, which required one-time dues of five dollars; and associate, which required dues of one dollar. Heldman welcomed men to join as associate members, and many did, including the highest-profile professional players, like Rod Laver; however, with the exception of her husband, Julius, she tried to limit full memberships to women so that her organization never lost track of its principal mission to promote the visibility and viability of women's tennis in the Open Era. The low dues policy, which collected only about one thousand dollars per financial year, also meant that a dozen or so key members in the WITF shouldered a far greater financial burden than the rest of the membership. The WITF's role as the prime manager of the women's professional tennis tour meant that the most established players fronted cash to Heldman in the form of prize-money splits and percentages of their endorsements. Heldman then disbursed what they literally called a "Slush Fund" to aspiring women professionals in need. In the first full season of the women's pro tour, Heldman paid advances to and travel expenses for more than a dozen non-topflight professionals to encourage more robust draws in Virginia Slims events.[13]

Women professionals certainly competed against one another as fiercely as did the men, but in the early years of open tennis, women professionals showed greater solidarity than their male peers. With agents like Mark McCormack and Donald Dell encouraging their clients to think more and more about money, male stars began to skip tournaments for exhibition matches, which guaranteed a high payout simply for showing up. Whether or not the fix was in on those matches remains uncertain, but spectators who attended certainly considered the quality of play at those matches and the effort of the top stars below what they gave in tournaments. Heldman decried the "appearance money that the top men pros and their agents demand and get" as the "worst offense" in the sport. The amounts that tournaments paid ranged from fifty thousand dollars to three hundred thousand dollars to ensure the cooperation of the game's best. WCT took that a step further by operating a "Bonus Pool" that compensated male professionals with "race horses, diamonds, an oil well, stocks or $25,000 in cash." Women professionals may not have liked the gimmicks of their male peers, but WCT never posed a major threat to women's professional tennis. In fact, Virginia Slims tournaments earned better television ratings than most WCT tournaments. Virginia Slims Circuit financials also compared favorably to Lamar Hunt's WCT and many of the events in the ITF Grand Prix.[14]

Gladys Heldman's ambitious plans for the 1973 Virginia Slims Circuit required her to shed other responsibilities. In 1972 she sold *World Tennis* in order to focus more of her energy on managing the women's professional tour. She made money on the sale and remained a contributor to the magazine, but without ownership of *World Tennis*, Heldman no longer had the public forum or the same access to business capital that she had leveraged so effectively in getting the Virginia Slims Circuit off the ground. With between eighteen and twenty-two tournaments and at least five hundred thousand dollars in prize money posted for the start of the 1973 tour, women's professional tennis appeared poised for its best season yet.[15]

The success of women's professional tennis bothered the men who ran the USLTA. They wanted the women professionals back under their control. In 1971 USLTA president Robert Colwell went after the eight women professionals who had withdrawn from the 1970 Pacific Southwest Tournament to play the Houston Racquet Club matches. The USLTA sought to restrict their activities because their ongoing privately funded tournaments kept the association from collecting the 6 percent sanction fee. Heldman outflanked Colwell by convincing Cullman to pull Philip Morris advertising dollars from the U.S. Open if the association penalized the women professionals. The USLTA quickly removed "experimental" restrictions on the women professionals for the upcoming 1972 season, but that resolved little. Heldman wanted the most money for her players, but the USLTA wanted the most money for itself. Either paying or avoiding sanction fees meant more for one at the expense of the other. Conflict loomed.[16]

Heldman's position as the head of the tour made her the prime target for the USLTA's ire. She personally put up the initial one thousand dollars to incorporate what became the WITF and the early women's professional tour. The USLTA did not forget or forgive that investment, because the association respected Heldman's knowledge of the game and her ability to make professional tennis profitable. In fact, after the 1970 Houston tournament, the USLTA continued to pay Heldman what amounted to a consulting fee for her guidance when it came to women's tennis. Heldman's interactions with the association's leadership convinced her that the USLTA did not intend to promote women's professional tennis as vigorously as it did men's professional tennis. She found her suspicions confirmed when the USLTA ignored her counsel for prize-money parity and continued to keep women off the executive committee, which decided most association policy. In 1972 she severed her ties with the USLTA in order to remove any conflicts of interest in making the Virginia Slims Circuit totally independent of the association's influence. At first the USLTA did not seem to mind Heldman's decision to go it alone, because the men who ran the associations did not believe in the popularity of women's sports as fully as Heldman and Philip Morris did. More importantly, they wanted Heldman and her big-tobacco backers to pay a 6 percent sanction fee. She refused and sued the association.[17]

The case came down to the legality of how Heldman had started the women's professional tour. Heldman maintained that she offered the women players professional contracts because the USLTA planned to suspend them for playing at the Houston Racquet Club instead of at the LATC. The court disagreed, maintaining the USLTA never explicitly issued the "threat of suspension" to the players. That distinction justified the court's ruling that Heldman wrongly manipulated the women professional players in claiming that the USLTA would have suspended them if they played in a non-USLTA-sanctioned event. In reaching the conclusion that Heldman offered "naught but imperfect shadows of self-interested conjecture," the court ignored the USLTA's six decades of suspending players for the smallest of infractions, a history that almost certainly would have resulted in the vindication of Heldman's claims to player suspensions, especially given the growing popularity and growing dollars entering women's professional tennis. In a letter dated December 16, 1971, from USLTA president Robert Colwell to "The Top U.S. Women Players," which specifically threatened potential ineligibility for "Wimbledon, Forest Hills, Federation Cup and Wightman Cup competitions" should the USLTA not secure sanction fees from the women's tour professional tournaments, the court's reasoning revealed a fear of gender equality that outweighed the evidence of the case. Incredulity directed at Heldman appeared throughout the opinion, with the court seemingly having no qualms that the professional tournaments the USLTA planned to sponsor offered less prize money to the women professionals than what Heldman had secured for the players.[18]

Heldman and her fellow petitioner King failed in their attempt to secure a preliminary injunction against the USLTA's plans to prohibit Virginia Slims professionals from competing in association-sanctioned tournaments. The pair discussed the loss with the players. All of them expressed gratitude for everything that Heldman had done for women's tennis, but some asked Heldman to release them from their WITF contracts on the Virginia Slims Circuit in order to play USLTA- and ILTF-sanctioned tournaments. Heldman decided that women's professional tennis stood the best chance of growing if she stepped away from managing what she had started. Her resignation as director of the Virginia Slims Circuit appeased the USLTA to the degree that they decided not to ban women professionals from participating in sanctioned tournaments. Women's professional tennis would go on to flourish but without the real founder of that movement and without the full acknowledgment in later years of the impact Heldman had made on the sport by the athletes whose very careers she had sacrificed so much to make.[19]

At the same time, women's professional tennis seemed to suffer another setback. On May 13, 1973, the San Diego Country Estates in Ramona, California, played host to an exhibition match between Bobby Riggs and Australian champion Margaret Court. The Estates developers believed the spectacle could help sell prospective units. Thus they got more than they bargained for as limousine after limousine brought the most prominent entertainers and celebrities from throughout California up an unfinished road, past the unfinished golf course, and to the one finished tennis court for the match. Star running back for the Buffalo Bills O. J. Simpson attended and predicted that the number one woman in the world, Court, would clean up the crusty old Californian Riggs. Bill Cosby likewise predicted a Court victory, as did Court's colleagues on the women's tour, like Rosemary Casals, who remarked on camera, "Bobby Riggs is living on his past . . . and I'd be surprised if he wouldn't have a coronary right there." When asked the straightforward question "Do you have anything nice to say about Bobby Riggs at this point?" by broadcaster Brent Musburger, women's tennis tour promoter Gladys Heldman answered equally straightforwardly, "No, not really." Male former professional players disagreed with Bill Talbert and Pancho Segura, both of whom predicted a Riggs win. After the first set, a Riggs victory seemed more and more likely, with Riggs "soft balling Margaret to death," in Segura's analysis. Riggs completed the so-called Mother's Day Massacre with a straight-set win over the consistently best woman professional in the world.[20]

Fortunately for women's professional tennis, Billie Jean King stepped up to lead both on and off the court. King had long enjoyed special success at Wimbledon since back in 1962 when, as a teenager, she beat the previous year's winner, Margaret Smith Court. The following year she made the Wimbledon final. In 1966 she won her first Wimbledon Singles Championships, a feat she repeated in 1967, 1968, 1972, 1973, and 1975. What mattered a great deal more for the history of the sport was the organizing of the Women's Tennis Association (WTA), which King led around the 1973 Championships. In preparation for the 1973 Wimbledon boycott, King had offered ATP leadership the solidarity of herself and a number of women professionals. The ATP paid the offer no mind, but they did set an example that inspired King. At the Hotel Gloucester, with players having just arrived for the tournament, King, Rosie Casals, Frankie Durr, and Ann Jones whipped the votes needed for the women professionals to form the WTA.[21]

The initial importance of the player union was overshadowed when on September 23, 1973, approximately 48 million television viewers watched King beat Bobby Riggs in the so-called Battle of the Sexes. The Riggs-versus-King showdown was long on sideshow and short on the rank-and-file work of what getting paid to play professional tennis actually took. At the same time, however, the excitement over women's professional tennis that came with King's defeating Riggs gave the sport an extra boost in the context of the wider movement for women's athletics that had recently opened following the passage of Title IX in the Education Amendments Act of 1972.[22] The WTA would make the most of the spectacle and the substance to grow their sport in the mid-1970s. As sports historian Kristi Tredway has argued, the WTA coordinated the discrete ILTF Women's Grand Prix series of mostly European tournaments with the Virginia Slims Series of mostly U.S. based events, an important development in the professionalization of women's tennis.[23]

Toward the end of 1973, the WTA brought on a New York lawyer named Martin Carmichael to serve as the union's first executive director. He struggled to secure sponsorships, and the players themselves drafted a "Code of Conduct" and formed a "Disciplinary Committee" to enforce rules governing member behavior. The next year, Julian "Jerry" Diamond replaced Carmichael in leading the WTA's day-to-day operations, a move that proved wise, as tournament purses and sponsorship deals increased substantially throughout 1974. Just as Heldman was the driving force behind the first Virginia Slims and women's professional tennis partnership, so was Diamond largely responsible for the second. After growing up in the Bronx during the Great Depression, Diamond moved to San Francisco during the 1950s, where he worked in newspapers and public relations. He gained some experience in sports marketing in 1963 when he helped to bring the Soviet Union basketball team to the United States. He initially looked askance at women's professional tennis, having watched the Virginia Slims San Francisco tournament lose money on January 6, 1971; however, because that same event broke even in 1972 and proved profitable in 1973, Diamond began to realize the demand for women's tennis. He made good in his first year working for the WTA, growing prize money to around one million dollars in 1974.[24]

In 1974 the Virginia Slims Circuit was the more commercially successful and innovative of the tournament circuits run through the WTA. That had a lot to do with the Virginia Slims marketing team, who took great care to make sure WTA professionals put on the best show for spectators and television viewers alike. They held press conferences in the finest restaurants in America and made sure that the press room always had fresh flowers, and they provided the players with hairstylists at every event. They sent a traveling exhibit of memorabilia to cities to create buzz before the players arrived. Most importantly, they hired longtime tennis fashion designer Ted Tinling to create special outfits for the women professionals who played Virginia Slims tournaments.[25]

Martina Navratilova, Virginia Wade, Olga Morozova, Nancy Gunter, Betty Stove, and Rosie Casals all wore Tinling's clothes during their Virginia Slims events. King herself wore dozens of different dresses that ran about $250 per outfit. The prime-time setting for most of these matches meant Tinling designed his wares with the elegance a viewer expected to see on an evening out about town. Black and white dresses, short skirts with high waistlines, and tops that laid shoulders bare dominated, as well as strapless bras paired with dipped necklines to accentuate the movements of the player when serving, retrieving shots, and stroking shots. Tinling understood the game as more than a sport. His designs thus stressed allure and poise while simultaneously trying to slenderize the player's body to titillate spectators with an experience much like watching a ballerina on stage. From the many seats of large indoor stadiums, spectators watched the players move. Belts and buttons with rhinestones and sequins strove to resemble the entertainment of Hollywood rather than the sweat of athletic competition. Athletic prowess but also sex appeal were probably on peoples' minds.[26]

But by the early 1980s, women's tennis needed a new injection of excitement, because the expansion of and quality of play on the men's side had prompted many spectators to prefer the faster tennis of WCT and ITF Grand

Prix events. Youth, smooth athletic movements, and beauty increasingly became the attributes players now needed—at least more than ever before—to strive for on the court. Off the court, the WTA issued a year-end calendar that displayed the female professionals looking their best. Sports marketing agents, even more than WTA leadership, also tried to push their player-clients to a new level of sexiness, because an attractive athlete was easier to sell to advertisers, who themselves believed that sex sold. For example, in 1983 Donald Dell's ProServ agency began to turn Elizabeth Sayers, a tennis champion unknown outside of her home country of Australia, into a global sex symbol. Through a "complete beauty makeover" and photo shoot, Sayers saw her exhibition and corporate event income climb from virtually nothing to more than a quarter of a million dollars in just a few months irrespective of any success she enjoyed in competitive tournaments. The WTA noticed the upswing in both Sayers's exposure and, more importantly, her income and realized that the financial best interest of its players and tournaments might be best served by emphasizing tennis shots as well as sex. As Dell remarked about Virginia Slims and WTA players, they were "a pleasure to watch for more reasons than the quality of their tennis."[27]

The increased visibility in the public's eye that televised tours gave female players meant that those women could expect to negotiate bigger and better endorsements and licensing contracts with companies. More than their male counterparts on tour, however, women players had to make sure they looked their best each and every time they stepped out onto the court. Agents such as Mark McCormack and Dell noted that a handsome player like Eliot Teltscher stood to benefit in terms of marketability from his good looks. Furthermore, agents told Jimmy Connors, John McEnroe, Brad Gilbert, and other male clients that their on-court misbehavior could cost them corporate sponsorships, as companies did not like risking a marketing campaign on an athlete known for erratic behavior in the spotlight. But those same agents did not really tell a male player that he needed to change something about his body in order to improve his marketability; the male player's body that produced his on-court performance belonged to the player and, perhaps, his coach.[28]

By contrast, sports agents regularly told women players to shape up their bodies. The reasons for that double standard were twofold: first, sports agents knew that when it came to marketing a woman player, companies and sponsors valued attractiveness more than victory; second, despite not earning a living competing on the court, male sports agents still felt they knew more about sports than the women who actually got paid to play each and every day. In confronting one of his women player-clients over her recent weight gain, Dell asked, "How are you going to be a top ten player when you are fifteen pounds overweight?" In that rhetorical question, the agent hinted that any change in her appearance that detracted from her on-court sex appeal could cost her even more money with sponsors than a drop in the rankings and subsequent drop in tournament prize money might cost her. "Name one player in the top ten who's even three pounds overweight," Dell said. With that demand, he drove the point home.[29]

Looks mattered, but so did a good story in the sport of tennis. For much of tennis history, spectators wanted the underdog, the outsider, to take on the establishment. Ever since Suzanne Lenglen had made the first international professional tour in 1926, anyone who made money in the game before 1968 was treated as a pariah or traitor by the men of the amateur associations who ran the game. Women, people from the working classes, migrants, ethnic and racial minorities, people from all walks of life became professional tennis players if they had the talent. With the transition of Dr. Richard Raskind to Dr. Renée Richards, professional tennis crossed one final barrier—that of physical gender itself.

From childhood, tennis, gender identity, and sexuality intermingled. Raskind had spent many hours on the courts, where as an adolescent he practiced strokes and found a first girlfriend in a fellow player. Brief and awkward intimate encounters with both a female sibling and a female summer camper contributed to a great deal of gender confusion by the time Raskind turned sixteen. By then one of the only times the teenager felt comfortable was playing tennis, where Raskind's athletic six-foot, one-inch height gave him a decisive advantage over the many friends he met through the game. But youth tennis also gave Raskind the opportunity to think about transitioning to become a man when, after having played an amateur tournament on the U.S. Military Academy's West Point courts, Raskind found his way to the local bookshop and noticed a copy of Lili Elbe's posthumously published memoir, *Man into Woman*. Raskind bought the book and fled to a hotel bathroom, where he read all about the Danish artist Einar Wegener's transsexual awakening and the first attempt at sexual reassignment surgery. In 1951 Raskind brought this expanded horizon with him to Yale. Freshman year in New Haven challenged Raskind, who felt disoriented save for his amateur tennis career. Regular practice trips to New York to play on the indoor courts of the city also gave Raskind the opportunity to visit Greenwich Village, where the teenager encountered people who did not conform to gender binaries. While Raskind had gone out before as Renée, the personal freedom college provided catalyzed that transition. Under the pretense of practicing tennis at Forest Hills, Raskind left for Manhattan to audition for the Satin Slipper Revue. At the home of the revue's owner, Renée had her first complete sexual encounter.[30]

At the same time, Christine Jorgensen returned to New York City having undergone sexual reassignment surgery in Denmark. Newspaper publicity surrounding Jorgensen's transition catalyzed city- and nationwide conversations about transsexuality. The grace with which Jorgensen embraced her newfound visibility encouraged Raskind to consider his own identity. Over time his story would come to rival Jorgensen's in influencing public discussions about people who are transgender.[31]

That experience, combined with collegiate tennis triumphs, complicated Raskind's sexual identity. As the top player in a sport that was very popular on his Ivy League campus, Raskind felt obligated to maintain a heterosexual relationship. At the same time, he attended therapy with a psychiatrist to discuss his sexuality and future plans to play tennis professionally. Toward the end of his time at Yale, he traveled to England and Paris to compete in the Prentice Cup, where he solicited prostitutes. After Europe, Raskind began medical school in Rochester, New York, and there Renée reappeared. Tennis touring momentarily suppressed her, because on trips to cities like Miami and Havana, Raskind spent evenings with prostitutes. Sex in committed relationships did not happen for Raskind, and that frustration renewed his need for therapy. Once again, a busy schedule, this time as a resident at Lenox Hill Hospital in New York City along with his amateur tennis career, left Raskind with little time for Renée. That changed with the death of Raskind's mother. He mutilated his genitals, cross-dressed more frequently, and encouraged his pregnant girlfriend to have an abortion so that they could avoid marrying. The end of that relationship effectively meant the beginning of Raskind's life as Renée.[32]

Raskind underwent hormonal therapy while also serving in the U.S. Navy. That treatment ended without Raskind's consent, and incompleteness spurred him to drive across the country stopping in small towns as Renée before returning to New York City to direct the residency program at Manhattan Eye and Ear Hospital. Dr. Raskind excelled as an eye surgeon and as a teacher of eye surgeons, but the surgery the physician wanted for himself had to be completed outside the United States. Raskind left his New York life behind, traveled to Europe, and then on to Casablanca, Morocco, intending to undergo sexual reassignment surgery. As a physician, however, he decided against the procedure there and returned to New York to resume his medical career in Manhattan, where he married and had a son. At the same time, he continued to compete at the highest level of amateur tennis, making the quarterfinals and the finals at the U.S. National Championships. Family life did little to solve Raskind's complicated gender identity, however, and he separated from his wife. He also resumed his hormone treatments, dressed as Renée every night, and finally underwent the surgery, this time in America. In 1975 at Physician's Hospital in Queens Dr. Roberto Granato performed what paperwork called a "sex change" to give Richard Raskind the anatomy of Renée Richards. Dr. Richards continued as Dr. Raskind in the medical profession, but over the following months and years Raskind changed all of his identifying and legal documents to Renée Richards. The paperwork included changing USLTA tournament registrations from the men's draw to the women's draw, and that change is what made Renée Richards famous. [33]

Most of the women tennis players did not support Richards's right to compete in their tournaments and on their tour. They felt uncomfortable competing against a big and strong player many knew from the men's amateur tennis circuit. Of greater concern to women's professionals was their belief that Richards's presence undermined their own tacit willingness to sexualize their sport in order to appeal to male viewers. They thought Richards was a sideshow. Gladys Heldman disagreed and wrote in defense of Richards, because she was undergoing similar mistreatment at the hands of the women professionals on whose behalf she worked tirelessly.[34]

Forced out of the tour she had founded, Heldman still worked long hours to expand women's tennis and to champion women in the workplace. That her ouster from Virginia Slims came, at least in part, by the established players meant Heldman felt even closer to outsiders than ever before. She pushed professional tennis events for women thirty-five and over despite the reluctance of sponsors to pay dollars for what they considered senior tennis. She established the Avon Futures Tour, which developed players for the WTA. The partnership between the beauty products company and women's professional tennis proved so successful that the WTA agreed to have Avon replace Virginia Slims as the premiere players' tour sponsor in 1979, until Virginia Slims renewed its primary sponsorship four years later. That success dovetailed

Heldman's new efforts to help talented women secure management positions at major firms. All the while, Heldman continued to write about tennis as a guest editorialist for *World Tennis* and in a variety of other publications.[35]

WTA members planned to boycott the 1976 Hawaiian tournament on their schedule because of Richards's intention to participate, until Heldman stated her intention to play the tournament herself, along with her tennis group from Houston, in solidarity with Richards. The women professionals relented and decided to play alongside Richards. Heldman lost money, though, for her support of Richards. After her $2.25 million sale of *World Tennis* in 1972 and her withdrawal from the day-to-day management of the Virginia Slims Circuit in 1973, Heldman founded and ran Heldman and Associates, an executive search firm that helped secure women executives positions in upper management or on boards of directors for the biggest companies in America. Her willingness to speak out for Richards cost her consultancy at least one corporate client and perhaps more. But Heldman voiced no regrets. "Gladys kept silent about Renée Richards, because it might have cost her a fee," Heldman later said about herself, and that was an outcome she would not accept. Her tombstone could instead list her very real accomplishments: placing women clients on thirty boards of Fortune 500 companies (a 50 percent increase in the number before Heldman and Associates); building *World Tennis* to a subscriber base of 125,000 at the time of the sale; and shepherding women's professional tennis through the tumultuous first decade of open tennis competition. The fact that a person with such an impressive list of accomplishments recognized the legitimacy of gender transitioning and sexual reassignment surgery of a professional tennis player as an important moment goes a long way in explaining why Heldman herself had such an outsized impact on sports history in the United States. She saw potential where other people did not. She championed causes long kept on the outside. Late in life she even cowrote a book of tennis instruction with Pancho Segura and Pancho Gonzales. She remained active with various professional tennis projects as well as other causes and avocations. When she had a few quiet minutes to herself at her Houston or Santa Fe homes, she spent them with her cats, Virginia and Slim.[36]

Renée Richards became a household name in the United States the following summer when she sued the USTA over its refusal to allow her to enter the women's draw of the 1977 U.S. Open. The case hinged on how the association, and by extension professional sports organizations, determined the sex of an athlete. Never in its long history had the association administered a "sex determination test" beyond simply looking at an athlete. On Richards they performed a "sex chromatin test," the so-called Barr body test, which ruled her genetically more man than woman. The WTA backed the use of the Barr body test, as did various affidavits from professional players who said they did not want to play against Richards. The history of tennis as a sport in which women had long ago and recently played dominant roles informed the Supreme Court of New York's decision to rule in Richards's favor. While sports scholar Lindsay Parks Pieper cautions against putting too much emphasis on the Richards decision, as the court issued a narrow ruling, the USTA nevertheless hosted a trans tennis professional for the first time when Richards played against Virginia Wade in the 1977 U.S. Open.[37]

Richards retired from professional tennis in 1981 after four seasons of top-flight play. The forty-seven-year-old began practicing medicine again in New York City. At the same time, Richards began coaching Martina Navratilova, herself no stranger to ostracism. Communism had spurred Navratilova to flee her native Czechoslovakia, and she defected to the West in New York City in 1975 having traveled to the United States to play in the U.S. Open. During the next half decade, Navratilova established herself as one of the top players on the WTA tour, renowned for her attacking style of play and intense rivalry with Chris Evert. In 1981 the press outed Navratilova and her lover Rita Mae Brown, the author of the classic lesbian bildungsroman *Ruby Fruit Jungle*. While Richards and Navratilova always treated each other with courtesy on the professional tour, the shared public vitriol each faced on account of their sexuality increased the bond between the two, which took the form of an athlete and coach arrangement. For the next year, Richards traveled with and coached Navratilova to the latter's best season up to that point, with singles titles in the Australian Open, the French Open, and Wimbledon. That summer Richards told Navratilova she planned to step away from coaching, and the two parted amicably; Richards returned to practice medicine full-time and Navratilova sat out the 1982 U.S. Open before resuming her dominance of women's professional tennis. After one of her major finals wins, Navratilova took the microphone and publicly thanked her coach, Renée Richards.[38]

After more than one hundred years, the most historic venues in the sport of tennis were finally open to anyone with game enough to get there.

Professional Tennis as Global Entertainment

Tennis's popularity with the American public began to slow somewhat toward the end of the first decade of open tennis. One industry survey actually noted a decline from 26.2 million Americans playing tennis in 1976 to 25.9 million people playing in 1977. In the latter of those years, players in the United States purchased 9.5 million tennis racquets along with spending $500 million on tennis shoes and $340 million on outfits to play in. Fortunately for the seventeen or so firms that made racquets, tens of millions of American consumers watched professional tennis on television, and some of those wanted to upgrade their racquets to match what they saw ATP and WTA players using in WCT, Grand Prix, and Virginia Slims matches. In 1978, 400,000 of those consumers would attend the first U.S. Open held at Flushing Meadows and watch their favorite professionals play in the USTA's new home for the U.S. Open.[1]

Over the next decade, the ATP, the WTA, and the sports agents who represented the players exercised greater influence over the game at the expense of the ITF, the USTA, Lamar Hunt's WCT, and the Virginia Slims Circuit. Nonetheless, the governance structure of the MIPTC held the influence of the professionals in check. The ITF representatives and the tournament representatives serving on the council could outvote the player representatives to set the year's Grand Prix playing calendar.[2] A handful of top players worked around the official schedule through the efforts of their IMG and ProServ sports agents, who secured for them prize-money guarantees for one-off exhibition matches in which television sponsorship dollars earned them high payouts. In one infamous example, ProServ's Donald Dell organized John McEnroe, Jimmy Connors, Vitas Gerulaitis, and Björn Borg for the four-man $250,000 Suntory Cup exhibition in Tokyo during the middle of WCT's River Oaks, Houston, tournament.[3] In that respect, at least, tennis in the late 1970s and '80s somewhat resembled the barnstorming professional tours of the pre–Open Era. The difference, of course, was the amount of money and the degree of control: the commercial contracts that sports agents negotiated for their managed athletes; the powerful position that player unions came to occupy.

In the mid-1980s, ITF president Philippe Chatrier looked optimistically at the future of the game just as trouble appeared on the horizon. A total of 109 national tennis associations now belonged to the ITF. Efforts to return tennis to the Olympics seemed promising. The Grand Slam tournaments made enough money to share with the ITF for growing tennis in developing countries. The women professionals on the Virginia Slims Circuit flourished. The MIPTC continued to grow professional tennis by expanding the Nabisco Grand Prix tour to include a season-ending Nabisco Masters tournament in December. That meant two additional tournaments for the 1986 season as the circuit got on the new schedule, a calendar that brought simmering problems forward. That year the ATP and the other stakeholders on the MIPTC sat down to try to revamp the Grand Prix calendar to include fewer tournaments with higher prize money. Consensus could not be reached between the players, the tournament directors, and the ITF, so the MIPTC agreed to revisit the issue throughout 1987.[4]

Over the coming year, the ATP membership installed new leadership, including Hamilton Jordan (former presidential chief of staff to Jimmy Carter), who articulated the players' dissatisfaction with the current status of the game in a critique titled "Tennis at the Crossroads." The report first emphasized how far tennis had come in the last twenty years with the administration of the Nabisco Grand Prix by the MIPTC before articulating the "problems" with the sport: the governing structure of the game in the MIPTC left the game disorganized; that disorganization made the sport confusing to consumers and more difficult for management companies such as IMG and ProServ to market to potential sponsors than necessary if a more unified structure existed. The players, sports management companies, the ITF, and the tournament directors may very well have agreed with the ailments, but the cure proposed was a different matter. The ATP advocated that the players begin to exercise more control over the game within the MIPTC in order to set the Grand Prix tour calendar and coordinate the commercialism of the sport. If the players could not achieve that additional control by way of reform of the current power structure, then they would "consider" forming an ATP Tour.[5]

The year 1988 proved the most consequential for the sport of tennis since the Open Era began twenty years earlier. In January the LTAA hosted the Australian Open at Flinders Park, a new National Tennis Centre with a fifteen-thousand-dollar set center court. In September, Seoul welcomed back tennis as an Olympic sport after a sixty-four-year absence from the Games. Less than two weeks earlier, West German wunderkind Steffi Graf became the fifth player in history to win the Grand Slam, joining the exclusive pantheon of Margaret Court, Rod Laver, Maureen Connolly, and Don Budge.[6] What mattered more for the history of the game took place during that same U.S. Open, not inside the stadium court but outside on a parking lot.

Two days before the start of the 1988 U.S. Open, the ATP presented its report advocating for an overhaul of professional tennis. The ITF leadership and tournament directors read, rejected, and publicly rebuked the proposal as the equivalent of the ATP placing a gun against the head of the MIPTC, which really controlled professional tennis. With the ATP board preparing to make a statement in response, the USTA locked the players out of the National Tennis Center press rooms. The following day, on August 30, Swedish professional Mats Wilander spoke for eighty-five of the world's top one hundred ranked players from a hastily erected ATP podium in a Flushing Meadows parking lot. The ATP would move ahead with a player-run professional tennis tour.[7]

The ITF and the Grand Slam tournament directors responded to the parking-lot presser by issuing invitations to U.S. Open players to join a revamped Grand Prix beginning in 1990. The invitations left the players with a lot of specific questions concerning the calendar, the number of weeks players needed to commit to playing, and, most importantly, how a proposed ITF computer ranking system would replace the ATP computer rankings that for decades had decided most of the spots in the Grand Slam draws. Few players seemed interested as the U.S. Open wound down and players departed New York for other parts of the world.[8]

The MIPTC quickly recognized the seriousness of the players' resolve. The ATP, the ITF, and the tournament directors talked throughout September, and on October 4, 1988, the MIPTC met to reform some parts of the Grand

Prix to meet ATP demands. The MIPTC planned to address commercial concerns through a five-year schedule of the most ambitious seasons in the sport's history. The MIPTC would divide the year into two main classifications of tournaments: one-million-dollar so-called World Series tournaments and five-hundred-thousand-dollar so-called Super Series tournaments. The calendar would allow players more rest between the season-ending ATP Masters and the resumption of the professional circuit with the Australian Open in January. Most importantly, the governance structure of the MIPTC would change to give the ATP constituency half rather than only a third of the voting strength when dealing with tournament directors for scheduling Grand Prix tournaments and with the ITF for decision making regarding the four historic major championships. In the case of a deadlocked vote, the MIPTC administrator reserved the tiebreaker.[9]

The ability of the ATP to resist these concessions, and to offer their own version of where they wanted tennis to go in the new decade beginning with the 1990 season, exemplified how strong the players themselves had become. First, the tour's name would change from the Nabisco Grand Prix to the ATP Tour. Second, the ATP Tour board rather than the MIPTC would govern the tour, make the schedule, designate the different classifications of the tournaments, and regulate all tournament matters. Third, the number of tournaments would decrease slightly, with thirty weeks of top-level tournaments falling to sixteen weeks, a decrease that would give players more rest and increase the importance of small and middling tournaments for players who were not in the top echelon of ATP rankings. The off-season would go from practically nonexistent under the Grand Prix to close to two months with the proposed ATP Tour. Fifth, whereas the MIPTC required that ranking players compete in all four Grand Slams, one remaining WCT event, and the season-ending Masters, the ATP Tour gave the players more discretion to pick and choose the tournaments they wanted to play. Less specifically, the ATP Tour claimed to offer better promotion, more money, and a better-organized playing calendar still anchored by the four Grand Slams and Davis Cup. The biggest difference in the MIPTC-led Grand Prix and the ATP-led tour was that in the latter the athletes gained real agency over the professional game.[10]

Determined to achieve player autonomy, the ATP board received the MIPTC-proposed compromise and "unanimously rejected" the Grand Prix in favor of the ATP Tour. At once ATP executives set about approaching tournament partners to build the new player-led tour while doing their best to not alienate the Grand Slam tournaments, which had just seen their influence diminish, as the ITF would now have less of a check over the professionals in making the playing calendar. By November 2 the ATP secured contracts from Mats Wilander, Stefan Edberg, Boris Becker, and Andre Agassi, along with thirteen other members of the men's twenty-five highest-ranking players.[11] Most of the rank-and-file players soon fell in line as did a robust number of tournament venues and sponsors. The inaugural ATP Tour schedule would include seventy-five tournaments across twenty-seven countries, including matches in the Soviet Union and China.[12]

The Grand Prix, which had tamed the once mighty WCT, went out with a whimper with a December 1989 doubles tournament at London's Royal Albert Hall. In January 1989 the ATP Tour would begin in Australasia with a singles tournament in Adelaide, Australia, and a doubles tournament in Wellington, New Zealand, in a run-up to the Australian Open. The ITF held onto the four Grand Slams, which continued to anchor the entire tennis season, and they put together a big money prize but an underwhelming season-ending exhibition called the Grand Slam Cup. They continued to run the Davis Cup. WCT died a quiet death in the late summer of 1990 with a final Tournament of Champions at the historic West Side Tennis Club in New York City. IMG represented dozens of the top professionals and signed a minimum-guarantee contract of $56.1 million to market much of the ATP season to television networks and sponsors. I.B.M. came on board as the main tour sponsor for an estimated $9 million over the next two years. The ATP Tour was now in reality the tennis year.[13]

The WTA never staged such a dramatic break from the ITF but nonetheless grew steadily in influence. Around the same time as the ATP breakaway, the WTA counted more than five hundred members across forty-five countries. Their 1989 season would include main circuit tournament and player development matches for over fifteen hundred women's tennis professionals. Their leadership also brokered a five-year contract with Philip Morris for continuing sponsorship of the Virginia Slims World Championship Series into the mid-1990s.[14]

The players, the national associations, and the international federation that governed tennis had long competed for both control of game and the degree of commercialization in the sport.[15] For four decades the touring professionals chipped away at USLTA and ILTF opposition to open tennis until in 1968 the best players in the world could play in the game's most historic tournaments. The game's global and commercial footprint grew exponentially over the next twenty years. From 1990 up to the present, the professional players themselves competed in the game whose direction they now, more than ever, controlled.

As with the Laver Cup a few years earlier, in April 2020 during the middle of the worldwide COVID-19 pandemic, Grand Slam champion Roger Federer once again suggested a new development with a long history in professional tennis. Why not merge the ATP Tour with the WTA Tour for a combined worldwide professional tennis calendar?[16] Time will tell. Whether or not these last twenty years have made for a fourth period in the growth of the game of tennis in the United States and around the world is for the forthcoming scholarship of sports historians to decide.

Notes

Abbreviations

ALT	*American Lawn Tennis*
CBIRC	State of California Business Incorporation Records Collection, California State Archives, Sacramento, CA
CHS	California Historical Society, San Francisco, CA
EDP	Edward Dickson Papers, Collection 662, Alfred Young Research Library, University of California at Los Angeles, Los Angeles, CA
FLTC	William M. Fischer Lawn Tennis Collection, St. John's University Archives and Special Collections, Queens Campus, New York, NY
GHP	Gladys Heldman Papers, Dolph Briscoe Center for American History, The University of Texas at Austin, Austin, TX
GMP	George MacCall Papers (6188), Penn State University Archives, Special Collections Library, Penn State University, University Park, PA
ITHF	International Tennis Hall of Fame, Newport, RI
LBC	Lawrence Baker Collection, International Tennis Hall of Fame, Newport, RI
LHP	Lamar Hunt Papers, Hunt Enterprise Archive, Kansas City, MO
MMC	Mark H. McCormack Papers (MS 700), Special Collections and University Archives, University of Massachusetts Amherst Libraries, Amherst, MA
NAACP-Tennis	National Association for the Advancement of Colored People Administrative File, Papers of the NAACP, Part 11, Series

A, Special subject files, 1912–1939, Discrimination—Sports [Tennis], Microfilm Reel 27, Frames 0454–0492 [reproduced from the Library of Congress] (Frederick, MD: University Publications of America, 1990).

OHC-ITHF   Oral History Collection, International Tennis Hall of Fame, Newport, RI

OM   Mark McCormack, "Operational Memorandum: International Management and Affiliated Companies," typescript dated, Dec. 26, 1967, Mark McCormack Personal File, MMC

RKC   Robert J. Kelleher Collection, International Tennis Hall of Fame, Newport, RI

SCWH   Seaver Center for Western History Research, Los Angeles County Natural History Museum, Los Angeles, CA

SCTA   Southern California Tennis Association

TPC-ITHF   Tennis Program Collection, International Tennis Hall of Fame, Newport, RI

TTC   Ted Tinling Collection, International Tennis Hall of Fame, Newport, RI

USLTA-Annals   Annals of the United States Lawn Tennis Association, typescript, n.d., Folder [no number] USLTA Development, William M. Fischer Lawn Tennis Collection, St. John's University Archives and Special Collections, Queens Campus, New York, NY

WT   *World Tennis*

Introduction

1. Christopher Clarey, "Event Honoring a Legend Is Inspired by the Ryder Cup," *New York Times*, Jan. 29, 2016, B14.

2. "Kramer Cup to Australia," *Melbourne Age*, Nov. 14, 1961, 22; Jack Kramer, "Kramer Prescribes a Tennis Cure," *Miami Herald*, Feb. 5, 1961, 2.

3. William C. Lufler, "Best Wishes and Good Fortune!," in *World Series of Professional Tennis 1963 Tour of the Game's Top Tennis Stars Program*, 31, TPC-ITHF; United States Professional Tennis Association, *USPTA: Our History, Our Members and Our Contribution to the Sport* (Morley, MO: Acclaim Press, 2017), 6–7, 12, 14.

4. Rod Laver with Larry Writer, *The Golden Era: The Extraordinary Two Decades When Australians Ruled the Tennis World* (Sydney: Allen & Unwin, 2020), 217, 323–24, 426; "The Kramer Cup," in *World Series of Professional Tennis 1963 Tour of the Game's Top Tennis Stars Program*, 21, TPC-ITHF; "Australia Win Kramer Cup," *London Observer*, Sept. 7, 1963, 20.

5. Laver, *Golden Era*, 9–10, 530–41; Kevin Jefferys, *British Tennis: From the Renshaws to the Murrays* (Worthing, Sussex: Pitch Publishing, 2019), 12–14.

6. Robert J. Lake, "Introduction to the History and Historiography of Tennis," in *The

Routledge Handbook of Tennis: History, Culture, and Politics, ed. Robert J. Lake (New York: Routledge, 2019), 1–16.

7. Heiner Gillmeister, *Tennis: A Cultural History* (London: Leicester University Press, 1998; Robert J. Lake, *A Social History of Tennis in Britain* (New York: Routledge, 2014); E. Digby Baltzell, *Sporting Gentlemen: Men's Tennis from the Age of Honor to the Cult of the Superstar* (New York: Free Press, 1995); Warren F. Kimball, *The United States Tennis Association: Raising the Game* (Lincoln: University of Nebraska Press, 2017); Susan Ware, *Game, Set, Match: Billie Jean King and the Revolution in Women's Sports* (Chapel Hill: University of North Carolina Press, 2011); Eric Allen Hall, *Arthur Ashe: Tennis and Justice in the Civil Rights Era* (Baltimore: Johns Hopkins University Press, 2014); Sundiata Djata, *Blacks at the Net: Black Achievement in Tennis,* 2 vols. (Syracuse, NY: Syracuse University Press, 2006/2008); Elizabeth Wilson, *Love Game: A History of Tennis from Victorian Pastime to Global Phenomenon* (Chicago: University of Chicago Press, 2016).

8. Rob Steen, *Floodlights and Touchlines: A History of Spectator Sport* (London: Bloomsbury, 2014), 84, 93, 112, 114, 173; Robert Peterson, *Cages to Jump Shots: Pro Basketball's Early Years* (Lincoln: University of Nebraska Press, 2002), 15, 32; Elliott Gorn and Warren Goldstein, *A Brief History of American Sports* (Champaign: University of Illinois Press, 2004), 131, 154, 164; Marc Maltby, *The Origin and Early Development of Professional Football* (New York: Routledge, 1997), xi.

9. Steen, *Floodlights and Touchlines,* 178–82; Gorn and Goldstein, *Brief History,* 133–34, 137–38, 140; S. W. Pope, *Patriotic Games: Sporting Traditions in the American Imagination, 1876–1926* (Knoxville: University of Tennessee Press, 2007), 29–32.

Chapter 1. Amateur Associations along the American Atlantic Coast

1. Walter Clopton Wingfield, A Portable Tennis Court for Playing Tennis, British Patent no. 685, filed Feb. 23, 1874, and provisionally issued Feb. 24, 1874, series 3, Subject Files, Oversize 6, folder Patent: "A New and Improved Portable Court for Playing the Ancient Game of Tennis," FLTC; Selden Cale, "A Short History of Tennis in America and England," typescript, 1–2, folder Illinois Sports, box A125, Works Progress Administration Collection, Manuscripts Division, Library of Congress, Washington DC; Gillmeister, *Tennis,* 223.

2. The discussion of grips and the analysis of tennis mechanics, stroke production, play, and strategy come from the author's dozen years of experience teaching tennis.

3. Gillmeister, *Tennis,* 34–38.

4. Advertisement for Slazenger tennis balls, *Slazengers Catalogue* (London: Slazengers Ltd., 1914), 19.

5. Cindy Aron, *Working at Play: A History of Vacations in the United States* (New York: Oxford University Press, 1999), 9–10, 67.

6. Burton Bledstein, *The Culture of Professionalism: The Middle Class and the Development of Higher Education in America* (New York: W. W. Norton, 1978), 59–60; Roy

Rosenzweig, *The Park and the People: New York's Central Park* (Ithaca, NY: Cornell University Press, 1992), 196, 199; Perry Duis, *Challenging Chicago: Coping with Everyday Life, 1837–1920* (Chicago: University of Chicago Press, 1998), 15, 177; William Wilson, *The City Beautiful Movement* (Baltimore: Johns Hopkins University Press, 1989), 248–49, 252; Peter Schmitt, *Back to Nature: The Arcadian Myth in Urban America* (Baltimore: Johns Hopkins University Press, 1990), 4, 70.

7. Stuart Blumin, *The Emergence of the Middle-Class Social Experience in the American City, 1760–1900* (New York: Cambridge University Press, 1996), 207–208, 213–14.

8. Howard Mumford Jones, *The Age of Energy: Varieties of American Experience, 1865–1915* (New York: Viking Press, 1971), 319.

9. Aron, *Working at Play*, 91, 206–207, 221–23, 238–40.

10. Jackson Lears, *Something for Nothing: Luck in America* (New York: Penguin, 2003), 156–58.

11. *1880 Annual Report*, folder 1.1, untitled cart box, Newport Casino Collection, ITHF; *1929 Annual Report*, folder 1.1, untitled cart box, Newport Casino Collection, ITHF.

12. Harvey Green, *Fit for America: Health, Fitness, Sport, and American Society* (New York: Pantheon, 1986), 182–91; Jackson Lears, *No Place of Grace: AntiModernism and the Transformation of American Culture, 1880–1920* (Chicago: University of Chicago Press, 1994), 108–109; Jackson Lears, *Rebirth of a Nation: The Making of Modern America, 1877–1920* (New York: Harper Perennial, 2009), 270; Oscar Handlin, *The Uprooted: The Epic Story of the Great Migration That Made the American People* (Boston: Little, Brown, 1973), 223–24; Elliott Gorn, *The Manly Art: Bareknuckle Prize Fighting in Urban America* (New York: Cornell University Press, 2010), 108; Thomas Schlereth, *Victorian America: Transformations in Everyday Life, 1876–1915* (New York: Harper Perennial, 1991), 220–21; Gail Bederman, *Manliness and Civilization: A Cultural History of Gender and Race in the United States, 1880–1917* (Chicago: University of Chicago Press, 1995), 15.

13. R. St. G. Walker, *Annual Reports of the Staten Island Cricket and Base Ball Club for the Year 1892* (New York: Michael & Strauss Printers, Feb. 6, 1893), 1–3, in series 3, Subject Files, Staten Island Cricket and Base Ball Club, no folder, FLTC; United States Lawn Tennis Association (USLTA), *Fifty Years of Lawn Tennis in the United States* (Norwood, MA: Plimpton Press, 1931), 13, 15. Recently, Robert Everitt and Richard Hillway have subjected both the Wingfield and Outerbridge origin stories to the highest detail of scrutiny. They conclude that Wingfield does deserve credit for originating the game and that Outerbridge may or may very well not deserve credit for first introducing lawn tennis in America. See Robert Everitt and Richard Hillway, *The Birth of Lawn Tennis: From the Origins of the Game to the First Championship at Wimbledon* (Kingston upon Thames, UK: Vision Sports Publishing, 2018), 496–500.

14. R. St. G. Walker, *Annual Reports of the Staten Island Cricket and Base Ball Club for the Year 1892*, 1–3, in series 3, Subject Files, Staten Island Cricket and Base Ball Club, no folder, FLTC; USLTA, *Fifty Years of Lawn Tennis*, 13, 15.

15. *Officers, Members, Constitution Rules and Reports of the West Side Tennis Club 1910 Organized 1882,* series 3, Subject Files, Cabinet File, 9–1, folder West Side Tennis Club 1903–1910, FLTC; *Schedule of Sanctioned Tournaments of the Lawn Tennis and Metropolitan Association* (New York: n.p., 1925) in folder New York Lawn Tennis Association Metropolitan LTA, 1925, series 3, Subject Files, Cabinet File, 9–1, folder West Side Tennis Club 1903–1910, FLTC.

16. "Tennis—Playing for Admiration," *The Sporting Life,* Aug. 30, 1917, 16.

17. N.A., *Outdoors: A Book of Healthful Pleasure* (Boston: Pope MFG. Co., 1894), 4–10.

18. Participating clubs and their representatives included Staten Island Cricket and Base Ball Club, represented by George Scofield Jr., William Donald, and E. H. Outerbridge; Athletic Department of Niantic Club, represented by Walter B. Lawrence and Ernest Mitchell; St. George's Club; Merion Cricket Club; Beacon Park Athletic Association, represented by James Dwight; Montclair Athletic Club, represented by Frederick Van Lenneys; Albany Tennis Club, represented by William Gould Jr., H. C. Littlefield, and Robert Oliver; Jersey City Lawn Tennis Club, represented by George Miller and H. E. Hart; Powelton Lawn Tennis Club, represented by H. Stockbridge Ramsdell; Philadelphia Cricket Club, represented by Richard Clay; Yale University Tennis Club, represented by W. H. Wood and E. Thorn; Franklin Archery Club, represented by W. H. Boardman and J. Fischer Satterthwaite; Elizabeth Lawn Tennis Club, represented by W. Hull Wickham, Edward Haines, and Edward Day; Short Hills Club, represented by Charles Henry and George Campbell Jr.; Germantown Cricket Club, represented by A.W.H. Powell and Alfred Cope; Orange Lawn Tennis Club, represented by Henry F. Hatch; Pioneer Tennis Club, represented by Berkeley Hostyn and Colles Johnston; Young America Cricket Club, represented by E. E. Denniston, Clarence Clark, and E. M. Wright Jr.; and Knickerbocker Base Ball Club, represented by H. P. Rogers and H. C. Bowers. The following clubs participated in the meeting via proxy representation: Johnstown Croquet, Archery, and Tennis Club; Nahant Sporting Club; Providence Lawn Tennis Club; Athletic Association of the University of Pennsylvania; Hawthorne Archery and Lawn Tennis Club; Myopia Club; Longman Cricket Club; Institute Lawn Tennis Club; Philadelphia Lawn Tennis Club; Amateur Lawn Tennis Club; Germantown Tennis "C" Club; Newark Cricket Club; Harrisburg Outdoor Club; Pittsburgh Cricket Club; and Belmont Cricket Club. For participating clubs and proxy representation, see USLTA-Annals.

19. USLTA-Annals.

20. Ibid.; Allison Danzig, "Spahiristike, History of the United States Lawn Tennis Association," in *The Fireside Book of Tennis: A Complete History of the Game and Its Great Players and Matches,* eds. Allison Danzig and Peter Schwed (New York: Simon & Schuster, 1972), 15–16. Members founded the All England Croquet Club in 1868, renamed it in 1877, began calling it the All England Lawn Tennis Club in 1882, and settled on the club's current name, the All England Lawn Tennis and Croquet Club (AELTC), in

1899. See John Barrett, *Wimbledon: The Official History of the Championships* (London: CollinsWillow, 2001), 1–3.

21. USLTA-Annals; Danzig, "Spahiristike," 15–16; "A Summer Transformation," *Music and Drama* 8, no. 205 (July 29, 1893): 4.

22. Kevin Jefferys, "The Heyday of Amateurism in Modern Lawn Tennis," *International Journal of the History of Sport* 26, no. 15 (Dec. 2009): 2236–52.

23. USLTA-Annals.

24. F.D.T. to James Dwight, Apr. 6, 1898, reprinted in "Questions and Answers," *ALT* 1, no. 3 (Mar. 10, 1898): 43–44.

25. Valentine Hall, *Lawn Tennis in America* (New York: D. W. Granbery, 1889), vii, 1–8, 67–69.

26. USLTA-Annals.

27. Robert J. Lake, Simon J. Eaves, and Bob Nicholson, "The Development and Transformation of Anglo-American Relations in Lawn Tennis around the Turn of the Twentieth Century," *Sports History Review* 49, no. 1 (May 2018): 1–22; Simon J. Eaves and Robert J. Lake, "Dwight Davis and the Foundation of the Davis Cup in Tennis: Just Another Doubleday Myth?," *Journal of Sport History* 45, no. 1 (Spring 2018): 1–23.

28. USLTA-Annals.

29. Ibid.

30. Hall, *Lawn Tennis in America*, 69; Gorn and Goldstein, *Brief History of American Sports*, 45, 68, 107, 109–110; David A. Hounshell, *From the American System to Mass Production, 1800–1932: The Development of Manufacturing Technology in the United States* (Baltimore: Johns Hopkins University Press, 1984), 189–214; Evan Friss, *The Cycling City: Bicycles and Urban America in the 1890s* (Chicago: University of Chicago Press, 2015), 202–204.

31. Lake, *Social History of Tennis*, 84–85; William Henry Wright, "Making Tennis Play," *Outing* 70 (Apr. 1917): 61–62, 64; USLTA-Annals.

32. Chris Bowers, *The International Tennis Federation: A Century of Contribution to Tennis* (New York: Rizzoli, 2013), 18–20; Kimball, *United States Lawn Tennis Association*, 41–43, 81; "Vincent Richards Is Suspended," *ALT* 13, no. 2 (May 15, 1919): 43–44; Holcombe Ward to the Executive Committee, Jan. 23, 1948, folder [no number] USTA Amateur Rule Committee 1948, box 14, LBC.

33. Vincent Richards Is Suspended," *ALT* 13, no. 2 (May 15, 1919): 43–44; Holcombe Ward to the Executive Committee, Jan. 23, 1948, folder [no number] USTA Amateur Rule Committee 1948, box 14, LBC.

34. Gorn and Goldstein, *Brief History of American Sports*, 68, 70, 109, 115, 120–21.

35. John Carvalho, "'An Honorable and Recognized Vocation': Bill Tilden Makes the USLTA Back Down," *Journal of Sports History* 36, no. 1 (Spring 2009): 83–98.

36. Allen M. Hornblum, *American Colossus: Big Bill Tilden and the Creation of Modern Tennis* (Lincoln: University of Nebraska Press, 2018), 11–12, 16, 20, 27, 29–30, 36–37, 45, 51, 55, 57–59.

37. Lawrence B. Rice, "Wm. T. Tilden 2nd; Master Player," *ALT* 16, no. 2 (May 15, 1922): 57.

38. "U.S.L.T.A. Will Not Send Tilden," *ALT* 16, no. 1 (Apr. 15, 1922): 39; Hornblum, *American Colossus*, 89; "How the Interpretation Is Viewed," *ALT* 18, no. 1 (Apr. 15, 1924); Stephen Wallis Merrihew, "There Are Two Classes of Player-Writers," *ALT* 18, no. 1 (Apr. 15, 1924): 38; "Tilden's Passing Shots," *ALT* 18, no. 1 (Apr. 15, 1924): 19; "Player-Writer Controversy Ends with Suddenness," *ALT* 18, no. 3 (June 15, 1924): 123–24; "Clean Sweep for United States in Davis Cup Match," *Brooklyn Daily Eagle*, Sept. 14, 1924, 46; "Amateur Rule Controversy Is Settled," *ALT* 18, no. 12 (Dec. 15, 1924): 627–29; S. Wallis Merrihew, "Player-Writers," *ALT* 18, no. 12 (Dec. 15, 1924): 643–44; William Tilden to the Members of the Executive Committee of the United States Tennis Association, Aug. 1, 1925, folder [no number] Tilden Controversy, FLTC; Tilden Articles Appeared in the *N.Y. World* on the Following Dates, typescript, n.d., folder [no number] Tilden Controversy, FLTC; Wireless Messages between [unintelligible, but presumably Holcombe] Ward, President Collom and Advisory Committee, July 9, 1928, folder [no number] Tilden Controversy, FLTC.

39. United States Lawn Tennis Association, Press Release Tilden USLTA, dated Aug. 24, 1928, folder [no number] Tilden Controversy, FLTC; Myrick Herrick to Joseph Wear, July 23, 1928, folder [no number] Tilden Controversy, FLTC; Myrick Herrick to Joseph Wear, July 28, 1928, folder [no number] Tilden Controversy, FLTC.

40. Edward Moss to Members of the Executive Committee, July 26, 1928, folder [no number] Tilden Controversy, FLTC; William Tilden to Samuel Collom, Aug. 17, 1928, folder [no number] Tilden Reinstatement Correspondence, FLTC; George Lott, "William Tatum Tilden," *WT* 13, no. 7 (Dec. 1965): 14, 17; "American Rules of the Three Bodies" reprinted in "The U.S.L.T.A. and Amateurism," *ALT* 21, no. 13 (Jan. 20, 1928): 644–45.

41. Minutes of Amateur Rule Committee Meeting, Feb. 16, 1948, folder [no number] USTA Amateur Rule Committee 1948, box 14, LBC.

42. Simon J. Eaves and Robert J. Lake, "The 'Ghosts' of Lawn Tennis Past: Exploring the Forgotten Lives of Early Working-Class Coaching-Professionals," *Sport in History* 36 (Nov. 2016): 498–521; Robert J. Lake, Dave Day and Simon J. Eaves, "Coaching and Training in British Tennis: A History of Competing Ideals," in Lake, *Routledge Handbook of Tennis*, 173–82.

43. "An Interview with Colonel James H. Bishop," *WT* 3, no. 5 (Oct. 1955): 16; Edward B. Dewhurst, *The Science of Lawn Tennis* (Philadelphia: Innes and Sons, 1910), 4; Charles M. Wood, "Professional Progress," in *Tennis: Builder of Citizenship*, ed. William P. Jacobs (South Carolina: Jacobs Press, 1943), 200–204; Maj. Thomas Cassady to Lawrence Baker, Feb. 19, 1948, folder [no number] USTA Amateur Rule Committee 1948, box 14, LBC; Holcombe Ward to Maj. Thomas Cassady, Mar. 11, 1948, folder [no number] USTA Amateur Rule Committee 1948, box 14, LBC.

44. Holcombe Ward to Tournament Committee Chairman, Jan. 8, 1948, folder [no number] USTA Amateur Rule Committee 1948, box 14, LBC.

45. "List of Tournaments," *ALT* 2, no. 1 (Apr. 15, 1908): 19–20; F. Dean McClusky, "The E.L.T.A. Junior Development Program," typescript, n.d., folder [no number] ELTA—History including Constitution, FLTC; "Harvard and Princeton Interscholastic," *ALT* 2, no. 2 (May 15, 1908): 30; Julian S. Myrick to E. L. Lounsbery, June 6, 1941, folder [no number] ELTA—History including Constitution, FLTC; "Home Players Win in Mexico," *ALT* 2, no. 2 (May 15, 1908): 36–39; "Indoor Tournament Ends Brilliantly," *ALT* 2, no. 2 (May 15, 1908): 35; "Ojai Valley Tournament," *ALT* 2, no. 2 (May 15, 1908): 40–41.

46. Gladys M. Heldman, "The Fans and The Players," typescript, n.d., no folder, box 25, GHP.

47. William M. Fischer, "History of the Eastern Lawn Tennis Association and Previous Metropolitan Organizations," typescript, n.d., folder [no number] ELTA—History including Constitution, FLTC; "Eastern Lawn Tennis Association," typescript, Jan. 11, 1947, folder [no number] ELTA—History including Constitution, FLTC.

48. Julian S. Myrick to E. L. Lounsbery, June 6, 1941, folder [no number] ELTA—History including Constitution, FLTC; Dean McClusky, "The E.L.T.A. Junior Development Program," typescript, n.d., folder [no number] ELTA—History including Constitution, FLTC.

49. "Eastern Lawn Tennis Association," typescript, Jan. 11, 1947, folder [no number] ELTA—History including Constitution, FLTC; Clarence Hobart to Stephen Wallis Merrihew, "The Basis of Representation," *ALT* 2, no. 1 (Apr. 15, 1908): 18.

Chapter 2. The West Coast Game

1. Carey McWilliams, *Southern California: An Island on the Land* (Salt Lake City: Peregrine Smith Books, 1983), 150; "California Tennis," *ALT* 2, no. 1 (Jan. 12, 1889): 14; H. Archie Richardson, "California Tennis Dates Back to 1870s," *Christian Science Monitor*, Apr. 28, 1948, unpaginated; "Championship of the Pacific Coast," Lawn Tennis Tournament entry form, July 4, 1888, scrapbook, Los Angeles Tennis Club Archive, Los Angeles, California; C. R. Yates, "Lawn Tennis on the Pacific Coast," *Outing* (July 1890): 271–79; USLTA-Annals.

2. Pacific States Lawn Tennis Association, *Constitution and Bylaws* (San Francisco: F.M.L. Peters & Co, 1890), folder Pacific States Lawn Tennis Association, box Pacific S-Pan, San Francisco Ephemera Collection, CHS. PSLTA founding clubs included the California Lawn Tennis Club of San Francisco, the Lakeside Lawn Tennis Club of Oakland, the East Oakland Lawn Tennis Club of East Oakland, the University Lawn Tennis Club of Berkeley, the Sausalito Lawn Tennis Club of Sausalito, the Belle Vue [Bellevue] Lawn Tennis Club of Alameda, the Versailles Lawn Tennis Club of Alameda, the Alameda Lawn Tennis Club of Alameda, the San Rafael Lawn Tennis Club of San Rafael, and the San Jose Lawn Tennis Club of San Jose.

3. Ibid.; Stephen S. B. to G. S. Smith, postcard, folder Tennis 1, box 73, C. S. Recreation—Tennis Collection, CHS; John James Smith postal card, folder Pastime Tennis

Club, box San Diego Co., California Ephemera Collection, CHS; Pacific States Lawn Tennis Association Championship Men's Doubles ticket, folder 200, box 275, California Ephemera Collection, Alfred Young Research Library, University of California Los Angeles; "California Tennis," *ALT* 2, no. 1 (Jan. 12, 1899): 14.

4. Federal Writers Project of the Works Progress Administration, *Los Angeles in the 1930s: The WPA Guide to the City of Los Angeles* (Berkeley: University of California Press, 2011), 49–50, 74; Kevin Starr, *Material Dreams: Southern California through the 1920s* (New York: Oxford University Press, 1990), 133.

5. Richardson, "California Tennis," unpaginated; Yates, "Lawn Tennis on the Pacific Coast," 271–79; "A Program of Recreation the Whole Year Through," *Los Angeles Times*, Jan. 3, 1928, C18.

6. William T. Tilden, *The Art of Lawn Tennis* (New York: George H. Doran Co., 1921), 29–30.

7. "Tournament Schedule," *ALT* 44, no. 1 (May 1950): 25, 27–28; "Tennis Factory: Perry Jones Is Champion Producer of Champions," *Life*, Aug. 7, 1950, 98–102, 105.

8. Wilson, *City Beautiful Movement*, 83, 175, 205, 304; Terrence McDonald, *The Parameters of Urban Fiscal Policy: Socioeconomic Change and Political Culture in San Francisco, 1860–1906* (Berkeley: University of California Press, 1986), 47–48, 138, 146, 174–75, 178–79, 208, 216, 219, 221; "Lawn Tennis at G. G. Park," postcard, folder Golden Gate Park, box SC, San Francisco Photo Collection, CHS; "Playing Tennis in Winter Time," postcard, folder Golden Gate Park, box SC, San Francisco Photo Collection, CHS; "2085—Tennis Court," postcard, folder Golden Gate Park, box SC, San Francisco Photo Collection, CHS; Mary Lea Heger Shane interview, July 18, 1968, Oral History Collection, Special Collections University of California Santa Cruz, Santa Cruz, California.

9. Ellsworth Vines interview, OHC-ITHF; Dr. Ford A. Carpenter, consulting meteorologist for the Los Angeles Chamber of Commerce, "Temperature and Rainfall at Los Angeles, California" (Wolfer Prg. Co., Los Angeles), n.p., reprinted in program to the 1932 Olympic Games titled *Olympic Games, July 30 to Aug. 14, 1932, Los Angeles County*, Call #cF868.L804, California History Section, California State Library, Sacramento.

10. John O. Pohlmann, "Alphonzo E. Bell: A Biography: Part I," *Southern California Quarterly* 46, no. 3 (Sept. 1964): 198. Bell was also one of the half dozen founders of the Los Angeles Tennis Club two decades later.

11. James. F. J. Archibald, "Lawn Tennis in California," *Overland Monthly* (Oct. 1892): 363–76.

12. "Lawn Tennis in the Bahamas," *ALT* 2, no. 1 (Apr. 15, 1908): 12–13; Dwight F. Davis, "The Establishment of an International Trophy: A Step toward Placing Tennis Competition on a Universal Basis," in USLTA, *Fifty Years of Lawn Tennis*, 22; Hazel Hotchkiss Wightman, Biographical File, Biographical Files Collection, ITHF.

13. "Wightman Cup Up Again," *New York Times*, Jan. 15, 1922, 113.

14. "Fourth Annual Church Cup Contest: New York Overwhelms both Boston and

Philadelphia—Kumagae Beats Williams and Wallace Johnson Downs Kumagae," *ALT* 15, no. 3 (June 15, 1921): 106–107; Francis Townshend Hunter interview, OHC-ITHF.

15. "Close Finish in East versus West Match, *ALT* 16, no. 2 (May 15, 1922): 48–49; "Los Angeles Has Views of Eastern Stars," *ALT* 16, no. 2 (May 15, 1922): 50.

16. Slew Hester interview, OHC-ITHF.

17. *Growth of Lawn Tennis in California* (San Francisco: Wright & Dixon, 1918), unpaginated; "Stage Finals in Tennis Tourney," *Los Angeles Herald*, July 30, 1921, A14; "Another California Prodigy," *ALT* 18, no. 3 (June 15, 1924): 14.

18. Articles of Incorporation of the Southern California Tennis Association, GC1145 #22140, SCWH.

19. Articles of Incorporation of Pacific Coast Sportsmen's Club, GC1145.1 #31970, SCWH; Warren Susman, *Culture as History: The Transformation of American Society in the Twentieth Century* (Washington, DC: Smithsonian Books, 2003), 78, 112; Sven Beckert, *The Monied Metropolis: New York City and the Consolidation of the American Bourgeoisie, 1850–1896* (Cambridge: Cambridge University Press, 2001), 130–31, 238–39, 247, 299; Articles of Incorporation of the Azusa Tennis Association, GC1145 #10896, SCWH; Articles of Incorporation of the Santa Monica Tennis Club Company, GC1145 #16140, SCWH; Articles of Incorporation of the Balboa Palisades Club, GC11415.1 #31981, SCWH; Application for Dissolution of Pacific Coast Sportsmen's Club, GC1145.1 #31970, SCWH.

20. Articles of Incorporation of the Southern California Tennis Association, GC1145 #22140, SCWH; Articles of Incorporation of the Los Angeles Tennis Club, GC1145 #23321, SCWH; "Nat Browne a President," *ALT* 14, no. 3 (June 15, 1920): 127; A.C.B. Gray, "Highlights of the Los Angeles Tennis Club," *Pacific Southwest Program*, 1930, Los Angeles Tennis Club Archive, Los Angeles, California.

21. Board of Directors to Los Angeles Tennis Club Members, Feb. 1, 1928, folder 7, box 17, EDP; Articles of Incorporation, Los Angeles Tennis Club, folder 93306, CBIRC; John Campbell to Los Angeles Tennis Club, May 27, 1952, Los Angeles Tennis Club, folder 93306, CBIRC.

22. Articles of Incorporation of the Southern California Tennis Association, GC1145 #22140, SCWH; Members' Resolution Approved Directors' Resolution for Amendment of Articles of Incorporation, Southern California Tennis Association, folder 90460, CBIRC.

23. Patricia Yeomans, *History and Heritage of the Los Angeles Tennis Club, 1920–1995* (Los Angeles: Los Angeles Tennis Club, 1995), 3, 12; Ted Tinling, *Love and Faults: Personalities Who Have Changed the History of Tennis in My Lifetime* (New York: Crown, 1979), 161–63; Pancho Gonzales with Cy Rice, *Man with a Racket: The Autobiography of Pancho Gonzales* (New York: A. S. Barnes, 1959), 47.

24. Robert W. Bagnall, NAACP, to Edward B. Moss, Executive Sec. USLTA, Dec. 24, 1929, Frame 455, NAACP-Tennis; Arthur E. Francis to Edward B. Moss, Dec. 26, 1929, Frame 459, NAACP-Tennis; "U.S. Lawn Tennis Association Admits Color Dis-

crimination," Dec. 27, press release, Frame 467, NAACP-Tennis; Albert E. Mac Dowell, Assistant Executive Secretary, American Tennis Association, to Robert W. Bagnall, NAACP Dir. of Branches, Dec. 28, 1929, Frame 473, NAACP-Tennis; Arthur E. Francis to Bagnall, Dec. 28, 1929, Frame 475, NAACP-Tennis; Dir. of Branches, NAACP to Arthur E. Francis, Dec. 31, 1929, Frame 481, NAACP-Tennis; "National Negro Aid Body Answers Lawn Tennis Association," Dec. 30, press release, Frame 477, NAACP-Tennis; Holcombe Ward to Lloyd W. Brooke, Aug. 3, 1943, folder 4.14.1, box 8, LBC; "Memorandum for Us at Conference with Alastair B. Martin," folder 4.14.1, box 8, LBC; Yeomans, *History and Heritage*, 13. For an overview of racial discrimination toward African Americans in tennis, see Djata, *Blacks at the Net*, vol. 1, 142–98.

25. "The Pacific Southwest Story," loose Pacific Southwest tournament program page, no date, folder 7, box 17, EDP; Isaac Jones to Chester Johnson, May 24, 1948, folder 7, box 17, EDP; Minutes of the Organization Meeting of the Board of Directors of the Tennis Patrons Association of Southern California, Mar. 2, 1928, folder 7, box 17, EDP; Articles of Association of the Tennis Patrons Association of Southern California, Sept. 4, 1927, folder 7, box 17, EDP; William Erie Fowler, "Tennis Patrons Association of Southern California," typescript, folder 7, box 17, EDP.

26. Robert Minton, *Forest Hills: An Illustrated History* (Philadelphia: J. B. Lippincott, 1975), 81, 105, 108–109; "In a Short Time It Will Be Too Late," *ALT* 18, no. 6 (July 15, 1924): 321; "Refreshment Charges at Forest Hills," *ALT* 18, no. 8 (Sept. 1, 1924): 410.

27. Sydney Wailes to Edward Dickson, Aug. 4, 1928, folder 18, box 5, EDP; E. Avery McCarthy to David Blankenhorn, Sept. 18, 1928, folder 18, box 5, EDP; E. Avery McCarthy to Edward Dickson, Sept. 19, 1928, folder 18, box 5, EDP; E. Avery McCarthy to Edward Dickson, Sept. 20, 1928, folder 18, box 5, EDP.

28. New Seating Diagram for the Los Angeles Tennis Club, 1928, folder 18, box 5, EDP; Pacific Southwest Championships Ticket Order Form, 1928, folder 18, box 5, EDP; Fred Perry, *My Story* (London: Hutchinson & Co., 1934), 208–211. Kay Francis, Gloria Swanson, Joan Bennett, Lilyan Tashman, Bette Davis, Helen Twelvetrees, Lupe Vélez, Norma Shearer, Constance Bennett, Carole Lombard, Madge Evans, Mary Pickford, Charles Chaplin, Harold Lloyd, William Powell, Ben Lyon, Charlie Farrell, Edmund Lowe, Theodore von Eltz, the Marx Brothers, Fredric March, Walter Huston, Robert Montgomery, Richard Barthelmess, Douglas Fairbanks, and Ralph Graves all made the tournament memorable to American and international players and fans alike.

29. Perry, *My Story*, 208–211.

30. Minutes and Financial Statements of the Tennis Patrons Association of Southern California and Pacific Southwest Sectional Tennis Championships, bound in large red volume, no folder number, box 35, EDP.

31. Kimball, *United States Tennis Association*, 90.

32. Articles of Incorporation, Tennis Patrons of Santa Monica, folder 237442, CBIRC; Articles of Incorporation, Tennis Patrons Association of San Diego, folder 281433, CBIRC; John Campbell to Tennis Patrons Association of San Diego, Aug. 4, 1953,

Tennis Patrons Association of San Diego, folder 281433, CBIRC; John Campbell to Tennis Patrons Association of San Diego, Dec. 23, 1953, Tennis Patrons Association of San Diego, folder 281433, CBIRC; Donald Pond to Bondholders, Mar. 15, 1947, folder 4, box 34, MSS-30, Daniel Cowan Jackling Papers, Stanford University Library and Special Collections, Palo Alto, California.

33. "Park Courts in 1907," *ALT* 29, no. 8 (Sept. 5, 1935): 27; "Public Parks Play in Greater New York," *ALT* 28, no. 5 (July 20, 1934): 36; "Public Parks Play in Springfield," *ALT* 28, no. 10 (Oct. 20, 1934): 25; "Public Parks' Rating," *ALT* 28, no. 14 (Feb. 20, 1935): 34–35; "Philadelphia's Public Park Courts," *ALT* 29, no. 2 (May 20, 1935): 47; Davison Obear, "Public Parks Play in St Louis," *ALT* 30, no. 8 (Sept. 5, 1936): 26–27; "Margaret Osborne, "Golden Gate Park Tennis Courts," *ALT* 31, no. 11 (Nov. 20, 1937): 9; Ned Wheldon, "Public Parks Championship," *ALT* 32, no. 8 (Sept. 5, 1938): 16–17; "Florida Public Courts Tournament," *ALT* 32, no. 13 (Jan. 20, 1939): 21; Californians in the East," *ALT* 29, no. 5 (July 20, 1935): 46; Jeane Hoffman, "Bouncing Around," *The Racquet* 46, no. 5 (Sept. 1952): 24–25; Alice Marble, "The State of the Tennis Union," *The Racquet* 46, no. 11 (Mar. 1953): 13, 32; Jeane Hoffman, "Bouncing Around," *The Racquet* 47, no. 4 (Aug., 1953): 28–29. For more on this "recreation revolution," see Greg Ruth, "Pancho's Racket and the Long Road to Professional Tennis," PhD diss., Loyola University Chicago, 2017, 102–140.

34. Bob Perry, "Tennis in Southern California," *WT* 1, no. 11 (Apr. 1954): 15; Jeane Hoffman, "Bouncing Around," *The Racquet* 46, no. 5 (Sept. 1952): 24–25.

35. Baltzell, *Sporting Gentlemen*, 34–35, 139, 152, 166, 221, 311, 392.

Chapter 3. The Cause Célèbre of the Pioneering Professional

1. "Peggy Writes to Polly," *ALT* 2, no. 1 (Apr. 15, 1908): 7; "Philadelphia Women Start Inter-Club Play, *ALT* 2, no. 2 (May 15, 1908): 28–29; "Metropolitan League Adopts Schedule," *ALT* 2, no. 1 (Apr. 15, 1908): 6; "From District Association," *ALT* 2, no. 1 (Apr. 15, 1908): 8.

2. Donald J. Mrozek, "The 'Amazon' and the American 'Lady': Sexual Fears of Women as Athletes," in *The New American Sport History: Recent Approaches and Perspectives*, ed. S. W. Pope (Urbana: University of Illinois Press, 1997), 198–214.

3. "Suzanne Lenglen Feels Free as a Pro," *New York Times*, Aug. 11, 1926, 18; "Suzanne Lenglen Tells of Kings and Queens She Meets," *Los Angeles Times*, Oct. 11, 1926, 12.

4. "Suzanne Lenglen Feels Free as a Pro," *New York Times*, Aug. 11, 1926, 18; Lynn Dumenil, *The Modern Temper: American Culture and Society in the 1920s* (New York: Hill and Wang, 1995), 98–144; Joshua Zeitz, *Flapper: A Madcap Story of Sex, Style, Celebrity, and the Women Who Made America Modern* (New York: Crown Publishing, 2006), 8–9, 135–45.

5. Charles Lenglen, "A Brief Biography of Suzanne Lenglen," 1–4, 11–13, *Suzanne Lenglen: North American Tour Souvenir Program*, 1926, folder Suzanne Lenglen North American Tour Souvenir Program, no box number, FLTC; "A Brief Biography of Su-

zanne Lenglen Written by Charles (Papa Lenglen) in 1926," reprinted as "Appendix" in Ted Tinling, *Tinling: Sixty Years in Tennis* (London: Sidgwick & Jackson, 1983), 220–22.

6. Lenglen, "Brief Biography of Suzanne Lenglen," 1–4, 11–13; "A Brief Biography of Suzanne Lenglen Written by Charles (Papa Lenglen) in 1926," reprinted in Tinling, *Tinling*, 220–22.

7. Tinling, *Love and Faults*, 2–5. On weather and the lawn tennis season in England, see Lake, *Social History of Tennis in Britain*, 18, 52, 163.

8. Tinling, *Love and Faults*, 6–9.

9. Gillmeister, *Tennis*, 191–95, 211, 225, 353n115.

10. Lenglen, "Brief Biography," 15.

11. Francis Townshend Hunter interview, OHC-ITHF.

12. Kathleen McKane Godfree interview, OHC-ITHF.

13. Mrs. Lambert Chambers, *Lawn Tennis for Ladies* (New York: Outing Publishing, 1910), 1–18, quotations on 3, 18. For more on women's tennis fashion during these years, see Suzanne Rowland, "Fashioning Competitive Lawn Tennis: Object, Image, and Reality in Women's Tennis Dress 1884–1919," in Lake, *Routledge Handbook of Tennis*, 173–82. For a sophisticated gender analysis of Chambers in social space, see David Gilbert, "The Vicar's Daughter and the Goddess of Tennis: Cultural Geographies of Sporting Femininity and Bodily Practice in Edwardian Suburbia," *Cultural Geographies* 18, no. 2 (Apr. 2011): 187–207.

14. H.B.L. Hart, "Winning the English Championships," *ALT* 13, no. 6 (Aug. 1, 1919): 252; Zeitz, *Flapper*, 23–24, 135–45.

15. Chambers, *Lawn Tennis for Ladies*, 9, 60–69; John Morrow Jr., *The Great War: An Imperial History* (London: Routledge, 2004), 284–85; Godfree interview, OHC-ITHF.

16. Godfree interview, OHC-ITHF; Tinling, *Love and Faults*, 24.

17. Molla Bjurstedt, *Tennis for Women* (New York: Doubleday, Page & Co., 1916), 164–75. As historian Mark Dyreson has pointed out, by the late nineteenth into the early twentieth century, tennis and many forms of athletic contests had become yardsticks with which social commentators measured American "superiority" vis-à-vis other nations. See Mark Dyreson, *Making the American Team: Sport, Culture, and the Olympic Experience* (Urbana: University of Illinois Press, 1997), 35–36. American attitudes of exceptionalism in sport continued into the 1920s when national figures like Babe Ruth became, in the words of Warren Susman, "sports heroes." See Susman, *Culture as History*, 141.

18. Tinling, *Love and Faults*, 24–26; "Suzanne Lenglen, The French Tennis Champion, Arrives," *Boston Globe*, Aug. 13, 1921, 1; Suzanne Lenglen, "Accepts Welcome as a Tribute to France," *Boston Globe*, Aug. 17, 1921, 9; John Hallahan, "Tennis Fans Sore on Suzanne for Default," *Boston Globe*, Aug. 17, 1921, 1, 9; Godfree interview, OHC-ITHF.

19. Charles C. Pyle, *World's Premiere: International Professional Tennis Matches*, Of-

ficial Program, 1, folder [no number] *Suzanne Lenglen: North American Tour Souvenir Program*, FLTC; Lenglen photograph, *ALT* 18, no. 4 (July 1, 1924): 181; Stephen Wallis Merrihew, "Organized Professional Lawn Tennis Has Its Inaugural," *ALT* 20, no. 10 (Oct. 14, 1926): 507–509; Joseph Claurice, "4,500 Baltimoreans Watch Professionals," *ALT* 20, no. 10 (Oct. 14, 1926): 507.

20. "C. C. Pyle Dies; Ex-Manager of Red Grange," *Chicago Daily Tribune*, Feb. 4, 1939, 17.

21. Jim Reisler, *Cash and Carry: The Spectacular Rise and Hard Fall of C. C. Pyle, America's First Sports Agent* (Jefferson, NC: McFarland, 2009), 111–15, 124–25.

22. British Pathé, "Suzanne Signs On 1926," newsreel, digitized at http://www.britishpathe.com/video/suzanne-signs-on/query/lenglen (accessed June 1, 2020).

23. Suzanne Lenglen, "Why I Became a Professional," in Charles C. Pyle, *World's Premiere: International Professional Tennis Matches*, Official Program, 14–15, folder [no number] *Suzanne Lenglen: North American Tour Souvenir Program*, FLTC.

24. Official Program unpaginated scorecard insert, folder [no number] *Suzanne Lenglen: North American Tour Souvenir Program*, FLTC; "Organized Professional Lawn Tennis Has Its Inaugural," *ALT* 20, no. 10 (Oct. 14, 1926): 507–509; Joseph Claurice, "4,500 Baltimoreans Watch Professionals," *ALT* 20, no. 10 (Oct. 14, 1926): 509; "Professionals and Reinstatement," *ALT* 20, no. 10 (Oct. 14, 1926): 515; "Professional Lawn Tennis," *ALT* 20, no. 10 (Oct. 14, 1926): 538; "The Pyle Troupe of Professionals," *ALT* 20, no. 11 (Nov. 15, 1926): 558–59; "Amateurs versus Professionals," *ALT* 20, no. 11 (Nov. 15, 1926): 560–62.

25. "Suzanne Lenglen and Pyle's Stars in Cincinnati," *ALT* 20, no. 11 (Nov. 15, 1926): 559; "Mlle. Lenglen Sees Chicago," *ALT* 20, no. 11 (Nov. 15, 1926): 559; "Professionals Are Interested," *ALT* 20, no. 11 (Nov. 15, 1926): 578; "A Pro Championship for the U.S.?," *ALT* 20, no. 11 (Nov. 15, 1926): 591; "Dates for Mlle. Lenglen's Tour," *ALT* 20, no. 11 (Nov. 15, 1926): 591; Leo J. Lunn, "Pyle Professionals in Chicago," *ALT* 20, no. 12 (Dec. 15, 1926): 606; Blanche K Ashbaugh, "Professionals in Northern California," *ALT* 20, no. 12 (Dec. 15, 1926): 607; "The Professionals in Denver," *ALT* 20, no. 12 (Dec. 15, 1926): 606; "The Professionals in Montreal," *ALT* 20, no. 12 (Dec. 15, 1926): 613; John Tunis, "The Professional Championship of France," *ALT* 20, no. 13 (Jan. 15, 1927): 655–57; "End of the Pyle Exhibitions," *ALT* 20, no. 14 (Feb. 15, 1927): 710; "Suzanne Ends Pyle Tour by Losing Set in Mixed Doubles," *Hartford Courant*, Feb. 15, 1927, 12; "The Pyle Delbers Disband," *ALT* 20, no. 15 (Mar. 15, 1927): 756.

26. "Organized Professional Lawn Tennis Has Its Inaugural," *ALT* 20, no. 10 (Oct. 14, 1926): 507–509. "Suzanne Again Scores in Garden," *Brooklyn Times Union*, Oct. 11, 1926, 16; "Suzanne Is Easy Winner," *Des Moines Tribune*, Oct. 13, 1926, 16; Leo Doyle, "Sports Topics," *Baltimore Evening Sun*, Oct. 15, 1926, 36; "Bostonians See Suzanne," *Brooklyn Times Union*, Oct. 17, 1926, 13; "Suzanne Lenglen Beats Mary K. Browne, 6–2, 6–2," *Sacramento Bee*, Oct. 20, 1926, 25; "8,500 in Gallery as Suzanne Made Montreal Debut," *Montreal Gazette*, Oct. 25, 1926, 18; "Buffalo in Grip of Suzanne's Speed," *Bos-*

ton Globe, Oct. 26, 1926, 14; "Suzanne and Mary in Ohio," *Dayton News Daily*, Oct. 28, 1926, 26; "Here and There Over the States," *New Castle News*, Nov. 3, 1926, 22; "Three Thousand See Suzanne at Columbus," *Akron Beacon Journal*, Nov. 5, 1926, 28; "Tennis Pros Show Wares," *Detroit Free Press*, Nov. 10, 1926, 18; Bill Powers, "Small Crowd Views Tennis Stars," *Cincinnati Enquirer*, Nov. 12, 1926, 15; "Suzanne-Helen Wills Net Match in the Making," *Minneapolis Daily Star*, Nov. 17, 1926, 12; "Suzanne Lenglen Up to Old Form," *Decatur Daily Review*, Nov. 19, 1926, 27; "Mlle. Lenglen to Introduce 'Pro' Tennis Here Tonight," *St. Louis Post-Dispatch*, Nov. 20, 1926, 18; "Mary Presses Suzanne," *Sacramento Bee*, Nov. 25, 1926, 19; "The Professionals in Denver," *ALT* 20, no. 12 (Dec. 15, 1926): 606; "Feret's Victory Is International Upset," *Victoria Daily Times*, Dec. 2, 1926; "Suzanne Lenglen Wins and Loses in Exhibition before 4000 People," *Vancouver Province*, Dec. 3, 1926, 32; "Suzanne Wins Singles but Loses in Doubles," *Victoria Daily Times*, Dec. 4, 1926, 15; "Star Collapses as Mary Browne Forces Contest," *Bakersfield Morning Echo*, Dec. 5, 1926, 8; "Mlle. Lenglen Again Beats Mary Browne, 8–6, 6–2," *Oakland Tribune*, Dec. 8, 1926, 36; "Lenglen, Browne Please Oakland Net Enthusiasts," *San Francisco Examiner*, Dec. 10, 1926, 34; "Suzanne Tremendous Hit," *Los Angeles Evening Express*, Dec. 29, 1926, 21; Paul Moore, "Sport Notes," *Corsicana Daily Sun*, Jan. 4, 1927, 9; "Suzanne Lenglen Keeps Calm at Dallas, Texas," *Fresno Morning Republican*, Jan. 5, 1927, 13; Larry Engelmann, *The Goddess and the American Girl: The Story of Suzanne Lenglen and Helen Wills* (New York: Oxford University Press, 1988), 280; "Suzanne Demonstrates Skill with Racquets at Coliseum," *Tampa Times*, Jan. 20, 1927, 19; "Suzanne Trims Mary with Ease," *Miami Herald*, Jan. 24, 1927, 10; "Suzanne Suspected of Falling in Love," *Washington Evening Star*, Jan. 26, 1927, 29; "Suzanne Ill, Quits after Losing Set," *Hartford Courant*, Feb. 10, 1927, 1; "Suzanne Unable to Appear in Singles of Program at Newark," *Hartford Courant*, Feb. 11, 1927, 12; "Peerless Suzanne Lenglen in Farewell Match Tonight," *Brooklyn Times Union*, Feb. 12, 1927, 22; "Suzanne's Visit Here Attracts Few," *Brooklyn Standards Union*, Feb. 13, 1927, 1; "Suzanne Ends Pyle Tour by Losing Set in Mixed Doubles," *Hartford Courant*, Feb. 15, 1927, 12.

27. British Pathé, "Suzanne Lenglen aka Mlle. Suzanne Lenglen (1926)," newsreel; British Pathé, "Suzanne Lenglen—Tennis (1930–1939)," newsreel; British Pathé, "Sportshots No. 18—Suzanne Lenglen (1933)," newsreel; British Pathé, "How I Play Tennis—by Mlle. Suzanne Lenglen (1925)," newsreel; British Pathé, "Fit As a Fiddle aka Fit As Fiddle (1925)," newsreel; British Pathé, "Suzanne Meets Helen (1926)," newsreel; British Pathé, "Suzanne Wins Shorts Version on Sleeve as Celebrates the Advent (1926)," newsreel; British Pathé, "Suzanne Wins Long Version on Sleeve as Celebrates the Advent (1926)," newsreel; British Pathé, "Where the Sun Is Shining (1924)," newsreel; British Pathé, "Suzanne Lenglen Breaks Wimbledon Record (1925)," newsreel; British Pathé, "Suzanne the Magnet (1925)," newsreel; British Pathé, "Out Takes / Cuts for Incomparable Suzanne in G 1302 (1926)," newsreel; British Pathé, "Suzanne Lenglen Breaks Wimbledon Record (1925)," newsreel; British Pathé, "Tennis (1924)," newsreel; British Pathé, "World's Tennis Rivals (1924)," newsreel; Brit-

ish Pathé, "Tennis (1921)," newsreel; British Pathé, "Incomparable Suzanne (1926)," newsreel; British Pathé, "Next Year—Joan (1925)," newsreel; British Pathé, "Suzanne Signs On (1926), " newsreel; British Pathé, "Incomparable Suzanne (1925)," newsreel; British Pathé, "Versatile Susanne (1925)," newsreel; British Pathé, "Tennis Film (1920–1929)," newsreel; British Pathé, "On Suzanne's Own Ground Too! (1927)," newsreel; British Pathé, "Tennis 'Greats' (1900–1952)," newsreel; British Pathé, "Junior Lawn Tennis Champs (1921)," newsreel; British Pathé, "Wimbledon's Jubilee (1926)," newsreel; British Pathé, "Five Reigns Reel 3 (1919–1929)," newsreel; British Pathé, "Peaceful Years Reel 3 (1919–1938)," newsreel; British Pathé, "Here's to Memory—Part 3 (1920–1939)," newsreel; British Pathé, "Emancipation of Women (1890–1930)," newsreel. All newsreels are digitized and archived by British Pathé at http://www.britishpathe.com/search/query/lenglen (accessed June 10, 2020). Alison Muscatine, "Tennis Dress, Anyone?," *Washington Post*, Sept. 5, 1989, C01.

28. May Sutton Bundy interview, OHC-ITHF. For a brief overview of the historical literature arguing that for the late nineteenth century and first two decades of the twentieth century, women's sports were primarily associational and centered on physical education, see Linda J. Borish, "Women in American Sport History," in *A Companion to American Sports History*, ed. Steven Reiss (New York: Wiley Blackwell, 2014), 503–519.

29. Engelmann, *Goddess*, 426.

30. Helen Hull Jacobs interview, OHC-ITHF; Wilson, *Love Game*, 71.

31. Jacobs interview, OHC-ITHF.

32. Suzanne Lenglen, *Lawn Tennis for Girls* (New York: American Sports Publishing, 1920), frontispiece, 4–15, 17–96, 98–100, esp. 98.

33. René Lacoste interview, OHC-ITHF.

34. Engelmann, *Goddess*, 282–83.

Chapter 4. Depression-Era Developments in Amateur and Professional Tennis

1. Lake, *Social History of Tennis*, 65, 67, 68, 81–82; Simon J. Eaves and Robert J. Lake, "The 'Ubiquitous Apostle of International Play,' Wilberforce Vaughan Eaves: The Forgotten International of Lawn Tennis," *International Journal of the History of Sport* 33, no. 16 (May 2017): 1963–81.

2. Dick Skeen, *Tennis Champions Are Made, Not Born* (Redwood City, CA: Cal-Pacific Color, 1976), 63–66.

3. Ibid.

4. Ibid.

5. "Mercer Beasley," *Sports Illustrated*, July 29, 1957, 64. In the interview for this article, Beasley counted having coached seventeen players who together combined to win eighty-four elite tournament titles in the United States.

6. Yeomans, *History and Heritage*, 11, 13–14; Ellsworth Vines interview, OHC-ITHF.

7. "Tilden Pro Champion of the World," *ALT* 25, no. 2 (May 20, 1931): 4–7; "Tilden Keeps World Professional Title," *ALT* 25, no. 15 (Mar. 20, 1932): 8–9; "Kozeluh Is Pro

Champion," *ALT* 26, no. 7 (Aug. 20, 1932): 36–39; "Martin Plaa Wins Professional Title," *ALT* 26, no. 10 (Oct. 20, 1932): 11–12; "Tilden Beats Vines in Their First Meeting," *ALT* 27, no. 13 (Jan. 20, 1934): 4–5; "Vines Wins in Washington," *ALT* 27, no. 13 (Jan. 20, 1934): 10–12; "Tilden Is Pro Indoor Champion," *ALT* 27, no. 13 (Jan. 20, 1934): 17–18; "American Pros Gain Sweep against French," *ALT* 27, no. 14 (Feb. 20, 1934): 4–7; "Vines and Tilden in Corn Belt," *ALT* 28, no. 2 (May 20, 1934): 32; "Pro Facts and Figures," *ALT* 28, no. 3 (June 20, 1934): 40–44; Allison Danzig, "The Pros 1870–1958," in *Jack Kramer Presents, World's Professional Championship Tennis: 1958 Tour of the Game's Top Stars,* tour program, 15, 21, TPC-ITHF; Vines interview, OHC-ITHF.

8. "Helen Jacobs Not Even Considering Pro Offer," *St. Petersburg Independent,* Jan. 4, 1935, 10. "When the Pros Were Amateurs," *ALT* 28, no. 11 (Nov. 20, 1934): 35; "Pros at Loggerheads," *ALT* 28, no. 14 (Feb. 20, 1935): 34; "Some Highlights on Tilden Troupers," *ALT* 28, no. 15 (Mar. 20, 1935): 21; "Peace among the Pros," *ALT* 29, no. 2 (May 20, 1935): 45; Vines interview, OHC-ITHF.

9. Perry, *My Story,* 11, 18–21.

10. Ibid., 23–29, 53, 67.

11. Ibid., 67, 87–89, 148–50, 176. For an analysis of Perry's move to professional tennis within the context of the LTA's stance on amateurism, see Kevin Jefferys, "Fred Perry and the Amateur-Professional Divide in British Tennis between the Wars," in Lake, *Routledge Handbook of Tennis,* 67–75.

12. Fred Perry, *An Autobiography* (London: Hutchinson, 1986), 108–113.

13. Ibid.

14. Ibid; "Perry Confounds Critics with Victory over Vines in Pro Tennis Bow," *Brooklyn Times Union,* Jan. 7, 1937, 9.

15. Perry, *Autobiography,* 113–16.

16. Ibid., 108–109, 111, 117–20.

17. Ibid.

18. "Perry Confounds Critics with Victory over Vines in Pro Tennis Bow," *Brooklyn Times Union,* Jan. 7, 1937, 9; "Perry Wins No. 2 in Cleveland," *ALT* 30, no. 13 (Jan. 20, 1937): 7; "Perry and Vines," *ALT* 30, no. 13 (Jan. 20, 1937): 17; "Vines' Comeback in Pittsburgh," *ALT* 30, no. 13 (Jan. 20, 1937): 27; "Vines Leading," *ALT* 30, no. 14 (Feb. 20, 1937): 7; "Vines and Perry," *ALT* 30, no. 14 (Feb. 20, 1937): 22; "The Pros in Philadelphia," *ALT* 30, no. 14 (Feb. 20, 1937): 28; "Vines Forges Ahead," *ALT* 30, no. 15 (Mar. 20, 1937): 10; "Vines Still Ahead," *ALT* 31, no. 1 (Apr. 20, 1937): 13; "Vines Denver Victory," *ALT* 31, no. 1 (Apr. 20, 1937): 17; "Perry-Vines Return to the Garden," *ALT* 31, no. 2 (May 20, 1937): 20–21; "Vines 32, Perry 29," *ALT* 31, no. 2 (May 20, 1937): 21; "The Pros Abroad," *ALT* 31, no. 3 (June 20, 1937): 25–26; "1,400 Watch Vines Defeat Perry in Straight Sets, 6–4, 6–4," *Scranton Tribune,* May 13, 1937, 16; "Vines and Perry End Their Tour," *ALT* 31, no. 4 (July 5, 1937): 32.

19. Dora Lurie, "Perry Beats Vines in Four Sets," *Philadelphia Inquirer,* Jan. 7, 1937, 21, 23; "Freddie Perry Defeats Vines," *Charlotte Observer,* Jan. 9, 1937, 10; "Perry Drubs

Vines Again," *Charlotte News*, Jan. 10, 1937, 12; "Vines Makes Short Work of Perry in 4-Set Match," *St. Louis Globe-Democrat*, Jan. 16, 1937, 7; "Vines Beats Perry in Straight Sets," *El Paso Times*, Jan. 17, 1937, 22; "Vines Beats Perry Again," *Boston Globe*, Jan. 19, 1937, 19; "Vines, Perry Square, Visiting Buffalo," *Bridgewater Courier-News*, Jan. 20, 1937, 15; "Freddie Perry Defeats Vines," *Charlotte Observer*, Jan. 23, 1937, 18; "Vines Trims Perry," *Billings Gazette*, Jan. 24, 1937, 9; "Vines Victor, Squares Series," *Richmond Times-Dispatch*, Jan. 26, 1937, 12, 13; "Vines Trims Perry in Richmond Match," *Charlotte News*, Jan. 27, 1937, 14; Wilton Garrison, "Vines Battles Perry Here Tonight," *Charlotte Observer*, Jan. 27, 1937, 10; "Perry Bows to Vines," *Scranton Tribune*, Feb. 1, 1937, 17; "Vines-Perry Match Attracts Interest," *Palm Beach Post*, Jan. 24, 1937, 19–20; "Perry Defeats Vines," *Fort Worth Star-Telegram*, Feb. 6, 1937, 10; "Weekend Sports," *Fort Worth Star-Telegram*, Feb. 8, 1937, 13; "Perry Wins and Cuts Vines' Lead," *Fort Worth Star-Telegram*, Feb. 11, 1937, 21; "Vines Takes Tenth Match from Perry," *Marysville Appeal-Democrat*, Feb. 13, 1937, 6; "Vines Defeats Fred Perry," *Petaluma Argus-Courier*, Feb. 17, 1937, 4; Rube Samuelsen, "Vines at His Best, Takes Perry, 6–3, 6–3, 6–4," *Pasadena Post*, Feb. 17, 1937, 6; "Perry Squares Matches with Ellsworth Vines," *Sacramento Bee*, Feb. 22, 1937, 27; Pat Slattery, "Terrific Smashing by Vines Thrills Large Court Crowd," *Vancouver Sun*, Feb. 25, 1937, 20–21; "Perry Is Winner," *La Grande Observer*, Feb. 27, 1937, 6; "Perry Beats Vines," *Austin American-Statesman*, Mar. 1, 1937, 3; Bob Goodwell, "Fred Perry Whips Vines, 3–6, 6–3, 8–6," *Salt Lake Tribune*, Mar. 3, 1937, 19; "Tilden, at Peak, Was Better Than Perry Now, Says Vines," *Brownsville Herald*, Mar. 5, 1937, 8; "Vines, Perry Even," *Minneapolis Star*, Mar. 9, 1937, 6; "Perry Beats Vines," *Reading Times*, Mar. 11, 1937, 10; "Pro Champion Plays English Tennis Ace Here Tonight," *St. Louis Post-Dispatch*, Mar. 12, 1937, 23; "Vines Wins, Takes Lead in Series with Fred Perry," *St. Louis Post-Dispatch*, Mar. 16, 1937, 16; "Vines Beats Perry," *Salt Lake Telegram*, Mar. 17, 1937, 16; "Vines Drops Perry," *Indianapolis News*, Mar. 18, 1937, 22; "Perry Beats Vines," *Birmingham News*, Mar. 19, 1937, 16; "Perry Gains 17th," *Louisville Courier-Journal*, Mar. 20, 1937, 21; "Vines Beats Perry," *Winnipeg Tribune*, Mar. 22, 1937, 17; "Perry Beats Vines," *Boston Globe*, Mar. 26, 1937, 31; "Perry Defeats Vines," *Pittsburgh Sun-Telegraph*, Mar. 30, 1937, 23; "Perry Loses to Vines," *Montreal Gazette*, Apr. 3, 1937, 16; "Perry, Vines Squared," *La Crosse Tribune*, Apr. 4, 1937, 15; "Vines Defeats Perry," *Chattanooga Daily Times*, Apr. 8, 1937, 9; "Vines Beats Perry," *Santa Rosa Press Democrat*, Apr. 14, 1937, 4; "Vines Whips Perry," *Amarillo Globe-Times*, Apr. 16, 1937, 15; "Perry Beats Vines," *Bridgewater Courier-News*, Apr. 17, 1937, 17; "Perry Tops Vines," *Bridgewater Courier-News*, Apr. 19, 1937, 16; "Vines Whips Perry," *Waterloo Courier*, Apr. 19, 1937, 10; "Vines Beats Perry," *Philadelphia Inquirer*, Apr. 21, 1937, 21; "Perry Beats Vines," *Los Angeles Times*, Apr. 24, 1937, 30; "Vines Defeats Perry," *Boston Globe*, Apr. 26, 1937, 8; "Vines Beats Perry," *Indianapolis Star*, Apr. 29, 1937, 18; "Perry Beats Vines," *Minneapolis Star Tribune*, May 1, 1937, 19; "Perry Beats Vines in Grueling Match," *New York Daily News*, May 2, 1937, 5; "Service Too Hot for Perry," *Leader-Post*, May 4, 1937, 16; "Service Too Hot for Perry," *Regina Leader-Post*, May 4, 1937, 16; "Perry Defeats

Vines," *Pomona Progress Bulletin*, May 6, 1937, 10; Jimmy Cowen, "Vines Vanquishes Perry 6–4, 6–1, 7–5, for 2-Match Lead in Series," *Louisville Courier-Journal*, May 7, 1937, 35; "Vines Beats Perry," *Miami Herald*, May 9, 1937, 42; "Perry Defeats Vines," *Allentown Morning Call*, May 10, 1937, 16; "Perry Beats Vines," *Spokesman-Review*, May 12, 1937, 15; "Perry Beats Vines," *Spokane Spokesman-Review*, May 12, 1937, 15; "Vines Beats Perry," *Tyler Morning Telegraph*, May 12, 1937, 6; "Vines Defeats Perry again at Scranton," *Wilkes-Barre Evening News*, May 13, 1937, 20.

20. Perry, *Autobiography*, 109, 121–23, 148–55.

21. Ibid., 125–26, 130–32.

22. Laura Hillenbrand, *Seabiscuit: An American Legend* (New York: Ballantine Books, 2002), 141–42; Al Laney interview, OHC-ITHF.

23. Don Budge interview, OHC-ITHF; "Don Budge 'Takes the Shilling,'" *ALT* 32, no. 11 (Nov. 20, 1938): 4–5.

24. Budge interview, OHC-ITHF; "Don Budge 'Takes the Shilling,'" 4–5.

25. Budge interview, OHC-ITHF; "Don Budge 'Takes the Shilling,'" 4–5. For more on nationalism and internationalism in sport during the 1930s, see Barbara J. Keys, *Globalizing Sport: National Rivalry and International Community in the 1930s* (Cambridge: Harvard University Press, 2006), 38, 62–63.

26. Gene Mako interview, OHC-ITHF.

27. Ibid.

28. Ibid.

29. John Bale, *The Brawn Drain: Foreign Student-Athletes in American Universities* (Urbana: University of Illinois Press, 1991), 44.

30. Mako interview, OHC-ITHF.

31. Ibid.

32. Ibid.; "Cramm Sentenced to a Year in Prison; He Was Blackmail Victim," *New York Times*, May 15, 1938, 6; Paul Fein, *Tennis Confidential: Today's Greatest Players, Matches, and Controversies* (Washington, DC: Potomac Books, 2003), 132, 144, 271–75.

33. John Van Ryn interview, OHC-ITHF.

34. The journalist Marshall Jon Fisher—who has written a vivid account of the 1937 Davis Cup tie between Germany and the United States—suggests that Bill Tilden was in fact the coach for the German squad. While Tilden certainly had an axe to grind with the USLTA, not all evidence supports this position. For Fisher's case and evidence, see Marshall Jon Fisher, *A Terrible Splendor: Three Extraordinary Men, A World Poised for War, and the Greatest Tennis Match Ever Played* (New York: Crown Publishers, 2009), 4–5, n. to pp. 4–5 on pp. 272–73. On how Gene Mako remembered the 1937 Davis Cup tie, listen to Mako interview, OHC-ITHF.

35. Frank Deford, *Big Bill Tilden: The Triumphs and the Tragedy* (New York: Simon and Schuster, 1976), 244–53.

36. Ibid.

37. Ibid., 250–59.

Chapter 5. Wartime Southern California Professionals

1. James Sparrow, *Warfare State: World War II Americans and the Age of Big Government* (New York: Oxford University Press, 2011), 113–16, 127; James E. Block, *A Nation of Agents: The American Path to a Modern Self and Society* (Cambridge: Harvard University Press, 2002), 305, 310, 318, 328, 330, 383, 412.

2. Holcolmbe Ward, Draft of Letter to Ranking Players, Jan. 2, 1948, folder [no number] USTA Amateur Rule Committee 1948, box 14, LBC.

3. Bobby Riggs interview, OHC-ITHF.

4. Ibid.

5. Ibid.

6. Ibid.

7. Ibid.

8. Ibid.

9. Ibid.

10. Bud Collins, *The Bud Collins History of Tennis: An Authoritative Encyclopedia and Record Book* (New York: New Chapter Press, 2010), 357–61, 386–89, 414–21, 454–61.

11. Bobby Riggs, *Court Hustler* (New York: J. B. Lippincott, 1973), 68, 70–71.

12. Ibid., 71; Riggs interview, OHC-ITHF.

13. Richard Overy, *Why the Allies Won* (New York: W. W. Norton, 1995), 190–98, 205–207; *Economic Report of the President Transmitted to Congress*, Jan. 8, 1947 (Washington, DC: U.S. Government Printing Office, 1947), 3, 23; William O'Neill, *A Democracy at War: America's Fight at Home and Abroad in World War II* (New York: Free Press, 1993), 75–76, 78–80, 82–84, 90, 98–101, 214–15, 218, 222.

14. Gorn and Goldstein, *Brief History of American Sports*, 179–80; Wanda Ellen Wakefield, *Playing to Win: Sports and the American Military, 1898–1945* (Albany: State University of New York Press, 1997), 61, 79–82; Steven Bullock, *Playing for Their Nation: Baseball and the American Military during World War II* (Lincoln: University of Nebraska Press, 2004), xi-xiii, 143–44.

15. Dan Maskell, *From Where I Sit* (London: Willow Books, 1988), 175–76; Deford, *Big Bill Tilden*, 234–37.

16. Gorn and Goldstein, *Brief History of American Sports*, 198, 200–202.

17. John Morton Blum, *V Was for Victory: Politics and American Culture during World War II* (New York: Harcourt Brace Jovanovich, 1976), 7, 9, 143; "The Draft: Navy Spanking," *Time*, May 24, 1943, 69.

18. Riggs, *Court Hustler*, 68, 72; Riggs interview, OHC-ITHF.

19. Riggs, *Court Hustler*, 68, 72; Riggs interview, OHC-ITHF.

20. Gene Tunney, "A Man Must Fight: A Champion's Autobiography," *Collier's Weekly*, Feb. 6, 1932, 7–9; Gene Tunney, "A Man Must Fight, Part II: The Fighting Marine, Part II," *Collier's Weekly*, Feb. 13, 1932, 12–13; Gene Tunney, "A Man Must Fight, Part III: The Championship of the A.E.F.," *Collier's Weekly*, Feb. 20, 1932, 14–15; Gene Tunney, "A Man Must Fight, Part IV: Upgrade toward the Championship," *Collier's Weekly*,

Feb. 27, 1932, 24–27; Gene Tunney, "A Man Must Fight, Part V: The Grab Feud," *Collier's Weekly*, Mar. 5, 1932, 14–15; Gene Tunney, "A Man Must Fight, Part VI: Meeting Carpentier," *Collier's Weekly*, Mar. 12, 1932, 16–17 ; Gene Tunney, "A Man Must Fight, Part VII: Getting Ready to Take Dempsey," *Collier's Weekly*, Mar. 19, 1932, 12–13; Gene Tunney, "A Man Must Fight, Part VIII: The First Dempsey Fight," *Collier's Weekly*, Mar. 26, 1932, 16–17; Gene Tunney, "A Man Must Fight, Conclusion: The Story of the Long Count," *Collier's Weekly*, Apr. 2, 1932, 12–13; Gene Tunney, *A Man Must Fight* (Boston: Houghton Mifflin, 1932).

21. Riggs, *Court Hustler*, 72.

22. "Screen and Net stars . . ." press release, folder Tennis 1, box 73, Recreation—Tennis collection, CHS; Riggs interview, OHC-ITHF; Riggs, *Court Hustler*, 72–74.

23. Williamson Murray and Allan R. Millett, *A War to Be Won: Fighting the Second World War* (Cambridge: Harvard University Press, 2000), 583–84; Riggs interview, OHC-ITHF; Riggs, *Court Hustler*, 72–74.

24. Gardnar Mulloy interview, OHC-ITHF; Samuel Stouffer, "The American Soldier in World War II: Athletes and Entertainers in Uniform," Research Brand, Information and Education Division, War Department, May 1945, available digitally at www.roper-center.cornell.edu (accessed May 10, 2016).

25. Ruth Stoefen to La Jolla Club Membership, Nov. 5, 1943, folder La Jolla Beach and Tennis Club, box L—Love, California Business Ephemera Collection, CHS.

26. "The Sexes," *ALT* 39, no. 4 (July 15, 1945): 14; Jean Hastings Ardell, *Breaking into Baseball: Women and the National Pastime* (Carbondale: Southern Illinois University Press, 2005), 102–103, 109–116.

27. George "Pat" Hughes, "Lawn Tennis Economics," *ALT* 39, no. 1 (May [n.d.], 1945): 25–26; Lt. Hal Surface Jr., "U.S. Army Sports Program," *ALT* 39, no. 4 (July 15, 1945): 12; Corporal John Kraft, "Parker vs. Budge in the Pacific," *ALT* 39, no. 4 (July 15, 1945): 13.

28. Bobby Riggs, *Tennis Is My Racket* (New York: Simon and Schuster, 1949), 8–10, 15–16, 160–61.

29. Ibid.

30. "Kramer Comes Through," *ALT: News Supplement* 49, no. 1 (July 2, 1938): 2; Jack Kramer, with Frank Deford, *The Game: My Forty Years in Tennis* (New York: G. P. Putnam's Sons, 1979), 20–23, 28, 30–31.

31. Peter Young, "The Big Game," *WT* 2, no. 12 (May 1955): 24; Edward Potter, "The Big Game," *WT* 7, no. 7 (Dec. 1959): 35–37.

32. Edward Potter, "The Big Game," *WT* 7, no. 7 (Dec. 1959): 35–37; Frank Eck, "Jack Kramer All-Conquering before Turning Professional," *Ithaca Journal*, Dec. 24, 1947, 13.

33. Kramer, *The Game*, 156–62.

34. Roy Miller, "Kramer Absolute Ruler," *ALT* 42, no. 5 (Aug. 1, 1948): 6–10.

35. Lake, *Social History of Tennis*, 153, 157.

36. Murray Janoff, "'Doomed' Pro Tourney Gets Late Reprieve," *ALT* 47, no. 2 (June 1948): 9, 32; Roy Miller, "Among the Pros," *ALT* 42, no. 3 (July 1, 1948): 32–33.

37. Janoff, "'Doomed' Pro Tourney," 9, 32; Miller, "Among the Pros," 32–33.

38. Kramer, *The Game*, 92, 192–94, 238–39.

39. "Bobby Riggs Presents World Championship Tennis Tour," 1949–50 tour program, TPC-ITHF; "Kramer Trounces Gonzales Neatly," *Shreveport Times*, Dec. 4, 1949; [No title, AP score report], *Cincinnati Enquirer*, Dec. 5, 1949, 27; "Gonzales Beats Kramer," *Boston Globe*, Dec. 6, 1949, 22; Karl Kaufmann, "Kramer Boosts Margin over Pancho Gonzales," *Ithaca Journal*, Dec. 8, 1949, 25; "Kramer Bats Gonzales for Twenty-Second Win," *Tulare Advance-Register*, Dec. 8, 1949, 6; Karl Kaufmann, "Kramer Boosts Margin over Pancho Gonzales," *Ithaca Journal*, Dec. 8, 1949, 25; Gale Talbot, "Gonzales Calls Kramer Land's Greatest Player," *Hackensack Record*, Dec. 13, 1949, 25; "Kramer Defeats Gonzales Again," *Asbury Park Press*, Dec. 14 1949, 13; Angelo Angelopolous, "Jake Requires but 37 Minutes to Beat Pancho," *Indianapolis News*, Dec. 16, 1949, 42; "All-Star Net Show," *Owensboro Messenger*, Dec. 16. 1949, 34; "Jack Kramer Whips Gonzales Again," *Alabama Journal*, Dec. 19, 1949, 10; "Kramer Defeats Pancho Gonzales," *Pittsburgh Press*, Dec. 20, 1949, 30; "Two Tennis Pros Head for London," *Fort Collins Coloradoan*, Dec. 22, 1949, 16; "Gonzales Beats Kramer," *Louisville Courier-Journal*, Dec. 27, 1949, 15; "Kramer Drubs Gonzales in London Net Match," *Syracuse Post-Standard*, Dec. 28, 1949, 12; "Kramer Says Gonzales Slow to Learn on Pro Net Tour," *Tampa Tribune*, Dec. 29, 1949, 15; "Segura Switches with Gonzales and Beats Kramer," *Orangeburg Times and Democrat*, Jan. 2, 1950, 11; "Flash! Gonzales Defeats Kramer," *Charlotte News*, Jan. 11, 1950, 21; "Gonzales Tops Kramer," *Long Branch Daily Record*, Jan. 12, 1950, 16; "Pancho Gonzales Defeats Kramer," *San Mateo Times*, Jan .13, 1950, 10; "Kramer Wins 39th Net Tussle from Gonzales," *Salt Lake City Deseret News*, Jan. 14, 1950, 4; "Kramer Takes 40th Victory over Gonzales," *Sacramento Bee*, Jan. 16, 1950, 18; "Gonzales Beats Kramer," *Pittsburgh Press*, Jan. 17 1950, 28; "Net Victory No. 11 for Gonzales over Kramer," *Jefferson City Post-Tribune*, Jan. 18, 1950, 9; "Gonzales Whacks Kramer Again," *Yuma Sun-Advertiser*, Jan. 19, 1950, 6; "Gonzales Beats Kramer Again," *Ithaca Journal*, Jan. 20, 1950, 13; "Kramer Stops Gonzales," *St. Louis Post-Dispatch*, Jan. 21, 1950, 6; "Gonzales Defeats Kramer," *Louisville Courier-Journal*, Jan. 23, 1950, 14; "Kramer, 42, Gonzales, 14," *St. Louis Post-Dispatch*, Jan. 24, 1950, 18; "Kramer Routs Gonzales," *Terre Haute Tribune*, Jan. 25, 1950, 11; Dick Hyland, "The Hyland Fling," *Los Angeles Times*, Jan. 28, 1950, 32; "Kramer Bests Gonzales," *Montana Standard*, Jan. 30, 1950, 8; "Gonzales Downs Kramer," *Eugene Guard*, Jan. 31, 1950, 9; "Jack Kramer Defeats Gonzales on Mainland," *Victoria Times Colonist*, Feb. 1, 1950, 16; "Kramer, 47, Gonzales, 15," *Munster Times*, Feb. 2, 1950, 21; "Kramer Subdues Gonzales Again," *Salem Statesman Journal*, Feb. 6, 1950, 9; "Kramer Overpowers Gonzales Again," *St. Cloud Times*, Feb. 8, 1950, 13; "Kramer Trounces Gonzales Again," *Los Angeles Times*, Feb. 9, 1950, 67; Joe Collier, "Kramer Turns Back Gonzales," *Tucson Citizen*, Feb. 13, 1950, 21; "Kramer Whips Gonzales," *Pasadena Independent*, Feb. 14, 1950, 25; "Kramer

Defeats Pancho Gonzales," *Pampa Daily News*, Feb. 16, 1950, 15; "Kramer Beats Gonzales in Oklahoma City Match," *Ponca City News*, Feb. 17, 1950, 9; "Gonzales Victor over Kramer," *Philadelphia Inquirer*, Feb. 18, 1950, 18; "Pancho Gonzales Defeats Kramer," *Pensacola News Journal*, Feb. 20, 1950, 2; "Tennis Pros Play Near," *Victoria Advocate*, Feb. 21, 1950, 6; "Kramer Beats Gonzales," *Fort Worth Star-Telegram*, Feb. 23, 1950, 39; "Gonzales Beats Kramer," *St. Louis Post-Dispatch*, Feb. 25, 1950, 6; "Kramer Leads, but Pancho Gets Tougher Every Day," *Austin American-Statesman*, Feb. 23, 1950, 40; "Kramer Tops Gonzales in Shreveport Match," *Birmingham News*, Feb. 27, 1950, 22; "Kramer Beats Gonzales," *Philadelphia Inquirer*, Feb. 28, 1950, 30; "Kramer, Gonzales Play Tonight at 8," *Birmingham News*, Feb. 28, 1950, 23; "Kramer Scores 62nd Victory over Gonzales," *Alabama Journal*, Mar. 2, 1950, 12; Gene Asher, "Kramer Trims Gonzales, Segura Defeats Parker," *Atlanta Constitution*, Mar. 5, 1950, 26; "Segura to Quit Pro Tennis Tour Soon," *Tallahassee Democrat*, Mar. 6, 1950, 6; "Kramer-Gonzales Troup Appears Here Tuesday," [*Gainesville*] *Florida Alligator*, Mar. 3, 1950, 8; "Kramer Blasts Gonzales," *Terre Haute Tribune*, Mar. 10, 1950, 24; "Kramer-Gonzales Net Feud Due for Coral Beach Club," *Palm Beach Post*, Mar. 10, 1950, 15; "Kramer Dubs Gonzales," *Dayton Journal Herald*, Mar. 13, 1950, 6; Bob Quincy, "Gonzales Says He'll Quit Tennis for a Year," *Charlotte News*, Mar. 16, 1950, 23; "Kramer Scores 70th Victory over Pancho," *Los Angeles Times*, Mar. 17, 1950, 61; "Kramer Trounces Gonzales 71st Time," *Philadelphia Inquirer*, Mar. 18, 1950, 20; "Net Pros Slated to Perform Here on Armory Court," *Hartford Courant*, Mar. 30, 1950, 15; "Gonzales Beats Kramer," *Tampa Tribune*, Apr. 3, 1950, 14; "Gonzales Beats Kramer," *Lubbock Morning Avalanche*, Apr. 3, 1950, 6; "Gonzales Snares Win over Kramer," *Los Angeles Times*, Apr. 9, 1950, 83; "Gonzales and Kramer Head for Binghamton," *Binghamton Press and Sun-Bulletin*, Apr. 9, 1950, 5; Jimmie Waters, "Kramer-Gonzales Duel Features Pro Net Program Here Tonight," *Elmira Star-Gazette*, Apr. 11, 1950, 14; Fred Box, "Kramer 'Sneaks' Past Gonzales in Armory Show," *Elmira Star-Gazette*, Apr. 12, 1950, 18; Bill Kennedy, "Kramer Topples Gonzales 11 to 9 in Third Set," *Glen Falls Post-Star*, Apr. 13, 1950, 17; "Kramer 67; Gonzales 33," *Munster Times*, Apr. 14, 1950, 31; "Kramer 77, Gonzales 24," *Moberly Monitor-Index*, Apr. 15, 1950, 7; "Norfolk Site of Gonzales, Kramer Meet," *Newport News Daily Press*, Apr. 9, 1950, 25; "Gonzales Beats Jack Kramer," *Asheville Citizen-Times*, Apr. 20, 1950, 28; "Gonzales Bows Again," *Rochester Democrat and Chronicle*, Apr. 22, 1950, 23; "Pancho Gonzales to Play Kramer in Columbia," *Orangeburg Times and Democrat*, Apr. 18, 1950, 9; "Tennis Pros to Give Exhibition Here," *Charleston Evening Post*, Apr. 24, 1950, 17; "Kramer Beats Gonzales," *St. Louis Post-Dispatch*, Apr. 28, 1950, 46; Bud Montet, "Good Show," *Baton Rouge Advocate*, Apr. 29, 1950, B2; "Kramer Defeats Gonzales in Local Pro Tennis Match," *Jackson Clarion-Ledger*, Apr 30, 1950, 20; George Short, "Jack Kramer Rips Gonzales in 31 Minutes Here; Riggs, Parker in Marathon," *Chattanooga Daily Times*, May 4, 1950, 22; "Gonzales Whips Kramer," *Birmingham News*, May 5, 1950, 43; "Kramer Beats Gonzales in Springfield Match," *Moberly Monitor-Index*, May 9, 1950, 11; "Kramer Meets Gonzales in Peoria Match," *Bloomington Pantagraph*, May

6, 1950, 9.; "Kramer, Gonzales Meet in 116th Match Tonight," *Minneapolis Star Tribune*, May 10, 1950, 23; "Kramer, Gonzales to Play at Rochester, *Winona Daily News*, May 11, 1950, 21; "Kramer Meets Gonzales as Pro Net Tour Comes Here Monday," *Iowa City Press-Citizen*, May 13, 1950, 10; "Grand Rapids," *Lansing State Journal*, May 18, 1950, 40; Robert Cromie, "Riggs' Tennis Show Opens in Arena Tonight," *Chicago Tribune*, May 19, 1950, 48; Dale Stevens, "Riggs, Park 'Featured' Players in Tennis Show," *Dayton Daily News*, May 21, 1950, 48; "Jack Kramer Wins Final Match from Gonzales," *Lansing State Journal*, May 22, 1950, 13.

40. Kramer, *The Game*, 186–87, 217–20.

Chapter 6. The Cultural Contexts of Mid-Century Women's Tennis

1. "Little Mo Is Named Top Female Athlete 3rd Time," *Toledo Blade*, Jan. 8, 1954, 30; Nelson Fisher, "Vacation from Tennis," *The Racquet* 45, no. 8 (Dec. 1951): 6; Kramer, *The Game*, 96; Nelson Fischer interview, Oral History Collection, San Diego Historical Society (now known as San Diego History Center), San Diego, California.

2. Elaine Taylor May, *Homeward Bound: American Families in the Cold War Era* (New York: Basic Books, 2008), 8, 13, 15, 17.

3. For a different read on women's tennis and fashion with an emphasis up to 1960, see Jaime Schultz, *Qualifying Times: Points of Change in U.S. Women's Sport* (Urbana: University of Illinois Press, 2014), 15–46. In a more recent work, Schultz has asked the larger question of how much sex really matters in popularizing women's sports. While she points out that the Women's Tennis Association was one of several sporting bodies that has sexualized women athletes, she concurs with other scholars that sex really doesn't "sell" women's sports. See Jaime Schultz, *Women's Sports: What Everyone Needs to Know* (New York: Oxford University Press, 2018), 54–56.

4. Tinling, *Love and Faults*, 23–32; Ted Tinling Biographical File, Biographical Files Collection, ITHF; folder 1.3.1, Tennis Players (small), 1932–1969, box 6, TTC; folder 1.3.2, Tennis Players (medium) 1939–1971, later undated, box 6, TTC; folder 1.3.2, Tennis Players (medium), 1939–1971, later undated, box 6, TTC; folder 1.2.1, Tennis Men 1956–1961, undated, box 6, TTC; folder 1.1.36, Separates (women), undated, box 5, TTC; "Sport: Build Up at Wimbledon," *Time*, July 4, 1949, unpaginated. Several *Time* magazine sources cited here are unpaginated, as many were accessed digitally via https://time.com/vault/.

5. Kramer, *The Game*, 93–95; Louise Brough Clapp interview, OHC-ITHF; "Sport: Build Up at Wimbledon," *Time*, July 4, 1949, unpaginated.

6. "Sport: Build Up at Wimbledon," *Time*, July 4, 1949, unpaginated; A. Steward, "Letter to the Publisher," *Time*, Aug. 1, 1949, unpaginated.

7. Royal Commission on the Press (Report), *House of Commons Debate*, vol. 467, cc2683-794, July 28, 1949, http://hansard.millbanksystems.com/ (accessed on Dec. 2, 2012).

8. Louise Brough Clapp interview, OHC-ITHF. Moran did, however, reapply to join

the amateur ranks only to see the SCTA refuse to back her bid for returned amateur status at the national level. See Minutes of a Specially Called Meeting of the Board of Directors of the Southern California Tennis Association, Dec. 17, 1953, folder [no number] Southern California Tennis Association 1953–1954, RKC. On how Moran compared to other female competitors at Wimbledon, see Janine van Someren and Stephen Wagg, "Wimbledon Women: Elite Amateur Tennis Players in the Mid-Twentieth Century," in Lake, *Routledge Handbook of Tennis*, 183–92.

9. Kramer, *The Game*, 93–95; Clapp interview, OHC-ITHF.

10. Tennis Tours broadside, folder [no number], box Teale-Thompkins, Business Ephemera Collection, CHS; *Bobby Riggs Presents World Championship Tennis Tour, 1950–1951* tour program, TPC-ITHF; "Forest Hills Crowds See National Tennis Upsets," *Life*, Sept. 23, 1946, 92; Kramer, *The Game*, 93–96.

11. Patricia Yeomans, *Southern California Tennis Champions Centennial, 1887–1987: Documents & Anecdotes* (Los Angeles: privately printed, 1987), 155; Dick Skeen, *Tennis Champions Are Made*, 4; Budge Patty, *Tennis My Way* (Tiptree, Essex: Anchor Press, 1951), 21.

12. Alice Marble, "Tennis Has Room for Both Amateur and Pro Games," *ALT* 41, no. 2 (June 15, 1947): 8; Jack Miller, "Net Queens Abdicate," *ALT* 41, no. 2 (June 15, 1947): 6–7; Mary Hardwick, "Pauline's Exodus Leaves Gap in Women's Racket Ranks," *ALT* 41, no. 2 (June 15, 1947): 8–9; "Tentative Schedule Drawn for Betz-Cooke Tour," *ALT* 41, no. 2 (June 15, 1947): 9; Sarah Palfrey Danzig interview, OHC-ITHF; David Lardner, "Thirty Years War," *New Yorker*, July 15, 1944, 65.

13. Jack Miller, "Net Queens Abdicate," *ALT* 41, no. 2 (June 15, 1947): 6–7; "New Pros Debut," *ALT* 41, no. 4 (July 15, 1947): 43; "Sarah Cooke Enjoys Pro Tour," *ALT: Weekly Supplement* 1, no. 5 (July 15, 1947): 2; Roy Miller, "Among the Pros," *ALT* 41, no. 3 (July 1, 1947): 28–29.

14. "Final European Appearance of the World's Greatest Tennis Players," *Belfast News-Letter*, Aug. 14, 1947, 2; "U.S. Netters Back from Tour," *Dayton Journal Herald*, Aug. 28, 1947, 16; "Tennis Stars to Compete," *Red Bank Daily Register*, Aug. 28, 1947, 14; Oscar Fraley, "Big Jake Expected to Join Pros at Top Rate," *Lead Daily Call*, Sept. 8, 1947, 2; David Condon, "Jack Kramer's Pro Contract Is Official Now," *Chicago Tribune*, Nov. 13, 1947, 38; "Pauline Betz Trims Sarah Cooke, 6–1, 6–2," *St. Louis Globe-Democrat*, Dec. 29, 1947, 17; "Exhibition Postponed," *Fort Lauderdale News*, Dec. 26, 1947, 12; "Net Pros Play Here Tonight in Exhibitions," *Fort Lauderdale News*, Jan. 14, 1948, 14; "Tennis Open Merely Hope, States Star," *Rochester Democrat and Chronicle*, Oct. 13, 1948, 27; "World's Best—Cincinnati's Sports and Boat Show," *Cincinnati Enquirer*, Feb. 29, 1948, 36; "Pauline Betz Headlines E. Genesee St. Armory Show," *Syracuse Post-Standard*, May 7, 1948, 19.

15. Eleanor Page, "Net Players Do a Bit as Comics, Too," *Chicago Tribune*, July 11, 1947, 15; Harold Ratliff, "Pro Tennis Gals: Plenty Good Showmen," *Casper Star-Tribune*, Sept. 1, 1947, 10.

16. Tennis Educational Foundation and the U.S. Lawn Tennis Association in Conjunction with President Eisenhower's Youth Fitness Program, *Tennis for Speed, Stamina, Strength, and Skill* (Book No. 1) (New York City: A. Derus Production, 1956), 2, in vertical file, FLTC; "Around the World," *WT* 4, no. 3 (Aug. 1956): 65; "Around the World," *WT* 4, no. 2 (July 1956): 57; Ned Potter, "The Story behind the USLTA Publicity Campaign," *WT* 4, no. 7 (Dec. 1956): 12–13; "Around the World," *WT* 5, no. 11 (Apr. 1958): 64; Gladys Heldman, "The Kelleher Regime," *WT* 15, no.1 (June 1967): 14. On the important educational role of comic books in shaping American youth during the Cold War, see Bradford W. Wright, *Comic Book Nation: The Transformation of Youth Culture in America* (Baltimore: Johns Hopkins University Press, 2003), xiii.

17. J. P. Shanley, "Sports on Video—Channel 5 to Present Tennis Matches Originating in Station's Studio," *New York Times*, Aug. 21, 1955, 105; "ALT has a vacancy . . .," *ALT* 2, no. 2 (May 15, 1908): 40–46; Richard Hillway and Geoff Felder, "Stephen Wallis Merrihew & ALT," *Journal of the Tennis Collectors of America* 29 (Autumn 2013): 452–56.

18. For example, see Grantland Rice, America's foremost sportswriter in the first half of the twentieth century, reflecting on women athletes during his career in his *The Tumult and the Shouting: My Life in Sport* (New York: A. S. Barnes, 1954), 237–46.

19. Alice Marble, "As I See It," *ALT* 41, no. 3 (July 1, 1947): 1, 30.

20. Alice Marble, *The Road to Wimbledon* (New York: Charles Scribner's Sons, 1946), 8–9, 11–12, 17.

21. Ibid., 22–33.

22. Ibid., 34–37.

23. Ibid., 37–47, 58, 107.

24. Ibid., 48–51, 60, 66–67, 73, 77–78, 80, 87, 93, 100, 103–104, 116–17.

25. Ibid., 118–19, 122–23, 137, 147–48, 157–60, 165–67; Don Budge interview, OHC-ITHF; Alice Marble, *Courting Danger: My Adventures in World-Class Tennis, Golden-Age Hollywood, and High-Stakes Spying* (Boston: St. Martin's Press, 1991), 207–234.

26. Danzig interview, OHC-ITHF; Marble, *Road to Wimbledon*, 157; *Alice Marble and Don Budge 1941 Professional Tennis Tour Program*, Pro Tours Case, Area Two, ITHF; Alice Marble designed "Tennis Themed Scarf," n.d., Tennis and Culture Accessories Case, Area Two, ITHF; Jill Lepore, *The Secret History of Wonder Woman* (New York: Alfred A. Knopf, 2015), 220–23, 239, 315; Doris Jane Hart interview, OHC-ITHF.

27. Althea Gibson, interview, OHC-ITHF.

28. Ibid.

29. Ibid.

30. Ibid.; Howard Cohn, "The Gibson Story," *ALT* 44, no. 3 (July 1, 1950): 6–7; Alice Marble, "A Vital Issue," *ALT* 44, no. 3 (July 1, 1950): 14; Marble, *Road to Wimbledon*, 148.

31. Gibson interview, OHC-ITHF.

32. Ashley Brown, "Swinging for the State Department: American Women Tennis Players in Diplomatic Goodwill Tours, 1941–59," *Journal of Sport History* 42, no. 3 (Fall 2015): 289–309; Akira Iriye, eds., *Global Interdependence: The World after 1945* (Cambridge: Harvard University Press, 2014), 547; Penny M. Von Eschen, *Satchmo Blows Up the World: Jazz Ambassadors Play the Cold War* (Cambridge: Harvard University Press, 2004), 27; Laura Belmonte, *Selling the American Way: U.S. Propaganda and the Cold War* (Philadelphia: University of Pennsylvania Press, 2008), 5, 7, 71, 176; Tom Engelhardt, *The End of Victory Culture: Cold War America and the Disillusioning of a Generation* (Amherst: University of Massachusetts Press, 2007), 300n; Stephen J. Whitfield, *The Culture of the Cold War* (Baltimore: Johns Hopkins University Press, 1996), 127–51; Reinhold Wagnleitner, *Coca-Colonization and the Cold War: The Cultural Mission of the United States in Austria during the Second World War* (Chapel Hill: University of North Carolina Press, 1994), 96, 114, 161, 276; Kurt Kemper, *College Football and American Culture in the Cold War Era* (Urbana: University of Illinois Press, 2009), 1–2; Robert Elias, *The Empire Strikes Out: How Baseball Sold U.S. Foreign Policy and Promoted the American Way Abroad* (New York: New Press, 2010), xi, 1–3, 286–89, 291–94; Russ Crawford, *The Use of Sport to Promote the American Way of Life during the Cold War: Cultural Propaganda, 1945–1963* (Lewistown, NY: Edwin Mellen Press, 2008), 2–3; Damion Thomas, *Globetrotting: African American Athletes in Cold War Politics* (Urbana: University of Illinois Press, 2012), 41–74.

33. Richard Espy, *The Politics of the Olympic Games* (Berkeley: University of California Press, 1981), 3–7; Alfred Senn, *Power, Politics, and the Olympic Games* (Urbana: University of Illinois Press, 1999), 97–110; Jules Boykoff, *Power Games: A Political History of the Olympics* (New York: Verso, 2016), 81–116; Toby Rider, *Cold War Games: Propaganda, the Olympics, and U.S. Foreign Policy* (Urbana: University of Illinois Press, 2016), 29–48.

34. William T. Tilden II, "Reminiscences," *WT* 1, no. 2 (July 1953): 13.

35. Gloria Butler, "The Tennis Story behind the Iron Curtain," *WT* 1, no. 1 (June 1953): 24, 29.

36. Ibid.

37. Thomas Borstelmann, *The Cold War and the Color Line: American Race Relations in the Global Arena* (Cambridge: Harvard University Press, 2001), x, 2–3, 6; Mary L. Dudziak, *Cold War Civil Rights: Race and the Image of American Democracy* (Princeton, NJ: Princeton University Press, 2000), 203–248.

38. "Around the World," *WT* 16, no. 11 (Apr. 1969): 93; Gibson interview, OHC-ITHF.

39. "Around the World," *WT* 16, no. 11 (Apr. 1969): 93; Gibson interview, OHC-ITHF.

40. Billie Jean King, with Cynthia Starr, *We Have Come a Long Way: The Story of Women's Tennis* (New York: McGraw-Hill, 1988).

Chapter 7. The "Kramer Karavan"

1. Fred Lillywhite recalls this tour in *The English Cricketers' Trip to Canada and the United States* (London: Kent & Co., 1860), v.

2. Steen, *Floodlights and Touchlines*, 92–93, 286, 290–91, 306–307. On basketball barnstorming, see Robert Peterson, *Cages to Jump Shots: Pro Basketball's Early Years* (Lincoln: University of Nebraska Press, 2002), 12, 59, 62–65, 73, 101. On baseball barnstorming and racial integration in the first third of the twentieth century, see Neil Lanct, "'A General Understanding': Organized Baseball and Black Professional Baseball, 1900–1930," in *Sport and the Color Line: Black Athletes and Race Relations in Twentieth Century America*, ed. Patrick Miller and David Wiggins (New York: Routledge, 2004), 30–52. While professional football never boasted peripatetic teams to the degree that baseball and basketball did, it was not until the mid-1930s that professional football teams really began to cement themselves in urban centers with populations large enough to discourage frequent regional travel in search of fans. On this change as told through the life of Joseph Carr, the president of what came to be called the National Football League from 1921 to 1939, see Chris Willis, *The Man Who Built the National Football League: Joe F. Carr* (Plymouth, Eng.: Scarecrow Press, 2010), 199–201, 244–66, 337–47.

3. Simon J. Eaves and Robert J. Lake, "The 'Ubiquitous Apostle of International Play,' Wilberforce Vaughan Eaves: The Forgotten International of Lawn Tennis," *International Journal of the History of Sport* 33, no. 16 (May 2017): 1963–81; Simon J. Eaves and Robert J. Lake, "Dwight Davis and the Foundation of the Davis Cup in Tennis: Just Another Doubleday Myth?," *Journal of Sport History* 45, no. 1 (2018): 1–23.

4. Don Budge, *Don Budge: A Tennis Memoir* (New York: Viking Press, 1969), 41, 95, 125–26, 141.

5. Jeane Hoffman, "Bouncing Around," *The Racquet* 47, no. 3 (July 1953): 26.

6. Minutes of a Specially Called Meeting of the Board of Directors of the Southern California Tennis Association, Dec. 17, 1953, folder [no number] Southern California Tennis Association 1953–1954, RKC; Minutes of the Organization Meeting of the Board of Directors of the Southern California Tennis Association, Jan. 21, 1954, folder [no number] Southern California Tennis Association 1953–1954, RKC; Ned Potter, "Passing Shots," *WT* 1, no. 10 (Mar. 1954): 37.

7. Minutes of the Organization Meeting of the Board of Directors of the Southern California Tennis Association, Jan. 21, 1954, folder [no number] Southern California Tennis Association 1953–1954, RKC.

8. J. Joubert and G. Heldman, "25 Years Ago," *WT* 3, no. 11 (Apr. 1956): 3; George McGann, "Frank Sedgman and the Pot of Gold," *The Racquet* 45, no. 10 (Feb. 1952): 6, 34, 36–37; "Around the World," *WT* 1, no. 4 (Sept. 1953): 33; "Around the World," *WT* 1, no. 6 (Nov. 1953): 36; Gardnar Mulloy, "USLTA Annual Meeting," *WT* 1, no. 9 (Feb. 1954): 10–14; "Around the World," *WT*, 3, no. 5 (Oct. 1955): 68.

9. Kramer, *The Game*, 134; Art Larsen and Gladys Heldman, "The Sporting Goods Representative," *WT* 2, no. 6 (Nov. 1954): 19; "Tennis Clinics," *WT* 2, no. 4 (Sept.

1954): 60–61; Edward Potter, "Vic Denny Is New USLTA Prexy," *WT*, 5, no. 10 (Mar. 1958): 12–13.

10. Peck & Snyder, *Price List of Outdoor Sports & Pastimes* (New York: n.p., ca. 1886), 36, Call# GV747, Trade Catalog Collection, Winterthur Museum and Library, Wilmington, Delaware; "Advertisements," *ALT* 14, no. 1 (Apr. 15, 1920): i–1; "Advertisement," *ALT* 28, no. 14 (Feb. 20, 1935): i; "Advertisement," *ALT* 34, no. 5 (July 20, 1920): i; *Wilson Tennis Equipment* product catalog for 1941, Call# .W7395 1941, Trade Catalog Collection, Hagley Museum and Library, Wilmington, Delaware; "Advertisement," *ALT* 37, no. 1 (Apr. 20, 1943): i; "Advertisement," *ALT* 37, no. 3 (June 20, 1943): 23; "Advertisement," *ALT* 37, no. 14 (May 1944): 24–25; "Advertisement," *ALT* 41, no. 1 (July 15, 1947): 22–23.

11. Jack Miller, "Jack Brightens Pro Scene," *ALT* 41, no. 12 (Jan. 1, 1948): 6–7; "Advertisement," *ALT* 41, no. 13 (Feb. 1, 1948): 20–21.

12. "Advertisement," *ALT*, 42, no. 11 (Dec. 1948): 20–1; "Advertisement," *ALT* 41, no. 13 (Feb. 1, 1948): 20–21; Kramer, *The Game*, 134–36.

13. Jeane Hoffmann, "Bouncing Around," *ALT* 44, no. 3 (July 1, 1950): 13; Hugh Stewart, "The Pro Tour: Success or Failure," *WT* 2, no. 1 (June 1954): 45; "End of Tour: Kramer Wins—On the Court and in the Bank," *WT* 1, no. 1 (June 1953): 27; "Around the World," *WT* 1, no. 2 (July 1953): 20.

14. "World Professional Championship . . .," *WT* 1, no. 1 (June 1953): 18; "10,000 P.O.C. World Tennis Championship of 1954," *WT* 1, no. 10 (Mar. 1954): 32–33.

15. Kramer, *The Game*, 187; Paul Tillich, "Is There a Judeo-Christian Tradition?," *Judaism* 1, no. 2 (Apr. 1952): 106–109; Burton J. Bledstein, *The Culture of Professionalism: The Middle Class and the Development of Higher Education in America* (New York: W. W. Norton, 1978), 80–83; William Leach, *Land of Desire: Merchants, Power, and the Rise of a New American Culture* (New York: Vintage, 1993), 3.

16. Tony Trabert interview, OHC-ITHF.

17. Hugh Stewart, "The Pro Tour: A Three-Day Account," *WT* 1, no. 8 (Jan. 1954): 26–27; "The Jack Kramer Tour Itinerary," *WT* 1, no. 9 (Feb. 1954): 39.

18. Hugh Stewart, "The Pro Tour: A Three-Day Account," *WT* 1, no. 8 (Jan. 1954): 26–27; "The Jack Kramer Tour Itinerary," *WT* 1, no. 9 (Feb. 1954): 39.

19. "Around the World," *WT* 1, no. 9 (Feb. 1954): 41; Hugh Stewart, "The Pro Tour: A Three-Day Account," *WT* 1, no. 8 (Jan. 1954): 26–27.

20. "Around the World," *WT* 1, no. 8 (Jan. 1954): 42.

21. Hugh Stewart, "The Pro Tour: Success or Failure," *WT* 2, no. 1 (June 1954): 45; "Around the World," *WT* 2, no. 1 (June 1954): 41; "Around the World," *WT* 1, no. 11 (Apr. 1954): 41; "The Pro Tour," *WT* 2, no. 2 (July 1954): 39.

22. Hugh Stewart, "The Pro Tour: Success or Failure," *WT* 2, no. 1 (June 1954): 45; "Around the World," *WT* 2, no. 1 (June 1954): 41; "Around the World," *WT* 1, no. 11 (Apr. 1954): 41; "The Pro Tour," *WT* 2, no. 2 (July 1954): 39.

23. Hugh Stewart, "The Pro Tour: Success or Failure," *WT* 2, no. 1 (June 1954): 45;

"Around the World," *WT* 2, no. 1 (June 1954): 41; "Around the World," *WT* 1, no. 11 (Apr. 1954): 41; "The Pro Tour," *WT* 2, no. 2 (July 1954): 39.

24. Jerome Scheur, "The Pro Tour: An excerpt from a letter, New Haven, Feb. 4," *WT* 1, no. 10 (Mar. 1954): 50; George McGann and Peter Hastings, "Professional Tennis Is Tougher Than Ever," *WT* 1, no. 10 (Mar. 1954): 17; "Around the World," *WT* 1, no. 11 (Apr. 1954): 41; Ann Olson, letter to the editors of *WT* magazine, *WT* 1, no. 11 (Apr. 1954): 2; Ned Potter, "Passing Shorts," *WT* 1, no. 10 (Mar. 1954): 37; Jack Kramer, "Our Young Players: An Analysis," *WT* 2, no. 4 (Sept. 1954): 20; "Around the World," *WT* 1, no. 6 (Nov. 1953): 34.

25. Don Budge, "Wembley Professional Tournament: Sedgman Wallops Gonzales," *WT* 1, no. 7 (Dec. 1953): 12; Mike Davies, *Tennis Rebel* (London: Stanley and Paul, 1962), 149–52.

26. "Around the World," *WT* 1, no. 9 (Feb. 1954): 41; Jack March, "Gonzales Retains World Pro Title," *WT* 2, no. 1 (June 1954): 50–52.

27. Jack March, "Gonzales Retains World Pro Title," *WT* 2, no. 1 (June 1954): 50–52.

28. George Lyttelton Rogers, "Segura Takes Pacific Coast Pro Event," *WT* 2, no. 5 (Oct. 1954): 34.

29. Frank Sedgman interview, OHC-ITHF.

30. Barry MacKay to Mark McCormack, Mar. 11, 1967, Mack, Barry (1967), Television Tennis, folder, box M0705 (453), MMC.

31. Richard Savitt interview, OHC-ITHF.

32. "1954 Schedule of Sanctioned Tournaments," *WT* 1, no. 1 (June 1953): 34–36; "The Rich Man's Game," *WT* 1, no. 1 (June 1953): 20–21. For an overview of the impact of widespread (but not universal) upward mobility on sports in the 1950s, see Kathryn Jay, *More Than Just a Game: Sports in American Life since 1945* (New York: Columbia University Press, 2004), 48, 60–69.

33. Gardnar Mulloy, "Is Tennis Dying?," *WT* 1, no. 3 (Aug. 1953): 12; "Around the World," *WT* 1, no. 3 (Aug. 1953): 20; "Around the World," *WT* 1, no. 5 (Oct. 1953): 32.

34. Sidney B. Wood Jr., "The Tennis Players' League," *WT* 1, no. 4 (Sept. 1953): 34.

35. Ibid.

36. Sidney B. Wood, Jr. "The Case for the Tennis Players' League," *WT* 1, no. 5 (Oct. 1953): 8; Gardnar Mulloy, "Is Tennis Dying?," *WT* 1, no. 3 (Aug. 1953): 12.

37. Sidney B. Wood, Jr. "The Case for the Tennis Players' League," *WT* 1, no. 5 (Oct. 1953): 8; Gardnar Mulloy, "Is Tennis Dying?," *WT* 1, no. 3 (Aug. 1953): 12.

38. Ray Robinson, "Sidney Wood: Tennis Tycoon," *WT* 1, no. 6 (Nov. 1953): 10–11.

39. "Around the World," *WT* 1, no. 7 (Dec. 1953): 30; Gardnar Mulloy, "USLTA Annual Meeting," *WT* 1, no. 9 (Feb. 1954): 10–14; Sidney Wood, "A TV National Round Robin," *WT* 1, no. 9 (Feb. 1954): 34.

40. Sidney Wood, "S-S-S-Sh, We're on the Air," *WT* 2, no. 1 (June 1954): 24–26; Bill Rockwell to Sidney Wood Jr., "A Letter to Sidney," *WT* 1, no. 5 (Oct. 1953): 8.

41. Sidney Wood, "S-S-S-Sh, We're on the Air," *WT* 2, no. 1 (June 1954): 24–26; Bill Rockwell to Sidney Wood Jr., "A Letter to Sidney," *WT* 1, no. 5 (Oct. 1953): 8.

42. Benjamin Rader, *In Its Own Image: How Television Has Transformed Sports* (New York: Free Press, 1984), 33–35.

43. Ibid., 35–38.

44. Donald Dell, *Minding Other People's Business: Winning Big for Your Clients and Yourself* (New York: Villard Books, 1989), 205; Barry MacKay to Mark McCormack, Mar. 11, 1967, Mack, Barry (1967), Television Tennis, folder, box M0705 (453), MMC.

45. Barry MacKay to Mark McCormack, Mar. 11, 1967, Mack, Barry (1967), Television Tennis, folder, box M0705 (453), MMC.

46. Ibid.

47. Sedgman interview, OHC-ITHF.

Chapter 8. The World Champion from "The Wrong Side of the Tracks"

1. Gonzales, *Man with a Racket*, 32; "Victorious Pancho to Turn Pro," *Ventura County Star-Free Press*, Sept. 19, 1949, 9.

2. Pancho Gonzales interview, OHC-ITHF; Gonzales, *Man with a Racket*, 35, 43–44; Rita Agassi Gonzalez, "The Power and the Fury: The Childhood That Produced the Great Pancho Gonzalez," *WT* 35, no. 4 (Sept. 1987): 24–27, 75, 77; Dave Lewis, "Once Over Lightly," *Long Beach Independent*, Feb. 14, 1948, 17–18; *The Official Report of the Xth Olympiad, Los Angeles*, 60, 64, 78–79,106, 149, 777.

3. "Central Juvenile Index," *Confidential Annual Report* for 1944, folder 2, box 1, LA County Coordinating Council Records, 1930–48, California Welfare Archives, USC Special Collections, Los Angeles, California; Gonzales, *Man with a Racket*, 25–26, 36, 43; Gonzales interview, OHC-ITHF.

4. "Mako Denies Taking Money for Exhibition," *Iowa City Daily Iowan*, Apr. 13, 1938, 3; Don Budge interview, OHC-ITHF. For more on this "recreational revolution," see Ruth, "Pancho's Racket," 102–140.

5. Perry T. Jones Biographical File, Biographical Files Collection, ITHF; Year: 1900; Census Place: San Bernardino Ward 2, San Bernardino, California; Roll: 97; Page: 9B; Enumeration District: 0225; Family History Library microfilm: 1240097; Year: 1920; Census Place: Los Angeles Assembly District 63, Los Angeles, California; Roll: T625_106; Page: 98A; Enumeration District: 166; Image: 902. In the 1930 census he reported his occupation as a managing accountant and his industry as building and loans. See Year: 1930; Census Place: Los Angeles, California; Roll: 134; Page: 4B; Enumeration District: 64; Image: 380.0; Family History Library microfilm: 2339869. In the 1940s census Jones reported his occupation as the Southern California Tennis Association and his industry as sports. Year: 1940; Census Place: Los Angeles, California; Roll: T627_405; Page: 62A; Enumeration District: 60–311; Baltzell, *Sporting Gentlemen*, 233.

6. Jim Murray, "Last of the Victorians," *Los Angeles Times*, Oct. 1, 1970, A20; Yeo-

mans, *Southern California Tennis Champions Centennial*, 67; Perry T. Jones, *Perry T. Jones Presents Fine Points of Tennis for Youth* (n.p.: Union Oil Company of California, 1958), 1. For the context on whiteness in which Jones operated, see Nell Irvin Painter, *The History of White People* (New York: W. W. Norton, 2010), 325, 341, 359–73.

7. Will Levington Comfort, "Tennis Playing Benefits Youth," *Los Angeles Times*, May 24, 1925, B3; William Plumer Jacobs, *Tennis, Builder of Citizenship: The Psychology and Technique of the Game as Taught in the Tennis Clinic* (Clinton, SC: Jacobs Press, 1941), 21, 27, 30–33, 37–41. Roosevelt's 1899 speech is reprinted in Theodore Roosevelt, *The Strenuous Life: Essays and Addresses* (New York: The Century Co., 1902), 1–24.

8. John T. Bailey, "How to Improve One's Game: A Series of Practical Articles for the Average Player," *ALT* 2, no. 15 (Mar. 15, 1909): 410–11; A. E. Bemish, *First Steps to Lawn Tennis* (London: Mills & Boon, 1922), 13–14; P. A. Vaile, *Modern Tennis* (New York: Funk & Wagnalls Co., 1915), vi; "Review of the Woodford Tennis Club," *ALT* 2, no. 15 (Mar. 15, 1909): 413.

9. Perry T. Jones to USLTA President John Holcombe Ward, Aug. 2, 1943, folder 4.14.1, box 8, LBC. African Americans first came to Los Angeles in large numbers during the 1920s. The work they found there can only be assessed on a case-by-case basis, as some of the city's 456 industries employed African Americans as full equals to white and Mexican workers while others separated them, paying them lower wages. See "Department of Research and Investigation in the National Urban League," 1926 Report, undated typescript, California Contemporary Culture 1926–1937 folder, box A874, Works Progress Administration Collection, Manuscripts Division, Library of Congress; Kramer, *The Game*, 20–23; "The Business of Pleasure," typescript, Sept. 14, 1939, Los Angeles Guide Sports folder, box A533, Works Progress Administration Collection, Library of Congress, Washington, D.C.; "Tennis Factory: Perry Jones Is Champion Producer of Champions," *Life*, Aug. 7, 1950, 98–102, 105; Gonzales interview, OHC-ITHF.

10. Gonzales, *Man with a Racket*, 48–49. For the association between race and male delinquency nationwide, see Luis Alvarez, *The Power of the Zoot: Youth Culture and Resistance during World War II* (Berkeley: University of California Press, 2008), 42–73. For the gendered origins of earlier juvenile reform efforts in Los Angeles, see Mary Odom, "City Mothers and Delinquent Daughters: Female Juvenile Justice Reform in Early 20th Century Los Angeles," in *California Progressivism Revisited*, ed. William Deverell and Tom Sitton (Berkeley: University of California Press, 1993), 175–99; Los Angeles County Plan of Coordinating Councils, *Why Have Delinquents?* (Los Angeles: Rotary Club of Los Angeles, 1933), 32, 41, 44–45.

11. Frank Sedgman interview, OHC-ITHF; John Van Ryn interview, OHC-ITHF.

12. Sedgman interview, OHC-ITHF; Van Ryn interview, OHC-ITHF.

13. Gonzales, *Man with a Racket*, 25–26, 36, 43; Gonzales interview, OHC-ITHF; John F. Lafferty, *The Preston School of Industry: A Centennial History* (Ione, CA: Preston School of Industry, 1994), 278–79; Leon Adams, "Boys 'Graduate' as Crooks at Reform School," unnamed San Francisco paper, July 10, 1923, newspaper clipping,

in Miscellaneous Records, Newspaper Clippings, Preston School of Industry, folder 3738:67, California Youth Authority Collection, California State Archives, Sacramento, California; "Notorious Crooks 'Graduates' of Preston," *San Francisco Daily News*, July 11, 1923, newspaper clipping in Miscellaneous Records, Newspaper Clippings, Preston School of Industry, folder 3738:67, California Youth Authority Collection, California State Archives, Sacramento, California; Leon Adams, "Only Two Per Cent of Boys Are Reformed at Preston," *California Daily News*, July 18, 1923, newspaper clipping, in Miscellaneous Records, Newspaper Clippings, Preston School of Industry, folder 3738:67, California Youth Authority Collection, California State Archives, Sacramento, California.

14. Southern California Timing Association, Inc., "SCTA Program Time Trials," Nov. 3, 1946, Elmrage, Calif., Nov. 3, 1946, SCTA, folder, Finn Race Files, box 11, Revs Institute, Naples, Florida; "What This Is All About—" SCTA Bulletin No. 2A, July 25, 1947, Harper Dry Lakes, Calif., July 6, 1947, SCTA, folder, Finn Race Files, box 11, Revs Institute, Naples, Florida; "Fourth Annual Bonneville National Speed Trials," *Souvenir Program*, Aug. 25–31, 1952, Bonneville, UT—Aug 23–31, 1954, folder, Finn Race Files, box 11, Revs Institute, Naples, Florida; Bobby Riggs interview, OHC-ITHF.

15. Gonzales interview, OHC-ITHF.

16. Ibid.

17. Ibid.; Deford, *Big Bill Tilden*, 98–99. The comments on stroke mechanics are based on the author's decade of experience coaching tennis technique.

18. Dave Lewis, "Once Over Lightly," *Long Beach Independent*, Feb. 14, 1948, 17–18; Gonzales interview, OHC-ITHF.

19. Gonzales interview, OHC-ITHF; "Proposed Changes in USLTA Amateur Regulations," June 6, 1943, Amateur Rule Committee folder 1, box 1, RKC; Hugh W. Stewart letter to Perry T. Jones, Nov. 20, 1953, Amateur Rule Committee folder 1, box 1, RKC; Minutes of Special Meeting of the Amateur Rule Committee, Dec. 11, 1953, Amateur Rule Committee folder 1, box 1, RKC.

20. Robert J. Lake, "A History of Social Exclusion in British Tennis: From Grass Roots to the Elite Level," in Lake, *Routledge Handbook of Tennis*, 460–69.

21. Gonzales interview, OHC-ITHF; Gonzales, *Man with a Racket*, 51–52.

22. Gonzales interview, OHC-ITHF; Gonzales, *Man with a Racket*, 51–52; Jim Murray, "Last of the Victorians," *Los Angeles Times*, Oct. 1, 1970, A20; "Pancho Ponders Mexican Citizenship," *Reno News*, Feb. 7, 1948, 8; Bion Abbott, "Gonzales Can't Make Up Mind on Net Offer, *Los Angeles Times*, Feb. 8, 1948, 14; "Gonzales Turns Down Mexican Net Offer," *Oakland Tribune*, Feb. 11, 1948, 18.

23. "Pancho Gonzales Wins National Clay Court Title," *Long Beach Press-Telegram*, July 19, 1948, A10; "Pancho Gonzales, Eric Sturgess in Tennis Finals," *Jacksonville Daily Journal*, Sept. 19, 1948, 14; "Sport: Build Up at Wimbledon," *Time*, July 4, 1949, unpaginated; "Clowning Gonzales Blasts Way to Amateur Tennis Crown," *Montana Standard*, Sept. 20, 1948, 8.

24. "Pancho Gonzales Wins National Tennis Crown," *Harlingen Star Farmer*, Sept. 20, 1948, 3; Oscar Frailey, "Young Mexican Wins National Net Title," *Amarillo Globe*, Sept. 30, 1948, 13; "Gonzales, as Amateur Tennis Champion, Poses Social Problem at Forest Hills," *Olean Times Herald*, Sept. 29, 1948, 13; "Ted Schroeder Defeats Gonzales Again," *Alton Evening Telegraph*, Oct. 11, 1948, 10; "Gonzales Finds Rough Sledding," *Amarillo Globe*, Oct. 19, 1948, 13; Stan Opoiowky, "Pancho Gonzales Ranked No. 1 Netman," *Portland Sunday Telegram and Sunday Press Herald*, Dec. 19, 1948, B2; Oscar Fraley, "Kramer Professes Sorrow at Schroeder's Setback, Though He Gains $50,000," *Reno News*, Sept. 11, 1949, 15; Ray Haywood, "Pancho Abdicates; To Miss Meet Here," *Oakland Tribune*, Sept. 19, 1949, 23; Gonzales, *Man with a Racket*, 34.

25. "Gonzales Joins Pro Net Ranks for $60,000," *Portland Press Herald*, Sept. 21, 1949, 18; "New Racket," *Inter Lake*, Sept. 23, 1949, 2; Richard "Pancho" Gonzales, "Amateur Tennis Champ Tells of Lure of 'Pro Dollars,'" *Tipton Daily Tribune*, Sept. 24, 1949, 4; Bobby Riggs, "To Fly When Pancho Launches Tour with Jack," *ALT* 43, no. 9 (Oct. 1949): 10; "Pancho Starts As Pro," *San Rafael Independent-Journal*, Oct. 25, 1949, 8; Al Schmahl, "Crowd Poor at Tennis Show Here," *Iowa City Press-Citizen*, May 16, 1950, 14; "Pancho Planning Ambitious Tennis Schedule for '49," *Ventura County Star-Free Press*, Apr. 6, 1949, 10.

26. Hamilton Chambers, "Highlights of 1949," *ALT* 43, no. 11 (Dec. 1949): 20; Bion Abbott, "The Pacific Southwest," *ALT* 43, no. 9 (Oct. 1949): 5.

27. John Boss, "Fans Cast Still Another Vote for Open Competition," *ALT* 43, no. 10 (Nov. 1949): 6–7, 14.

28. Alice Marble, "Kramer, Gonzales & Co.," *ALT* 43, no. 11 (Dec. 1949): 26; *Bobby Riggs Presents World Championship Tennis Tour*, 1949–1950, tour program, TPC-ITHF.

29. Jeane Hoffman, "Bouncing Around," *ALT* 43, no. 11 (Dec. 1949): 20; Edward C. Potter, Jr., "World Rankings for 1949," *ALT* 43, no. 10 (Nov. 1949): 3; Jeane Hoffman, "Kramer Karavan" cartoon, *ALT* 43, no. 11 (Dec. 1949): 20; Jeane Hoffman, "Bouncing Around," *ALT* 43, no. 12 (Jan. 1950): 15; Jeane Hoffman, "Bouncing Around," Pancho Gonzales in bed cartoon, *ALT* 44, no. 1 (May 1950): 11–12; Joan Raulet, "Capsule Court News," *ALT* 43, no. 13 (Feb. 1950): 21; "Kramer Holds Pro Tour Lead," *ALT* 43, no. 14 (Mar. 1950): 27.

30. "Kramer Holds Pro Tour Lead," *ALT* 43, no. 14 (Mar. 1950): 27; Mayer Brandschain, "Pancho Surprises, Upsets Kramer in Inquirer Event," *ALT* 44, no. 1 (May 1950): 11–12; Pancho Gonzales Testimony, "Court Transcript," 129–30, in *Richard A. Gonzalez v. The International Professional Tennis Players Association*, No. 63-CA-689 CC (C.D.C.A. June 13, 1963), case file, National Archives and Records Administration–Riverside, [NARA-Riverside] Riverside, California; hereafter *Gonzalez v. IPTPA*.

31. Jeane Hoffman, "Bouncing Around," Pancho Gonzales in bed cartoon, *ALT* 44, no. 1 (May 1950): 14.

32. Jeane Hoffman, "Bouncing Around," *ALT* 44, no. 5 (Aug. 1, 1950): 14; Jeane Hoffman, "Bouncing Around," *ALT* 44, no. 3 (July 1950): 12; "Capsule Court News,"

ALT 44, no. 2 (June 1950): 10; H.E.B., "Editorials," *ALT* 44, no. 7 (Sept. 1950): 14; Jeane Hoffman, "Bouncing Around," *ALT* 44, no. 2 (June 1950): 12; "Capsule Court News," *ALT* 44, no. 7 (Sept. 1950): 14.

33. Jeane Hoffman, "Bouncing Around," *ALT* 44, no. 5 (Aug. 1, 1950): 13–14; Ned Potter, "Ned Potter Says . . .," *ALT* 44, no. 3 (July 1950): 14; Pat O'Toole, "Segura Stops Kovacs in Surprise Finale," *ALT* 44, no. 3 (July 1950): 10, 29; John Michaels, "There's Gold in Them 'Thar Forest Hills," *ALT* 44, no. 6 (Aug. 15, 1950): 12, 28; "Capsule Court News," *ALT* 44, no. 5 (Aug. 1, 1950): 10; Jeane Hoffman, "Bouncing Around," *ALT* 44, no. 7 (Sept. 1950): 20.

34. Al Stump, "All Dressed Up and No Place to Play," *Sport*, Aug. 1955, 10, 71–73.

35. Ibid.

36. Linton Baldwin, "Where's Pancho," *The Racquet* 47, no. 1 (May 1953): 7–8; Al Stump, "All Dressed Up and No Place to Play," *Sport*, Aug., 1955, 10, 71–73.

37. Arthur Marx, "They're All Afraid of Gonzales," *Sport*, July 1952, 33, 75–76; Jerome Scheuer, "For the Defense," *The Racquet* 47, no. 4 (Aug. 1953): 25.

38. Jack March, "Gonzales Wins Pro Title," *WT* 1, no. 2 (July 1953): 31; Tony Mottram, "Seixas Is Wimbledon Champ," *WT* 1, no. 2 (July 1953): 5–8, 32–33.

39. Jack March, "Gonzales Wins Pro Title," *WT* 1, no. 2 (July 1953): 31; Tony Mottram, "Seixas Is Wimbledon Champ," *WT* 1, no. 2 (July 1953): 5–8, 32–33.

40. "End of Tour: Kramer Wins—On the Court and in the Bank," *WT* 1, no. 1 (June 1953): 27; *Jack Kramer Presents the World's Professional Championship Tennis, 1955–1956*, tour program, TPC-ITHF.

41. *Jack Kramer Presents the World's Professional Championship Tennis, 1955–1956*, tour program, 29, TPC-ITHF.

42. Ibid., 3, 13, 29.

43. Ibid., 3.

44. Ibid, 3, 13, 29.

45. Jim Russell, "Rosewall, Hoad Remain Amateurs," *WT* 3, no. 7 (Dec. 1955): 22–23.

46. Ibid.

47. "Around the World," *WT* 1, no. 6 (Nov. 1953): 36.

48. Kramer, *The Game*, 212–14; Dell, *Minding Other People's Business*, 87.

49. "Complaint for Injunctive Relief," 2, in *Gonzalez v. IPTPA*.

50. The International Professional Tennis Players' Association, "Our Inauguration," 1–6, in *Gonzalez v. IPTPA*. The players were M. A. "Mal" Anderson, Jack Arkinstall, Luis Ayala, Earl "Butch" Buchholz Jr., Ashley Cooper, Michael Davies, Andrés Gimeno, Richard "Pancho" Gonzales, Robert Haillet, Rex Hartwig, Lewis Alan Hoad, Jack Kramer, Barry MacKay, Ken McGregor, Kurt Nielsen, Alex Olmedo, Dinny Pails, Paul Remy, Mervyn Rose, Kenneth Rosewall, Frank Sedgman, Pancho Segura, and Anthony "Tony" Trabert.

51. "Around the World," *WT* 9, no. 10 (Mar. 1962): 61; "Aussie Net Great Rod Laver Signs $110,000 Contract for Big Pro Tour," *Hartford Courant*, Dec. 30, 1962, 39.

52. "Complaint for Injunctive Relief," 1–10, in *Gonzalez v. IPTPA*.

53. "Court Transcript," 154–78, in *Gonzales v. IPTPA*; "Famous Tours of Tennis History," in *World Series of Professional Tennis 1963 Tour of the Game's Top Tennis Stars* program, 24, TPC-ITHF; "Around the World," *WT* 8, no. 6 (Nov. 1960): 46; Walter Bingham, "A Legend Dies on the Court," *Sports Illustrated*, July 8, 1963, 18–19.

54. Judge comments, "Court Transcript," 178, in *Gonzalez v. IPTPA*.

55. "Interlocutory Findings of Fact, Conclusions of Law and Order," 2–3, in *Gonzalez v. IPTPA*.

Chapter 9. Tennis Opens

1. "Around the World," *WT* 9, no. 10 (Mar. 1962): 61; "Around the World," *WT* 9, no. 6 (Nov. 1961): 56; "Around the World," *WT* 9, no. 7 (Dec. 1961): 56, 65.

2. Noel Brown, "I Was a Pro," *WT* 1, no. 1 (June 1953): 19.

3. Ibid.; Gladys Heldman, "Around the World," *WT* 1, no. 1 (June 1953): 18.

4. "Around the World," *WT* 9, no. 5 (Oct. 1961): 68–69, 74; "Around the World," *WT* 9, no. 9 (Feb. 1962): 67–68; "Around the World," *WT* 9, no. 10 (Mar. 1962): 61; "Welcome Tennis Fans," in *World Series of Professional Tennis 1963 Tour of the Game's Top Tennis Stars* program, 3, TPC-ITHF; Rod Laver with Larry Writer, *Rod Laver: An Autobiography* (Chicago: Triumph Books, 2016), 138–40, 152, 155–57; Herb Ralby, "Boston Buoys Tennis," *Boston Globe*, July 7, 1964, 39; "U.S. Professional Tour," *WT* 13, no. 1 (June 1965): 31; "Around the World," *WT* 13, no. 1 (June 1965): 75–76; Mal Anderson, "The Pros Play New York," *WT* 13, no. 1 (June 1965): 36–39.

5. "M. Anthony Trabert Affidavit," [7], in *Gonzales v. IPTPA*; "U.S.P.L.T.A Membership List," [1–10], in *Gonzalez v. IPTPA*.

6. "Twenty-Five Years Ago," *WT* 4, no. 5 (Oct. 1956): 11.

7. Gloria Butler, "Four Wimbledon Questions," *WT* 1, no. 2 (July 1953): 26; "The Open Tournament and the Specter of Jack Kramer," *WT* 8, no. 10 (Mar. 1961): 28–29; "Around the World," *WT* 8, no. 11 (Apr. 1961): 60–61, 63–65.

8. Edward C. Potter to Gladys Heldman, *WT* 13, no. 5 (Oct. 1965): 2.

9. "Around the World," *WT* 13, no. 3 (Aug. 1965): 75; Lance Tingay, "Wimbledon Presses On," *WT* 13, no. 4 (Sept. [misprinted on magazine as Oct.] 1965): 58–59; Lake, *Social History of Tennis*, 154. For a comparative account of what follows regarding the LTA's role in the push for open tennis, see Lake, *Social History of Tennis*, 223–34.

10. "Around the World," *WT* 13, no. 3 (Aug. 1965): 75; Lance Tingay, "Wimbledon Presses On," *WT* 13, no. 4 (Sept. [misprinted on magazine as Oct.] 1965): 58–59.

11. Lance Tingay, "Wimbledon Presses On," *WT* 13, no. 4 (Sept. [misprinted on magazine as Oct.] 1965): 58–59.

12. Ibid.

13. George McGann, "75 Years with the USLTA: A History of Hassles, Squabbles, and Controversies," *WT* 3, no. 8 (Jan. 1956): 11–13; Alan Trengove, *The Story of the Davis Cup* (London: Stanley Paul & Co., 1985), 11, 565; "Comes the Tennis Revolution," *Sports Illustrated*, Feb. 24, 1958, 23–25.

14. "Tennis Faces Backward," *Sports Illustrated*, July 18, 1960, 10; Gilbert Rogin, "Low Point for Tennis," *Sports Illustrated*, Sept. 19, 1960, 36; Ann Wetzel to Edwin Baker, *WT* 13, no. 8 (Jan. 1966): 8.

15. "Around the World," *WT* 8, no. 4 (Sept. 1960): 63; "Around the World," *WT* 8, no. 10 (Mar. 1961) 45; "Around the World," *WT* 9, no. 5 (Oct. 1961): 69; "Around the World," *WT* 8, no. 12 (May 1961): 45; Lance Tingay to Ned Potter, *WT* 13, no. 8 (Jan. 1966): 4; Gladys Heldman, "A Senior International Championship," *WT* 14, no. 10 (Mar. 1967): 14.

16. "Around the World," *WT* 9, no. 9 (Feb. 1962): 68; Jean Borotra, "The Case for the Authorized Player," *WT* 7, no. 11 (Apr. 1960): 14.

17. "Around the World," *WT* 9, no. 8 (Jan. 1962): 53; "Around the World," *WT* 9, no. 9, (Feb. 1962): 67–68; "Around the World," *WT* 9, no. 10 (Mar. 1962): 61; Jack Pollard, "'Mystery Man' Wins Jan. Marlboro Award," *WT* 13, no. 8 (Jan. 1966): 32–33.

18. George MacCall, "National Tennis League," handwritten history, no date, folder 1, box 1, GMP; Biography of Robert Joseph Kelleher, Legal-Licensing Corporation of America 4/67–10/67 folder [no number], box 3, LBC; Gladys Heldman, "Captain George MacCall," *WT* 13, no. 4 (Sept. [misprinted on magazine as Oct.] 1965): 12–13.

19. "Around the World," *WT* 14, no. 6 (Nov. 1966): 54; "Around the World," *WT* 14, no. 11 (Apr. 1967): 68; Around the World," *WT* 14, no. 12 (May 1967): 79.

20. Robert Shepherd Jr. to George MacCall, Apr. 26, 1965, folder 18, box 2, GMP; Arthur Ashe to George MacCall, Nov. 13, 1967, folder 9, box 1, GMP; Joe Henderson, "Gonzales to Coach U.S. Davis Cup Team," *Los Angeles Times*, Mar. 17, 1965, C5; Joe Hendrickson, "Davis Cuppers in Good Hands," unknown publication, n.d, folder 15, box 2, GMP; Pancho Gonzales, "The Davis Cup," unknown publication, Nov. 1966, folder 2, box 2, GMP; Bob Galt, "Courtside with Pancho," unknown publication, n.d., folder 15, box 2, GMP; Richard A. Gonzales Player Agreement, Sept. 30, 1968, folder 15, box 2, GMP; Tennis Championships Incorporated, promotional brochure, folder 5, box 2, GMP; "Around the World," *WT* 15, no. 6 (Nov. 1967): 66.

21. Gladys Heldman, "The Best and Worst of 1966," *WT* 14, no. 9 (Feb. 1967): 12; "Around the World," *WT* 13, no. 12 (May 1966): 85; "Around the World," *WT* 14, no. 5 (Oct. 1966): 74; "Around the World," *WT* 14, no. 4 (Sept. 1966): 77, 79.

22. Around the World," *WT* 14, no. 8 (Jan. 1967): 70, 74–75, 79–80; David Gray, "The Pros at Wimbledon" *WT* 15, no. 5 (Oct. 1967): 74–75; "Around the World," *WT* 14, no. 6 (Nov. 1966): 50.

23. "Around the World," *WT* 14, no. 9 (Feb. 1967): 66, 73–74.

24. "Around the World," *WT* 15, no. 4 (Sept. 1967): 73; "Around the World," *WT* 15, no. 3 (Aug. 1967): 85.

25. Lake, *Social History of Tennis*, 225; "Around the World," *WT* 15, no. 3 (Aug. 1967): 87; David Gray, "The Pros at Wimbledon," *WT* 15, no. 5 (Oct. 1967): 74–75.

26. "The British Defy Ban on Open Tennis," *WT* 15, no. 6 (Nov. 1967): 44–45; "Around the World," *WT* 14, no. 12 (May 1967): 84; "Around the World," *WT* 15, no.

2 (July 1967): 75; "Around the World; *WT* 15, no. 3 (Aug. 1967): 84–85; "Around the World," *WT* 14, no. 1 (June 1966): 83.

27. "A Forward Step," *WT* 15, no. 9 (Feb. 1968): 12–13; Marty Mulligan, "Interview with the President of the ILTF," *WT* 15, no. 9 (Feb. 1968): 45.

28. Jean Borotra, "The Problem Facing Tennis in the World Today," Extracts of the Press Conference Held in Chicago, Jan. 19, 1961, International Lawn Tennis Federation 1937–1967 folder [no number], box 6, LBC; Perry T. Jones to William Clothier, Apr. 9, 1965, folder 11, box 1, GMP; "Report of the Committee of Management on the Subject of Amateurism," ILTF, Mar. 30, 1968, folder 3, box 1, GMP.

29. Jean Borotra, "The Problem Facing Tennis in the World Today," Extracts of the Press Conference Held in Chicago, Jan. 19, 1961, International Lawn Tennis Federation 1937–1967 folder [no number], box 6, LBC; Perry T. Jones to William Clothier, Apr. 9, 1965, folder 11, box 1, GMP; "Report of the Committee of Management on the Subject of Amateurism," ILTF, Mar. 30, 1968, folder 3, box 1, GMP.

30. Jean Borotra to George MacCall, Apr. 2, 1968, folder 11, box 2, GMP; Jean Borotra to George MacCall, Apr. 4, 1968, folder 11, box 2, GMP.

31. Draft Protocol, n.d., folder 11, box 2, GMP; "Around the World," *WT* 15, no. 11 (Apr. 1968): 76–77; Jean Borotra to George MacCall, cable, Apr. 23, 1968, folder 11, box 2, GMP; Jean Borotra to George MacCall, cable, Apr. 24, 1968, folder 11, box 2, GMP; French Open 1968 Contract, Apr. 26, 1968, folder 11, box 2, GMP; Roger Cirotteau to George MacCall, May 2, 1968, folder 11, box 2, GMP; Mr. Darmon to George MacCall, cable, May 9, 1968, folder 11, box 2, GMP; Jean Borotra to George MacCall, cable, May 13, 1968, folder 11, box 2, GMP; Jean Bassompierre to George MacCall, May 13, 1968, folder 11, box 2, GMP; George MacCall to Borotra Tenisfedet, cable, May 16, 1968, folder 11, box 2, GMP; George MacCall to Borotra Tenisfedet, cable, May 20, 1968, folder 11, box 2, GMP.

32. Mark Kurlansky, *1968: The Year That Rocked the World* (New York: Ballantine Books, 2004), xvii-xviii, 9–13, 15–17, 33, 35, 375; "Around the World," *WT* 16, no. 3 (Aug. 1968): 71, 73; Lance Tingay, "The French Championships," *WT* 16, no. 3 (Aug. 1968): 20–23.

33. Lance Tingay, "The French Championships," *WT* 16, no. 3 (Aug. 1968): 20–23; Roger Cirotteau to George MacCall, May 7, 1968, folder 11, box 2, GMP; Jean Borotra to George MacCall, June 10, 1968, folder 11, box 2, GMP.

34. Lance Tingay, "The French Championships," *WT* 16, no. 3 (Aug. 1968): 20–23; Roger Cirotteau to George MacCall, May 7, 1968, folder 11, box 2, GMP; Jean Borotra to George MacCall, June 10, 1968, folder 11, box 2, GMP.

35. Tony Kennedy, "U.S. Amateurs on a Mission," unknown newspaper clipping, June 30, 1968, unpaginated, in folder 4, box 2, GMP; "Eight of Each," unknown newspaper clipping, June 30, 1968, unpaginated, in folder 4, box 2, GMP.

36. Richard Evans, "Open Wimbledon," *WT* 16, no. 4 (Sept. 1968): 30–41.

37. George MacCall, "Employment History," n.d., folder 1, box 1, GMP; National Tennis League Cash Flow Statement Mar. 1 through Dec. 31, 1968, folder 18, box 1,

GMP; Life Insurance Policies in Force, n.d., folder 18, box 1, GMP; "Memorandum of Agreement," n.d., folder 1, box 1, GMP; "Professional Tennis Proposal," June 26, 1968, folder 4, box 1, GMP; George MacCall to Lamar Hunt, July 13, 1968, folder 4, box 1, GMP; Bob Briner to George MacCall, Feb. 24, 1969, folder 6, box 1, GMP; "National tennis league," typescript, seemingly written by George MacCall in a question-and-answer note format, n.d., folder 1, box 1, GMP; "Hunt Purchases Control of All Top Tennis Pros," *Philadelphia Inquirer*, July 29, 1970, 22.

Chapter 10. The Rise and Demise of World Championship Tennis

1. Robert Moore, "A History of World Championship Tennis," unpublished typescript [2–3], no box, LHP. My thanks to Bob Moore, corporate archivist for Hunt Enterprises and friend of the late Lamar Hunt, for providing me with a copy of his unpublished "History of World Championship Tennis," which I draw on throughout this section, as well as access to Hunt's personal papers and the private print and television archive of World Championship Tennis housed in the SubTropolis cave complex, the largest civilian climate-controlled underground storage facility in the country, located off of Northeast Underground Drive in Kansas City, Missouri.

2. Moore, "History of World Championship Tennis," typescript [3], LHP.

3. For a discussion of the NFL-AFL merger in trenchant analysis of post-WWII professional football, see Michael Oriad, *Brand NFL: Making and Selling America's Favorite Sport* (Chapel Hill: University of North Carolina Press, 2007), 19–21. For more detail on Hunt's specific role in the AFL, see Michael MacCambridge, *Lamar Hunt: A Life in Sports* (Kansas City, MO: Andrews McMeel, 2012), 156–62. A second biography of Hunt is also strong on his important role in professional football, soccer, baseball, and basketball, yet lighter on analyzing his role in bringing profitability to professional tennis in his WCT venture. See David Sweet, *Lamar Hunt: The Gentle Giant Who Revolutionized Professional Sports* (Chicago: Triumph Books, 2010), 7–8, 31–62, 64–69, 110–37, 139–67, 170–74.

4. Moore, "History of World Championship Tennis," typescript [3–4], LHP.

5. Robert C. Trumpbour, "Stadiums, Arenas, and Audiences," in *A Companion to American Sports History*, ed. Steven Reiss (New York: John Wiley and Sons, 2014), 577.

6. Moore, "History of World Championship Tennis," typescript [14], LHP.

7. Ibid.; Robert Moore, "WCT Tours: 1971–1990," typescript [1–2], LHP. I again offer my thanks to Bob Moore for sharing with me his unpublished and in-house year-by-year and month-by-month match results for WCT tournaments. As before, I have added pagination in brackets.

8. For a detailed account of the Cowboys-versus-Texans competition, see John Eisenberg, *Ten-Gallon War: The NFL's Cowboys, the AFL's Texans, and the Feud for Dallas's Pro Future* (Boston: Houghton Mifflin Harcourt, 2012).

9. "List of Cities Where WCT Has Had Tournaments" as of January 13, 1987, typescript, box 13, LHP; Moore, "WCT Tours: 1971–1990," typescript [1–2], LHP.

10. Moore, "History of World Championship Tennis," typescript [14], LHP; Moore, "WCT Tours: 1971–1990," typescript [1–2], LHP.

11. Moore, "WCT Tours: 1971–1990," typescript [1–2], LHP.

12. Michael MacCambridge, *America's Game: The Epic Story of How Pro Football Captured a Nation* (New York: Anchor Books, 2005), 130–34.

13. Moore, "WCT Tours: 1971–1990," typescript [1–4], LHP; "What Is WCT?," photocopy, n.d., 3, 6–7, box 13, LHP.

14. William Woy, "Dear," WCT sponsorship rights typescript, n.d., 1, box 13, LHP; "A Chronological History of World Championship Tennis," typescript, n.d., [4–5], box 13, LHP; Rich Koster, *The Tennis Bubble: Big-Money Tennis: How It Grew and Where It's Going* (New York: New York Times Book Co., 1976).

15. "The WCT Complaint," *Pro Tennis: The Official Newspaper of World Championship Tennis* 2, no. 5 (Mar. 17, 1983): 7–10; Mike Davies, "Mike Davies Comments," in *Official WCT Tennis Calendar, 1973–74* (Chicago: Johns-Byrne Co., n.d.), 3–6, in box 13, LHP; Moore, "WCT Tours: 1971–1990," typescript [5–6, 22–23], LHP.

16. Kramer, *The Game*, 104–107.

17. Ibid., 108–111.

18. Ibid., 112–13, 115–20.

19. Gladys Heldman, "My Ad," typescript, n.d., no folder, box 25, GHP.

20. Kramer, *The Game*, 81, 272, 275–79.

21. Gladys Heldman, "My Ad," typescript, n.d., no folder, box 25, GHP.

22. David Goldblatt, *The Games: A Global History of the Olympics* (New York: W. W. Norton, 2016), 287; Joseph Ivy to Louis Carruthers, Aug. 14, 1934, Media 1932–1962 folder [no number], box 6, LBC; Louis Carruthers to Lawrence Baker, Sept. 5, 1934, Media 1932–1962 folder [no number], box 6, LBC; Lawrence Baker to Walter Merrill, Sept. 6, 1935, Media 1932–1962 folder [no number], box 6, LBC; Lawrence Baker to Henry Luce, June 24, 1948, Media 1932–1962 folder [no number], box 6, LBC; Minutes of Meeting of the Amateur Rule Committee, Sept. 3, 1958, Amateur Rule Committee 1958–1963 folder [no number], box 1, RKC.

23. Donald Hobart to Lawrence Baker, May 14, 1964, Media 1963–1977 folder [no number], box 6, LBC; Robert Kelleher to James Dickey, May 6, 1964, Media 1932–1962 folder [no number], box 6, LBC; Renville McCann to Robert Kelleher, May 11, 1964, Media 1932–1962 folder [no number], box 6, LBC; "How To's of Tennis—Part V," television script, no date, Media 1932–1962 folder [no number], box 6, LBC.

24. USLTA Membership: 1958–1971, folder [no number], box [no number], LBC; Wilmer Allison to Ralph Westcott, June 21, 1960, Open Tennis 1960–1961 folder [no number], box 7, LBC.

25. Gladys Heldman, "The Kelleher Regime," *WT* 15, no. 1 (June 1967): 14, 16; Licensing, Corporation of America, "A Proposal to Help Popularize Interest in Tennis throughout the United States," Legal-Licensing Corporation of America 10/66–3–67 folder [no number], box 3, LBC; USLTA Grants Endorsement Rights to Licensing Corporation of America in Major Policy Action, press release, Apr. 5, 1967, Legal— Licensing Corporation of America 4/67–10/67 folder [no number], box 3, LBC; Fred

J. Podesta to Robert J. Kelleher, Feb. 23, 1967, Legal—Madison Square Garden, 1967–1968 folder [no number], box 3, LBC.

26. H. W. Colburn to Edgar Mooney, July 3, 1967, Legal—Licensing Corporation of America 4/67–10/67 folder [no number], box 3, LBC.

27. Alastair Martin, "Report by the President of the United States Lawn Tennis Association: A Statement of Opinion and Objectives," Apr. 14, 1970, International Lawn Tennis Federation, 1969–1977 folder [no number], box 6, LBC; Alastair Martin to Members of the Executive Committee, July 24, 1970, International Lawn Tennis Federation, 1969–1977 folder [no number], box 6, LBC; Lawrence Baker to James Dickey, June 30, 1960, Open Tennis 1960–1961 folder [no number], box 7, LBC.

28. *Gladys M. Heldman and Billie Jean King v. United States Lawn Tennis Association* 73. Civ 162, Opinion, for the United States District Court Southern District of New York, opinion issued Feb. 7, 1973, [7–8], in Legal—Gladys Heldman, 1973 folder [no number], box 2, LBC.

29. J. Howard Frazer to Robert Colwell, May 19, 1971, in Legal—Gladys Heldman, 1973 folder [no number], box 2, LBC.

30. Robert Caro, *The Power Broker: Robert Moses and the Fall of New York* (New York: Vintage, 1975), 619, 654, 772, 1061–1062, 1082–1113.

31. Slew Hester interview, OHC-ITHF.

32. William Hester III, "William E. Hester, Jr.," *WT* 15, no. 3 (Aug. 1967): 38–39; Michelle Nickerson and Darren Dochuk eds., *Sunbelt Rising: The Politics of Place, Space, and Region* (Philadelphia: University of Pennsylvania Press, 2013), 16.

33. Slew Hester, "How to form your Own Tennis Club," *WT* 15, no. 4 (Sept. 1967): 44–46; Hester interview, OHC-ITHF.

34. Slew Hester, "How to form your Own Tennis Club," *WT* 15, no. 4 (Sept. 1967): 44–46; Hester interview, OHC-ITHF.

35. Hester interview, OHC-ITHF.

36. Ibid.

37. Ibid.

38. Ibid.

39. Ibid.

40. Ibid.; USTA, "Year by Year: U.S. Open Attendance," http://2014.usopen.org/en_US/about/history/years.html (accessed June 7, 2016); Kurt Badenhausen, "Business Is Booming at the U.S. Open," *Forbes*, Sept. 10, 2015, http://www.forbes.com/sites/kurtbadenhausen/2015/09/10/business-is-booming-at-the-u-s-open/#46dc179290c5 (accessed June 7, 2020); Liz Kobak, "U.S. Open More Profitable Than Super Bowl," *World Tennis* online, http://www.worldtennismagazine.com/archives/9855 (accessed June 7, 2020).

41. Dave Gallup, "Tennis in Need of Super Circuit," *Cincinnati Enquirer*, May 30, 1970, 20.

42. Richard Finn, "Fans' Practice Guide for the Open," *Pro Tennis: The Official News-*

paper of World Championship Tennis 1, no. 16–17 (Sept. 2, 1982): 12; William Woy, "Dear," WCT sponsorship rights typescript, n.d., "Appendix A" [6], box 13, LHP.

Chapter 11. The Impact of Sports Agents and Agencies on Professional Tennis

1. Mark McCormack to Frank Barclay, Sept. 9, 1965, Gonzales, Pancho, Client File, box M3405 (0002), MMC. At the time of this writing, Special Collections and University Archives staff at the University of Massachusetts Amherst Libraries are continuing to process the sizable MMC. I have given the most complete citation available based upon when I conducted research in the MMC, though those citations may not match exactly with its current and ongoing organization.

2. Donald Dell, *Never Make the First Offer Except When You Should: Wisdom from a Master Dealmaker* (New York: Portfolio, 2009), 108–109.

3. Summerall, Pat, client folder; Sugar, Leo, client folder; Humphrey, Buddy, client folder; Krupa, Joe, client folder, all in box M3494 (0184), MMC. That conclusion is drawn from the comparison of these applications to those of clients from elite sports such as Billie Jean King's Representation Agreement found in King, Billie Jean, client folder, Rep Agreement 1972–1982, box M3162 (6219), MMC.

4. Rod Laver, with Bud Collins, *The Education of a Tennis Player* (New York: Simon and Schuster, 1971), 257–58.

5. Ibid.

6. Ibid., 258; Janet A. Horvath to Mr. Howard Friedman, Apr. 28, 1971, folder, Rod Laver, Kodacorp, box M3594 (0487/0158), MMC.

7. Richard R. Alford to Richard D. Moody and American Express, July 29, 1969, folder, Rod Laver, Club Continental, LTD., box M3594 (0487/0158), MMC.

8. Peter A. Kuhn to Richard R. Alford, Aug. 24, 1972 folder, Adidas Apparel, 1969–1972, box M3512 (0106), MMC; Hartmut Klar, Adidas Export Department, to Richard Alford, Aug. 7, 1972, folder, Adidas Apparel, 1969–1972, box M3512 (0106) MMC; Advertisement, Puritan Sports Company, Rod Laver Company (large brown accordion folder), box M3657 (1358) (0158), MMC; Rod Laver Press Kit, Rod Laver Tennis Wear Collections by Vivo by Susan Thomas and the Puritan Sportswear Corp, Rod Laver Company (large brown accordion folder), box M3657 (1358) (0158), MMC.

9. David Armstrong to Palm Desert Property Representative, Nov. 10, 1976, folder, Rod Laver, Palm Desert Property, box M3657 (0158), MMC; David Armstrong to Michael J. Narracott, Dec. 22, 1975, Rod Laver Hyatt Hotel Corporation folder, box M3657 (0158), MMC; Mike Narracott to David Armstrong, Oct. 29, 1975, Rod Laver Hyatt Hotel Corporation folder, box M3657 (0158), MMC; Mike Narracott to Bill Carpenter, Jan. 13, 1975, Rod Laver, Hilton Head folder, box M3657 (0158), MMC; David Armstrong to Mike Narracott, Oct. 28, 1975, Mass Mutual, Rod Laver folder, box M3657 (1358/0158), MMC; Mike Narracott to David Armstrong, Feb. 22, 1977, Professional International Inc., Rod Laver folder, box M3657 (1358/0158) MMC; Statement of Financial Condition of The Rod Laver Company, Dec. 31, 1970, Corre-

spondence, Rod Laver Co. folder, box M3657 (0158), MMC; Securities and Exchange Commission Registration Statement for Automated Player Machines, Inc., Apr. 16, 1970, Automated Play Machine, 1969 through 1971 folder (brown accordion folder), box M3594 (0487/0158) MMC; Contract between Rodney Laver and Rucanor Corporation, Mar. 1970, Rod Laver, Rucanor folder, box M3512 (0106), MMC.

10. Arnold Palmer Breeder Program Binder, no folder name or number, box M3747 (097), MMC; Jack Nicklaus Breeder Program Binder, no folder name or number, box M3747 (097), MMC; Brooks Robinson Breeder Program Binder, no folder name or number, box M3747 (097), MMC.

11. Laver, *Education of a Tennis Player*, 258–59.

12. Rod Laver to David Armstrong, n.d., Professional International Inc., Rod Laver folder, box M3657 (0158), MMC; Dick Bradlee's Tennis Colleges advertisement, Professional International Inc., Rod Laver folder, box M3657 (0158), MMC; David Armstrong to Dick Bradlee, Dec. 22, 1975, Professional International Inc., Rod Laver folder, box M3657 (0158), MMC.

13. Mark McCormack, *The 110% Solution* (New York: Villard Books, 1990), 17–18; Mark McCormack, *The Terrible Truth about Lawyers: How Lawyers Really Work and How to Deal with Them Successfully* (New York: Beach Tree Books, 1987), 163.

14. Mark McCormack, *Staying Street Smart in the Internet Age: What Hasn't Changed about the Way We Do Business* (New York: Viking, 2000), 150, 249; McCormack, *The 110% Solution*, 11–12, 39–40, 63–64; Mark McCormack, *On Selling* (West Hollywood, CA: Dove Books, 1996), 180–81.

15. IMG to Future Inc., Sept. 1978, King, Billie Jean, Client K: Rep Agreement 1974–1982, folder, box M3162 (0159), MMC; Contract Summary for Billie Jean King as of June, 1980, King, Billie Jean, Client K: Summaries & Prior K's 1978 folder, box M3162 (0159), MMC.

16. Billie Jean King Measurements, Mar. 15, 1980, King, Billie Jean, Fact Sheet 1979, folder, box M3162 (0159), MMC; Billie Jean King Fact Sheet, King, Billie Jean, Fact Sheet 1979, folder, box M3162 (0159), MMC; Patrick Alcox & John Nay to Tennis Committee, June 13, 1980, King, Billie Jean, Fact Sheet 1979, folder, box M3162 (0159), MMC; McCormack, *Staying Street Smart*, 249.

17. McCormack, *Terrible Truth about Lawyers*, 12, 173–74. No master client list can be found in the McCormack collection. These figures are a best estimate based on the firm's individual client records held as MMC file room holdings. Again, my thanks to the University of Massachusetts Amherst library staff for making this material available to me.

18. Dell, *Minding Other People's Business*, 39; Dell, *Never Make the First Offer*, 33–34; Mark McCormack, *On Communicating* (Los Angeles: Dove Books, 1996), 5; McCormack, *Staying Street Smart*, 256.

19. Memorandum of Initial Meeting, May 2, 1967, NFL Negro Union Memo, folder, box M0705 (0453), MMC; Richard R. Alford to William H. Carpenter, June 28, 1967, NFL Negro Union Memo folder, box M0705 (0453), MMC.

20. Mark McCormack, "Operational Memorandum: International Management and Affiliated Companies," typescript dated, Dec. 26, 1967, Mark McCormack Personal File, MMC (hereafter, OM), 10, 25.

21. My thanks to the Special Collections and University Archives staff at the University of Massachusetts Amherst Libraries for providing me with these figures.

22. For a passing reference to McCormack and IMG in *New Yorker* writer Herbert Warren Wind's collected essays on the tennis boom, see Herbert Warren Wind, *Game, Set, and Match: The Tennis Boom of the 1960s and '70s* (New York: E. P. Dutton, 1969), 144.

23. Donald Dell, "Q&A with Tennis Hall of Famer Donald Dell," *USTA*, n.d., https://www.usta.com/Pro-Tennis/Feature/QA_with_Donald_Dell/ (accessed Mar. 1, 2017); Dell, *Never Make the First Offer*, 108–109.

24. Gordon R. Lasenbury to Irwin Goldberg, Nov. 5, 1974, Betsey Negelsen and Fabergé Cosmetics File, no folder, box M3421 (0124), MMC; McCormack, *Terrible Truth about Lawyers*, 12.

25. McCormack, *Staying Street Smart*, viii, 8; ESPN Staff writer, "Tiger Richest Athlete in History," *ESPN News Service*, Oct. 2, 2009, http://espn.go.com/golf/news/story?id=4524640 (accessed Mar. 1, 2017).

26. These figures come from a tabulation of the chronological files in the Mark McCormack Collection, Special Collections, University of Massachusetts Amherst. My thanks to the Special Collections and University Archives staff at the University of Massachusetts Amherst Libraries for providing me with these figures.

27. Mark McCormack to Donald L. Dell, Dec. 30, 1968 (MS 700), MMC; available digitally at https://credo.library.umass.edu/view/collection/mums700.

28. Donald Dell Biographical File, Biographical Files Collection, ITHF.

29. Dell, *Minding Other People's Business*, 7, 25–26; Donald Dell Diary Card, White House Diary Card File, alphabetical arrangement D, LBJ Presidential Library, Austin, Texas; White House Formal Invitation, May 27, 1968, White House Central File, S02, box 4, LBJ Presidential Library, Austin, Texas; Donald Dell Social Events Card, White House Social Events Cards Collection, alphabetical arrangement D, LBJ Presidential Library, Austin, Texas; Dell, *Never Make the First Offer*, 16–18, 177–79.

30. White House Dinner for Israeli Prime Minister, Jan. 27, 1976, "Press Guests at State Dinners—Lists and Memos (6)" folder, box 23, Ron Nessen Papers, Gerald R. Ford Presidential Library, Ann Arbor, Michigan; "Prayer Brunch for Professional Athletes: Appendix 'B,'" The Daily Diary of President Gerald R. Ford, Feb. 15, 1976, Scanned from the President's Daily Diary Collection (box 80), Gerald R. Ford Presidential Library, Ann Arbor, Michigan.

31. Dell, *Minding Other People's Business*, 3–5, 38.

32. Ibid., 39–40.

33. Ibid., 28.

34. Ibid., 49–50.

35. Ibid., 19.

36. Ibid., 48–49, 59, 97; Dell, *Never Make the First Offer*, 13, 170.

37. John Lewis Gaddis, *The Cold War: A New History* (New York: Penguin Books, 2007), 231, 238–53.

38. Dell, *Minding Other People's Business*, 71–72.

39. Richard Nixon, *The Memoirs of Richard Nixon* (New York: Grosset & Dunlap, 1978), 544–80.

40. Dell, *Minding Other People's Business*, 71–72.

41. Ibid., 21; Dell, *Never Make the First Offer*, 103.

42. For the play on words, see Cameron Crowe, dir., *Jerry Maguire* (Gracie Films, TriStar Pictures, 1996).

43. Charles Korr, *The End of Baseball as We Knew It: The Players Union, 1960–1981* (Urbana: University of Illinois Press, 2002), 5.

44. Robert Trumpbour, *The New Cathedrals: Politics and Media in the History of Stadium Construction* (Syracuse, NY: Syracuse University Press, 2007), 35–58.

45. Mark H. McCormack, *Arnie: The Evolution of a Legend* (New York: Simon and Schuster, 1967), 221–44.

46. Arthur Ashe, Yale University talk, Feb. 11, 1991, folder 5/5, Speaking Engagements 1991, box 5, Arthur Ashe Collection, Schomburg Center for Research in Black Culture, New York Public Library, New York.

47. Mark H. McCormack memorandum to Brian Roggenburk, Feb. 12, 1985, Wimbledon/MHM Corr. 1985 folder [actually a black box], box M0105 (1198), MMC.

48. Perry, *My Story*, 192–94; Rob Steen, *Floodlights and Touchlines*, 93.

49. Robert J. Lake, "The Wimbledon Championships, the All England Lawn Tennis Club, and 'Invented Traditions,'" *International Journal of Sport Communication* 11, no. 1 (Mar. 2018): 52–74; Chris Gorringe, *Holding Court: Inside the Gates of the Wimbledon Championships* (London: Arrow Books, 2009), 54–55.

50. McCormack, OM, 16.

51. Jay Michaels to Mark McCormack, Jan. 28, 1969, Wimbledon: Correspondence 1967–1970 folder, M0105 (1198), MMC.

52. Ibid.

53. All England Lawn Tennis & Croquet Club, Television Rights Sales table, 1989 Wimbledon, folder, Wimbledon Historical: Video Cassettes, 1987–1994, box M0105 (1198), MMC; All England Lawn Tennis & Croquet Club, Television Rights Sales table, 1990 Wimbledon, folder, Wimbledon Historical: Video Cassettes, 1987–1994, box M0105 (1198), MMC.

54. Richard Savitt interview, OHC-ITHF.

55. Ibid.

Chapter 12. Women's Professional Tennis in the Early Open Era

1. Mark McCormack to Noman Blake, Dec. 31, 1968, Wimbledon: Correspondence 1967–1970 folder, box M0105 (1198), MMC.

2. "Tennisdom's Woman of the Year," *The Racquet* 45, no. 7 (Nov. 1951): 9, 40–41.

3. Front matter, *WT* 1, no. 1 (June 1953): 3, back cover; front matter, *WT* 1, no. 5 (Oct. 1953), 3; Sarah Palfrey Danzig interview, OHC-ITHF; Gladys M. Heldman to Harold Lebair, Dec. 2, 1953, Amateur Rule Committee 1953 folder, box 1, RKC.

4. Gonzales, *Man with a Racket*, 114–15; The USLTA Amateur Rule: A Talk by Harold A. Lebair, chairman, before the Tennis Writer's Association, Feb. 26, 1953, Amateur Rule Committee 1953 folder, box 1, RKC; Minutes of the Amateur Rule Committee, Nov. 16, 1953, Amateur Rule Committee 1953 folder, box 1, RKC; Susan Ware, *Game, Set, Match*, 31–32; Gladys Heldman to George Weissman, Feb. 7, 1974, no folder, box 8, GHP.

5. Gladys Heldman, "Seven Heavenly Days," *WT* 16, no. 4 (Sept. 1968): 20, 22; Gladys Heldman, "Forest Hills," *WT* 16, no. 6 (Nov. 1968): 14, 16; Gladys Heldman, "The Dilemma," *WT* 16, no. 8 (Jan. 1969): 14, 16; Gladys Heldman, "Forest Hills 1969," *WT* 16, no. 12 (May 1969): 16; Gladys Heldman, "Open Tennis, Registered Players, and Confusion," *WT* 16, no. 3 (Aug. 1968): 16, 18.

6. Gladys Heldman, "Mixed Memories," typescript, n.d., no folder, box 25, GHP; Gladys Heldman to David Lott, Nov. 16, 1981, no folder, box 25, GHP; Gladys Heldman, "Throw the Rascals Out," *WT* 16, no. 5 (Oct. 1968): 14.

7. Kramer, *The Game*, 31–32, 79–80, 83–86; "Around the World," *WT* 16, no. 6 (Nov. 1968): 84.

8. Billie Jean King with Frank Deford, *Billie Jean* (New York: Viking Press, 1982), 43–44, 58; Robert Lipsyte, "Little Myth America," *Los Angeles Times*, Dec. 28, 1975, Q36; "Around the World," *WT* 16, no. 1 (June 1968): 78.

9. Jack Gallagher, "Eight Top Fem Netters Defy USLTA," *Houston Post*, Sept. 24, 1970, D1–D2. For a further elaboration on the views King held at the time, see Billie Jean King, "A Role for the USLTA," *WT* 16, no. 8 (Jan. 1969): 58–59.

10. Gladys Heldman to George Weissman, Feb. 7, 1974, no folder, box 8, GHP.

11. Philadelphia—$50,000.00 W.I.T.F. financial statements, folder [no number], box 22, GHP.

12. WPT Income statement, Women's Pro Tour Income 1972–1973 folder [no number], box 22, GHP; Philadelphia—$50,000.00 W.I.T.F. financial statements, folder [no number], box 22, GHP; Women's International Tennis Federation Cash Basis statement, Women's International Tennis Federation Financials folder [no number], box 22, GHP; Kathleen Kemper to Gladys Heldman, no date, WPT Receipts—1973 folder [no number], box 22, GHP; World Tennis/Women's International Tennis Federation Expenses Incurred by Julius D. Heldman and Not Otherwise Reimbursed, Feb. 1973, Bank Account—WITF (1973) folder [no number], box 22, GHP; Apr. 1973 Disbursements statement, Bank Account—WITF (1973) folder [no number], box 22, GHP; Sanction for San Francisco and Los Angeles Tournaments $2,000 deposit slip, Women's Pro Tour Deposits 1971–1973 folder [no number], box 22, GHP; Women's Pro Tour Income Statement—1972, Women's Pro Tour Deposits 1971–1973 folder [no number], box 22, GHP; Gladys Heldman to George Weissman, Feb. 7, 1974, no folder, box

8, GHP; Gladys Heldman to George Weissman, Feb. 7, 1974, no folder, box 8, GHP; Women's Pro Tour Financials 1/1/73 to 4/25/73 folder [no number], box 22, GHP.

13. Women's International Tennis Federation Cash Basis statement, Women's International Tennis Federation Financials folder [no number], box 22, GHP; Slush Fund memo, undated, Travel & Entertainment, WPT Receipts—1973 folder [no number], box 22, GHP; Expenses Paid by WPT, typed list beginning Apr. 6, 1971, WPT Receipts—1973 folder [no number], box 22, GHP.

14. Gladys Heldman, "Stay Away from Exhibitions," typescript, undated, no folder, box 25, GHP; Gladys Heldman, typescript that begins with "The Best pro Event for the . . .," typescript, undated, no folder, box 25, GHP; Mary Prusko, "Gladys Heldman and Slims," *New York News World*, Mar. 24, 1977, B10–11; Virginia Slims Tour Balance Sheets, Women's Pro Tour Financials, 1971–1973, Women's International Tennis Federation Financials folder [no number], box 22, GHP; Women's International Tennis Federation Cash Basis statement, Women's International Tennis Federation Financials folder [no number], box 22, GHP.

15. Gladys Heldman, "Wimbledon Revisited," typescript, Receipts 1978 folder [no number], box [no number, unprocessed], GHP.

16. Robert Colwell to Gladys Heldman, Dec. 28, 1971, in Legal—Gladys Heldman, 1973 folder [no number], box 2, LBC; Robert Colwell, "Statement Issued to Press," Sept. 8, 1971, in Legal—Gladys Heldman, 1973 folder [no number], box 2, LBC; Robert Colwell to Gladys Heldman, Dec. 17, 1971, in Legal—Gladys Heldman, 1973 folder [no number], box 2, LBC; UPI Teletype, "The President Elect of the United States Lawn Tennis . . .," no date, Articles folder [no number], box 1, GHP.

17. William C. Perry to Frederick Leydig, Dec. 5, 1972, WPT Receipts—1973 folder [no number], box 22, GHP; Stanley Malless to Gladys Heldman, Sept. 26, 1972, Articles folder, box 1, GHP; *Gladys M. Heldman and Billie Jean King v. United States Lawn Tennis Association* 73. Civ 162, Opinion, for the United States District Court Southern District of New York, opinion issued Feb. 7, 1973, in Legal—Gladys Heldman, 1973 folder [no number], LBC.

18. *Gladys M. Heldman and Billie Jean King v. United States Lawn Tennis Association* 73. Civ 162, Opinion, [18–21, 28 of the Opinion], for the United States District Court Southern District of New York, opinion issued Feb. 7, 1973, in Legal—Gladys Heldman, 1973 folder [no number], box 2, LBC.

19. Patty Reese to Gladys Heldman, Jan. 5, 1973, Articles folder, box 1, GHP; Patty Anne Reese contract, signed Aug. 8, 1972, Articles folder, box 1, GHP; "USLTA and Virginia Slims Circuits to Combine This Year," Press Release, June 19, 1973, in Legal—Gladys Heldman, 1973 folder [no number], box 2, LBC; Shari Barnam to Gladys Heldman, Mar. 28, 1989, no folder, box 7, GHP; Billie Jean King to Gladys Heldman, Mar. 17, 1989, no folder, box 7, GHP; Shari Barnam to Gladys Heldman, Apr. 10, 1989, no folder, box 7, GHP.

20. Curry Kirkpatrick, "Mother's Day Ms. Match," *Sports Illustrated*, May 21, 1973,

35–37; Richard Muscio [uploader], "Mother's Day Massacre: Margaret Court vs. Bobby Riggs," YouTube video, uploaded Nov. 19, 2014, https://www.youtube.com/watch?v=E1Ueec50rVw (accessed June 7, 2020).

21. King, *Billie Jean*, 2, 15, 20, 34, 62–64.

22. Ware, *Game, Set, Match*, 1, 8–14.

23. Kristi Tredway, "The Original 9: The Social Movement That Created Women's Professional Tennis, 1968–73," in Lake, *Routledge Handbook of Tennis*, 411–19.

24. Wayne Kalyn, "Jerry Diamond Is a Ladies Man," *Pro Tennis Magazine*, Feb. 1983, 18–22.

25. Robert F. Tracey, "Vintage Films, Horse Racing, Tennis Celebrities: All Part of the Philip Morris' Marketing Mix," outline of presentation made in Louisville, Oct. 16, 1978, Philip Morris Records, Master Settlement Agreement, https://www.industry-documents.ucsf.edu/docs/prlw0107 (accessed June 19, 2020).

26. Gladys Heldman, Ted Tinling Lunch notes, no date, T Correspondence folder, box 1, GHP; Gladys Heldman to Don [unintelligible], Mar. 1, 1979, T Correspondence folder, box 1, GHP; folder 1.1.32, (Virginia Slims), 1976–1978, box 5, TTC.

27. Dell, *Minding Other People's Business*, 129–30. For a social theory–based account of the sexualization of women tennis professionals after the Open Era, see John Vincent "'You've Come a Long Way Baby,' but When Will You Get to Deuce?: The Media (Re)presentation of Women's Tennis in the Post Open Era," in Lake, *Routledge Handbook of Tennis*, 223–33. On the WTA's role in a more recent advertising campaign, see Travis R. Bell and Janelle Applequist, "Veiled Hyper-Sexualization: Deciphering *Strong as Beautiful* as Collective Identity in WTA's Global Ad Campaign," in Lake, *Routledge Handbook of Tennis*, 234–44.

28. Dell, *Minding Other People's Business*, 74–76, 79.

29. Ibid.

30. Renée Richards, *Second Serve: The Renée Richards Story* (New York: Stein and Day, 1983), 36–42, 54–55, 61–65, 67, 69–73.

31. Joanne Meyerowitz, *How Sex Changed: A History of Transsexuality in the United States* (Cambridge: Harvard University Press, 2002), 51–97, 277–78.

32. Richards, *Second Serve*, 78, 82, 84, 89, 91, 96–97, 101, 103, 106, 110–12, 114, 117, 127, 130, 133, 135, 139, 144.

33. Ibid., 165, 173, 178, 181, 199–201, 203, 211–14, 234, 246, 253, 256–57, 264, 268, 270, 273, 276–77, 280–81, 289–90, 293.

34. Gladys Heldman, "Renee Richards," typescript, undated, Articles to CBS 1976 folder, box 19, GHP.

35. "Proposal for Royal Crown: A Series of Women's 35 Tennis Events," O Correspondence folder, box 1, GHP; Gladys Heldman to Charlene Crafton, Nov. 16, 1978, C Correspondence folder, box 1, GHP; Gladys Heldman to Herb FitzGibbon, Apr. 7, 1979, F Correspondence folder, box 1, GHP; Supplement to the *Savannah News-Press*, "$25,000 Avon Futures Tennis Championship," Mar. 13–17, 1977, in no folder,

box 8, GHP; "Gladys Medalie Heldman," *Advantage*, May-June, 1978, 7; Ted Tinling to Gladys Heldman, March 26, 1980, no folder, box 12, GHP; Gladys Heldman to Kay Hutchinson, Feb. 5, 1979, H Correspondence folder, box 1, GHP; Anne Hyde to Gladys Heldman, March 23, 1979, H Correspondence folder, box 1, GHP; Wendy Overton to Gladys Heldman, February 12, 1979, O Correspondence folder, box 1, GHP; Ron Bookman to Gladys Heldman, September 26, 1975, Copyright folder, box 27, GHP.

36. Patricia Lasher, *Texas Women: Interviews & Images* (Austin: Shoal Creek Publishers, 1980), 63–67; Paula Moore, "Who Is Gladys Heldman?," *Southwest Airlines Magazine*, July 1980, 61–66.

37. Richards v. US Tennis Assn, 93 Misc.2d 713 (1977) *Renee Richards, Plaintiff v. United States Tennis Association et al., Defendants*, Supreme Court, Special Term, New York County, Aug. 16, 1977; Lindsay Parks Pieper, "Break Point: Renée Richards and the Significance of Sex and Gender in Women's Tennis," in Lake, *Routledge Handbook of Tennis*, 432–39.

38. Richards, *Second Serve*, 365–73; Martina Navratilova with George Vecsey, *Being Myself* (New York: Grafton, 1986), 179, 220–21.

Conclusion

1. Alexander McNab, "Beyond the Boom: Today's Tennis Market," *Tennis USA: The Official Publication of the USTA* (July 1978): 22–25; William Woy, "Dear," WCT sponsorship rights typescript, n.d., 1, box 13, LHP; Mike Bartlett, "New York, New York: A Tennis Watchers' Guide to the Big Apple," *Tennis USA: The Official Publication of the USTA* (July 1978): 29–31.

2. "The Next Step," *International Tennis Weekly: The Official Newspaper of the Association of Tennis Professionals* 13 (Nov. 6, 1988): 2.

3. Gladys M. Heldman, "Stay Away from Exhibitions," typescript, n.d., no folder, box 25, GHP; "Connors Subdues McEnroe in Tokyo," *Paducah Sun*, Apr. 14, 1980, 16.

4. Philippe Chatrier, "Review of the Year," *The International Tennis Federation: President's Newsletter* (Apr. 1985): unpaginated; Philippe Chatrier, "Wimbledon Aiding the Tennis World," *The International Tennis Federation: President's Newsletter* 74 (Mar. 29, 1985): unpaginated; Philippe Chatrier, "Rewarding Progress on Three Issues," *The International Tennis Hall of Fame: President's Newsletter* 92 (Dec. 12, 1986): unpaginated.

5. Prepared by the Association of Tennis Professionals, "Tennis at the Crossroads: A Critique of the Opportunities and Problems Facing Men's Professional Tennis," n.d, n.p., 1–8, no folder, box 27, GHP.

6. "National Tennis Centre," *Sydney Morning Herald*, Jan. 4, 1988, 48; Frank Keating, "Home Sounds Off in a Courteous Land," *London Guardian*, Sept. 21, 1988, 12; Peter Alfano, "Open Victory Gives Graf a Grand Slam," *New York Times*, Sept. 11, 1988, section 8, 1.

7. "Chronology of Events," *International Tennis Weekly: The Official Newspaper of the Association of Tennis Professionals* 13 (Nov. 6, 1988): 4; "Banned from U.S. Open Press

Facilities, Players Hold Parking Lot Press Conference," *International Tennis Weekly: The Official Newspaper of the Association of Tennis Professionals* 13 Special (Sept. 11, 1988): 4; "Status of Top 100 Players on Commitment to New Tour," *International Tennis Weekly: The Official Newspaper of the Association of Tennis Professionals* 13 Special (Sept. 11, 1988): 4.

8. Michael Curet, "ITF Hands Out Invitations for 'Elite' Circuit," *International Tennis Weekly: The Official Newspaper of the Association of Tennis Professionals* 13 Special (Sept. 11, 1988): 2; "Players Have Questions about ITF Tour," *International Tennis Weekly: The Official Newspaper of the Association of Tennis Professionals* 13 Special (Sept. 11, 1988): 2.

9. M. Marshall Happer III to All Proposed Grand Prix of Tennis Tournaments, Oct. 25, 1988, no folder, box 27, GHP.

10. "Player Contract for the 1990 ATP Tour," n.d., no folder, box 27, GHP.

11. "Statement from the Association of Tennis Professionals," November 2, 1988, London, no folder, box 27, GHP.

12. "ATP Promises Indoor Seven of the World's Best," *Sydney Morning Herald*, Jan. 21, 1989, 69. The original schedule featured seventy-seven matches, but public pressure against South African apartheid finally convinced the ATP to eliminate tournaments in Cape Town and Johannesburg. See "ATP Reverses Stand on South Africa," *Indianapolis Star*, Aug. 30, 1989, 39.

13. "Young Mac's No Brat," *Sydney Morning Herald*, Dec. 10, 1989, 96; Mike Dickson, "McEnroe in Final," *London Guardian*, Jan. 1, 1990, 25; Thomas Bonk, "New Men's Pro Tour Having Difficult Time Getting Started," *Los Angeles Times*, Nov. 12, 1989, 76; "W.C.T. Out of Business," *New York Times*, Aug. 28, 1990, B11; Mark McCormack to Ned McCormack, Oct. 10, 1992, MMC, available digitally at http://credo.library.umass.edu/view/full/mums700-b0021-f008-i001 (accessed June 20, 2020); "McEnroe, Agassi to Play Cup Singles for U.S.," *Tampa Tribune*, Mar. 28, 1989, C2; Thomas Bonk, "Martina Not Ready to Give Skiing a Thumbs Down," *Los Angeles Times*, Feb. 18, 1990, 109.

14. Merrett R. Stierheim, "Dear Tennis Patron," in Virginia Slims of Albuquerque Tennis Tournament Program, Aug. 14–20, 1989, no folder, box 7, GHP.

15. Robert J. Lake, "Tennis Governance: A History of Political Power Struggles," in Lake, *Routledge Handbook of Tennis*, 341–50.

16. Christopher Clarey, "With Men's and Women's Tennis Halted, a Merger Idea Gains Steam," *New York Times*, Apr. 27, 2020, D6.

Selected Bibliography

Archival Sources

Biographical Files Collection, International Tennis Hall of Fame, Newport, RI

California Business Ephemera Collection, California Historical Society, San Francisco, CA

California Ephemera Collection, Alfred Young Research Library, University of California Los Angeles, Los Angeles, CA

California Welfare Archives, USC Special Collections, Los Angeles CA

California History Section, California State Library, Sacramento, CA

California Youth Authority Collection, California State Archives, Sacramento, CA

C. S. Recreation—Tennis Collection, California Historical Society, San Francisco, CA

Edward Dickson Papers, Collection 662, Alfred Young Research Library, University of California at Los Angeles, Los Angeles, CA

Finn Race Files, Revs Institute, Naples, FL

Daniel Cowan Jackling Papers, Stanford University Library and Special Collections, Palo Alto, CA

Gladys Heldman Papers, Dolph Briscoe Center for American History, The University of Texas at Austin, Austin, TX

George MacCall Papers (6188), Penn State University Archives, Special Collections Library, Penn State University, University Park, PA

Lamar Hunt Papers, Hunt Enterprise Archive, Kansas City, MO

Lawrence Baker Collection, International Tennis Hall of Fame, Newport, RI

Los Angeles Tennis Club Archive, Los Angeles, CA

Mark H. McCormack Papers (MS 700), Special Collections and University Archives, University of Massachusetts Amherst Libraries, Amherst, MA

Newport Casino Collection, International Tennis Hall of Fame, Newport, RI

Oral History Collection, International Tennis Hall of Fame, Newport, RI

Oral History Collection, San Diego History Center, San Diego, CA

Oral History Collection, Special Collections University of California Santa Cruz, Santa Cruz, CA

President's Daily Diary Collection, Gerald R. Ford Presidential Library, Ann Arbor, MI

Robert J. Kelleher Collection, International Tennis Hall of Fame, Newport, RI

Ron Nessen Papers, Gerald R. Ford Presidential Library, Ann Arbor, MI

San Francisco Ephemera Collection, California Historical Society, San Francisco, CA

San Francisco Photo Collection, California Historical Society, San Francisco, CA

Seaver Center for Western History Research, Los Angeles County Natural History Museum, Los Angeles, CA

State of California Business Incorporation Records Collection, California State Archives, Sacramento, CA

Tennis Program Collection, International Tennis Hall of Fame, Newport, RI

Ted Tinling Collection, International Tennis Hall of Fame, Newport, RI

Trade Catalog Collection, Hagley Museum and Library, Wilmington, DE

United States District Court for the Southern District of California Central Division, civil case files, National Archives and Record Administration-Riverside [NARA-Riverside], Riverside, CA

White House Central File, LBJ Presidential Library, Austin, TX

White House Diary Card File Collection, LBJ Presidential Library, Austin, TX

White House Social Events Cards Collection, LBJ Presidential Library, Austin, TX

William M. Fischer Lawn Tennis Collection, St. John's University Archives and Special Collections, Queens Campus, New York, NY

Works Progress Administration Collection, Manuscripts Division, Library of Congress, Washington DC

Published Player and Promoter Memoirs and Instructional Materials

Ashe, Arthur, and Arnold Rampersad. *Days of Grace: A Memoir*. New York: Alfred A. Knopf, 1993.

Bemish, A. E. *First Steps to Lawn Tennis*. London: Mills & Boon, 1922.

Betz, Pauline. *Wings on My Tennis Shoes*. London: Sampson Low, Marston, 1949.

Bjurstedt, Molla. *Tennis for Women*. New York: Doubleday, Page, 1916.

Brookes, Dame Mabel. *Crowded Galleries*. London: William Heinemann, 1956.

Brown, Tom, with Lee Tyler. *As Tom Goes By: A Tennis Memoir*. McKinleyville, CA: Fithian Press, 2006.

Budge, Don, with Frank Deford. *Don Budge: A Tennis Memoir*. New York: Viking Press, 1969.

Chambers, Mrs. Lambert. *Lawn Tennis for Ladies*. New York: Outing Publishing, 1910.

Court, Margaret Smith. *Court on Court: A Life in Tennis*. New York: Dodd, Mead, 1975.

Davies, Mike. *Tennis Rebel*. London: Stanley and Paul, 1962.

Dell, Donald. *Minding Other People's Business: Winning Big for Your Clients and Yourself*. New York: Villard Books, 1989.

———. *Never Make the First Offer Except When You Should: Wisdom from a Master Dealmaker*. New York: Portfolio, 2009.

Dewhurst, Edward B. *The Science of Lawn Tennis*. Philadelphia: Innes and Sons, 1910.

Gonzales, Pancho, with Cy Rice. *Man with a Racket: The Autobiography of Pancho Gonzales*. New York: A. S. Barnes, 1959.

Goolagong, Evonne, and Bud Collins. *Evonne! On the Move*. New York: Dutton, 1975.

Gorringe, Chris. *Holding Court: Inside the Gates of the Wimbledon Championships*. London: Arrow Books, 2009.

Hall, Valentine. *Lawn Tennis in America*. New York: D. W. Granbery, 1889.

Hart, Doris. *Tennis with Hart*. New York: J. B. Lippincott, 1955.

Jacobs, Helen Hull. *Beyond the Game: An Autobiography*. Philadelphia: J. B. Lippincott, 1936.

Jacobs, William Plumer. *Tennis, Builder of Citizenship: The Psychology and Technique of the Game as Taught in the Tennis Clinic*. Clinton, SC: Jacobs Press, 1941.

Jones, Perry T. *Perry T. Jones Presents Fine Points of Tennis for Youth*. N.p.: Union Oil Company of California, 1958.

King, Billie Jean, with Frank Deford. *Billie Jean*. New York: Viking Press, 1982.

Kramer, Jack, with Frank Deford. *The Game: My 40 Years in Tennis*. New York: G. P. Putnam's Sons, 1979.

Laver, Rod, with Larry Writer. *Rod Laver: An Autobiography*. Chicago: Triumph Books, 2016.

Laver, Rod, with Bud Collins. *The Education of a Tennis Player*. New York: Simon and Schuster, 1971.

Lenglen, Suzanne. *Lawn Tennis for Girls*. New York: American Sports Publishing, 1920.

Lloyd, Chris Evert, with Neil Amdur. *Chrissie: My Own Story*. New York: Simon & Shuster, 1982.

Marble, Alice. *Courting Danger: My Adventures in World-Class Tennis, Golden-Age Hollywood, and High-Stakes Spying*. Boston: St. Martin's Press, 1991.

———. *The Road to Wimbledon*. New York: Charles Scribner's Sons, 1946.

Maskell, Dan. *From Where I Sit*. London: Willow Books, 1988.

McCormack, Mark H. *Arnie: The Evolution of a Legend*. New York: Simon and Schuster, 1967.

———. *The 110% Solution*. New York: Villard Books, 1990.

———. *McCormack on Communicating*. West Hollywood, CA: Dove Books, 1996.

———. *McCormack on Managing*. New York: Random House, 1995.

———. *McCormack on Negotiating*. New York: Random House, 1995.

———. *McCormack on Selling*. West Hollywood, CA: Dove Books, 1996.

———. *Staying Street Smart in the Internet Age: What Hasn't Changed about the Way We Do Business*. New York: Viking, 2000.

———. *The Terrible Truth about Lawyers: How Lawyers Really Work and How to Deal with Them Successfully*. New York: Beach Tree Books, 1987.

———. *What They Don't Teach You at Harvard Business School about Executive Travel: Hit the Ground Running*. New York: Dove, 1996.

———. *What They Don't Teach You at Harvard Business School: Notes from a Street-Smart Executive*. New York: Bantam, 1984.

———. *What They Still Don't Teach You at Harvard Business School: Selling More, Managing Better, and Getting the Job Done in the '90s*. New York: Bantam, 1989.

Mulloy, Gardnar. *Advantage Striker*. London: Allan Wingate Publisher, 1959.

———. *As It Was: Reminiscences from a Man for All Seasons*. New York: Flexigroup, 2009.

———. *The Will to Win: An Inside View of the World of Tennis*. New York: A. S. Barnes, 1959.

Navratilova, Martina, with George Vecsey. *Being Myself*. New York: Grafton, 1986.

Patty, Budge. *Tennis My Way*. Tiptree, Essex: Anchor Press, 1951.

Perry, Fred. *An Autobiography*. London: Hutchinson, 1986.

———. *My Story*. London: Hutchinson, 1934.

Richards, Renée. *Second Serve: The Renée Richards Story*. New York: Stein and Day, 1983.

Riggs, Bobby, with George McGann. *Court Hustler*. New York: J. B. Lippincott, 1973.

Riggs, Bobby. *Tennis Is My Racket*. New York: Simon and Schuster, 1949.

Sedgmen, Frank. *Frank Sedgman Presents the World's Greatest Tennis: Tournament of the Game's Top Tennis Stars*. St. Kilda, Australia: Frank Sedgman, 1954.

Skeen, Dick. *Tennis Champions Are Made, Not Born*. Redwood City, CA: Cal-Pacific Color, 1976.

Tilden, William T. *My Story: A Champion's Memoir*. New York: Hellman Williams, 1948.

———. *The Art of Lawn Tennis*. New York: George H. Doran Co., 1921.

Tinling, Ted, with Rod Humphries. *Love and Faults: Personalities Who Have Changed the History of Tennis in My Lifetime*. New York: Crown, 1979.

Tinling, Ted. *Tinling: Sixty Years in Tennis*. London: Sidgwick & Jackson, 1983.

Vaile, P.A. *Modern Tennis*. New York: Funk & Wagnalls, 1915.

Secondary Sources

Adelman, Melvin. *A Sporting Time: New York City and the Rise of Modern Athletics, 1820–70*. Urbana: University of Illinois Press, 1986.

Alamillo, José. "Richard 'Pancho' González, Race and the Print Media in Postwar Tennis America." *The International Journal of the History of Sport* 26, no. 7 (2009): 947–65.

Alvarez, Luis. *The Power of the Zoot: Youth Culture and Resistance during World War II*. Berkeley: University of California Press, 2008.

Ardell, Jean Hastings. *Breaking into Baseball: Women and the National Pastime*. Carbondale: Southern Illinois University Press, 2005.

Aron, Cindy. *Working at Play: A History of Vacations in the United States*. New York: Oxford University Press, 1999.

Arsenault, Raymond. *Arthur Ashe: A Life*. New York: Simon and Schuster, 2019.

Ashe, Arthur. *A Hard Road to Glory: A History of the African American Athlete, 1619–1918*. New York: Amistad Press, 1993.

———. *A Hard Road to Glory: A History of the African American Athlete, 1919–1945*. New York: Amistad Press, 1993.

———. *A Hard Road to Glory: A History of the African American Athlete, Since 1946*. New York: Amistad Press, 1993.

Bale, John. *The Brawn Drain: Foreign Student-Athletes in American Universities*. Urbana: University of Illinois Press, 1991.

Baltzell, E. Digby. *Sporting Gentlemen: Men's Tennis from the Age of Honor to the Cult of the Superstar*. New York: Free Press, 1995.

Barrett, John. *Wimbledon: The Official History of the Championships*. London: Collins Willow, 2001.

Beckert, Sven. *The Monied Metropolis: New York City and the Consolidation of the American Bourgeoisie, 1850–1896*. Cambridge: Cambridge University Press, 2001.

Bederman, Gail. *Manliness and Civilization: A Cultural History of Gender and Race in the United States, 1880–1917*. Chicago: University of Chicago Press, 1995.

Bell, Marty. *Carnival at Forest Hills: Anatomy of a Tennis Tournament*. New York: Random House, 1975.

Bell, Travis R. and Janelle Applequist, "Veiled Hyper-Sexualization: Deciphering *Strong as Beautiful* as Collective Identity in WTA's Global Ad Campaign." In Lake, *Routledge Handbook of Tennis*, 233–44.

Belmonte, Laura. *Selling the American Way: U.S. Propaganda and the Cold War*. Philadelphia: University of Pennsylvania Press, 2008.

Bledstein, Burton J. *The Culture of Professionalism: The Middle Class and the Development of Higher Education in America*. New York: W. W. Norton, 1978.

Block, James E. *A Nation of Agents: The American Path to a Modern Self and Society*. Cambridge: Harvard University Press, 2002.

Blum, John. *V Was for Victory: Politics and American Culture during World War II*. New York: Harcourt Brace Jovanovich, 1976.

Blumin, Stuart. *The Emergence of the Middle-Class Social Experience in the American City, 1760–1900*. New York: Cambridge University Press, 1996.

Bodo, Peter. *The Courts of Babylon: Tales of Greed and Glory in a Harsh New World of Professional Tennis*. New York: Scribner, 1995.

Borish, Linda J. "Women in American Sport History." In *A Companion to American Sports History*, edited by Steven Reiss, 503–519. New York: Wiley Blackwell, 2014.

Borstelmann, Thomas. *The Cold War and the Color Line: American Race Relations in the Global Arena*. Cambridge: Harvard University Press, 2001.

Bowers, Chris. *The International Tennis Federation: A Century of Contribution to Tennis*. New York: Rizzoli, 2013.

Boyer, Paul. *By the Bomb's Early Light: American Thought and Culture at the Dawn of the Atomic Age*. Chapel Hill: University of North Carolina Press, 1994.

Boykoff, Jules. *Power Games: A Political History of the Olympics*. New York: Verso, 2016.

Braudy, Leo. *The Frenzy of Renown: Fame and Its History*. New York: Vintage, 1997.

Brown, Ashley. "Swinging for the State Department: American Women Tennis Players in Diplomatic Goodwill Tours, 1941–59." *Journal of Sport History* 42, No. 3 (Fall 2015): 289–309.

Bullock, Steven. *Playing for Their Nation: Baseball and the American Military during World War II*. Lincoln: University of Nebraska Press, 2004.

Caro, Robert. *The Power Broker: Robert Moses and the Fall of New York*. New York: Vintage, 1975.

Collins, Bud. *The Bud Collins History of Tennis: An Authoritative Encyclopedia and Record Book*. New York: New Chapter Press, 2010.

Crawford, Russ. *The Use of Sport to Promote the American Way of Life during the Cold War: Cultural Propaganda, 1945–1963*. Lewistown, NY: Edwin Mellen Press, 2008.

Cross, Gary. *An All-Consuming Century: Why Consumerism Won in Modern America*. New York: Columbia University Press, 2002.

Cummings, Parke. *American Tennis: The Story of a Game and Its People*. Boston: Little, Brown, 1957.

Daley, Arthur. "Vincent Richards, The First Boy Wonder." In *The Fireside Book of Tennis*, edited by Allison Danzig and Peter Schwed, 187–89. New York: Simon & Schuster, 1972.

Danzig, Allison. "Spahiristike, History of the United States Lawn Tennis Association." In *The Fireside Book of Tennis: A Complete History of the Game and Its Great Players and Matches*, edited by Allison Danzig and Peter Schwed, 15–16. New York: Simon & Schuster, 1972.

Davis, Dwight F. "The Establishment of an International Trophy: A Step Toward Placing Tennis Competition on a Universal Basis." In USLTA, *Fifty Years of Lawn Tennis in the United States*, 69–72. New York: USLTA, 1931.

Deford, Frank. *Big Bill Tilden: The Triumphs and the Tragedy*. New York: Simon and Schuster, 1976.

Djata, Sundiata. *Blacks at the Net: Black Achievement in Tennis*, 2 vols. Syracuse, NY: Syracuse University Press, 2006/2008.

Dudziak, Mary L. *Cold War Civil Rights: Race and the Image of American Democracy*. Princeton, NJ: Princeton University Press, 2000.

Duis, Perry. *Challenging Chicago: Coping with Everyday Life, 1837–1920*. Chicago: University of Chicago Press, 1998.

Dumenil, Lynn. *The Modern Temper: American Culture and Society in the 1920s*. New York: Hill and Wang, 1995.

Dyreson, Mark. *Making the American Team: Sport, Culture, and the Olympic Experience*. Urbana: University of Illinois Press, 1997.

Eaves, Simon J. and Robert J. Lake. "Coaching and Training in British Tennis: A History of Competing Ideals." In Lake, *Routledge Handbook of Tennis*, 173–82.

———. "Dwight Davis and the Foundation of the Davis Cup in Tennis: Just another Doubleday Myth?" *Journal of Sport History* 45, no. 1 (Spring 2018): 1–23.

———. "The 'Ghosts' of Lawn Tennis Past: Exploring the Forgotten Lives of Early Working-Class Coaching-Professionals." *Sport in History* 36 (Nov. 2016): 498–521.

———. "The 'Ubiquitous Apostle of International Play,' Wilberforce Vaughan Eaves: The Forgotten International of Lawn Tennis." *The International Journal of the History of Sport* 33, no. 16 (May 2017): 1963–81.

Eisenberg, John. *Ten-Gallon War: The NFL's Cowboys, the AFL's Texans, and the Feud for Dallas's Pro Future*. Boston: Houghton Mifflin Harcourt, 2012.

Elias, Robert. *The Empire Strikes Out: How Baseball Sold U.S. Foreign Policy and Promoted the American Way Abroad*. New York: New Press, 2010.

Engelhardt, Tom. *The End of Victory Culture: Cold War America and the Disillusioning of a Generation*. Amherst: University of Massachusetts Press, 2007.

Engelmann, Larry. *The Goddess and the American Girl: The Story of Suzanne Lenglen and Helen Wills*. New York: Oxford University Press, 1988.

Espy, Richard. *The Politics of the Olympic Games*. Berkeley: University of California Press, 1981.

Evans, Richard. *Open Tennis, 1968–1988: The Players, the Politics, the Pressures, the Passions, and the Great Matches*. New York: Penguin, 1989.

Everitt, Robert and Richard Hillway, *The Birth of Lawn Tennis: From the Origins of the Game to the First Championship at Wimbledon*. Kingston upon Thames, UK: Vision Sports Publishing, 2018.

Fein, Paul. *Tennis Confidential: Today's Greatest Players, Matches, and Controversies*. Washington, DC: Potomac Books, 2003.

Fischer, Lucy. *American Cinema of the 1920s: Themes and Variations*. New Brunswick, NJ: Rutgers University Press, 2009.

Fisher, Marshall Jon. *A Terrible Splendor: Three Extraordinary Men, A World Poised for War, and the Greatest Tennis Match Ever Played*. New York: Crown, 2009.

Fraterrigo, Elizabeth. *Playboy and the Making of the Good Life in Modern America*. New York: Oxford University Press, 2009.

Friss, Evan. *The Cycling City: Bicycles and Urban America in the 1890s*. Chicago: University of Chicago Press, 2015.

Galenson, David W. "The Impact of Economic and Technological Change on the Careers of American Men Tennis Players, 1960–1991." *Journal of Sport History* 20 (Summer 1992): 127–50.

Gilbert, David. "The Vicar's Daughter and the Goddess of Tennis: Cultural Geographies of Sporting Femininity and Bodily Practice in Edwardian Suburbia." *Cultural Geographies* 18, no. 2 (Apr. 2011): 187–207.

Gillmeister, Heiner. *Tennis: A Cultural History*. London: Leicester University Press, 1998.

Goldblatt, David. *The Games: A Global History of the Olympics*. New York: W. W. Norton, 2016.

Goldman, Eric F. *The Crucial Decade: America, 1945–1955*. New York: Alfred A. Knopf, 1956.

Goldstein, Warren. *Playing for Keeps: A History of Early Baseball*. Ithaca, NY: Cornell University Press, 2009.

Gordon, Robert J. *The Rise and Fall of American Growth: The U.S. Standard of Living since the Civil War*. Princeton, NJ: Princeton University Press, 2016.

Gorn, Elliott. *The Manly Art: Bare-Knuckle Prize Fighting in America*. Updated ed. Ithaca, NY: Cornell University Press, 2010.

Gorn, Elliott, and Warren Goldstein. *A Brief History of American Sports*. Champaign: University of Illinois Press, 2004.

Grant, Barry Keith, ed., *American Cinema of the 1960s: Themes and Variations*. New Brunswick, NJ: Rutgers University Press, 2008.

Green, Harvey. *Fit for America: Health, Fitness, Sport, and American Society*. New York: Pantheon, 1986.

Greenberg, David. *Republic of Spin: An Inside History of the American Presidency*. New York: W. W. Norton, 2016.

Hall, Eric Allen. *Arthur Ashe: Tennis and Justice in the Civil Rights Era*. Baltimore: Johns Hopkins University Press, 2014.

Handlin, Oscar. *The Uprooted: The Epic Story of the Great Migration That Made the American People*. Boston: Little, Brown, 1973.

Hillenbrand, Laura. *Seabiscuit: An American Legend*. New York: Ballantine Books, 2002.

Hillway, Richard, and Geoff Felder. "Stephen Wallis Merrihew & American Lawn Tennis." *Journal of the Tennis Collectors of America* 29 (Autumn 2013): 452–56.

Hornblum, Allen. *American Colossus: Big Bill Tilden and the Creation of Modern Tennis*. Lincoln: University of Nebraska Press, 2018.

Hounshell, David A. *From the American System to Mass Production, 1800–1932: The Development of Manufacturing Technology in the United States*. Baltimore: Johns Hopkins University Press, 1984.

Iriye, Akira, ed., *Global Interdependence: The World after 1945*. Cambridge: Harvard University Press, 2014.

Jackson, Kenneth. *Crabgrass Frontier: The Suburbanization of the United States*. New York: Oxford University Press, 1987.

Jay, Kathryn. *More Than Just a Game: Sports in American Life since 1945*. New York: Columbia University Press, 2004.

Jefferys, Kevin. *British Tennis: From the Renshaws to the Murrays*. Worthing, Sussex: Pitch Publishing, 2019.

———. "Fred Perry and the Amateur-Professional Divide in British Tennis between the Wars." In Lake, *Routledge Handbook of Tennis*, 67–75.

——. "The Heyday of Amateurism in Modern Lawn Tennis." *International Journal of the History of Sport* 26 (Dec. 2009): 2236–52.

——. "The Triumph of Professionalism: The Road to 1968." *International Journal of the History of Sport* 26, no. 15 (2009): 2253–69.

Jones, Howard Mumford. *The Age of Energy: Varieties of American Experience, 1865–1915*. New York: Viking Press, 1971.

Kemper, Kurt. *College Football and American Culture in the Cold War Era*. Urbana: University of Illinois Press, 2009.

Keys, Barbara J. *Globalizing Sport: National Rivalry and International Community in the 1930s*. Cambridge: Harvard University Press, 2006.

Kimball, Warren F. *The United States Tennis Association: Raising the Game*. Lincoln: University of Nebraska Press, 2017.

King, Billie Jean, with Cynthia Starr. *We Have Come a Long Way: The Story of Women's Tennis*. New York: McGraw-Hill, 1988.

Koster, Rich. *The Tennis Bubble: Big-Money Tennis: How It Grew and Where It's Going*. New York: New York Times Book Co., 1976.

Korr, Charles. *The End of Baseball As We Knew It: The Players Union, 1960–1981*. Urbana: University of Illinois Press, 2002.

Kurlansky, Mark. *1968: The Year That Rocked the World*. New York: Ballantine Books, 2004.

Lafferty, John F. *The Preston School of Industry: A Centennial History*. Ione, CA: Preston School of Industry, 1994.

Lanct, Neil. "'A General Understanding': Organized Baseball and Black Professional Baseball, 1900–1930." In *Sport and the Color Line: Black Athletes and Race Relations in Twentieth Century America*, edited by Patrick Miller and David Wiggins, 30–52. New York: Routledge, 2004.

Lake, Robert J. "A History of Social Exclusion in British Tennis: From Grass Roots to the Elite Level." In Lake, *Routledge Handbook of Tennis*, 460–69.

——. *A Social History of Tennis in Britain*. New York: Routledge, 2014.

——. "Introduction to the History and Historiography of Tennis." In Lake, *Routledge Handbook of Tennis*, 1–16.

——, ed. *The Routledge Handbook of Tennis: History, Culture, and Politics*. New York: Routledge, 2019.

——. "Tennis Governance: A History of Political Power Struggles." In Lake, *Routledge Handbook of Tennis*, 341–50.

——. "The Wimbledon Championships, the All England Lawn Tennis Club, and 'Invented Traditions.'" *International Journal of Sport Communication* 11, no. 1 (Mar. 2018): 52–74.

Lake, Robert J., Simon J. Eaves, and Bob Nicholson. "The Development and Transformation of Anglo-American Relations in Lawn Tennis around the Turn of the Twentieth Century." *Sports History Review* 49, no. 1 (May 2018): 1–22.

Lasher, Patricia. *Texas Women: Interviews & Images*. Austin, TX: Shoal Creek Publishers, 1980.

Laver, Rod, with Larry Writer. *The Golden Era: The Extraordinary Two Decades When Australians Ruled the Tennis World*. Sydney: Allen & Unwin, 2019.

Leach, William. *Land of Desire: Merchants, Power, and the Rise of a New American Culture*. New York: Vintage, 1993.

Lears, Jackson. *No Place of Grace: Antimodernism and the Transformation of American Culture, 1880–1920*. Chicago: University of Chicago Press, 1994.

———. *Rebirth of a Nation: The Making of Modern America, 1877–1920*. New York: Harper Perennial, 2009.

———. *Something for Nothing: Luck in America*. New York: Penguin, 2003.

LaFeber, Walter. *Michael Jordan and the New Global Capitalism*. New York: W. W. Norton, 2002.

Lepore, Jill. *The Secret History of Wonder Woman*. New York: Alfred A. Knopf, 2015.

Lewis, Tom. *Divided Highways: Building the Interstate Highways, Transforming American Life*. Ithaca, NY: Cornell University Press, 2013.

Lhamon, W. T., Jr. *Deliberate Speed: The Origins of a Cultural Style in the American 1950s*. Cambridge: Harvard University Press, 2002.

MacCambridge, Michael. *America's Game: The Epic Story of How Pro Football Captured a Nation*. New York: Anchor Books, 2005.

———. *Lamar Hunt: A Life in Sports*. Kansas City, MO: Andrews McMeel, 2012.

Maltby, Marc. *The Origin and Early Development of Professional Football*. New York: Routledge, 1997.

May, Elaine Tyler. *Homeward Bound: American Families in the Cold War Era*. New York: Basic Books, 2008.

McDonald, Terrence. *The Parameters of Urban Fiscal Policy: Socioeconomic Change and Political Culture in San Francisco, 1860–1906*. Berkeley: University of California Press, 1986.

McPhee, John. *Levels of the Game*. New York: Farrar, Straus, and Giroux, 1969.

McWilliams, Carey. *Southern California: An Island on the Land*. Salt Lake City: Peregrine Smith Books, 1983.

Meyerowitz, Joanne. *How Sex Changed: A History of Transsexuality in the United States*. Cambridge: Harvard University Press, 2002.

Minton, Robert. *Forest Hills: An Illustrated History*. Philadelphia: J. B. Lippincott, 1975.

Morrow Jr., John. *The Great War: An Imperial History*. London: Routledge, 2004.

Mrozek, Donald J. "The 'Amazon' and the American 'Lady': Sexual Fears of Women as Athletes." In *The New American Sport History; Recent Approaches and Perspectives*, edited by S. W. Pope, 198–214. Urbana: University of Illinois Press, 1997.

Murray, Williamson, and Allan R. Millett. *A War to Be Won: Fighting the Second World War*. Cambridge: Harvard University Press, 2000.

Nickerson, Michelle, and Darren Dochuk, eds. *Sunbelt Rising: The Politics of Space, Place, and Region*. Philadelphia: Pennsylvania University Press, 2011.

Nunis, Doyce B., Jr., ed. *Los Angeles and Its Environs in the Twentieth Century: A Bibliography of a Metropolis*. Los Angeles: Ward Ritchie Press, 1973.

O'Neill, William. *A Democracy at War: America's Fight at Home and Abroad in World War II*. New York: Free Press, 1993.

Odom, Mary. "City Mothers and Delinquent Daughters: Female Juvenile Justice Reform in Early 20th Century Los Angeles." In *California Progressivism Revisited*, edited by William Deverell and Tom Sitton, 175–99. Berkeley: University of California Press, 1994.

Oriad, Michael. *Brand NFL: Making and Selling America's Favorite Sport*. Chapel Hill: University of North Carolina Press, 2007.

Overy, Richard. *Why the Allies Won*. New York: W. W. Norton, 1995.

Painter, Nell Irvin. *The History of White People*. New York: W. W. Norton, 2010.

Pieper, Lindsay Parks. "Break Point: Renée Richards and the Significance of Sex and Gender in Women's Tennis." In Lake, *Routledge Handbook of Tennis*, 432–39.

Peterson, Robert. *Cages to Jump Shots: Pro Basketball's Early Years*. Lincoln, NE: Bison Books, 2002.

———. *Pigskin: The Early Years of Pro Football*. New York: Oxford University Press, 1997.

Piketty, Thomas. *Capital in the Twenty-First Century*. Cambridge: Harvard University Press, 2014.

Pohlmann, John O. "Alphonzo E. Bell: A Biography: Part I." *Southern California Quarterly* 46 (Sept. 1964): 197–222.

Pope, S. W. *Patriotic Games: Sporting Traditions in the American Imagination, 1876–1926*. Knoxville: University of Tennessee Press, 2007.

Potter, David. *People of Plenty: Economic Abundance and the American Character*. Chicago: University of Chicago Press, 1954.

Rader, Benjamin. *In Its Own Image: How Television Has Transformed Sports*. New York: Free Press, 1984.

Reisler, Jim. *Cash and Carry: The Spectacular Rise and Hard Fall of C. C. Pyle, America's First Sports Agent*. Jefferson, NC: McFarland, 2009.

Rice, Grantland. *The Tumult and the Shouting: My Life in Sport*. New York: A. S. Barnes, 1954.

Rider, Toby. *Cold War Games: Propaganda, the Olympics, and U.S. Foreign Policy*. Urbana: University of Illinois Press, 2016.

Riess, Steven. *City Games: The Evolution of American Urban Society and the Rise of Sports*. Urbana: University of Illinois Press, 1989.

Roberts, Selena. *A Necessary Spectacle: Billie Jean King, Bobby Riggs, and the Tennis Match That Leveled the Game*. New York: Crown, 2005.

Rosenzweig, Roy. *The Park and the People: New York's Central Park*. Ithaca, NY: Cornell University Press, 1992.

Rowland, Suzanne. "Fashioning Competitive Lawn Tennis: History, Culture, and Politics." In Lake, *Routledge Handbook of Tennis*, 173–82.

Schlereth, Thomas. *Victorian America: Transformations in Everyday Life, 1876–1915*. New York: Harper Perennial, 1991.

Schmitt, Peter. *Back to Nature: The Arcadian Myth in Urban America*. Baltimore: Johns Hopkins University Press, 1990.

Schultz, Jaime. *Qualifying Times: Points of Change in U.S. Women's Sports*. Urbana: University of Illinois Press, 2014.

———. *Women's Sports: What Everyone Needs to Know*. New York: Oxford University Press, 2018.

Seebohm, Caroline. *Little Pancho: The Life of Tennis Legend Pancho Segura*. Lincoln: University of Nebraska Press, 2009.

Senn, Alfred. *Power, Politics, and the Olympic Games*. Urbana: University of Illinois Press, 1999.

Sparrow, James. *Warfare State: World War II Americans and the Age of Big Government*. New York: Oxford University Press, 2011.

Starr, Kevin. *Material Dreams: Southern California through the 1920s*. New York: Oxford University Press, 1990.

Steen, Rob. *Floodlights and Touchlines: A History of Spectator Sport*. London: Bloomsbury, 2014.

Susman, Warren. *Culture as History: The Transformation of American Society in the Twentieth Century*. Washington, DC: Smithsonian Books, 2003.

Sweet, David. *Lamar Hunt: The Gentle Giant Who Revolutionized Professional Sports*. Chicago: Triumph Books, 2010.

Thomas, Damion. *Globetrotting: African American Athletes in Cold War Politics*. Urbana: University of Illinois Press, 2012.

Tredway, Kristi. "The Original 9: The Social Movement That Created Women's Professional Tennis, 1968–73." In Lake, *Routledge Handbook of Tennis*, 411–19.

Trengrove, Alan. *The Story of the Davis Cup* (London: Stanley Paul & Co., 1985.

Trumpbour, Robert. "Stadiums, Arenas, and Audiences." In *A Companion to American Sports History*, edited by Steven Reiss, 577–97. New York: John Wiley and Sons, 2014.

———. *The New Cathedrals: Politics and Media in the History of Stadium Construction*. Syracuse, NY: Syracuse University Press, 2007.

United States Professional Tennis Association. *USPTA: Our History, Our Members, and Our Contribution to the Sport*. Morley, MO: Acclaim Press, 2017.

United States Lawn Tennis Association. *Fifty Years of Lawn Tennis in the United States*. Norwood, MA: Plimpton Press, 1931.

Van Someren, Janine, and Stephen Wagg. "Wimbledon Women: Elite Amateur Tennis Players in the Mid-Twentieth Century." In Lake, *Routledge Handbook of Tennis*, 183–92.

Vincent, John. "'You've Come a Long Way Baby,' but When Will You Get to Deuce?: The Media (Re)presentation of Women's Tennis in the Post Open Era." In Lake, *The Routledge Handbook of Tennis*, 233–44.

Von Eschen, Penny M. *Satchmo Blows Up the World: Jazz Ambassadors Play the Cold War*. Cambridge: Harvard University Press, 2004.

Wagnleitner, Reinhold. *Coca-Colonization and the Cold War: The Cultural Mission of the United States in Austria during the Second World War*. Chapel Hill: University of North Carolina Press, 1994.

Wakefield, Wanda Ellen. *Playing to Win: Sports and the American Military, 1898–1945*. Albany: State University of New York Press, 1997.

Ware, Susan. *Game, Set, Match: Billie Jean King and the Revolution in Women's Sports*. Chapel Hill: University of North Carolina Press, 2011.

Whitfield, Stephen J. *The Culture of the Cold War*. Baltimore: Johns Hopkins University Press, 1996.

Willis, Chris. *The Man Who Built the National Football League: Joe F. Carr*. Plymouth, England: Scarecrow Press, 2010.

Wilson, Elizabeth. *Love Game: A History of Tennis from Victorian Pastime to Global Phenomenon*. Chicago: University of Chicago Press, 2016.

Wilson, William. *The City Beautiful Movement*. Baltimore: Johns Hopkins University Press, 1989.

Wind, Herbert Warren. *Game, Set, and Match: The Tennis Boom of the 1960s and '70s*. New York: E. P. Dutton, 1970.

Wright, Bradford. *Comic Book Nation: The Transformation of Youth Culture in America*. Baltimore: Johns Hopkins University Press, 2003.

Yeomans, Patricia. *History and Heritage of the Los Angeles Tennis Club, 1920–1995*. Los Angeles: Los Angeles Tennis Club, 1995.

———. *Southern California Tennis Champions Centennial, 1887–1987: Documents & Anecdotes*. Los Angeles: privately printed, 1987.

Zeitz, Joshua. *Flapper: A Madcap Story of Sex, Style, Celebrity, and the Women Who Made America Modern*. New York: Crown, 2006.

Index

Greg Ruth is an independent scholar.

SPORT AND SOCIETY

A Sporting Time: New York City and the Rise of Modern Athletics, 1820–70
   Melvin L. Adelman
Sandlot Seasons: Sport in Black Pittsburgh   *Rob Ruck*
West Ham United: The Making of a Football Club   *Charles Korr*
Beyond the Ring: The Role of Boxing in American Society   *Jeffrey T. Sammons*
John L. Sullivan and His America   *Michael T. Isenberg*
Television and National Sport: The United States and Britain   *Joan M. Chandler*
The Creation of American Team Sports: Baseball and Cricket, 1838–72
   George B. Kirsch
City Games: The Evolution of American Urban Society and the Rise of Sports
   Steven A. Riess
The Brawn Drain: Foreign Student-Athletes in American Universities   *John Bale*
The Business of Professional Sports   *Edited by Paul D. Staudohar and*
   James A. Mangan
Fritz Pollard: Pioneer in Racial Advancement   *John M. Carroll*
A View from the Bench: The Story of an Ordinary Player on a Big-Time Football
   Team (*formerly* Go Big Red! The Story of a Nebraska Football Player)
   George Mills
Sport and Exercise Science: Essays in the History of Sports Medicine
   Edited by Jack W. Berryman and Roberta J. Park
Minor League Baseball and Local Economic Development   *Arthur T. Johnson*
Harry Hooper: An American Baseball Life   *Paul J. Zingg*
Cowgirls of the Rodeo: Pioneer Professional Athletes   *Mary Lou LeCompte*
Sandow the Magnificent: Eugen Sandow and the Beginnings of Bodybuilding
   David Chapman
Big-Time Football at Harvard, 1905: The Diary of Coach Bill Reid
   Edited by Ronald A. Smith
Leftist Theories of Sport: A Critique and Reconstruction   *William J. Morgan*
Babe: The Life and Legend of Babe Didrikson Zaharias   *Susan E. Cayleff*
Stagg's University: The Rise, Decline, and Fall of Big-Time Football at Chicago
   Robin Lester
Muhammad Ali, the People's Champ   *Edited by Elliott J. Gorn*
People of Prowess: Sport, Leisure, and Labor in Early Anglo-America
   Nancy L. Struna
The New American Sport History: Recent Approaches and Perspectives
   Edited by S. W. Pope
Making the Team: The Cultural Work of Baseball Fiction   *Timothy Morris*
Making the American Team: Sport, Culture, and the Olympic Experience
   Mark Dyreson
Viva Baseball! Latin Major Leaguers and Their Special Hunger   *Samuel O. Regalado*

The University of Illinois Press
is a founding member of the
Association of University Presses.

———————————————

Composed in 11.25/14 Arno Pro
with DIN 1451 display
by Jim Proefrock
at the University of Illinois Press
Manufactured by Sheridan Books, Inc.

University of Illinois Press
1325 South Oak Street
Champaign, IL 61820-6903
www.press.uillinois.edu